The Original Story

The Original Story

GOD, ISRAEL, AND THE WORLD

John Barton and Julia Bowden

WILLIAM B. EERDMANS PUBLISHING COMPANY
Grand Rapids, Michigan / Cambridge, U.K.

© 2004 John Barton and Julia Bowden
All rights reserved

First published 2004
in the United Kingdom by
DARTON, LONGMAN AND TODD LTD
1 Spencer Court
140–142 Wandsworth High Street
London SW18 4JJ

This edition published 2005
in the United States of America by
WM. B. EERDMANS PUBLISHING CO.
255 Jefferson Ave. S.E., Grand Rapids, Michigan 49503 /
P.O. Box 163, Cambridge CB3 9PU U.K.
www.eerdmans.com

Printed in the United States of America

10 09 08 07 06 05   7 6 5 4 3 2 1

Library of Congress Cataloging-in-Publication Data

ISBN 0–8028–2900–7

Text design by Kevin van der Leek Design Inc.
Set in Knockout and Kepler Std

Contents

0.0 Before We Start . . .

MORE THAN TWO THOUSAND years ago, the people of a small nation in the Middle East believed they had encountered God. This was not unusual at the time, but their record of the encounter, and of their thoughts about it, resulted in a collection of writings unique in the ancient world. This is the collection normally referred to in English as the Old Testament, or sometimes as the Hebrew Bible.

Unfortunately, the Old Testament has an image problem nowadays. Many people think it is both boring and barbaric, but closer study shows that it is an extraordinary document still well worth getting to know. It contains stories about the involvement of God with Israel as a nation and with individuals within that nation. Like the literature of most peoples in ancient times, the story is sometimes bloody and not always very inspiring. Yet, through its account of heroes, villains, and ordinary people we encounter ideas about God, and about God's involvement in the world, that can still challenge us today.

The Old Testament also contains poems, hymns, proverbs, laws, and prophecies. These fill out our knowledge about the life of Israel in various periods of time, as well as raising many religious issues that are often subtle and sophisticated. The Old Testament stands alongside literature from Greek and Roman times as part of the heritage of the ancient world that is too little known in the modern one. Human insights into religious questions do not 'progress' in the way that scientific knowledge does: often, very ancient literature still has the power to speak to the modern reader. However, sometimes we need more help to understand books from long ago than to read, for example, a modern novel. Many of the ideas will be strange; references to events that were well known to the original readers will be obscure to us; literary styles and conventions will be unfamiliar. This book is intended to open up the Old Testament for readers in the twenty-first century.

REASONS FOR READING THE OLD TESTAMENT

The majority of people who read the Old Testament probably do so, at least initially, for religious reasons. These books are the Holy Scriptures of Jews, part of the Bible of Christians, and deeply respected by Muslims. The way they are often printed — in double columns and on special paper, sometimes with gold edges — supports the idea that as a religious text they are different from all other books. Religious believers approach the Bible in the expectation that they will learn from it things they could not learn from any other source, and that it will be relevant to their own questions and concerns.

However, there are at least two other reasons why someone might decide to study the Old Testament. One is that it is great literature on a par with other major works from the past – Greek tragedies or the plays of Shakespeare, for example. In modern times, as religious commitment to the Bible has faded for many people, there has come to be more interest in it as a classic work of literature. People who see it as the word of God need have no quarrel with others who read it mainly out of a literary interest. It has something to offer on that level, too.

Another reason for being interested in the Bible is simply its great importance in the history of western culture. Many writers and thinkers in the past were steeped in the language and imagery of the Bible. Stories from both the Old and the New Testaments were as familiar to them as the story of their own families. By and large, the Old Testament has passed out of modern culture. Journalists still sometimes seem to think we will pick up references to it. For example, they may talk about an unequal struggle between an apparently weak and an apparently powerful person or institution as a 'David and Goliath' contest – assuming we know the story in the first book of Samuel, chapter 17, where the shepherd-boy David, with nothing but a catapult, kills the giant Goliath who is heavily armed. Yet most people now know no more than a few fragmentary stories of this kind. If you read any major work of English literature, you need notes to explain all the references to biblical people and ideas that in the past were taken for granted. Studying the Bible can put you in touch with a great deal of this information.

USING THIS BOOK

The layout

In planning this book we have taken it for granted that many readers will come to it with a combination of these three reasons for reading the Old Testament: religious, literary, and cultural. Therefore, it should be equally accessible to those with and without a religious commitment and, at the same time, it is meant to be useful to people whose interest in the Old Testament is mainly literary or cultural.

In addition, the book is planned in a flexible manner so that it does not necessarily have to be read straight through. Each chapter offers explanations of key vocabulary, additional information related to the main text and easy-to-follow cross-references that can help the reader navigate the whole book for relevant information on a particular topic.

 alerts readers to useful hints or common misunderstandings about the subject under discussion.

presents scholarly (or other appropriate) quotations on the subject in hand.

 points out related additional information.

provides supplementary information about key personalities.

Many readers will need some but not all of this additional information, and can move freely between chapters according to their particular interests.

The book also has a linked website at **www.theoldtestament.co.uk** where the reader will find further information, images and links to sites related to the topics covered in this book.

The contents

Section 1: The Basics – An Introduction to the Old Testament
This section is meant for someone studying the Old Testament for the first time, and assumes no previous knowledge at all. Most people will need to read this before they can tackle the rest of the book.

Section 2: Major Themes in the Old Testament
This section is the heart of the book, and the chapters here are longer than elsewhere. Whether or not you have a religious commitment, you cannot fail to see that the Old Testament is mainly about religious questions – like so much other literature from the ancient world. These chapters look in detail at six issues, all of them still alive today for anyone concerned with religious questions. These are:

- the character of God
- God's relationship to particular groups of people, and especially the Jews
- what it means to be human
- how we should live
- why human beings suffer
- whether God can be known and, if so, how.

However, none of these themes as they appear in the Old Testament can be understood without some knowledge of the historical, social, and literary background from which they arose. Therefore, the rest of the book provides a lot of the necessary background information.

Section 3: History and the Old Testament
This section looks in detail at the history of ancient Israel, explaining why our knowledge is full of gaps but at the same time presenting what can be known. Our exploration of the topic involves study both of the biblical text and of archaeological evidence.

Section 4: The Institutions of the Old Testament
This section takes a more sociological look at Israel, examining the various groups that made it up and the social institutions by which they lived. Here you will find detailed accounts of prophecy, worship, wisdom literature, history-writing, law, and apocalyptic writing.

Section 5: Methods, Text, and Interpretation
This final section explains some of the techniques scholars use to study the Old Testament and introduces some of the great figures in Old Testament scholarship.

Other points to note
Unless otherwise stated, quotations from the Old Testament come from the New Revised Standard Version.

In the interests of inclusiveness, the abbreviations BCE (Before the Common Era) and CE (Common Era) have been used after dates instead of the traditional Christian terms of BC (Before Christ) and AD (Anno Domini – in the year of the Lord).

The dates of kings and rulers used represent a broad consensus of scholars and follow those in Siegfried Herrmann's *A History of Israel in Old Testament Times* (translated by John Bowden, 1983). The double dates offered reflect the fact that the Hebrew year did not begin on 1 January, but in either the autumn or the spring.

And finally . . . a word about Hebrew
Most European languages are related to each other – some closely, such as English and German, others more distantly, such as Welsh and Russian. However, Hebrew belongs to a completely different family of languages, usually called 'Semitic'. They include Akkadian, the ancient language of Mesopotamia; Aramaic; the languages of Ethiopia; and Arabic. Apart from the odd word borrowed from Hebrew, such as 'hallelujah' or 'cherubim', English has no vocabulary in common with the Semitic languages, which makes them hard to learn for an English-speaking person. Compare, for example, the words for 'night' in European languages:

English	night
German	*Nacht*
Greek	*nux*
Latin	*nox*
French	*nuit*
Italian	*notte*
Welsh	*nos*
Swedish	*natt*

There are huge differences, but you can see that they all go back to some shared ancestor. The Hebrew for night is *lay-elah* – a totally unrelated word.

Nearly all the Old Testament is in Hebrew. The only exceptions are a few chapters in Ezra and Daniel, which are in Aramaic. In ancient times, Hebrew was a small local language, the language of Palestine, whereas its cousin, Aramaic, was spoken all over the Middle East and in the first millennium BCE became the international language of diplomacy: Persians communicated with Egyptians in Aramaic. By the time of Jesus, Aramaic had become the language of everyday speech in Palestine, though people could still understand Hebrew and some, such as the community at Qumran where the Dead Sea Scrolls were written, still wrote religious texts in Hebrew. Hebrew never totally died out but passed through various changes right through the Middle Ages and into the modern world, but it was the original biblical form of it that was revived by the founders of the modern state of Israel to be the national language. Of course, thousands of new words have had to be coined to cover areas of vocabulary the Bible does not contain – you can buy a sheep using Biblical Hebrew but not a cappuccino!

It is possible to write Hebrew words using our alphabet with a few accents to mark long and short vowels, and in this book we will use a number of Hebrew words 'transliterated' into the alphabet we normally use: *elohim* (God), *nabi'* (prophet), *mishpat* (justice), *ehyeh* (I am), *eretz* (land). Nevertheless, Hebrew has its own distinctive alphabet (actually the remote ancestor of our own, via the Greek alphabet), which it shares with Aramaic. This alphabet is written from right to left – so Hebrew books open at the 'back'– though still from the top to the bottom of the page. One peculiarity is that all the letters stand for consonants, with the vowels marked by adding various dots and dashes, rather as in shorthand. The dots and dashes appear above or below the letter they follow, or occasionally in the middle of the letter. (This is feasible because in Hebrew you never get one vowel following another without a consonant between.) Thus 'word', *dabar*, is written:

that is,

```
r  b  d
   a  a
```

In practice, you soon get used to reading in this way. In many contexts the vowel signs (known as the 'pointing') can be left out, because they can be guessed – just as in English no one would have difficulty in reading 'th ct st n th mt' as 'the cat sat on the mat', because it is a familiar phrase and you can soon work out the vowels. In biblical times, in fact, all texts were 'unpointed', though a few consonants did double-duty as vowel markers, rather as 'y' in English can be a consonant (as at the beginning of 'yoghurt') or a vowel (as at the end of 'every'). The vowel signs were invented in the first few centuries CE, when traditional pronunciation of Hebrew was passing away and it needed to be recorded.

Here is the Hebrew alphabet:

א ב ג ד ה ו ז ח ט י כ

ל מ נ ס ע פ צ ק ר שׁ שׂ ת

And here are a few Hebrew words we will encounter in this book:

הַלְלוּ יָה	*hallelu-jah*	praise the Lord
כְּרוּבִים	*kerubim*	cherubim
נָבִיא	*nabi'*	prophet
אֱלֹהִים	*'elohim*	God
טוֹב	*tob*	good
בְּרִית	*berith*	covenant

Here, finally, is the divine name YHWH:

יהוה

and for a more detailed discussion of this word, see chapter 2.1 'Watchmaker or Living God?'

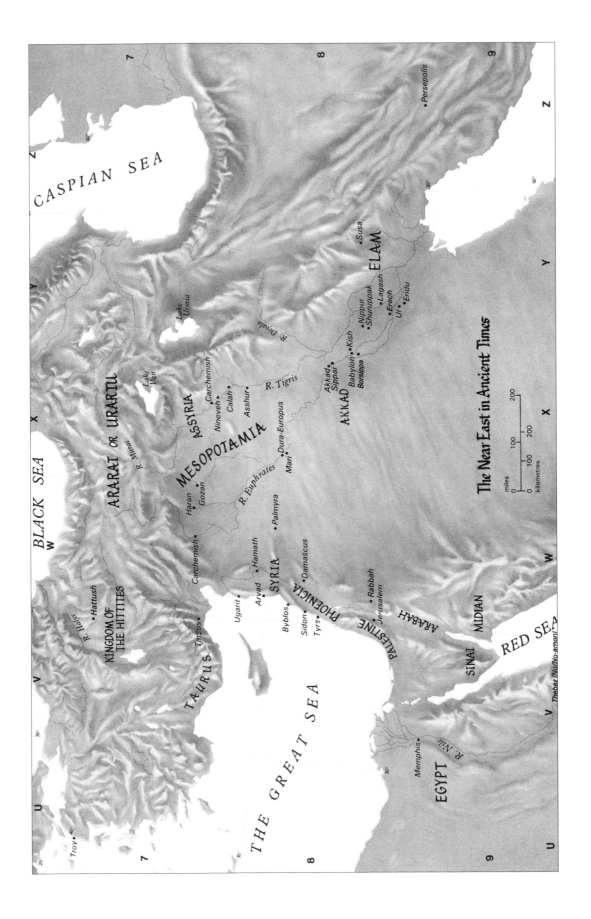

The Near East in Ancient Times

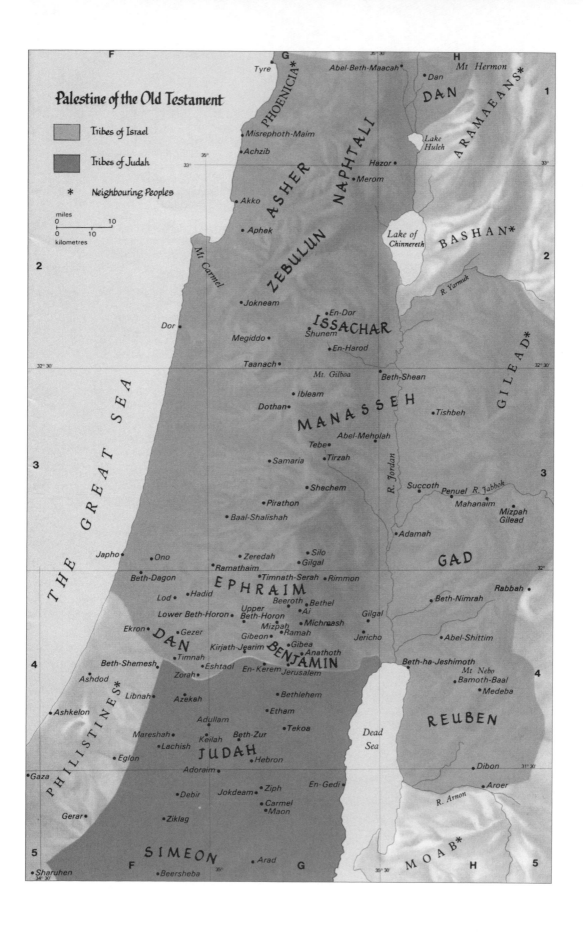

Palestine of the Old Testament

Tribes of Israel

Tribes of Judah

* Neighbouring Peoples

miles
0   10
0   10
kilometres

Tyre

PHOENICIA*

Abel-Beth-Maacah

Mt Hermon

Dan

DAN

ARAMAEANS*

Misrephoth-Maim

Achzib

Lake Huleh

ASHER

NAPHTALI

Hazor

Merom

Akko

Lake of Chinnereth

BASHAN*

Aphek

ZEBULUN

Mt Carmel

Jokneam

R. Yarmuk

Dor

En-Dor

ISSACHAR

GILEAD*

Shunem

Megiddo

En-Harod

THE GREAT SEA

Taanach

Mt. Gilboa

Beth-Shean

Ibleam

Dothan

MANASSEH

Tishbeh

Tebe

Abel-Meholah

Samaria

Tirzah

R. Jordan

Shechem

Succoth

Penuel R. Jabbok

Pirathon

Mahanaim

Mizpah Gilead

Baal-Shalishah

Adamah

Japho

Ono

Zeredah

Silo

GAD

Gilgal

Ramathaim

Rimmon

Timnath-Serah

Beth-Dagon

EPHRAIM

Lod   *Hadid*

Beeroth   Bethel

Beth-Nimrah

Rabbah

Lower Beth-Horon

Upper Beth-Horon

Ai

Gilgal

Ekron *Gezer*

Gibeon *Ramah*

Michmash

Jericho

Mizpah

Kirjath-Jearim

Gibea

Abel-Shittim

DAN

Timnah

Anathoth

BENJAMIN

Beth-Shemesh

Eshtaol

En-Kerem Jerusalem

Beth-ha-Jeshimoth

Zorah

Mt Nebo

Ashdod

Bamoth-Baal

Libnah

Azekah

Bethlehem

Medeba

Ashkelon

Etham

REUBEN

PHILISTINES*

Adullam

Tekoa

Mareshah

Keilah

Beth-Zur

Dead Sea

Lachish

Eglon

JUDAH

Hebron

Dibon

Adoraim

Debir

Jokdeam   *Ziph*

En-Gedi

Aroer

Gaza

Carmel

R. Arnon

Maon

Gerar

Ziklag

SIMEON

Arad

MOAB*

Sharuhen

Beersheba

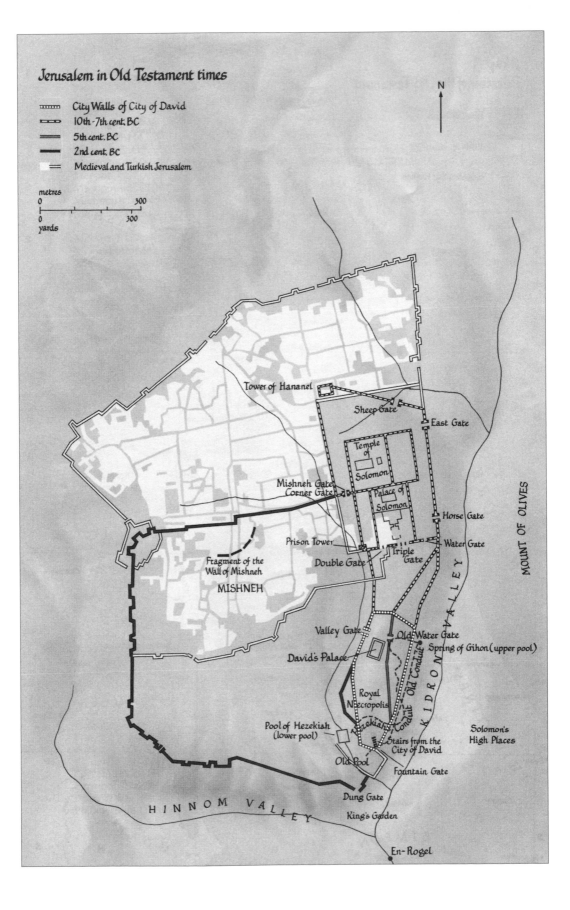

Jerusalem in Old Testament times

City Walls of City of David
10th-7th cent. BC
5th cent. BC
2nd cent. BC
Medieval and Turkish Jerusalem

metres
0   300
0   300
yards

N

Tower of Hananel
Sheep Gate
East Gate
Temple of Solomon
Mishneh Gate
Corner Gate
Palace of Solomon
Horse Gate
Prison Tower
Water Gate
Fragment of the Wall of Mishneh
Double Gate
Triple Gate
MISHNEH
MOUNT OF OLIVES
Valley Gate
Old Water Gate
David's Palace
Spring of Gihon (upper pool)
Royal Necropolis
KIDRON VALLEY
Pool of Hezekiah (lower pool)
Solomon's High Places
Stairs from the City of David
Old Pool
Fountain Gate
Dung Gate
King's Garden
HINNOM VALLEY
En-Rogel

Section I

The Basics — An Introduction to the Old Testament

1.1 Old Testament or Hebrew Bible?
THE SCRIPTURES OF JEWS AND CHRISTIANS

THE BASICS

- 'The Old Testament' is not a very exact term — different faith communities have different ideas about which books should be included and in what order they should be arranged.
- The Old Testament is sometimes referred to as 'The Hebrew Bible', 'The Hebrew Scriptures', 'The First Testament' or 'The Tanakh (or Tanak)'.

MANY READERS OF THIS book will have encountered the Old Testament as the first, and by far the longer, part of a Christian **Bible** that is organized into two sections: the Old Testament and the New Testament. However, some may have one that also contains a third section called the **Apocrypha**, and even if you have a two-part Bible, you may find that the Old Testament section contains some books not found in other two-part Bibles. Finally, if you buy a Jewish Bible you will find that it contains only the Old Testament books, but that these are arranged differently from the books in a Christian Bible. Our first task is therefore to try to explain this confusing situation.

THE CONTENTS OF THE CANON
Biblical books are said, both in Judaism and in Christianity, to be 'canonical' or part of the **canon**. Where the New Testament is concerned, all Christian Churches agree on which books are canonical: there are twenty-seven of them, and there has been no serious dispute about this since the fourth century CE at the latest. With the Old Testament, the picture is much more complicated.

Jews and Protestant Christians agree about which books belong in what Christians call the Old Testament, and Jews often call the Hebrew Bible or Hebrew Scriptures. However, Catholics recognize some extra books, which they refer to as **deuterocanonical**. In practice, the Catholic Old Testament

The word **bible** comes from a Greek word meaning 'books' and reflects the fact that the Bible is not one book but a collection of books by different authors at different times.

Apocrypha is the name given to the collection of books which are included in the Greek version of the Old Testament (the Septuagint) but not in the Hebrew Scriptures. These books are often also called 'deuterocanonical' books.

The word **canon** comes from a Greek term referring to a measuring rod and it is used to denote those books accepted as being genuine, authoritative and inspired for a particular religion. Therefore, in Jewish and Christian terms, the canon is the official list of books included in the Bible.

The word *deuteros* in Greek means 'second', and so books of the Old Testament referred to as deuterocanonical are those which many view as of only secondary importance. The collection of deuterocanonical books linked with the Old Testament is also known collectively as the Apocrypha.

THE CANONICAL BOOKS OF THE OLD TESTAMENT

GENESIS	The history of the world from the creation to the deeds of the 'patriarchs' — Abraham, Isaac, Jacob, and Joseph.	*These five books are sometimes called the Pentateuch, meaning a work in five parts, or the Books of Moses, or (in Judaism) the Torah.*
EXODUS	The Israelites in Egypt, their escape, the giving of the Law on Mount Sinai.	
LEVITICUS	Further laws.	
NUMBERS	Stories about the Israelites on their way to the Promised Land.	
DEUTERONOMY	Laws given by Moses just before Israel entered the Promised Land.	
JOSHUA	The conquest of the Promised Land.	*The books from Joshua to Esther (or sometimes Genesis to Esther) are often referred to as the 'historical' books.*
JUDGES	Exploits of early Israelite heroes.	
RUTH	A Moabite woman becomes part of Israel and an ancestor of Daniel.	
1 SAMUEL	Israel ruled by Samuel, the last 'judge', and Saul, the first king.	
2 SAMUEL	The reign of King David.	
1 KINGS	The reign of Solomon, and the early kings of the two kingdoms into which Israel split on his death.	
2 KINGS	The decline and fall of the two kingdoms.	
1 CHRONICLES	An alternative account of everything from Genesis to 2 Samuel.	
2 CHRONICLES	An alternative account of the story told in Kings.	
EZRA	Rebuilding Israel after its exile to Babylonia.	
NEHEMIAH	Further rebuilding under the governor, Nehemiah.	
ESTHER	A story of how the Jews were saved from persecution during the reign of a Persian king.	
JOB	The story of a good man who suffers severely and debates his suffering with his friends.	*The books from Job to Song of Solomon are sometimes called 'wisdom' books or 'didactic' (which means 'teaching') books.*
PSALMS	Hymns, prayers, and songs.	
PROVERBS	Wise sayings attributed to King Solomon.	
ECCLESIASTES	Sceptical sayings about the meaning of life.	
SONG OF SOLOMON	A collection of love-poems (sometimes also called the Song of Songs).	
ISAIAH	Lengthy prophecies attributed to a prophet who lived in Jerusalem in the eighth century BCE.	*The books from Isaiah to Malachi are called the 'prophetic' books.*
JEREMIAH	The longest prophetic book; Jeremiah lived in the seventh century BCE and saw the downfall of Jerusalem.	
LAMENTATIONS	Laments about the fall of Jerusalem.	
EZEKIEL	The visions of a younger contemporary of Jeremiah.	
DANIEL	Stories and prophecies from a Jew deported to Babylonia.	
HOSEA	Prophecies from the same period as Isaiah.	
JOEL	Poems and prophecies in a time of natural disaster.	
AMOS	Prophecies of doom from a contemporary of Hosea.	
OBADIAH	A short prophecy against the Edomites, neighbours of Israel who helped to destroy it in the sixth century BCE.	
JONAH	The prophet who preached repentance in Nineveh after escaping from a big fish which had swallowed him.	
MICAH	Prophecies by a contemporary of Isaiah.	
NAHUM	Predictions of God's destruction of the Assyrian city, Nineveh.	
HABAKKUK	God's judgement on Jerusalem, by a contemporary of Jeremiah.	
ZEPHANIAH	An attack on the injustice of Israelite life in the time of Jeremiah.	
HAGGAI	The words of a prophet who returned from exile in Babylonia.	
ZECHARIAH	Prophecies from a contemporary of Haggai.	
MALACHI	Attacks on abuses in Israel after the exile.	

THE DEUTEROCANONICAL BOOKS OF THE OLD TESTAMENT (THE APOCRYPHA)

TOBIT	A story about loyal Jews living in Assyria after the fall of the northern kingdom of Israel.
JUDITH	A story of how a Jewish heroine defeated the commander of a foreign army when it was attacking an Israelite town.
THE WISDOM OF SOLOMON	Further teaching attributed to Solomon.
SIRACH or ECCLESIASTICUS	Proverbial sayings by a teacher of the second century BCE, Jesus son of Sira.
BARUCH	Reflections on the Jewish exile by Jeremiah's secretary, Baruch. (Chapter 6 is sometimes printed separately and called The Letter of Jeremiah.)
SUSANNAH (or DANIEL 13)	A short detective story about Daniel.
BEL AND THE DRAGON (or DANIEL 14)	Two short stories about Daniel, poking fun at idols.
1 MACCABEES	Wars fought against the enemies of Israel in the second century BCE.
2 MACCABEES	A more legendary account of some of the events in 1 Maccabees.

contains these books on equal terms with the others, and they are often used for readings in church. These deuterocanonical books all have a Jewish origin, but from early in the Christian era Jews did not regard them as canonical, though at one time many Jews had had a high regard for them. The early Church used them freely, and it was not until the fourth century CE that any serious doubts were expressed about their status.

In the sixteenth century, at the time of the **Reformation**, Protestants decided that these books — which Jews by then definitely regarded as uncanonical — ought not to be part of the Old Testament. The Catholic Church, however, strongly affirmed that they should remain in the Bible. At that time, Protestants began to refer to these extra books as *apocrypha,* a Greek word originally meaning 'hidden books'. This term stuck, and nowadays these books, if they are included at all, are placed in a special section called 'The Apocrypha' in Protestant Bibles.

Other Christian Churches such as the Greek Orthodox and Ethiopian Churches have Old Testament canons that contain still other books, but these are not likely to be encountered much in the West. Two books found in the Greek Orthodox, but not in the Catholic Bible, did find their way into the Protestant Apocrypha: a book called 1 Esdras, and a short prayer of repentance called the Prayer of Manasseh. Otherwise, the Apocrypha of Protestants contains the same works as the 'deuterocanonical' books of the Catholic Old Testament.

All this is very complicated, and the detailed differences do not matter very much in practice. What does need to be grasped is that 'the Old Testament' is not a very exact term, quite unlike the New Testament whose contents are fixed and agreed on by everyone. The Old Testament is and always has been fuzzy at the edges. Everyone agrees on its basic core, but then there is an area of uncertainty. This is linked with the way the biblical canon developed.

The **Reformation** is the name given to the religious movement in the sixteenth century CE which sought to reform the Roman Catholic Church by reasserting the importance of the teaching and authority of the Bible over the Pope. This movement resulted in the establishment of a variety of Protestant groups such as the Church of England.

THE ORDER OF THE BOOKS OF THE OLD TESTAMENT IN THE JEWISH TRADITION

TORAH:
Genesis
Exodus
Leviticus
Numbers
Deuteronomy

PROPHETS:
Joshua
Judges
Samuel
Kings
Isaiah
Jeremiah
Ezekiel
The 'Twelve' (Hosea, Joel, Amos, Obadiah, Jonah, Micah, Habakkuk, Nahum, Zephaniah, Haggai, Zechariah, Malachi)

WRITINGS:
Psalms
Job
Proverbs
Ruth
Song of Solomon
Ecclesiastes
Lamentations
Esther
Daniel
Ezra-Nehemiah
Chronicles

Torah is the Hebrew word meaning 'teaching' or 'instruction' — although it is often translated, perhaps somewhat restrictively, as 'Law'. It is frequently used as a collective title for the first five books of the Old Testament, but can be used in a wider sense to refer to all or almost any part of the Old Testament, the oral teachings of Judaism and the traditional Jewish law.

Pentateuch is a common collective term for the first five books of the Old Testament — Genesis, Exodus, Leviticus, Numbers, and Deuteronomy. It is derived from the Greek word *pente* meaning 'five'. In the Jewish tradition, these are sometimes referred to as the five books of Moses.

A **synagogue** is a place where Jews meet to read the Scriptures and pray together.

THE ARRANGEMENT OF THE CANON

To make matters more complex still, the different communities — Jewish, Catholic, and Protestant — that use the Old Testament do not agree about how to arrange it. So if you buy a Bible you may be puzzled by the *order* of the books as well as by the contents! In simple terms, Christian Bibles group books of similar types together in the order History—Teaching—Prophecy. The Protestant order is the same as the Catholic one, but with the deuterocanonical/apocryphal books left out completely or printed together in a section between the Old and New Testaments. In Catholic Bibles, the deuterocanonical/apocryphal books are included in appropriate places, next to the books from the main list that they are most like. Hence, the 'wisdom' books in Catholic Bibles are arranged: Job, Psalms, Proverbs, Song of Solomon, Ecclesiastes, *Wisdom of Solomon, Ecclesiasticus/Sirach* (the books in italics being the deuterocanonical ones).

Jewish Bibles are arranged in a different way altogether. Within Judaism, instead of the arrangement History—Teaching—Prophecy, the order is **Torah**—**Prophets**—**Writings**. In this instance, 'Torah' means the **Pentateuch**, so the first five books are identical to the Christian arrangement. However, then come the prophetic books, and these are thought of as including some of the 'histories' (Joshua, Judges, Samuel, Kings). After that, there is a miscellaneous section ('Writings') which contains the teaching books, such as Job and Proverbs, and some further 'histories', such as Chronicles and Esther. The historical reasons for these different arrangements are hard to discover, but they do suggest rather different ways of reading the various books.

Christians, whose Old Testament progresses from history, through teaching, and into prophecy seem to see the books as moving from the past, through the present, and into the future. This is quite significant once we remember that the next books in a Christian Bible will be the Gospels. You read the end of the book of Malachi, turn the page, and you are in St Matthew's Gospel, with its stress on how prophecies found their fulfilment in Jesus. Therefore, in a way the Old Testament builds up to a climax at the end, with prophecy as its aim and goal.

For Jews, the Bible works in a quite different way. The most important part is the beginning, the Torah. In these five books God reveals his laws to Israel through Moses. Whereas passages from other biblical books can be read from printed Bibles in the **synagogue**, for the Torah there are sacred handwritten scrolls, kept in a special chest, called the 'Ark', which has pride of place in the synagogue. These scrolls are handled with the utmost reverence. The rest of the Bible is seen as a sort of commentary on the Torah, whose importance lies in the teaching it gives to help people keep the laws more perfectly. So there is no sense that the Bible builds up to a climax. It is more like a set of concentric circles, with the Torah as the vital central one, and ripples spreading out more faintly as we move into the Prophets and the Writings.

Torah scrolls in the Ark at Liberal Jewish Synagogue in London
(Photo: J. Bowden)

A **covenant** is a solemn, binding, mutual agreement between two parties. In biblical terms this usually refers to the relationship between God and his people. The Hebrew word for covenant is *berith* (pronounced buh-reeth, with the stress on the second syllable).

NAMING THE SCRIPTURES

For the earliest Christians, only what we now call the Old Testament was 'Scripture'. The sayings of Jesus and stories about him in the Gospels, and the letters of teachers such as Paul were highly important, but they were not yet referred to as 'Scripture'. When early Christian writers talk about 'Scripture', they mean the Old Testament. That is clear within the New Testament itself, where we find phrases such as 'Scripture says' or 'it is written' as a way of introducing Old Testament passages.

 'The term "Old Testament" cannot be used if we see it as a word that puts down the Jewish faith. But it becomes valuable when we realize that it roots all that we say about Christ in the proper and original soil of Israel's faith.' (Lawrence Boadt, *Reading the Old Testament: An Introduction,* Paulist Press, 1984)

However, once the books of the New Testament had come to be referred to as 'Scripture' too, then some way had to be found of distinguishing them from the older Jewish Scriptures. Fairly soon Christian writers began to talk about the Scriptures 'of the *old* **covenant**', by contrast with those 'of the *new* covenant'. In this they drew on the language of the New Testament Letter to the Hebrews (see Hebrews 7:22, 8:13, and especially 9:15), which speaks of a 'new covenant' made in Christ which extended God's original covenant with the Jewish people so as to include non-Jews — by then many Christians were non-Jews. The word 'covenant' in Greek is *diatheke* (pronounced dee-a-thee-kee), so the old Scriptures came to be called *he palaia diatheke*, 'the old covenant'. In Latin, 'covenant' is *testamentum*: hence our term 'Old Testament'. Before long most people no longer picked up the reference to 'covenant' in the word 'Testament', and the majority of Bible-readers today probably are unaware of it: for them 'Testament' means just 'a section of the Bible'.

Nevertheless, in recent times some people, both Jews and Christians, have come to feel that the term 'Old Testament' can sound dismissive — as though '*old* covenant' means a covenant which is inferior compared with the new one. Jews themselves have seldom used the term 'Old Testament' anyway, since for them there is no new one with which to contrast it, but the feeling that it can sound offensive leads

 Do not confuse the Ark of the Covenant and the ark in a synagogue with Noah's Ark, which uses a different Hebrew word! The ark in which the scrolls are kept is the most important item in a synagogue. The idea of the ark in a synagogue is based on the Ark of the Covenant. This was a large wooden box covered with gold that was said to contain the two tablets given to Moses on which God had written the Law. The box was constructed according to God's specific instructions (Exodus 25:10–22) and was eventually housed in the Temple in Jerusalem. You can find out more about the Ark of the Covenant and about Noah's Ark in 3.6 'Digging Up the Old Testament'.

The **Tanakh** or **Tanak** is a term used for the Hebrew Bible based on the sequence of the initial Hebrew letters of the names of the three sections of the Hebrew Bible: Torah (Law), Nebiim (prophets), Ketubim (writings): TNK.

to the use of alternative English terms. The commonest is 'Hebrew Bible' or 'Hebrew Scriptures', which does not contain the apparent suggestion of being out of date or inferior. However, it is not a perfect term because parts of the 'Hebrew Bible' are actually not in Hebrew but in Aramaic, a different though related language. Moreover, a version of the Old Testament which contains the deuterocanonical books is not identical to the version accepted by Jews, so it cannot really be referred to as the 'Hebrew Bible'. This term also creates a problem about what to call the 'New Testament' if there is no longer anything called the 'Old Testament'. A different solution used by some writers is to use the terms 'First Testament' and 'Second Testament' for the two sections of the Bible, and some Jews in modern times prefer simply to use the term **Tanak** or **Tanakh** for the Hebrew Bible.

In this book we shall use 'Old Testament' and 'Hebrew Bible' fairly interchangeably. Both are in current use, and for many people it does not much matter which is used. When speaking of the place of these books in Christianity, it makes sense to call them 'the Old Testament'; when concentrating on their Jewish context, 'Hebrew Bible' is more appropriate. Whichever we use, we are not trying to express a judgement about their religious status, just to identify the (fuzzy-edged) body of writings that is the subject of this book.

1.2 The Story So Far
ISRAEL TELLS ITS STORY

T H E   B A S I C S

- The history of Israel from the Old Testament's point of view begins with the creation of the world and, although Maccabees provides some ideas about the time between the Persian era and the first century BCE, peters out during the fifth or fourth centuries BCE when the Persian Empire was in control of Palestine.
- The history of Israel in the Old Testament is not history in the modern sense of the word, but gives the reader an important opportunity to understand what the biblical authors believed about God, his people, and the world.

IN OTHER PARTS OF this book we shall look at the problems in reconstructing the history of ancient Israel on the basis of the texts and archaeological evidence available to us today. However, before we can do that, it is essential to have an idea of the Old Testament's own presentation of the history — the story that ancient Israelites told themselves about their past. In ordinary political terms Israel was a tiny nation constantly ruled and oppressed by larger neighbours, yet the Old Testament tells its story as though Israel was the most important nation on earth. All of human history, according to the Old Testament, found its focus in the story of Israel. In this chapter we shall retell the story *from the Old Testament's own point of view*. Only in that way can we read the biblical texts with empathy, understanding how things looked to their authors — however far from the historical reality their self-image may actually have been.

THE BEGINNING

If we were writing the history of Britain or America, we should begin with the earliest historical (or prehistoric) evidence available. We should not begin with the creation of the world! But the Old Testament does begin there. It sees the story of Israel as belonging in a cosmic context. The God who is always there behind Israel's history is the God who created not just the nation but the whole universe. So the Bible begins with the creation of the world and the first humans

Abraham is viewed as the great father of the Jewish people. His name was changed by God from Abram (meaning 'exalted father') to Abraham (meaning 'father of a multitude') to indicate the significance of the promises made by God to Abraham and his descendants, namely that God would give Abraham his own land and descendants that would be as numerous as stars in the sky — not bad considering that Abraham was at that point a hundred years old and that his wife, Sarah, was unable to have children! Still, Abraham is regarded as a model of faith because he believed God's promises and, on the strength of them, was prepared to journey hundreds of miles to this new land of Canaan. Well-known episodes in Abraham's story include his negotiating with God in an attempt to save the cities of Sodom and Gomorrah (Genesis 18:16–33), and his having his obedience tested when he was instructed by God to sacrifice his son Isaac (Genesis 22:1–14).

Aetiologies, based on the Greek word *aitia* which means 'cause', are explanations of the origins of something.

to live on earth (Genesis 1–11), before it narrows down the story to **Abraham**, the ancestor of the Jewish people (from Genesis chapter 12).

In his account of the beginnings of the human race the biblical story-teller gives explanations for various features of human life — what are technically called **aetiologies**. The narrator explains the origins of human sin and violence, and of arts and crafts (Genesis 3 and 4), explains how humankind was nearly annihilated by a great flood (Genesis 6–9), and then goes on to account for the origins of the many human languages (Genesis 11, the story of the Tower of Babel). Only then does he turn his attention to the origins of the Hebrews, who are to be the subject of the rest of the biblical story.

THE PATRIARCHS

The rest of the book of Genesis tells the story of the 'fathers', as the Bible calls them: the **patriarchs** as they have come to be known in biblical studies. Their story is summed up in Deuteronomy 26:5:

> 'A wandering Aramean was my ancestor; he went down into Egypt and lived there as an alien, few in number, and there he became a great nation, mighty and populous.'

The 'wandering Aramean' was Abraham's grandson, **Jacob**. He took his family to Egypt because of a famine in Palestine, where Abraham had previously settled after leaving Mesopotamia, far to the east of the Promised Land. His son **Joseph** had gone to Egypt before him, sold into slavery by his jealous brothers. In Egypt, the descendants of Jacob multiplied until 'a new king arose over Egypt, who did not know Joseph' (Exodus 1:8).

Patriarchs is a term used in biblical studies to describe the key ancestors or father figures of the Israelites, specifically Abraham, Isaac, Jacob, and Jacob's twelve sons after whom the later tribes of Israel were named.

Jacob was the son of Isaac and Rebekah. Well-known episodes in Jacob's story include him deceiving his father in order to steal the blessing which was rightfully his elder brother Esau's (Genesis 27:1–38), and having a vision of angels ascending and descending on a ladder that reached from earth to heaven in which God assured him that he was the inheritor of the promises made between God and Abraham (Genesis 28:11–15). However, he is perhaps most important as a result of the new name given to him by God — 'Israel', so that his descendants, grouped in twelve tribes named after his sons, became known as the 'children of Israel' and his name was also given to the land.

Joseph was the favourite son of Jacob. He was sold into slavery in Egypt by his brothers because they hated his dreams and the special coat he had been given by Jacob. However, since 'the Lord was with Joseph' (Genesis 39:2, 23) he eventually became governor of Egypt, steered the country through seven years of famine and was reunited with his father and brothers who came to live with him in Egypt. His story is the one made famous by the musical *Joseph and the Amazing Technicolor Dreamcoat* (Andrew Lloyd Webber & Tim Rice, 1972).

THE EXODUS, THE WANDERINGS IN THE WILDERNESS, AND THE GIVING OF THE LAW

'When the Egyptians treated us harshly and afflicted us, by imposing hard labour on us, we cried to the LORD, the God of our ancestors; the LORD heard our voice and saw our affliction, our toil, and our oppression. The LORD brought us out of Egypt with a mighty hand and an outstretched arm, with a terrifying display of power, and with signs and wonders. . . .'

(Deuteronomy 26:6–8)

It was under **Moses**, according to the book of **Exodus**, that God rescued his people from their slavery in Egypt. Through a series of miracles with which God plagued the Egyptians he gradually wore them down, until in the end he killed all their first-born sons (Exodus 12:29–32). Then Moses led Israel out and brought them safely across the Red Sea, which lies between Egypt and the Promised Land of Israel. Because of the people's sinfulness, they had to wander in the desert for forty years before they were allowed to re-enter the land. During that time, Moses led them to Mount Sinai where they received the Ten Commandments and other laws, and God entered into a covenant with them. He promised to be their God; they in turn promised to be his people and to remain loyal to him. This was a promise that they constantly broke in their later history.

ENTRY INTO THE PROMISED LAND AND CONQUEST

According to the Bible, Moses was not allowed to enter the land God had promised, but this was accomplished under his successor, Joshua. The occupation of the land was achieved partly through violent campaigns of conquest but also partly through gradual infiltration. However, in the end Israel was fully in control of an area reaching from Syria and Lebanon in the north to the borders of Egypt in the south, the whole

Moses is arguably one of the greatest characters of the Old Testament and his role in the history of Israel was of paramount importance as he is credited with taking a group of slaves into the wilderness and shaping them into a theocracy — a nation under God. Born in slavery in Egypt, Moses grew up in the royal palace before running away to escape punishment for the murder of a slave driver, only to return to lead the Israelites out of slavery in Egypt and towards the land God had promised their ancestors. Well-known episodes in his story include him receiving his call from God at the burning bush (Exodus 3), parting the sea so that the Israelites could escape the Egyptian forces following them as they left Egypt (Exodus 14), and being given the Ten Commandments on Mount Sinai (Exodus 20). He is viewed as Israel's great leader, combining the roles of prophet, priest, law-giver and covenant maker, and has been described as 'a divinely inspired genius' (Lawrence Boadt, *Reading the Old Testament: An Introduction,* Paulist Press, 1984). His story has been popularized by the classic film *The Ten Commandments,* directed by Cecil B. DeMille (1956), and in the recent animated feature film *The Prince of Egypt* (Dreamworks, 1998).

The word **exodus** literally means 'way out' and refers to the departure of the Israelites from Egypt under the leadership of Moses. Exodus is also the name of the second book in the Old Testament in which these events are retold.

THE TEN PLAGUES WHICH GOD SENT ON EGYPT (EXODUS 7:14–12:42)

THE WATER OF THE NILE TURNING TO BLOOD

A PLAGUE OF FROGS

A PLAGUE OF GNATS

A PLAGUE OF FLIES

THE SICKNESS AND DEATH OF ANIMALS

A PLAGUE OF BOILS

HUGE HAILSTORMS

A PLAGUE OF LOCUSTS

THREE DAYS OF COMPLETE DARKNESS

THE DEATH OF THE FIRST-BORN MALES

Whether or not natural explanations can be found for these plagues, for those writing the history of Israel in the Old Testament these things were supreme examples of God acting in history to save his people.

A map showing the territories where Israel had control at this stage and detailing the division of the land according to tribes.

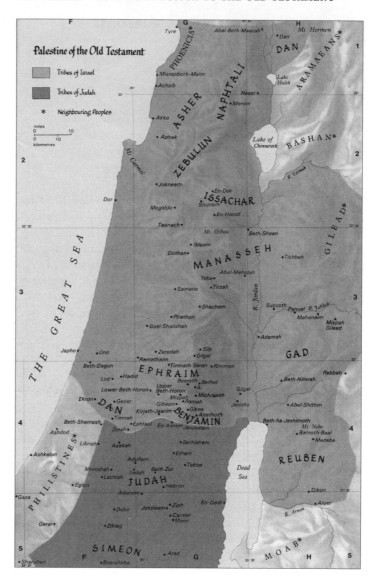

Although the Old Testament does not record that **Samson** ever rallied an army against Israel's enemies as some of the judges had done, the stories about him suggest he waged a one-man war against the Philistines. He is depicted as a legendary strong man — among other things, he kills a lion with his bare hands (Judges 14:5–6) and a thousand Philistines using the jaw bone of a donkey (Judges 15:14–17). He is only defeated by Delilah, who tricks him into revealing the source of his strength (his hair!) and hands him over to the Philistines. However, in a final act of defiance, resulting in his own death, Samson pulls down the pillars supporting a huge house full of Philistines celebrating victory over the Israelites (Judges 16:23–30). His story features in another famous biblical epic, *Samson and Delilah*, directed by Cecil B. DeMille (1949).

THE TWELVE JUDGES OF ISRAEL

OTHNIEL

EHUD

SHAMGAR

DEBORAH (WITH BARAK)

GIDEON

TOLA

JAIR

JEPHTHAH

IBZAN

ELON

ABDON

SAMSON

of Palestine west of the River Jordan, and a good deal of territory to its east. It is a matter of great controversy among Old Testament scholars how close this picture is to being accurate but no one can doubt that that is how the Old Testament itself sees it. By the time of Joshua's death, Israel was, it seems, firmly in possession of all the land God had promised to Abraham when he brought him from Mesopotamia.

THE JUDGES

The biblical book of Judges tells how Joshua was succeeded by a whole string of tribal leaders, the 'judges', who ruled over the newly settled nation one after another. The main task of these leaders was to defend the Israelites from various enemy peoples who made raids into the Promised Land from surrounding areas. Probably the most famous 'judge' was **Samson**, who saved his people from attack by the Philistines who had settled in the southwestern part of Palestine.

SAMUEL AND THE BEGINNINGS OF THE MONARCHY

The last, and in many ways the greatest, of the judges was **Samuel**. Samuel was given to his parents by God in answer to prayer (1 Samuel 1–2), and he turned into a leader who combined many functions: he was a prophet, a judge, a priest, and a ruler all in one. Under his rule Israel began to develop a greater national unity, but as the threat from the Philistines grew larger, they began to ask for a king 'like all the nations'. The Old Testament is unclear about whether this desire for a king was a good thing or a bad one. Some chapters in the first book of Samuel say that Samuel was opposed to it, but others show him as taking the lead himself in finding a king. One way or the other, a **monarchy** was established and a king was eventually found in the person of **Saul**. Saul was from the tribe of Benjamin and he won a series of victories over the Philistines. However, he was apparently a complex character who for some reason forfeited God's favour and did not fulfil his original destiny. Thus, the way was clear for a new king who would establish a lasting dynasty: David.

Samuel is the Old Testament character who is the vital link between the judges and the kings of Israel, and the accounts present him in a variety of roles. As a leader he is seer, prophet, judge, priest and kingmaker, and he thus makes an important contribution to both the history and religion of Israel. As kingmaker he has a unique role in Israel's history and it is he who sets out the idea of kingship in the context of the covenant so that the king is answerable to God (I Samuel 12:14–15). In Samuel is established the idea that an individual prophet could be both a religious and a political figure.

A **monarchy** is a form of government with a king or queen as its head.

Saul was the first king of Israel and is initially described as a handsome man who 'stood head and shoulders above everyone else' (I Samuel 9:2). The Old Testament account presents him in the role of a judge administering justice (I Samuel 14:38-44), in the role of a prophet (I Samuel 10:10) and in the role of a priest (I Samuel 13:9). However, there is relatively little evidence of these aspects of his role in the text and the emphasis is on his charismatic role as a valiant military leader who built up a well-organized army which enjoyed considerable suc-cess against Israel's enemies. In this way, Saul's reign fulfilled the people's hopes for a king. However, the overwhelming feeling one gets from reading the account of his reign is that Saul was a failure and was rejected by God (I Samuel 15:11). He quarrels with Samuel (I Samuel 13), he disobeys God's laws (I Samuel 15), he sets up a monument to himself (I Samuel 15:12), he uses witchcraft (I Samuel 28), he slaughters God's priests (I Samuel 22:11–19), and becomes increasingly mentally unstable — something which shows itself in his insane jealousy of David and his several attempts on David's life. Indeed, Saul's paranoia about David meant that he eventually put more energy and resources into trying to kill him than into ruling Israel effectively, and in the end Saul appears a broken man (I Samuel 28) and kills himself on the battlefield. His reign thus ends in tragedy, although the lament over Saul and his sons attributed to David perhaps gives an insight into the popularity of Saul and the gratitude that most Israelites felt towards him, 'O daughters of Israel, weep over Saul. . . . How the mighty have fallen in the midst of the battle!' (2 Samuel 1:24–25).

The two traditions in I Samuel are known as 'pro-monarchic' — favourable to the idea of a king for Israel — and 'antimonarchic' — against the idea of a king for Israel. The promonarchic tradition is believed to be the earlier of the two traditions, and it presents the idea of a king for Israel as being the only way to create the sort of unity among the tribes needed to overcome the threat of the Philistines. This tradition characterizes Samuel as a local wise man (Hebrew roeh meaning 'seer') to whom God reveals the identity of the man who should be anointed king, and presents Saul as a charismatic leader who leads Israel to victory over the Philistines. On the other hand, the antimonarchic tradition characterizes Samuel as a national prophet (Hebrew shophet meaning 'judge') who is unwilling to grant the people's demand for a king because he views it as an act of rebellion against the nation's one true king, God. And even though the potential problems of kingship are clearly set out (I Samuel 8:10–18), the people are portrayed as wanting a king because other nations had one and without one they felt powerless. Saul is eventually chosen as king by lot, and not by God's revelation, and turns out to be somewhat unfaithful to God's ideals (I Samuel 13:13–14).

Later writers of both the Old and New Testaments view **David** as Israel's greatest king, the one promised an eternal dynasty by God and from whom the Jewish Messiah would be descended (2 Samuel 7:12–16). He was a good statesman, aware of the need to keep the northern tribes, as well as his own southern tribes, united under his kingship. At the beginning of his reign, he even brought Saul's grandson, Mephibosheth, into his household — a move that enabled him to placate the northern tribes and at the same time to keep an eye on the previous king's relative who might become the focus for any plots to overthrow him (2 Samuel 9). David also showed mercy to his enemies (2 Samuel 19: 16–23), but was an excellent military leader who strengthened his forces by setting up a paid standing army and who fought hard in order to establish peace and security for Israel by defeating its enemies (2 Samuel 8:1–14). As a result of this peace he was also able to secure vital trade routes and to encourage peace between nations through trade. Furthermore, David established a new capital in Jerusalem — a geographically strong site but also a neutral site for the tribes — where he set up a civil service and a system of justice under which authority could also be delegated to judges in different parts of the country (2 Samuel 8:15). In addition, he brought to Jerusalem the Ark of the Covenant, the sacred box said to contain the two tablets on which God had written the Law and a powerful symbol of God's presence with his people, and created a permanent priesthood to serve God there (2 Samuel 6). So, for the first time, David centralized religion and politics and ruled over a united Israel — the 'Golden Age' of Israel.

However, in spite of all this success the Old Testament accounts in I and 2 Samuel are no whitewash as they also record David's failures. His weakness for women is recounted, with David arrogantly pursuing any woman he wanted without a thought for the consequences (2 Samuel II) and allowing them to manipulate him. In the latter years of his reign, old tribal rivalries also surfaced and led to rebellions, and this demonstrates a weakness in his control and a loss of contact with the people as a whole at that stage (2 Samuel 15–19 — Absalom's rebellion). A census imposed on the people was an additional cause of discontent (2 Samuel 24), and

there are indications that he did not administer justice as efficiently as he had once done. Nevertheless, for the biblical authors, David's successes outweighed his failures, and he passed into tradition as the ideal king who combined power with goodness and who kept the covenant.

Solomon was the first man to become an Israelite king simply as the result of his birth. The Old Testament writers state that, with God's blessing, he became a great and wise king (I Kings 3:12–13 and I Kings 4:29–34). He was a fortunate leader because he inherited a strong and stable kingdom, but he also worked hard to consolidate Israel's position by increasing its wealth, its trade, its army and its political alliances. He developed an efficient central administration and was also responsible for a large building programme which included the great Temple in Jerusalem to house the Ark of the Covenant (I Kings 5–7). However, the heavy taxes and forced labour he demanded from the people to cover his luxurious lifestyle and building programmes created great resentment (I Kings 5:13–18) and he was further criticized for having numerous foreign wives whom he allowed to worship their pagan gods. In the view of later generations, such things constituted violations of the covenant. Solomon was thus held responsible for the breakup of the united kingdom created by David, and any historical analysis of Solomon's reign includes references to his undoubted successes being tempered by mention of his failures.

DAVID, SOLOMON, AND THE UNITED MONARCHY

There are several stories about how **David** emerged into prominence, not all consistent with each other. In one he was a harpist whom Saul sought out when he was troubled in mind, to soothe him by his playing (1 Samuel 16:14–23); in another he first emerged as a simple shepherd who killed Goliath, the great Philistine warrior, and was rewarded by Saul with a generalship (1 Samuel 17:12–58). However, the Old Testament is absolutely clear that David was intended by God to replace Saul, and to be the founder of a long line of kings. David represented Judah, the tribe which had settled in the south of Palestine, whereas Saul's following had come from the northern tribes. David's great achievement was to unite north and south to a degree that had not been seen before, and to establish a capital city in Jerusalem, which he captured from its native inhabitants. (Until then it had lain outside Israelite territory.) David not only conquered peoples who tried to invade Israel, he also (according to the Old Testament) extended the boundaries of the state so as to build something we could call an empire, taking in many surrounding peoples such as the Edomites, Ammonites, and Moabites, and even the Syrians. It was only under David and his son and successor, Solomon, that Israel was a really major power in the Middle East.

The latter part of David's reign was dogged by family feuding, as his sons vied with each other to succeed him, and the second book of Samuel gives us a vivid picture of the court intrigues during this period. Finally, however, **Solomon** was established as David's successor, and he extended the boundaries of the state still further, even making an alliance by marriage with the major power, Egypt. He built lavish monuments in Jerusalem, including a great temple, and traded far and wide in alliance with the people of Tyre (in what is now Lebanon). The famous story of the coming of the Queen of Sheba to Jerusalem presents him as one of the greatest emperors the world had ever seen. But we also learn from the first book of Kings that Solomon failed to understand the importance of old tribal loyalties, and that his kingdom was fragile because it did not rest on wholehearted loyalty to his God. Solomon's final years were problematic, with tribal rebellions and plots against his life, and on his death the united kingdom he had inherited from his father quickly fell apart.

THE DIVIDED MONARCHY AND EXILE

The Old Testament tells the story of the divided kingdoms after Solomon's death as one of decline and fall, so for the most part the second book of Kings makes gloomy reading. The northern kingdom, whose capital moved around until it eventually settled at Samaria, was never stable, and kings came and went, often assassinating their predecessors and then being assassinated themselves. The southern kingdom, Judah, enjoyed a more peaceful existence internally, but it was troubled by frequent attacks from outside and some-

Elijah is a prophet featured principally in stories about the northern kingdom of Israel in 1 Kings 17–19, 21 and 2 Kings 1–2. In Jewish tradition he came to represent 'Prophecy' in the same way that Moses represented the 'Law'. Since he did not die, but was taken up to heaven in a chariot of fire (2 Kings 2:11–12), later Jewish belief also held that Elijah would return to earth to announce the coming of the Messiah — the one chosen by God to establish a great age of peace and prosperity for all people. Well-known episodes in Elijah's story include him being fed by ravens whilst in hiding (1 Kings 17:2–7), raising a young boy from the dead (1 Kings 17:8–24), and encountering God on Mt Horeb, not in wind, earthquake, or fire, but in a silent whisper (1 Kings 19:11–13).

Israel was the name given by God to Jacob (Genesis 32:28), his descendants became 'Israelites' and King David ruled over the kingdom of Israel. However, when the nation became divided into northern and southern kingdoms in around the tenth century BCE the term 'Israel' was used to denote the northern kingdom and the southern kingdom was called Judah. Confusingly, therefore, 'Israel' in the Old Testament sometimes means the whole 'people of God' and sometimes just the northern kingdom. Although both kingdoms were eventually overthrown and many of their population exiled, the southern kingdom outlasted the northern one, and the people became known as Jews ('people from Judah'). Nevertheless, as such people were still technically descendants of Israel (Jacob) the term 'Israelites' can still be used of them. On 14 May 1948 the name Israel was chosen for the modern state of Israel.

times even from its northern neighbour, Israel. The north was frequently disloyal to its God, with its kings worshipping Baal, the God of Tyre. King Ahab in particular tussled with the prophet **Elijah** over this issue, but Elijah showed the greater power of the true God when he held a contest with the prophets of Baal to see whether they or he could make fire fall from heaven (see 1 Kings 18). Eventually Samaria fell to the Assyrians, a mighty empire based in what is now Iraq.

Judah survived more than a century after the fall of Israel, but despite the work of two great reforming kings, Hezekiah and Josiah, it never regained the glories of the days of David and Solomon. In the end it fell to the armies of the Babylonians under King Nebuchadnezzar, and 'Judah went into exile out of its land' (2 Kings 25:21). Then there was a period of half a century or so in which the Judean leadership was in **exile** in Babylonia. Worship at the Temple in Jerusalem, which lay in ruins, ceased. God seemed to have abandoned his people, as the book of Lamentations records.

THE RETURN AND REBUILDING

There is no continuous history of Israel after the end of 2 Kings, and the books of Chronicles simply tell essentially the same story, though with different interests — less on political matters and more on the religious life of the nation. But 2 Chronicles ends with a few verses, repeated at the beginning of the book of Ezra, which tell us that the Persian king, Cyrus, who had conquered the Babylonian Empire, allowed those Jews who wished to do so to return and rebuild their temple:

> *'Thus says King Cyrus of Persia: the LORD, the God of heaven, has given me all the kingdoms of the earth, and he has charged me to build him a house at Jerusalem, which is in Judah. Whoever is among you of all his people, may the LORD his God be with him! Let him go up.'*
>
> (2 Chronicles 36:23, cf. Ezra 1:2–4)

The story of how this happened, together with later rebuilding of the walls and fortifications of Jerusalem, is related in a rather scrappy way in the books of Ezra and Nehemiah, and confirmed by the prophets Haggai and Zechariah. We do not get any clear picture of the time-scale involved, but we do get a definite impression that a Jewish state was re-established in Palestine, centred on Jerusalem, though it existed under the authority of a Persian governor.

THE LATER HISTORY

After this the main books of the Old Testament tell us no more about the history of Israel. Esther relates the story of a plot to kill all the Jews in the Persian Empire, which is thwarted through the intervention of Esther herself, the wife of the Persian emperor Ahasuerus (=Xerxes). But otherwise only the books of Maccabees in the **Apocrypha** fill in the history between the early Persian emperors and the first century BCE. It is as if, although Jewish life went on naturally, the official history of it in the Hebrew Bible had come to an end. The Jewish historian Josephus, who wrote in the first century CE and knew a lot about the time after the Persian Empire gave way to Greek rulers based in either Egypt or Syria, explicitly says that there was no more official history. He explains this by saying that there were no more 'prophets'. It may seem odd to us that you would need a *prophet* to have access to history, but that is how many people saw it at that time. The Old Testament account peters out in the age of the Persian kings (some time in the fifth or fourth century BCE). History did not stop, but 'sacred' history — the history of the special time in which God directed his people's story — was felt to have ended.

HISTORY AND STORY

To repeat a point made at the beginning: this chapter has summarized the history of Israel *as the Old Testament presents it*. The story the Bible tells is not, we believe, based on pure fiction; but the *story* is not *history* in anything like a modern sense of that word. Indeed, what a modern historian can say about each of the periods described here is often very different from what the Old Testament tells us.

But without having in our minds the Old Testament's own version of events we cannot understand what the biblical authors are talking about. We need to empathize with their version before we can grasp what they were trying to say about God, his people, and the world.

In biblical studies, the **Exile** refers to the period in Israel's history in the sixth century BCE when many of its people were taken captive and deported from Israel to Babylon. It should not be confused with the Exodus, which refers to the departure of the Israelites from Egypt under the leadership of Moses!

Apocrypha is the name given to the collection of books which are included in the Greek version of the Old Testament (the Septuagint) but not in the Hebrew Scriptures. For more information, see 1.1 'Old Testament or Hebrew Bible?'

1.3 Where and Who on Earth?

THE GEOGRAPHY AND PEOPLES OF THE OLD TESTAMENT WORLD

THE BASICS

- The Israel of the Old Testament was a very small territory whose fortunes depended, to a large extent, on its neighbours.
- Major players in Israel's history included the Egyptians, the Assyrians, the Babylonians, and the Persians; others included the Syrians, the Phoenicians, the Philistines, the Ammonites, the Moabites, and the Edomites.

THE OLD TESTAMENT RECORDS primarily the religious ideas of people in ancient Israel. The main reason for studying these ideas is that they may turn out to be still important today. However, 'ideas' never exist in a vacuum: they arise from particular sets of circumstances in particular places. You do not need to be an expert in ancient geography to study the Old Testament, but it does help to have a clear picture in mind of the physical environment in which ancient Israel lived — especially as so much of its literature is a reflection on specific events which, of course, always happen in particular places. What is needed is some grasp of the geography of Palestine itself and of Israel's place in the wider world.

THE LAND

What should we call the area where the history of Israel took place? Traditionally it has been called either 'Palestine' or the 'land of Israel'; but both these terms have become involved in modern disputes between Israelis and Palestinians, so that in using either of them there can be a political judgement. Both are so useful, however, that we are almost bound to run this risk. The Old Testament itself usually calls the country 'Canaan', and its pre-Israelite inhabitants 'Canaanites'. However, it also often speaks simply of 'the land', in Hebrew *ha-aretz*. Because this land is at the focus of our interest in this book, it is easy to think of it as

The Hebrew word *ha-aretz* (pronounced haa-aa-rets, with the stress on the second syllable) literally means 'the land' but it is the way the biblical authors often refer to the land they believe was given to them by God.

The word 'Palestine' has its roots in the word 'Philistine', as it is the Greek form of the Hebrew word that is written in English as Philistine. Until 1948, when the modern state of Israel was founded, Palestine was the name in general use to describe the geographical region which, more or less, incorporates the area of the modern state of Israel and an area to the east of the River Jordan. This is a relatively small area, about the size of the country of Wales or the state of Vermont in the USA.

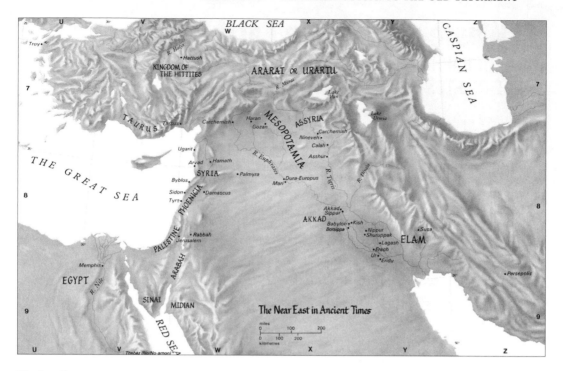

The Near East in Ancient Times

The Fertile Crescent is the name given to a crescent-shaped region which extends from Egypt in the southwest to what is now Iran in the southeast. Agriculture was possible in this fertile area and so people could live in settled villages and towns; outside it the terrain was mostly desert, making only a nomadic lifestyle possible.

'... [T]he political and historical geography of Palestine exhibits two dominant traits: the country has rarely been politically unified; and the country has rarely been politically independent.' (John L. McKenzie SJ, *Dictionary of the Bible*, Geoffrey Chapman, 1966)

In biblical studies, the Exile refers to the period in Israel's history in the sixth century BCE when many of its people were taken captive and deported from Israel to Babylon.

large and important and people are often surprised to learn just how small it is. The distance 'from Dan to Beersheba', which the Old Testament often uses as an indication of the extent of the land from the furthest town in the north to the furthest south, is less than 240 kilometres. Yet, this is the place where events took place that have influenced the whole of world history.

Another misperception is a tendency to think that the southern kingdom of Judah must have been larger than the northern kingdom of Israel, because it is there that the house of David ruled, and the Old Testament is written largely from a Judean perspective. In fact, for most of its history the northern kingdom was considerably larger, as well as more prosperous and fertile, than Judah. By the time of the **Exile** in the sixth century, Judah, which was all that was left of the two kingdoms by then, was about the size of an average English county. It was this very small area that made up the province of Judah or 'Yehud' under the Persians. Population estimates vary a lot, but we should probably think of the total population of Israel at its height in hundreds of thousands. These were not large and important kingdoms, but pocket-sized states.

THE TERRAIN

Nowadays many people have visited Israel and may have quite a clear picture of the terrain. It is not, as Bible readers often seem to think, mainly desert! The desert does encroach on the south of the country, and outside Jerusalem one is soon in the wilderness going down to the Dead Sea. However, much of the land is strikingly fertile, confirming the Bible's talk of 'a land flowing with milk and honey', though it never

The Dead Sea is an area of water 85 km long by 16 km at its widest and is at the lowest point on the earth at nearly 400 m below sea level. The River Jordan and other streams flow into it but there is no escape for the water, which suffers heavy evaporation. This means that the water in the Dead Sea is about twenty-five per cent salt — a density that allows people to float effortlessly and which means that no fish can survive. (Photo: J. Bowden)

yielded so much produce as it has come to do in recent times through modern agricultural methods.

An overview of the land shows that it can be divided into several vertical sections, each having its own particular characteristics. Firstly, there is a vertical section running along the Mediterranean coast in the form of a plain, broken only by Mount Carmel which is a spur of the central hill country. The second vertical section forms a transition between this coastal area and the central hills. It is called the Shephelah and is made up of a series of limestone hills of moderate height. The central hills form the third vertical section and begin in the north in Galilee, and move south incorporating the Samarian hills and the Jerusalem hills. They are broken at one point by the valley of Jezreel which is a triangular and fertile plain running northwest to southeast from the coastal plain to the Jordan Valley. This Jordan Valley forms the fourth vertical section and is part of the rift valley that extends into Africa. It is mostly below sea level and in places has a desert climate. Hills rising to the east of this valley form the fifth section. These hills rise to heights of 1100 metres before they form a plateau which stretches out towards Damascus.

The area occupied by the northern kingdom of Israel in the Old Testament consists of the alternating ridges and valleys in the south of the region, the 'hill country of Ephraim', separated by the plain of Jezreel, leading to the far north and the Galilean plateau, which is again largely hilly. There is also a relatively narrow coastal plain. Although we think of the northern kingdom as a unity, and as the legacy of the northern tribes of Israel, in practice the Galilean area is distinct from the Ephraimite territory that was really the heartland of the northern kingdom.

The southern kingdom of Judah forms a geographically distinct area, centred on hill country to the south of Jerusalem, between Hebron and Bethlehem. Immediately to the north of Jerusalem lies the more open country occupied in early times by the tribe of Benjamin, which had an uncertain status between the two kingdoms though eventually it came to belong with Judah.

CLIMATE

The climate of the land is Mediterranean or 'sub-tropical', with rain in the winter but a largely dry summer, in which temperatures (especially in the more barren areas) can soar into the high 30s Celsius. The rainfall tends to be in three main periods: the end of October (what the Bible calls the 'early rain'); the chief winter rain (January–February); and the 'late rain' in May. However, failure in rainfall was common, as we can see from accounts of severe drought and consequent famine in the Old Testament — for example, the major drought in the time of Elijah described in 1 Kings 17–18. For this reason, life in Palestine was precarious, especially in the south, the territory of Judah, where the desert begins. People were aware of the possible harmful effects of too much rain, as the Flood Story shows us, but in general they saw rain as a blessing from God that could not be taken for granted.

THE MAJOR POWERS OF THE ANCIENT WORLD

Since Palestine was a very small area, its fate nearly always depended on what was happening beyond its borders. Palestine was at a midway point in what is sometimes called the Fertile Crescent and was a kind of crossroads between much larger centres of power. It was a vital land bridge to Africa for Europe and Asia and was therefore a major trade and war route between different nations. Hence, for most of its history Israel lived in land fought over by one or other of the great powers located at opposite ends of the Fertile Crescent.

In the second millennium BCE the dominant power in the area was Egypt, which had a large empire extending right across Palestine. In the first millennium, Palestine was subject to invasion from the east, by the Assyrians and Babylonians, the peoples of what the ancient Greeks called **Mesopotamia**. At times, a third area had to be reckoned with: the area north of Israel, in what are now Lebanon and southern Turkey. It was only during the reigns of David and Solomon (in the tenth century BCE) — if then — that Israel could afford to go its own way; throughout the rest of its existence one or another of the major powers in the region called the tune. Even in times when Israel enjoyed reasonable freedom to order its own internal affairs, its foreign policy was dictated by whichever of the great powers was in the ascendant. Stepping out of line brought swift retribution.

The Egyptians

Not very far to the west of Israel, on the other side of the Sinai peninsula which is mostly desert, lies Egypt. Egypt had one of the earliest civilizations known to us, and its culture was already highly developed by the third millennium BCE. We know that its empire included Palestine by the end of the second millennium because of a large collection of documents, the El Amarna Letters, which represent correspondence between the Egyptian king (the Pharaoh) and his officials in Jerusalem.

Mesopotamia is literally in Greek 'the land between two rivers'. These two rivers are the Tigris and the Euphrates, which flow from the mountains of Armenia, in modern-day Turkey, to the Persian Gulf. They provide vital irrigation and allowed ancient civilizations to flourish in the area.

However, Egyptian power over the area had waned well before 1000 BCE, and it became possible for the small nations of Syria and Palestine to start leading an independent existence. Egypt did not become a major player in Palestinian politics again until the fourth century BCE, after the conquests of Alexander the Great. At many times people in Israel thought that the Egyptians might help them when they were being threatened by Mesopotamian nations. The book of Isaiah tells us that in the days of Hezekiah, towards the end of the eighth century BCE, delegations of diplomats hurried back and forth between Jerusalem and Egypt (Isaiah 18–19 refers to these negotiations). Unfortunately, by then the Egyptians, though they could still posture, could do nothing practical to help: 'Egypt's help is worthless and empty' (Isaiah 30:7).

The Assyrians

One of the major power centres in Mesopotamia that affected Israel was the city of Asshur which gave its name to the Assyrians, whose power base was in the part of Mesopotamia that is now Iraq. From our point of view the period of Assyrian power that is most important lies between the ninth and the seventh centuries BCE, the period of the divided monarchy, when Israel and Judah were separate nations. The Assyrians were intent on conquering the whole of the world as they knew it and, over a long period, they set their sights on dominating Syria and Palestine, in the hope eventually of taking control of Egypt. Even in periods when Assyria was not expansionist, however, Israel owed a lot to Assyrian influence, not least in some aspects of its religious thought. Even though Egypt was geographically nearer to Israel, Israel was always closer in its ways of thinking to Mesopotamia — Mesopotamians spoke languages that were related, though distantly, to Hebrew, and their religious thought was also in some ways similar. However, this did not prevent the northern kingdom of Israel from falling to the Assyrian king Sennacherib in the late 720s BCE.

The Babylonians

The other major power centre in Mesopotamia that affected Israel was Babylon, and by the end of the seventh century BCE dominance in Mesopotamia had moved from Asshur to the city of Babylon. The Babylonians conquered and took over the empire of the Assyrians, and it was a Babylonian king, Nebuchadnezzar, who conquered Judah and sacked the city of Jerusalem at the beginning of the sixth century BCE. Babylon was an area of very high culture: its 'hanging (i.e. terraced) gardens' were reckoned as one of the wonders of the ancient world. Moreover, much is known about the Babylonians from their written records, such as the Babylonian Chronicles. Many Jews were deported to Babylonia, as the area around Babylon is known, and despite the fact that some eventually returned to Palestine, there was a large Jewish community in Mesopotamia from that time onwards, one that was highly influential in later Jewish life.

The Medes, the Persians, and the Greeks

Later in the sixth century BCE, power in the ancient world moved still further south and east. The Medes were from the northern part of what is now Iran and the Persians were from the southern part. The Medes had entered into an alliance with Babylon in order to overthrow the Assyrians, but enjoyed limited power, as the Persian king Cyrus, in his turn, took control over the whole Babylonian Empire in around 550 BCE. The Persians eventually achieved the great prize their predecessors had never managed to win, and conquered Egypt, creating the greatest empire the world had ever seen, and one that lasted nearly two centuries, down to the time of Alexander the Great. It was only at that time that Israel finally came under the influence of lands outside the Fertile Crescent, as Greek power and culture started to spread to the peoples of the Middle East.

ISRAEL'S IMMEDIATE NEIGHBOURS

If we now move in closer and focus on the more immediate surroundings of Israel, we should notice that there were several smaller states in the region which, like Israel itself, were subject to the larger swings of power in the Middle East, yet also spent plenty of energy in alternately forming alliances with, and warring against, each other. From the first two chapters of the book of Amos, we can see how all these immediate neighbours of Israel were regarded as forming a kind of family of nations. Amos condemns all of them for various sins, mainly what we could call war crimes, and runs through them in the following order: Aram, the Philistines, Tyre, Edom, Ammon, and Moab.

The Syrians

The largest of Israel's immediate neighbours was Syria — really a collection of smaller states with shifting boundaries. The Syrians were known to Israel as Arameans and their country is referred to in the Old Testament as Aram. The major Syrian capital was Damascus, just as it is today. Damascus lies little more than fifty miles northeast of the Sea of Galilee, so in periods of hostility between Israel and Aram it was a fairly immediate danger. In the ninth century BCE, the time of King Ahab, the northern kingdom of Israel seems to have oscillated between fighting the Arameans and making temporary alliances with them, as neighbouring states have done throughout human history.

The Phoenicians

To the west of Aram, along the northern sea-coast of Palestine, lay the kingdom of Tyre, often referred to now (as it was by the ancient Greeks) as Phoenicia. This was an area rich in forests, and we read that its king, Hiram, provided Solomon with the timber he needed for his ambitious building proj-

With all these different groups in the Old Testament it is important not to get too confused! The Syrians, with their capital in Damascus, are easily confused with the Assyrians, with their capital in Asshur in Mesopotamia. Moreover, the Syrians are known as Arameans in the Old Testament, since their land is referred to as Aram, and care must be taken not to confuse them with Armenians — the name given to people from an ancient kingdom corresponding to an area in modern Turkey, Iran and part of the former USSR. Just to confuse the issue even further, the Syrians were referred to by the Babylonians and Assyrians as Amorites — in turn not to be confused with the Ammonites who come from another of Israel's neighbours, Ammon!

ects and with workmen skilled in using it (1 Kings 5:1–12). It was also the Phoenicians who developed the alphabet with its simple system of vowels and consonants which was borrowed by the Greeks and is the basis of our written language today.

The Philistines

The area to the immediate southwest of Judah, where the Gaza strip is now to be found, was occupied by the Philistines. Here they created five city-states — Ekron, Ashdod, Askelon, Gaza, and Gath. The Philistines probably came originally from Crete, settled in Palestine at around the same time as the tribes of Israel arrived there, and rose to prominence as a threat against Israel in the time of Samuel, Saul, and David. One of the reasons for this rise appears to have been their knowledge of iron, a metal far superior to the weapons of Israel made of soft copper. Indeed, the Old Testament records that it was the Philistine dominance in battles against the Israelites that led them to demand a king. The Philistines spoke a European language related to Greek, rather than one belonging to the Semitic language-family like the Israelites and their other neighbours. From the reign of David onwards the area once occupied by the Philistines was taken over into Judah, though in his day it is clear that the Philistine commander Ittai the Gittite (i.e. Gathite, from the Philistine town of Gath) was still regarded as a foreigner (2 Samuel 15:19). The Philistines took back their independence after the death of Solomon and, although they were not strong enough to threaten Judah or Israel again, existed until the Assyrian invasion of the area in the eighth century BCE.

The Ammonites, Moabites, and Edomites

Israel had three other neighbours who were important at various points in its history. Two of these lay on the other side of the Dead Sea, in what is now the kingdom of Jordan: *Ammon* and *Moab*. Then, to the south of Judah, was *Edom*. These kingdoms seem to have formed part of David's 'empire', and had strong affinities with Israel, speaking languages that were very close to Hebrew. Anyone who reads Hebrew can read, for example, the Moabite Stone, or victory stone erected by the Moabite king Mesha, who is mentioned in 2 Kings 3:4 as a contemporary of King Ahab.

1.4 The Way They Tell It
TYPES OF LITERATURE IN THE OLD TESTAMENT

THE BASICS

- The Old Testament is made up of many books of many different literary types.
- Types of literature represented in the Old Testament include narrative, wisdom, prophecy, poetry, law, and apocalyptic writing.

P EOPLE SOMETIMES SAY THAT the Old Testament is not a single book, but a whole library. This is true, and important. But not only is the Old Testament made up of many books, it is made up of books of many different types. A library of English literature would not contain only novels, or only books of poems. It would be made up of a variety of different kinds of book, some fiction, some non-fiction, including poems, plays, books of history, novels, and short stories. And some of these types could be divided further — for example, there are lyric poems, narrative poems, comic poems, and so on.

The same is true of the Old Testament. It contains books of different types. What is more, some of the individual books have sections that are of different kinds — just as in English, for example, there are novels that contain poems. In this chapter we look at a few examples of different 'genres', that is, types of Hebrew literature.

NARRATIVE

A bit more than half of the Old Testament consists of *narrative*: books that describe sequences of events. Traditionally these are known as the 'historical books', and in the Christian arrangement of the Old Testament everything from Genesis to Esther falls under that heading. We use the word 'narrative' here because it is more neutral than 'history'. 'History' seems to imply that the events being described actually hap-

When scholars talk about 'books' in the Old Testament it is worth remembering that these works of literature were in fact written in the form of scrolls. The text was written in columns on strips of papyrus, leather or parchment which were then attached to one another to form one continuous strip. This strip was then attached to a stick at each end and could be wound forwards or backwards so that the required portion of the text was visible. Jews still produce and use scrolls in their synagogues. It was not until about the second century CE that people began to produce writing in the form of a codex. In this form, pages of writing were bound between covers and read by turning the pages — just like a book today.

The scholar John Drane says of the Old Testament, 'It is the sheer diversity of its contents that partly helps to explain its perennial appeal . . . there is something here for everyone's taste and for many different moods and emotions' (John Drane, *Introducing the Old Testament*, Lion Publishing, 2000).

Jonah is the reluctant prophet who is the subject of the book of Jonah. God asks Jonah to go to the Assyrian capital of Nineveh to preach the message to the people there that they must turn away from their evil ways and seek God's forgiveness, but Jonah refuses because, as foreigners, he would rather see them destroyed and sets off in a boat in the opposite direction! However, God gets his own way in the end because the crew throw Jonah overboard and he ends up inside the stomach of a fish which takes him safely ashore. This time, he does what God asks and the people of Nineveh repent and are forgiven. But Jonah is annoyed at the outcome and God has to remind him that he is the God of 'all' people as well as the God of the Jews.

Ruth is a Moabite woman who has great faith in God and, in spite of the problems of being a foreigner in Israel, follows her mother-in-law, Naomi, to Bethlehem. Later, she marries Boaz, and together they turn out to be the great-grandparents of David, Israel's greatest king — showing that foreigners, too, are loved and blessed by God. For more about the book of Ruth, see 3.5 'Loyal Subjects?' and 5.4 'A Good Read?'

pened, whereas 'narrative' could be used both for historical accounts and for fiction. It can also cover stories that lie between the two — such as the kind of historical drama that we often see on television, sometimes called 'faction' (fact + fiction) because it mixes real events with imaginary ones.

Biblical scholars argue a lot about how historically accurate various Old Testament narratives are, and about how far they were *intended* to be historical. For example, there is not much doubt that the books of Kings were meant to recount real history. On the other hand, many would think that **Jonah** was a deliberate fiction, a good story told to make various important points about the character of God. But there is no doubt that there did exist an overall genre we would call 'narrative', even though there is no Hebrew word for it. All the nations of the ancient Near East told stories: sometimes in prose, sometimes in verse, sometimes to recount historical events, sometimes for pure entertainment. The Old Testament literature is no exception. Here are some examples of different kinds of narrative in the Old Testament:

* stories about the beginnings of things: Genesis 1–11
* stories of ancestors and heroes of the past: Genesis 12–50, Judges, Elijah and Elisha
* short stories focused on individuals: **Ruth**, Jonah
* long, elaborate, realistic stories something like novels: 2 Samuel
* snippets taken from official records: much of the contents of 2 Kings.

Two short excerpts will illustrate how different narrative sections of the Old Testament can be:

The king was deeply moved, and went up to the chamber over the gate, and wept; and as he went, he said, 'O my son Absalom, my son, my son Absalom! Would that I had died instead of you, O Absalom, my son, my son!' (2 Samuel 18:33)

Here King David is lamenting his son, who has just been killed in battle fighting against David's own army. Although Absalom has become his enemy, David cannot stifle his love for him. In this little scene we have a realistic portrayal of grief and love, such as we might find in a novel.

Compare this with the following:

In the fifty-second year of King Azariah of Judah, Pekah son of Remaliah began to reign over Israel in Samaria; he reigned for twenty years. (2 Kings 15:27)

This is the kind of note that appeared in the ancient world in 'annals', lists of the important dates and events of this or that king's reign, such as the Babylonian Chronicles. They are reported without any emotion, and are simply a kind of official record.

One of the features of Old Testament narrative that seems a bit odd to modern readers is that material of these two types (and of many others) is often mixed up together. This is like finding extracts from the football results, the editorial, reports of foreign correspondents, and letters to the editor all blended into a single newspaper item! One of the tasks in studying the Old Testament is recognizing the different types of narrative material that sometimes exist side by side even within a single chapter.

PROPHECY

At the end of the Old Testament, in its Christian arrangement, we meet the books of the prophets — though a few prophets, such as Nathan and Elijah, already appear in the 'historical' books. Prophets, like 'wise men', existed in many cultures in the ancient world. They were people who felt impelled to speak in the name of the gods. They thought the gods had given them a message which they must communicate, whether it brought them honour, or disgrace and suffering. Often it was a message about political affairs. Prophets might appear as if from nowhere, suddenly standing up to challenge a king or other ruler: Elijah seems to have been like this when he suddenly appeared to confront King Ahab and tell him there was to be a long drought (see 1 Kings 17:1), and so was Amos, who tells us that he was not a prophet by profession but felt a sudden call to prophesy (see Amos 7:14–15). Or they might actually be employed by rulers because they could foretell the outcome of military campaigns, and therefore were useful to the nation. You can find a story about such prophets in 1 Kings 22, where King Ahab consults them before going into battle.

The typical way for prophets to express themselves was through **oracles**:

The Babylonian Chronicles are a series of tablets which summarize the principal events of the reigns of the kings of Babylon. The Babylonian Chronicle for 605–594 BCE even refers to Nebuchadnezzar taking his troops to capture Jerusalem in 597 BCE.
(© Copyright The British Museum)

An **oracle**, in this sense, is a short saying given in the name of God.

> *Hear the word of the LORD, O people of Israel:*
> *for the LORD has an indictment against the inhabitants*
> *of the land.*
> *There is no faithfulness or loyalty,*
> *and no knowledge of God in the land.*
> *Swearing, lying, and murder,*
> *and stealing and adultery break out;*
> *bloodshed follows bloodshed.*
> *Therefore the land mourns,*
> *and all who live in it languish.* (Hosea 4:1–3)

As this oracle illustrates, the great prophets of the eighth and seventh centuries BCE (Amos, Hosea, Isaiah, Micah, Jeremiah) often foretold disaster on their people, claiming that national

In biblical studies, the **Exile** refers to the period in Israel's history in the sixth century BCE when many of its people were taken captive and deported from Israel to Babylon. For more about this period, see 3.4 'Refugee Status.'

·ı· Many Christians emphasize the importance of these so-called 'messianic prophecies'. The writer of the Gospel of Matthew in the New Testament was particularly keen on making links between events that the prophets had foretold and events in the life of Jesus, and he used these as proof that Jesus was indeed the awaited Jewish Messiah promised in the Old Testament. For example, he claims that Jesus' miraculous conception was foretold by Isaiah (Matthew 1:2–23 and Isaiah 7:14), that Jesus' birth in Bethlehem was foretold by Micah (Matthew 2:5–6 and Micah 5:2), that Jesus making Galilee his home was foretold by Isaiah (Matthew 4:13–16 and Isaiah 9:1–2, 42:7), and that Jesus and his teaching would be rejected by the Pharisees (Matthew 15:7–9 and Isaiah 29:13). In addition, many details of Jesus' suffering and death in the last few hours of his life appear to echo Isaiah's prophecies (Matthew 27:26 and Isaiah 53:5; Matthew 27:29 and Isaiah 53:3; Matthew 27:31 and Isaiah 53:7; Matthew 27:38 and Isaiah 53:12). However, it is worth remembering that such links are not always that clear or universally accepted and that the Jewish people still await the arrival of the Messiah – a person specially chosen by God who will signal the beginning of a great age of peace and prosperity for all people.

sin would bring national downfall. Probably it was the prophets' disciples who first remembered their oracles. But later they came to be collected into books. This may have begun to happen when the great disaster of the **Exile** (in the sixth century BCE) seemed to have vindicated the prophets.

This collecting was often not very systematic, however, and the prophetic books are consequently hard to read, because many chapters seem to be a jumble of oracles from different situations. It is as if we were to print out a whole series of e-mails from many different times and situations, simply joining them end to end. What is more, later editors often incorporated their own compositions into the prophetic books, so that these acquired the same high status as the original prophet's teachings. The result is that the books of the prophets are some of the most complicated books in the Bible. Isaiah, in particular, contains sayings that range from the eighth to about the fourth century BCE, often arranged thematically rather than in date order. A lot of effort has been devoted by modern scholars to trying to reconstruct the original teaching of the prophets — but also to understanding the ideas and motives of the editors.

In later times people came to believe that the prophets had spoken not just about the events of their own day, but about what would come about in the remote future. This is the traditional Christian idea of the prophet: someone who can look into a far-off time and foretell exactly what would happen then. Christians naturally were especially interested in oracles that concerned a future royal figure, the 'Messiah', who became an important element of Jewish hope in the last couple of centuries BCE — though never so important within the pages of the Old Testament itself as Christians have tended to think. In Judaism, though the predictions of the prophets are not ignored, prophets tend to be valued more for their moral teaching (a theme that has been important for Christians, too). But it is fair to say that in both Judaism and Christianity the prophets' *original* message has tended to be obscured by later ideas and theories about prophecy. Modern scholarship has been important in reconstructing what this original message really was.

LAW

All societies need laws to regulate their lives, and ancient Israel was no exception. The laws that have come down to us in the Old Testament are all 'embedded' in narrative, specifically in the stories about the ancestors of Israel wandering in the deserts between Egypt and Palestine on their way to the Promised Land. They appear in Exodus, Leviticus, Numbers, and Deuteronomy, and it is said that they were given to Israel through Moses.

Other ancient cultures also attributed their laws to a great lawgiver — in Athens, for example, people believed the laws had been established by someone called Solon, and in Mesopotamia various kings were credited with lawgiving. Of these, the most famous was King Hammurabi of Babylon, who lived in the early second millennium BCE — a good thousand years before most of the texts in the Old Testament. The so-called *Code of Hammurabi* preserves very old Babylonian laws, and some are quite close in style and content to laws in the Pentateuch. This may not mean that the Israelites borrowed them directly, but it does show that there was a common legal culture in the ancient Near East in which Israel shared.

For example, all these ancient societies had laws about what to do with dangerous animals. In Exodus 21:28–29 we find the 'law of the goring ox':

> *When an ox gores a man or a woman to death, the ox shall be stoned, and its flesh shall not be eaten; but the owner of the ox shall not be liable. If the ox has been accustomed to gore in the past, and its owner has been warned but has not restrained it, and it kills a man or a woman, the ox shall be stoned, and its owner also shall be put to death.*

Rough justice, but you can see the point. We react in a similar way, though less ferociously, when people fail to muzzle pit bull terriers that have already proved dangerous. The *Code of Hammurabi* contains a provision too similar for the resemblance to be accidental:

> *If an ox, when it was walking along the street, gored a nobleman to death, that case is not subject to claim. If a nobleman's ox was a gorer and his city council had made it known to him that it was a gorer, but he did not pad its horns or tie up his ox, and that ox gored to death a member of the aristocracy, he shall give one half mina of silver.* (Code of Hammurabi 250–51)

These laws are all expressed in the form 'If/When X happens, then Y is to be done', and this is the usual form in ancient Near Eastern laws. The Old Testament also contains a much less common form, the simple 'imperative': 'Do/Do not do X' or 'You shall/shall not do X'. The major examples of this are in the Ten Commandments (Exodus 20:2–17 and Deuteronomy 5:1–21):

> *You shall not murder.*
> *You shall not commit adultery.*
> *You shall not steal.*
> *You shall not bear false witness against your neighbour.*

These short formulas are a kind of summary of more detailed legislation, and are a special feature of Israelite law codes. They may have been one of the distinctive aspects of the laws that were given to Moses. Alternatively, they may reflect later thinking about the essentials of law and the central moral issues in human life. In that case, they could owe something to the teaching of the prophets. In any study

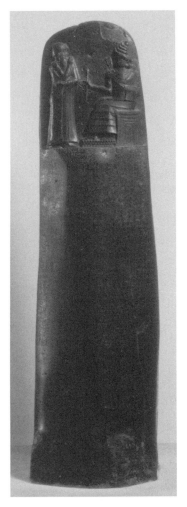

The Code of Hammurabi is one of the most famous ancient law codes. It comprises 282 laws engraved in cuneiform script on a black stone stele (pillar) 2.25 metres high. It is now on display in the Louvre Museum in Paris and was discovered in 1901 by a French archaeologist in the city of Susa, on the borders of present-day Iran and Iraq. Hammurabi was King of Babylon (1792–1750 BCE) and his memorial stele had probably been taken as a trophy of war to Susa from Babylon at some point. The Code of Hammurabi is interesting to biblical scholars because it contains a number of striking similarities to some of the laws of the Old Testament. (Code of Hammurabi, Louvre, Paris/Bridgeman)

of Old Testament ethics, attention to legal texts is obviously essential.

WISDOM

Proverbs circulate in all human cultures, although usually no one knows where they come from. Nowadays we learn them from our families and friends, but at times they get collected into small books. Victorian ladies used them as texts for samplers, and in the past they were often used as convenient short texts for students to copy out when they were learning to write.

> A **proverb** is a short saying which is believed to encapsulate a general truth.

All the cultures in the ancient world had proverbs of this kind, and often they passed from one part of the world to another as people travelled, especially for purposes of trade. There too they were used in schools for writing practice, and we have many texts from ancient Egypt and Mesopotamia that consist of lists of such 'wise' sayings. In the Old Testament the book of Proverbs consists mainly of this kind of material:

> *Hatred stirs up strife, but love covers all offences.*
> *On the lips of one who has understanding wisdom is found,*
>   *but a rod is for the back of one who lacks sense.*
> *The wise lay up knowledge, but the babbling of a fool brings*
>   *ruin near.* (Proverbs 10:12–14)

There are various theories about where such sayings ultimately come from. Some of those in the book of Proverbs reflect life in the Israelite village: 'Those who till their land will have plenty of food, but those who follow worthless pursuits have no sense' (Proverbs 12:11). Others seem to imply life at the royal court: 'When you sit down to eat with a ruler, observe carefully what is before you, and put a knife to your throat if you have a big appetite' (Proverbs 23:1–2).

It may be that old 'folk' sayings from time immemorial have been recorded alongside teachings from more élite circles around the king. Obviously, even old folk-proverbs can have been written down only by people who could write! Such people may have lived mainly in royal circles, at least during the pre-exilic period, and may have been 'official' scribes — what we might call Secretaries of State. One whole section of the book of Proverbs (Proverbs 22:17–24:34) is related in some way to an Egyptian 'wisdom book', *The Teaching of Amen-em-opet*. Probably it was 'borrowed' by Israelite scribes.

> The word **secular** suggests a view of the world which rejects religion, or regards it as of little importance.

> The word **exodus** literally means "way out" and refers to the departure of the Israelites from Egypt under the leadership of Moses.

The atmosphere of the proverbial 'wisdom' literature (found in Job and Ecclesiastes as well as in Proverbs) is rather '**secular**' by comparison with much of the rest of the Old Testament. God is mentioned at times, but there is nothing about the special Israelite ideas of God linked to themes such as the **Exodus** or the giving of the land; nor about the divine Law or the Ten Commandments. The concern is with what will 'work' in life — with leading a sensible and balanced life, at peace with others and with yourself. The 'theology' there is in wisdom seems to be about a general divine providence governing the order of the world, not about miracles or divine intervention in human affairs. Quite similar religious ideas are found in Egyptian and Mesopotamian wisdom, which often refers vaguely to 'the gods' or 'the divine', rather than to particular named gods.

What is more, the teaching in Proverbs is never said to come from God — unlike, for example, the teaching of the prophets, which often uses the formula 'Thus says the LORD'. It is presented as the teaching of a father or mother to his or her children, not as divine revelation:

> *My child, do not forget my teaching,*
> *but let your heart keep my commandments;*
> *for length of days and years of life*
> *and abundant welfare they will give you.* (Proverbs 3:1–2)

POETRY

In Hebrew as in English it is possible to distinguish between prose and verse, though the dividing line is not quite so clear in Hebrew literature. Among the parts of the Old Testament that are in verse one very important book is the **Psalter**. Some of the psalms seem to be hymns composed for public worship. Others are more like English 'lyric poems', reflecting the concerns of the individual. But both types may have been used in both ways — just as Christian hymnbooks contain poems that were originally private but have been adopted for public use, and on the other hand public hymns can be used by individuals in private prayer.

All of the psalms are religious in content, and in fact we do not possess any 'secular' poetry from ancient Israel, though no doubt there was some. The psalms are nearly all addressed to God. They either praise and thank him for his goodness or his generosity, or pray to him for deliverance from distress and trouble. Some of them concern the king, and these may have been written for use in the Temple at Jerusalem, which was in a way a kind of royal chapel. Others seem suitable for use at any place of worship.

Many are laments, and may have been uttered by people specially trained to pray them on behalf of others — this may help to explain why the distress the sufferer is in often has many varied, even incompatible features, with complaints of illness, poverty, and oppression by enemies all mentioned within a single psalm. The psalm was a multi-purpose text, reusable on many different occasions when someone was in trouble.

Although biblical tradition ascribes many of the psalms to David, it is hardly ever possible to discover how old particular psalms are, though a few have features that we know go back a long way in the ancient Near East. Typical of Hebrew poetry is the phenomenon called **parallelism**:

> *For he will deliver you from the snare of the fowler,*
> *and from the deadly pestilence;*

The **Psalter** is the name given to the book of Psalms.

Parallelism in Hebrew poetry is where one line either repeats the idea of the previous line with variations, or else draws a contrast with it.

> he will cover you with his pinions,
>> and under his wings you will find refuge... [repetition]
>
> You will not fear the terror of the night,
>> or the arrow that flies by day,
> or the pestilence that stalks in darkness,
>> or the destruction that wastes at noonday.   [contrast]
>>>>>>>> (Psalm 91:3–6)

This feature definitely goes back a long way in the ancient world, and particularly in the form known as 'step parallelism', which we find especially in some 'psalms' that appear outside the book of Psalms, embedded within narrative texts:

> He sank, he fell,
>> he lay still at her feet;
> at her feet he sank, he fell;
>> where he sank, there he fell dead. (Judges 5:27)

This comes from the very bloodthirsty story of the death of Sisera, which you can find in Judges 4–5. Texts that preserve this kind of parallelism, in which something is repeated and something new added in each line, are generally thought to be very old. Psalm 29 is an example, probably resting on an old **Canaanite** text about the weather-god:

Canaanite is the name given by the Old Testament to a pre-Israelite inhabitant of the land of Israel (Canaan).

> The voice of the LORD is over the waters;
>> the God of glory thunders,
>> the LORD, over mighty waters.
> The voice of the LORD is powerful;
>> the voice of the LORD is full of majesty.
> The voice of the LORD breaks the cedars;
>> the LORD breaks the cedars of Lebanon. (Psalm 29:3–5)

APOCALYPTIC

Nowadays the word 'apocalypse' suggests the end of the world. This does connect with the genre known as 'apocalyptic' in the Bible, but rather indirectly. To explain this we have to describe the genre more closely. Apocalyptic literature in the ancient world was literature that recorded information supposed to have been specially revealed, usually to people of long ago. In this it was not unlike prophecy, but it differed from most prophecy because it was usually expressed in symbolic language, unlike the more direct way that God addresses the prophets. For example, forthcoming events such as battles were described as if they were going to be fought between various animals, which symbolized the earthly powers involved. Four great world empires are described in the book of Daniel as four great 'beasts'. One was like a lion, with eagle's wings; one was like a bear; one was like a winged leopard; and a fourth (the Greek Empire that threatened the Jews in the second century BCE) was so terrible it seemed to be made of bits of many different animals, with iron teeth and ten horns (see Daniel 7:3–8). Thus the apocalyptic vision was a kind of code, and only those in the know, the writer and those who understood him, could decode it correctly.

The information passed on in this cryptic way was most often about coming events, and these were sometimes so vast in scale that they did amount to 'the end of the world' — at least, of the world as the writers and their contemporaries knew it. Often the writers hoped for a new world beyond the present state of affairs. Thus in Revelation 21:1 in the New Testament we read that there will be 'a new heaven and a new earth'. Consequently when people use the word 'apocalypse' today it is usually this idea of the end of the present world that they have in mind. Yet, it is important to see that originally apocalyptic literature was first and foremost about the revealing of mysterious knowledge. It just happens that much of this knowledge was about future disaster.

However, there are apocalypses that reveal other kinds of knowledge. For example, the books of Enoch (which did not get into the Old Testament, but were important for some of the New Testament writers) reveal information about the nature of the stars and planets. Another important apocalyptic work, the book of Jubilees, claims to reveal what God told Moses about the *beginning* of the world rather than the end of it — more than is there in Genesis.

Not much apocalyptic literature was accepted into the Bible, and in the Old Testament only Daniel is really of this kind, though some parts of Isaiah and Zechariah are quite like apocalypses.

The book of Revelation is the only example in the New Testament. It is there that we find the word 'apocalypse' for the first time — it begins 'The revelation [Greek: *apokalypsis*] of Jesus Christ…'. The Old Testament has no special word for apocalyptic books, and probably they were thought of as a special type of prophecy.

From all this we can see how varied the literature of ancient Israel was. Even though what we have in the Old Testament is probably only a fraction of what was written in Israel, it is a highly diverse collection of different types of work. Sometimes even a single book will contain material of diverse types — narrative can also contain poems and laws, for example. And many books, such as those of the prophets, are extremely complex and need careful analysis. Cataloguing the library that is the Old Testament is no easy task!

Do not confuse the words 'apocalyptic' and 'apocryphal'. The name given to the collection of books which are included in the Greek version of the Old Testament but not in the Hebrew Scriptures is the Apocrypha. Thus, any book in this category may be called 'apocryphal' literature. However, to make matters worse, the term 'apocryphal' can also be applied to books completely outside the canon, or indeed to any story which appears to be of dubious authenticity. (For more on the Apocrypha and the canon of the Old Testament, see I.I 'Old Testament or Hebrew Bible?')

Section 2

Major Themes in the Old Testament

2.1 Watchmaker or Living God?
THE OLD TESTAMENT VIEW OF GOD

THE BASICS

- There are many images of God in the Old Testament, and God is presented as both **immanent** and **transcendent**.
- The God of the Old Testament is called by many names — each suggesting something about how the biblical authors viewed God's nature. God's role as the creator of the world is a popular topic in the 'Science versus Theology' debates of the twenty-first century.

ON 23 NOVEMBER 1654 the French thinker Blaise Pascal (1623–62) had a visionary experience in which he came to the conviction that 'the God of Abraham, Isaac, and Jacob' is not 'the God of the philosophers', and that it is the former a Christian should believe in. He was drawing a contrast between ideas of God that can be worked out by human beings and the God revealed in the pages of the Bible and experienced firsthand: known, rather than known about.

What Pascal had in mind as 'the God of the philosophers' was the kind of God later described by William Paley (1743–1805) in his famous comparison of God with a watchmaker in his book *Natural Theology* (1802). This way of thinking argues that we can see, from the order and pattern of the world, that it must have been designed by a rational and purposeful mind — just as you can see by looking at the workings of a watch that it cannot possibly have come into being by accident. However, the problem with the comparison is that the watchmaker who has made a watch then leaves it, and need take no further part in how it functions. People soon said that Paley's God, like the watchmaker, set up the universe in the beginning, but had no further involvement with it. For practical purposes God is an absentee, a distant creator who has no 'hands-on' interest in the world he has made (a theory often known as **deism**). Pascal was contrasting such a God with the living God of the Jewish and Christian tradition,

When applied to God, the term **immanent** means that God is involved in the world and present in it. Do not confuse this term with 'imminent', which means 'coming soon'!

When applied to God, the term **transcendent** means that God is greater than the world and in some sense is beyond it and outside human experience.

Deism is a term for a belief in the existence of God, but as one who does not intervene in the normal course of human affairs.

the God who relates to particular people and is involved in their everyday lives: the 'God of Abraham, Isaac, and Jacob'.

In this chapter we shall look at the idea of God in the Old Testament, and ask whether this God is really different from 'the God of the philosophers'. This will involve presenting Old Testament ideas about God so far as possible in the Old Testament's own terms. There is no doubt that the Old Testament does not speak in the same language as western philosophy, but it will still prove possible to make some useful comparisons.

A GOD INVOLVED IN THE WORLD

Anyone who begins to read the Old Testament will soon come to appreciate Pascal's distinction, because the God we encounter in its pages is very much a 'hands-on' God. We can see this in four ways.

1. Creation: the potter's hands

As early as the second chapter of Genesis we find a picture of God as a potter, making the world, and human beings in it, in the most 'hands-on' way imaginable: taking clay in his hands and shaping it. 'The LORD God formed man from the dust of the ground' (Genesis 2:7). Later, when he creates the first woman, God does so by taking one of the man's ribs, closing up the wound, and then shaping the rib into a human being (Genesis 2:21–22). This is typical of what many scholars think is the earliest layer of writing in the Pentateuch, the so-called 'J' source. God, for this writer, is a person like us, though of course very much more powerful. In the next chapter he can even be found 'walking in the garden at the time of the evening breeze' (Genesis 3:8) and talking face to face with Adam and Eve.

The writers of the Old Testament do not seem to have been able to imagine a God who made the world, and then went away and left it to its own devices. For them, God is intimately involved in all that goes on, and there is nowhere that God is absent. We find this fact celebrated in the Psalms, too:

> *Where can I go from your spirit?*
>   *Or where can I flee from your presence?*
> *If I ascend to heaven, you are there;*
>   *if I make my bed in Sheol, you are there....*
> *For it was you who formed my inward parts;*
>   *you knit me together in my mother's womb....*
>   *My frame was not hidden from you*
> *when I was being made in secret,*
>   *intricately woven in the depths of the earth.*
> *Your eyes beheld my unformed substance.*
>   (Psalm 139:7–8, 13, 15–16)

The writer is saying that the God who created the world is also the God who made me, and who continues to be concerned with me. He will not abandon me; on the other hand, I cannot escape him even if I want to.

2. A special relationship: God and his people

To say that the God of the Old Testament is 'the God of Abraham, Isaac, and Jacob' has an obvious truth, in that the Old Testament presents God as greatly concerned with a particular people, Israel, which is seen as consisting of the descendants of these three **patriarchs**.

For most of the writers of the Old Testament it is obvious that the God of Israel has dominion over the whole world, and is not a 'local' god. There were believed to be local gods in many nations in the ancient world, indeed there were even gods associated with particular households, and it seems that there were times when some Israelites believed in such gods. Thus, although we do not know how old this story really is, in the account of how Jacob and his wives fled from his uncle Laban we read that Rachel took with her the household gods and hid them in the luggage (see Genesis 31:25–35). Yet the God of Israel is not a local god, but rules over the whole world. So, Amos asks, 'Did I not bring Israel up from the land of Egypt, *and the Philistines from Caphtor and the Arameans from Kir?*' (Amos 9:7, our emphasis), indicating that every nation on earth owes its history to the God Israel worships.

However, this does not detract from the fact that God has a special relationship with this one nation, Israel. The Old Testament, as we have seen, sets the history of Israel in the context of world history, but there is no doubt where God's interest specially lies, for that history quickly narrows down (from Genesis 12 onwards) to Abraham and his descendants. Even when the Old Testament talks in rather general terms of what God is like, as it occasionally does, his characteristics are closely linked to how he acts towards Israel. Thus in Exodus 34:6–7 God proclaims to Moses what he is like:

> The LORD, the LORD,
> a God merciful and gracious,
> slow to anger,
> and abounding in steadfast love and faithfulness,
> keeping steadfast love for the thousandth generation,
> forgiving iniquity and transgression and sin,
> yet by no means clearing the guilty,
> but visiting the iniquity of the parents
> upon the children
> and the children's children
> to the third and fourth generation.

Similar passages can be found in Numbers 14:18, Nehemiah 9:17, Psalms 86:15, 103:8, and 145:8, Nahum 1:3, and Jonah 4:2. Such examples are very much focused on how God acts within Israel, rather than a generalization about his activity towards the whole human race. 'Steadfast love' and 'faithfulness' are part of his special covenant relationship with Israel,

Patriarchs is a term used in biblical studies to describe the key ancestors or father figures of the Israelites, specifically Abraham, Isaac, Jacob, and Jacob's twelve sons, after whom the later tribes of Israel were named.

not an aspect of his relationship with humankind as such, and it is in Israel's history that the tension between 'forgiving iniquity' and yet 'visiting the iniquity of the parents upon the children' is worked out.

3. Miracles: a God who intervenes

Another of the ways in which the Old Testament God is as distant as possible from the remote watchmaker is seen in his continual interventions in the world he has made, through what we would call **miracles**. The entire existence of Israel depends on a series of divine interventions, changing what would otherwise have been the natural course of events. Thus the very fact that Abraham had any descendants who could turn into the people of Israel is seen as miraculous, for Sarah, his wife, was past the normal child-bearing age when God appeared to her and Abraham and told them that they would have a child.

In the same way, it is only through God's acts of power that the people are brought out of their slavery in Egypt, and given the Promised Land. God intervenes (through 'the angel of the LORD') to kill all the firstborn sons of the Egyptians, and it is only then that Pharaoh releases them (Exodus 12). Even after that, Pharaoh still sends his army to pursue the Israelites, and God has to drown them in the Red Sea to keep his people safe (Exodus 14). Yet here we already hit a problem for the modern reader of the Old Testament. God's miraculous interventions are not always what we might regard as morally defensible. Although his love for Israel apparently entailed killing thousands of Egyptians, the point for the writers of the Old Testament is simply that the God of the Old Testament is a highly interventionist God. Miracles are a big part of his repertoire of actions.

Sometimes it is suggested that the Old Testament does not really have a category we could call 'miracles', because everything was thought to derive from God: people did not have an idea that certain events were 'natural' and others 'supernatural'. However, the very fact that events such as the birth of Abraham's son Isaac, the death of the firstborn, and the crossing of the Red Sea are singled out for mention suggests that they are very unusual — so contrary to what anyone might expect. People in Israel knew that women could not have babies after the menopause, that there were not normally plagues that singled out firstborn children, and that water did not suddenly part to allow armies to pass across on dry ground. In making these things happen God was doing something special, 'wonderful deeds' as they put it (in Hebrew *niphla'oth*, pronounced niph-laa-oath, with the stress on the final syllable).

4. A personal God: the divine names

In the Old Testament God is portrayed as a personal God who has a name, or rather a whole series of names. The name most commonly used for God in the Old Testament is writ-

A **miracle** can be defined as an event which is the result of a direct intervention of God that breaks all known laws of nature.

 'The miracle is only in the *timing* of such fortunate events. . . . For the Ancient Near East, there were no lucky chances or accidental happenings; all things were the result of divine will. When the ordinary pattern changed dramatically, then it was a sign to be read and understood by all.' (Lawrence Boadt, *Reading the Old Testament — An Introduction,* Paulist Press, 1984)

When Abraham's wife Sarah hears God's message that she is going to have a son, the Old Testament records that she laughed, principally because she was 90 years old and Abraham was 100! God's reaction to her laughter is, 'Is anything too wonderful for the LORD?' (Genesis 18:14). Later, when her son is born, she laughs again and calls him 'Isaac' — a name formed from the Hebrew word meaning 'he laughs'. You can read the whole mysterious story about this in Genesis 18 and Genesis 21:1–7, and a tale of a similarly miraculous birth to a barren woman in I Samuel 1–2, which relates the story of Hannah and the birth of her son, Samuel.

ten in Hebrew as the four letters YHWH. However, we do not know for sure how this **tetragrammaton** was pronounced in ancient times since the Hebrew language was originally written without vowels, and by New Testament times there was a taboo against saying God's name aloud anyway because it was considered too holy. The best modern guess is that it was pronounced Yahweh. It also occurs in shorter forms, such as Yahu (pronounced yahoo!) and Yah, and we sometimes meet it as part of names. Thus, Isaiah in Hebrew is *Yeshayahu* ('Yahweh will save').

Once the taboo about the divine name came into force, people started to say 'the Lord' whenever they encountered YHWH in the biblical text: in Hebrew this is *Adonai* (pronounced uh-doa-nigh). This is the reason why we often meet 'the LORD' in capital letters in English translations of the Bible: it is a signal that the name YHWH is there in the text. When Hebrew did start to be written with vowels, people adopted the strange custom of adding the *vowels* of *Adonai* to the *consonants* of YHWH: the vowels were a reminder that you must say *Adonai*, and there was never any intention that the hybrid word this produced was actually to be read out loud. Misunderstanding this, later generations tried to read the resulting 'word' as if it were a real word, and it came out as *Yehowah*, which is the origin of the English 'Jehovah', a word that never really existed. No one knows what YHWH originally meant, if indeed it meant anything, but there were speculations about it, to which we will return later in this chapter.

Of course, there are many other names for God in the Old Testament and some of these begin with the element 'El'. El was the chief God among the Canaanites, who lived in Palestine before the Israelites, and it seems that some of them sometimes worshipped him alongside, or even instead of, YHWH. El came, as it were, in local versions: El-Elyon, El-Shaddai, El-Olam. Biblical translations 'translate' these names as 'God Most High', 'God Almighty', and 'the Everlasting God', but these translations rest on ancient guesses rather than really telling us what the names mean. What is clear is that over time these names, which were originally the names of other gods, came to be understood as titles of YHWH.

From our perspective, it is rather strange to think that God would have a name at all. In the later Old Testament period Israelites also stopped thinking of YHWH as a name that distinguished their god from other people's gods, and treated it simply as a pointer to the only God. Like us, they also started to refer to him simply by the word 'god', in Hebrew *Elohim* (pronounced el-oa-heem, with the stress on the last syllable). In the Pentateuch, where the earlier texts still say YHWH, later layers often say simply *Elohim*, 'God' — not a name, but just the ordinary noun for 'God', 'a god', or even, since the word is plural in form anyway, 'gods'. For our present purposes, though, the fact that God did have a

יהוה

The Hebrew word used for the name of God in the Old Testament, YHWH, is sometimes referred to as the **tetragrammaton** — literally 'the four letters'.

'Why does God have so many names? It's no mistake. It's not a case of sloppy editing. It's because the multiple names best characterize the awesomely complex figure of God.' (Bernhard Lang, 'Why God Has So Many Names', in *Bible Review*, August 2003)

name or names is important, because it shows how personal he was originally thought to be: not an abstract principle, but a person (or Person).

Interestingly, it is perhaps worth noting at this point that God in the Old Testament is always treated as male. On occasion he sometimes has feminine features:

> But Zion said, 'The LORD has forsaken me,
>   my Lord has forgotten me.'
> Can a woman forget her nursing-child,
>   or show no compassion for the child of her womb?
>
> (Isaiah 49:14–15)

— but he is predominantly thought of in masculine terms, and always referred to as 'he'. In fact, by the end of the Old Testament period people were quite clear that God was not sexual at all, and so was strictly neither male nor female. Nevertheless, the tendency to treat God as essentially a male figure has persisted.

A GOD WHO TRANSCENDS THE WORLD

In Christian theology God is said to be both 'immanent' and 'transcendent'. The book of Jeremiah expresses this idea:

> Am I a God near by, says the LORD, and not a God far off? . . .
>   Do I not fill heaven and earth? says the LORD.
>
> (Jeremiah 23:23–24)

The transcendent aspect of God in the Old Testament needs to be taken account of because, in some ways, it brings him nearer to 'the God of the philosophers' than do the aspects at which we have previously looked.

1. Creation: the word of command

Whereas Genesis 2 (the 'J' account) sees God as the potter working clay into human beings, Genesis 1 (the 'P' account) stresses that a mere word from God is enough to make the world exist. Eight times in this chapter God speaks, and some feature of the world comes into being. He does not need, as it were, to get his hands dirty.

There is little doubt that there was to some extent a development over time from the more 'hands-on' view of God to this picture of him as the supreme sovereign uttering his words of command. It is mainly in texts from after the **Exile** that we find an emphasis on God's more 'transcendent' aspects; and, apart from Genesis 1, the part of the Old Testament that presents this idea most strongly is Isaiah 40–55. This is a section of the book of Isaiah generally thought to date from the sixth century, and it was written by a prophet who lived shortly before the fortunes of Israel revived after the long years of domination by the Babylonians. This prophet, usually referred to as the 'Second Isaiah', stresses that God is supreme over the whole world:

In biblical studies, the **Exile** refers to the period in Israel's history in the sixth century BCE when many of its people were taken captive and deported from Israel to Babylon.

Even the nations are like a drop from a bucket,
  and are accounted as dust on the scales. . . .
All the nations are as nothing before him;
  they are accounted by him as less than nothing and empti-
  ness. (Isaiah 40:15, 17)

He was the sole creator of the universe:

I made the earth,
  and created humankind upon it;
it was my hands that stretched out the heavens,
  and I commanded all their host. (Isaiah 45:12)

The theme of God's sovereign creation is also developed in the Psalms:

By the word of the LORD the heavens were made,
  and all their host by the breath of his mouth. . . .
For he spoke, and it came to be;
  he commanded, and it stood firm. (Psalm 33:6, 9)

Comparing Old Testament texts with myths from other ancient cultures suggests that the idea that all God had to do was speak the word is unusual, if not actually unique, among the cultures Israel lived alongside. Usually the idea was that the gods had to work on some already existing material, which presented something of a challenge to them. However, the later writings in the Old Testament emphasize that God had a totally free hand. The created world is, as Second Isaiah saw it, trivially small in comparison with him, and creating it was the work of a moment.

2. God's universal scope

We saw that the God of the Old Testament has a particular concern for Israel, yet is not limited in scope to one single nation: he controls the affairs of all the nations. This too is strongly highlighted by Second Isaiah. He sees the exile of Israel as an act brought about by YHWH — whereas some Israelites thought it showed the gods of Babylon had defeated him. In the same way, the takeover of the Babylonian Empire by Cyrus II the Great, founder of the Persian Empire, was an act of YHWH:

Who has roused a victor from the east,
  summoned him to his service?
He delivers up nations to him,
  and tramples kings under foot. . . .
Who has performed and done this,
  calling the generations from the beginning?
I, the LORD, am first,
  and will be with the last. (Isaiah 41:2, 4)

The prophet can even call Cyrus God's 'anointed one' (Isaiah 45:1), a title usually reserved for the Israelite king. Of course, Cyrus would have been surprised to know that it was the God of the Israelites dictating his fortunes!

God's universal sovereignty means that everything in heaven and earth (i.e., from an Israelite perspective, the whole universe) exists to praise him, as we see in a psalm such as Psalm 148:

> *Praise the LORD from the heavens;*
> *praise him in the heights!*
> *Praise him, all his angels;*
> *praise him, all his host!*
>
> *Praise him, sun and moon;*
> *praise him, all you shining stars! . . .*
>
> *Praise the LORD from the earth,*
> *you sea monsters and all deeps,*
> *fire and hail, snow and frost,*
> *stormy wind fulfilling his command! . . .*
>
> *Kings of the earth and all peoples,*
> *princes and all rulers of the earth!*
> *Young men and women alike,*
> *old and young together!* (Psalm 148:1–3, 7–8, 11–12)

YHWH here is still the God of Israel, but he is also very much more than that: a God of universal scope and authority.

3. Providence: a God whose actions are hidden

As well as intervening in the world he has made through miraculous acts, God is also seen in the Old Testament as working through a *secret providence*. As the book Sirach or Ecclesiasticus (in the **Apocrypha**) puts it, 'Many things greater than these lie hidden, for I have seen but few of his works' (Sirach 43:32). From this point of view, God is so great that his power is displayed not only in miracles, but also in the whole drift and direction of history, and often we cannot see what he is doing.

There are two narratives in the Old Testament where God's hidden hand is particularly important to the way the story is told. These are the story of Joseph (Genesis 37–50) and the story of the court of David (2 Samuel 9–20, 1 Kings 1–2). In both these stories most events seem to unfold according to ordinary human patterns of motivation and action, rather as they would in a novel. Yet, in both cases the reader becomes aware that God is somehow involved in what is happening, and has purposes of his own which he is bringing to fruition.

In the Joseph story, this is made explicit towards the end when Joseph speaks to his brothers who had sold him as a slave. By doing so they had unwittingly caused him to travel

Apocrypha is the name given to the collection of books which are included in the Greek version of the Old Testament (the Septuagint) but not in the Hebrew Scriptures. These books are often also called 'deuterocanonical' books.

to Egypt, and so he was there when the Egyptians needed a shrewd official who could make provision for them in a time of great famine. In the process he was also able to provide for his family — including of course his hostile brothers — when the famine also affected them in Palestine:

> *Joseph said to them, 'Do not be afraid! Am I in the place of God? Even though you intended to do harm to me, God intended it for good, in order to preserve a numerous people, as he is doing today.'* (Genesis 50:19–20)

In the story of David, we are not given even this much indication of God's purposes behind the historical events. Yet after a tale of much violence, all the possible pretenders to David's throne except Solomon have been eliminated — nearly all through ordinary human means, rather than by divine intervention — and 'the kingdom was established in the hand of Solomon' (1 Kings 2:46). And there cannot be much doubt in the reader's mind that this is exactly what God wanted to happen all along, for when Solomon was born we are told that 'the LORD loved him' (2 Samuel 12:24). The interplay of human and divine action here is very complicated and is never spelled out for us; but there can be no doubt that God is involved in the process in a subtle way.

4. A super-personal God

A God who has a name, even a mysterious one such as YHWH, is bound to seem rather human: he is a person alongside other persons. However, the Old Testament also contains indications that God is beyond personality in our sense, and goes beyond our power to imagine him. One way in which this comes out is in the Old Testament's opposition to **anthropomorphism**. As we saw, in Genesis 2 God walks in the garden — so presumably he has a body, including legs to walk on. In Isaiah 6, the prophet sees him 'sitting on a throne' — so he must have something to sit on! Yet, in later books of the Bible people become much more reticent about describing God in these human terms. We see this most clearly in Ezekiel, who lived more than a hundred years later than Isaiah, in the early sixth century BCE. Ezekiel, like Isaiah, saw a vision of God, but where Isaiah was able to say, quite simply, 'I saw the Lord' (Isaiah 6:1), Ezekiel writes this:

> *There was something like a throne, in appearance like sapphire; and seated above the likeness of the throne was something that seemed like a human form. Upward from what appeared like the loins I saw something like gleaming amber, something that looked like fire enclosed all round; and downwards from what looked like the loins I saw something that looked like fire, and there was a splendour all round. Like the bow in a cloud on a rainy day, such was the appearance of the splendour all round. This was the appearance of the likeness of the glory of the LORD.* (Ezekiel 1:26–28)

Anthropomorphism is the act of making God seem like a human being by ascribing human characteristics to God, often in an attempt to make God more understandable.

'The appearance of the likeness of the glory of the LORD': that is as close as Ezekiel dares to come to saying that what he saw was God. If you saw God, you would see a figure that looked human — that is clear. Nevertheless, the prophet immediately stresses that of course God is *not* human, only 'human-like'. Here we have a move away from imagining God as a person like us, and a realization that he must in reality be very *un*like us.

The name YHWH, which is very different from most divine names in the ancient world in not having an obvious meaning, came in time to be seen as a sort of symbol of the mysteriousness of God. The verb 'to be' in Hebrew is *hayah*, and there are forms of it that come quite close to YHWH, especially the form which in Hebrew can express the present or future and is known as the 'imperfect'. 'He is/he will be' in Hebrew is *yihyeh*, which is not so far from *yahweh*. In Exodus 3 Moses, who has just seen God in the burning bush, asks God what his name is, and God replies, 'I am what I am' or 'I will be what I will be' (*ehyeh asher ehyeh*). This looks like a pun on the holy name YHWH, but scholars do not agree on what it means. One likely explanation is that it is a kind of refusal to answer the question. You want to know who I am — but 'I will be who I will be'. This is like the line in some fairytales or pantomimes: 'We shall see what we shall see!' It gives absolutely nothing away. Like Ezekiel's vision, this scene is a way of stressing the mystery of God, the fact that we can know little or nothing about him.

There are other scholars who think that the name YHWH really was connected with the verb 'to be', so that this is not just a pun. That is certainly what ancient translators of this text thought. In the **Septuagint**, Exodus 3:14 is translated, 'I am the one who is' (Greek *ho ōn*). This expresses a profound idea about God, that he is the one who supremely exists — who is, we might say, the most real being there is. In the Middle Ages philosophers reflected a great deal on this text, and developed the idea that God is not *a* being, but Being itself — the Ultimate Reality. That is a lot to read out of the puzzling words in Exodus, and probably the ancient Israelites had not got that far in their quest to understand God. It does remind us, though, that the God of Abraham, Isaac, and Jacob — as he is described in the very next verses (Exodus 3:15–16) — is not necessarily so far from 'the God of the philosophers' as we began by suggesting.

A note on God and creation

In a chapter discussing God's relationship to the world, the subject of creation itself needs addressing. It is obvious that the Old Testament presents God as the Creator of everything that exists; and this belief is found not only in Genesis, but also in Second Isaiah, in the Psalms, and indeed in many other places in the Old Testament. However, readers of the Bible are often asked to consider whether taking this fact seriously means that they ought to be **creationists**.

According to an ancient account, seventy scholars were originally involved in translating the Hebrew Scriptures into Greek. For this reason, based on the Latin word for seventy, the **Septuagint** is the name given to the Greek version of the Old Testament. It is sometimes abbreviated to LXX (the Roman numerals for seventy).

Creationist is the term applied to a person who believes that the story of the creation of the world in Genesis 1 is correct, irrespective of any scientific explanations about the beginning of the universe.

The response to this question by someone who wants to take the Bible seriously but who is also convinced by modern scientific accounts of the beginning of the universe is usually based around four points. The first of these is that believing that God is indeed the Creator does not necessarily mean thinking that the author of Genesis 1 got the details right. Second Isaiah is just as certain that God is the Creator of the world, but does not tell us the order of events in its creation. Thus, you can believe that Genesis is right about the fact of creation without thereby being committed to the detail. A second point is that it is possible that the detailed account in Genesis 1 is not intended to be taken literally, but is a poetic reflection on the nature of creation. The author tells us about the divine 'order' of things, sorting them into categories much as do some of the psalms (see Psalm 148 above), but not really about the 'order' in which they came to be. Third, some people aim to achieve some kind of compromise between the Bible and the scientific evidence by suggesting that the 'days' of creation in Genesis 1 stand for much longer periods of time. This allows the reader to accept the veracity of both God's creation of the world and, for example, the scientific theory of evolution proposed by **Charles Darwin**. Other people attempt a similar compromise between the Bible and scientific evidence when assessing the so-called 'Big Bang' theory for the creation of the universe, stating that it was God who was responsible for the spark of energy that caused the great explosion. However, those believers who wish to accept the scientific explanations of creation and evolution, and who are content simply to put God at the beginning of the process or in the gaps, should be wary. In his book *The Blind Watchmaker* (1986), Richard Dawkins, one of the most modern advocates of the theory of evolution, argues that the process of evolution alone is capable of producing the diversity and complexity of life on earth and that there is no need

In 1654, an Irish Archbishop, James Ussher, announced that the world was created at 9 a.m. on 23 October 4004 BCE. He had used the biblical genealogies as the basis for his calculation. Of course, the modern Jewish calendar is also reckoned from the date of creation according to the Old Testament — for this reason, the Jewish equivalent to the year 2004 is 5764.

Up until the mid 1850s it was generally believed that life began in the Garden of Eden much as the book of Genesis described. However, **Charles Darwin**'s publication of *The Origin of Species* in 1859 brought the scientific truth of the biblical account into question. In his book, Darwin suggested that only organisms that are well suited to their environment survive and that only the strongest organisms survive. He suggested that these organisms then reproduce and pass on their advantageous characteristics to their young. Since species are, therefore, constantly changing or evolving, Darwin said that humans and apes must have a common ancestor — a claim that caused scandal. However, it is worth noting that Darwin's theory of natural selection was discussing only the beginnings of life, and not the beginnings of the universe. For this reason, Darwin's theory does not actually discount God as the source of all beginnings. Yet, his ideas about natural selection caused outrage amongst the creationists, and the opposition of the Church to his views caused Darwin to turn from Christianity to agnosticism.

Although the teaching of evolution in schools is still an issue in some American states, Darwin's theory of evolution remains very widely accepted amongst scientists and the public alike; and Darwin was, in fact, eventually buried in Westminster Abbey in London.

The fact that most cultures have a story, many of them in a poetic format, about how the world was created has often been used as a starting point for analysis of the biblical stories of creation. It is claimed that the biblical stories are simply one more example of a people pondering the question of their origins and composing a story to give a starting point to their history and a meaning and a purpose to their lives and the world around them. One example from the ancient Near East is the Hymn to Ra, the god honoured by the Egyptians as creator and ruler. Discovered in the 1860s, this poetic account written in hieroglyphics on papyrus includes the idea that Ra spoke and living creatures appeared

out of nothing — a concept familiar to readers of the biblical account of the seven days of creation.

However, perhaps the most well-known story is the Enuma Elish, the Babylonian creation story in the form of a hymn of praise to the god Marduk who first formed earth from the body of Tiamat, the conquered goddess of the sea. In this story, Marduk uses half her body to form the heavens and half to form the earth, and mixes the blood of another god, Kingu, with dust from the earth to create humankind. For more on the Babylonian creation story and how the term 'myth' might be applied to the biblical creation stories, see 3.1 'Tall Stories?'

The 'Big Bang' theory states that a dense concentration of matter and energy exploded around fifteen million years ago, resulting in particles and energy matter being thrown together into hot lumps which formed stars. According to this theory, these stars clustered together in groups, called galaxies, and some of the stars then exploded and re-formed to produce new stars like the sun and the earth. Since, by chance, the earth was held in orbit around the sun and since, due to its position, water and air were present, life forms began to appear. Such an explanation for creation is included in the popular modern book by Stephen Hawking, *A Brief History of Time* (Bantam, 1995).

Speaking of Paley's theory about God and the creation of the world, Richard Dawkins says that his argument '. . . is made with passionate sincerity and is informed by the best biological scholarship of his day, but it is wrong, gloriously and utterly wrong. The analogy between telescope and eye, between watch and living organism, is false. All appearances to the contrary, the only watchmaker in nature is the blind force of physics, albeit deployed in a very special way. A true watchmaker has foresight: he designs his cogs and springs, and plans their interconnections, with a future purpose in his mind's eye. Natural selection, the blind, unconscious, automatic process which Darwin discovered, and which we now know is the explanation for the existence and apparently purposeful form of all life, has no purpose in mind. It has no mind and no mind's eye. It does not plan for the future. It has no vision, no foresight, no sight at all. If it can be said to play the role of watchmaker in nature, it is the *blind* watchmaker' (Richard Dawkins, *The Blind Watchmaker: Why the Evidence of Evolution Reveals a Universe Without Design*, 1986).

to involve a supernatural force, such as God, at any stage. Finally, some people would simply point out that the Bible is not a scientific document, but a document about religious faith. With this stance, being committed to it means thinking that it got its theology right, but not necessarily that it is also right about scientific questions such as the way the world came into being. Thus, science and theology are not in conflict because they are about two ways of seeing the world, each with its own proper sphere of activity.

There are clearly some big questions here about the nature of religious belief and the nature of our commitment to a scientific view of the world, which can't be solved in a book about the Old Testament. On the other hand, although some may find the points made above helpful, they do not really resolve the difficulties fully.

For example, the word 'day' in Hebrew is used everywhere else in the Old Testament to mean a period of twenty-four hours, just as in English. The fact that the days of creation have 'an evening and a morning' surely means that they are meant literally. Therefore, one might say that trying to reconcile the Bible and science by denying this is a fudge — a compromise that does justice neither to the text nor to science. Furthermore, it may be true that we can live with Genesis 1 only by treating it as poetry, not as a statement of sober fact, but it is not at all clear that the original writers saw it that way. Indeed they seem to have presented it as the best account known to them of how things actually happened.

Perhaps it might be more honest to say that either the scientific account of the origins of the universe or the account in Genesis 1 must be wrong; logically, of course, they could both be wrong, but they can't both be right.

In the end, the question for the reader may be more one about the nature of the Bible's authority. For some people, being committed to the Bible means believing that it is always right, whatever the evidence to the contrary. However, it is noticeable that many people who are very firmly committed to Genesis 1 do not treat the Bible as quite such an oracle on other subjects. Often, for example, they are not nearly so worried about questions like the implausibly long lives of some of the figures in Genesis (Methuselah is said to have lived to be 969 in Genesis 5:27), or the exact details of some of the battles in the historical books. You may feel that these are less important than the details of the creation, but the Old Testament itself reports them all in much the same way. So the person who is convinced by a scientific account but who wants to go on affirming the authority of the Bible in some sense may need to rethink what is meant by that authority. It will have to mean something compatible with the Bible's containing errors of fact. On the other hand, you may feel that the authority of Scripture is so great that it overrules scientific evidence, however strong. This is a very difficult position to hold in the modern world, but it is intellectually coherent.

Of course, for some readers, these issues will not be problems because they have no commitment to the Bible anyway. However, those with some kind of faith commitment to the Old Testament should see that the question of 'creationism' cannot be resolved just on its own terms: it involves much bigger questions about how we read the Bible and what kind of information we go to it for.

2.2 The Chosen People?
GOD'S RELATIONSHIP WITH ISRAEL

T H E   B A S I C S

- The concepts of election and covenant are central to the relationship between God and his people as presented in the Old Testament.
- It is a matter for debate how ancient, and how unique in the ancient Near East, such ideas really are, and modern scholarship suggests that the Old Testament's picture of the situation may be a rather idealized one.

YHWH is the primary way God's name appears in the Old Testament. It is simply four Hebrew consonants which many scholars believe may have been pronounced Yahweh. For a more detailed examination of this issue, see 2.1 'Watchmaker or Living God?'

In biblical studies, the word **election** is a technical term which relates to God's choice of particular people, or of a group of people, for certain purposes which involve a special relationship with him.

A **covenant** is a solemn, binding, mutual agreement between two parties; the covenants between God and his people are an important feature of the Old Testament. The Hebrew word for covenant is *berith*. It is pronounced buh-reeth, with the stress on the second syllable, although Jews in Britain and America nowadays often pronounce the word 'brit'.

'YHWH IS THE GOD of Israel and Israel is the people of YHWH.' That is not an actual quotation from the Old Testament, but it sums up very well one of its main themes. All the way through the Old Testament the assumption is that there is a special relationship between Israel and the God named YHWH. This idea is sometimes described as the theme of Israel's **election** — God's choice of Israel as his people — and is often presented in the Old Testament as connected with God's **covenant** with them.

However, modern biblical scholars do not always think that the Bible's own account of the history of Israel's ideas corresponds to the way those ideas really developed; and nowhere is this truer than in the case of the ideas of election and covenant. In this section we shall look at what the Old Testament tells us about these themes if it is read uncritically, and then go on to explain how people now think they actually developed over time. The two versions are strikingly different.

'The special relationship between God and Israel in the Old Testament is defined in the doctrine of election and expressed in the language of the covenant.' (G.E. Wright, 'The Old Testament Against Its Environment', *Studies in Biblical Theology*, Number 2, Naperville, Illinois, 1950)

GOD AND ISRAEL ACCORDING TO THE OLD TESTAMENT

According to the Old Testament itself, Israel understood itself as the people of YHWH from the very earliest times. Indeed, YHWH had a relationship with some individuals even before there was an Israel, since he made himself known to Adam and Eve, and to Noah. However, it was in selecting Abraham that he first narrowed down his choice to the ancestor of a single people (Genesis 12). He guided Abraham's family as they moved from Mesopotamia to Palestine, and then he made a covenant with Abraham under which he promised that Abraham's descendants would become very numerous and would inhabit this land for ever.

> 'Look towards heaven and count the stars, if you are able to count them.... So shall your descendants be.... To your descendants I give this land, from the river of Egypt to the great river, the river Euphrates.' (Genesis 15:5, 18)

From this point on, the Old Testament can be read as the story of how God's promises to Abraham gradually found their fulfilment. The people were often disobedient, but God always remained true to his promises. Even if he sometimes had to punish them for a time, he was always there to bless them again afterwards.

Seen in this light the Old Testament can be described as a record of God's **salvation history** with Israel. The **Pentateuch** and the historical or narrative books of the Bible — Joshua, Judges, Samuel, Kings — develop this way of seeing the history of Israel. They see history from the perspective of an unfolding divine purpose as they trace the various trials and tribulations that Israel went through in the course of its life in Palestine. That history contained much failure and distress, but through it all Israel remained the people of YHWH, and he would never abandon them: 'you shall be my treasured possession out of all the peoples' (Exodus 19:5).

1. The covenant with Noah

According to Genesis 9:9–17, God established a covenant with Noah. This covenant is essentially a promise by God that he will never again destroy humankind, as he had done in the great Flood, and he gives the rainbow as a sign of his promise. When it rains, people will see the rainbow and will remember that God has promised never again to let the rain turn into a destructive deluge, drowning all life.

A 'covenant' here means a solemn promise. There is no suggestion that the people with whom the covenant is made have any obligations towards God, simply that God has imposed an obligation on himself. Indeed, the covenant with Noah applies not just to Israel (which of course at this stage does not yet exist), but to the whole of humanity, and indeed to 'every living creature' (Genesis 9:12, 15, 16) — animals as well as human beings, and obviously there cannot be any question of animals being under obligations. The covenant with Noah is a pure act of kindness on God's part.

Nevertheless, at the same time as he makes the covenant, God also issues a demand, though it seems not to be linked in any way to the promise. The demand is that human beings should respect the blood of all living creatures. In the case of animals, humans must not consume the blood when they eat meat: this is the origin of one of the main food laws in

The term **salvation history** refers to the idea of history being seen as the unfolding of a divine purpose rather than as a series of random events. It is a translation of the German word *Heilsgeschichte*, which refers to 'the mighty acts of God in history'.

Pentateuch is a common collective term for the first five books of the Old Testament — Genesis, Exodus, Leviticus, Numbers, and Deuteronomy. It is derived from the Greek word *pente* meaning 'five'. In the Jewish tradition, these are sometimes referred to as the five books of Moses.

Judaism, which says that blood must be drained from meat before it is sold for food. In the case of human beings, they must not shed blood at all, and anyone who does so is to be executed as a murderer (Genesis 9:4–6). In later times, Jews came to see these laws as examples of moral rules binding on all human beings, since they had been given to Noah, who was the ancestor of the whole human race (because everyone except his family had been wiped out by the Flood). For this reason, these universal moral rules are sometimes described as the 'Noahite' or 'Noahide' Laws.

2. The covenant with Abraham

Genesis also presents God's covenant with Abraham as essentially a promise to him by God. The promise has two elements:

- Abraham will become the ancestor of a very large people
- This people will come to occupy the Promised Land.

There are the beginnings of a fulfilment for this promise within the story in Genesis. Abraham becomes the father of Isaac (Genesis 21), and though he only settles temporarily in Palestine he does acquire a small piece of land in it, a cave in which he can bury his wife when she dies (Genesis 23). However, it is clear that the real fulfilment will come about a long time in the future. Genesis is already looking forward to the stories in Exodus and Joshua of how YHWH led Abraham's descendants out of Egypt, where they had become slaves, and led them into the Promised Land so that they could conquer its native inhabitants and settle there for good.

Just as the covenant with Noah has a 'sign' in the form of the rainbow, the sign of the covenant with Abraham is the **circumcision** of all his male descendants (Genesis 17:9–14). From this point on, only those who are circumcised can become members of the people of YHWH. So in a sense there is a condition attached to this covenant: the obligation, for males, to be circumcised: 'Any uncircumcised male who is not circumcised in the flesh of his foreskin shall be cut off from his people; he has broken my covenant' (Genesis 17:14).

Yet the way the story is told does not give the impression that this disobedience would call the whole covenant relationship with God into question. The individual would have to be excluded from the people, but the covenant with the whole nation would remain in force. So, again, even in the covenant with Abraham it is primarily the element of divine promise, and not of human obligation, that is stressed.

3. The covenant with Moses

As the Old Testament tells it (and remember that we are concerned at the moment only with that, not with the question of what actually happened historically), the next covenant was made with Moses. When he brought the people to

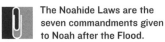

The Noahide Laws are the seven commandments given to Noah after the Flood. They specify that people should worship only God, should not blaspheme, murder, steal, commit adultery or be cruel to animals, and should establish a just rule of law to enable people to live in harmony with each other. Jews regard these laws as the basic framework for all people for a moral and spiritual life and view any religion that upholds these laws as an acceptable way for a non-Jew to serve God.

Circumcision is the cutting off of the foreskin of the penis. In Judaism this is done on the eighth day after birth and is an important sign of being Jewish, since the Old Testament presents circumcision as an instruction by God as a sign of the covenant made with Abraham and his descendants (Genesis 17:9–10).

Mount Sinai, he and some of the 'elders' of Israel saw a vision of YHWH, and ate and drank in his presence (Exodus 24). Before the meal, sacrifices were offered, and the blood from the slaughtered animals was splashed on an altar and on the people with the words, 'See the blood of the covenant that the LORD has made with you' (Exodus 24:8).

In this case, it is made clear that God's covenant with Israel is a two-sided arrangement, a kind of bargain or contract. God promises to bless the people, but they in turn have to pledge their loyalty to God, which they do in the words, 'All the words that the LORD has spoken we will do' (Exodus 24:3). These 'words' of God are said to be written in 'the book of the covenant' (Exodus 24:7). As the book of Exodus now stands, we are clearly meant to think that this book contained all the laws that now appear in Exodus 21–24 (and for that reason this collection of laws is usually referred to by scholars as 'the Book of the Covenant'). Yet what the people pledge themselves to obey must also include the Ten Commandments (Exodus 20), which are not in 'the book' but are inscribed on two stone tablets. Thus, the covenant made through Moses is a binding contract. YHWH promises to be true to Israel, but Israel in turn must promise to be true to him, and must obey all his laws.

This 'Mosaic' covenant is later recalled at the end of the settlement of the Promised Land, in the book of Joshua (Joshua 24). The people have defeated their enemies in the land, but they are tending to worship the gods of these conquered enemies instead of remaining completely loyal to YHWH. Joshua challenges them to reaffirm their allegiance to YHWH, which they do:

> *The people said to Joshua, 'The LORD our God we will serve, and him we will obey.' So Joshua made a covenant with the people that day, and made statutes and ordinances for them at Shechem. Joshua wrote these words in the book of the law of God....* (Joshua 24:24–26)

This is a kind of renewal of the covenant made with Moses rather than a new covenant, and at this point it is worth noting that something similar apparently happened again much later, during the days of the divided monarchy. In this case, King Josiah seems to have discovered an old copy of the book of the law in the Temple,

> *...and made a covenant before the LORD, to follow the LORD, keeping his commandments, his decrees, and his statutes, with all his heart and all his soul, to perform all the words of this covenant that were written in this book. All the people joined in the covenant.* (2 Kings 23:3)

So, the Mosaic covenant is what Old Testament scholars generally mean when they refer to 'the covenant' without further identification. Since in Judaism 'the covenant' more commonly means the covenant with Abraham, this can be confusing. Indeed, the word *berith* (*brit*) is sometimes used by Jews as a shorthand way of referring to circumcision which, as we have seen, is the sign of the covenant with Abraham.

4. The covenant with David

All the covenants we have looked at so far are covenants between God and a large group of people: the descendants of Noah or Abraham, the whole people of Israel led by Moses. However, there is another covenant in the Old Testament that is made instead between God and a single person: the covenant with David. This is described in 2 Samuel 7 and in Psalm 89:

> ... 'I have made a covenant with my chosen one,
> I have sworn to my servant David:
> "I will establish your descendants for ever,
> and build your throne to all generations."' (Psalm 89:3–4)

This covenant is not presented as any kind of alternative to the Mosaic covenant, as though David and his dynasty somehow took over God's promises made to the whole of Israel. It is simply a different issue. God is presented here as entering into a solemn agreement with David that will guarantee that his descendants will always be kings in Israel. It is on this basis that the rebellion of the northern tribes, after the death of Solomon, can be presented as rebellion against God: he had chosen the line of David, and no one else had any right to be king over any part of Israel (see 1 Kings 12:19–20).

When the line of David's descendants ceased to rule after the **Exile**, some people felt that this was a sign that God had broken his covenant with David:

> You have renounced the covenant with your servant;
> you have defiled his crown in the dust. (Psalm 89:39)

However, others thought that God would still remain loyal to the promises he had made with David, and so there would eventually be a new king from among David's descendants. This hoped-for new king is the figure we know as the Messiah.

5. The 'new covenant' of Jeremiah

Through the prophet Jeremiah, speaking when Israel had gone into exile, the Old Testament also makes reference to a 'new covenant':

> ... not ... like the covenant that I made with their ancestors when I took them by the hand to bring them out of the land of Egypt — a covenant that they broke, though I was their husband, says the LORD. But this is the covenant that I will make with the house of Israel after those days, says the LORD: I will put my law within them, and I will write it on their hearts; and I will be their

In biblical studies, the **Exile** refers to the period in Israel's history in the sixth century BCE when many of its people were taken captive and deported from Israel to Babylon.

'Messiah', from the Hebrew word meaning 'anointed one', is a term used to denote a person specially chosen by God who, according to the Jews, will appear in the future to signal the beginning of a great age of peace and prosperity for all people. The idea that the future Messiah will come from the line of David, regarded as Israel's greatest king, is seen as part of the covenant agreement between God and David set out in the Old Testament. However, there are very few texts in the Old Testament itself that talk of the renewal of God's covenant with David through the coming of the Messiah. Nevertheless, the messianic hope became important in some branches of Judaism after the Old Testament was largely finished — and of course it was very important for the writers of the New Testament who identified Jesus as the Messiah and applied to him the title Christ, the Greek word for 'anointed one'.

God, and they shall be my people. (Jeremiah 31:32–33)

Clearly what this has in mind is a new and improved version of the covenant that had been made through Moses ('the covenant that I made...when I took them by the hand to bring them out of the land of Egypt'). For Jeremiah, it seemed that the people had broken the Mosaic covenant by their disobedience, and that is why YHWH had sent them into exile. However, he was sure that at some point in the future that covenant would be renewed. Moreover, what is remarkable about the new form of covenant he envisaged is that, though it will still involve the people in obeying the law, God himself will make sure that they are able to do it. This is because God will put his law 'within' them and 'write it on their hearts', so that 'they shall all know me, from the least of them to the greatest' (Jeremiah 31:34).

Early Christians believed that this prophecy of a 'new covenant' had come to fulfilment through Jesus Christ, and so for them this text in Jeremiah became very important. However, from an Old Testament point of view it is not a very central passage, though it does show how important the Mosaic covenant was — a completely new relationship between YHWH and Israel would be modelled on it.

GOD AND ISRAEL: THE HISTORICAL REALITY

As we have seen, the Old Testament presents God's relationship with Israel as depending, from the very earliest times, on an act of election by him. God singled Israel out from all the other nations and, by entering into a special relationship with its ancestors, guaranteed his presence with the people at all times from then on. In its earlier phases, this relationship was largely unconditional — though God always wanted Israel to obey him — but from at least the time of Moses, it was seen as a two-sided contract, the 'Mosaic covenant'. This contractual aspect became so important that by the time of Jeremiah even God's unconditional promise was phrased in the form of a covenant, though one so 'new' that God himself would take the initiative in making sure that the people were capable of keeping its terms and conditions.

However, modern reconstructions of how ideas about these themes *actually* developed in ancient Israel have suggested that the Old Testament's own picture of the process is rather an idealized one and that later ideas have been read back into earlier times. Such a tendency is common in a traditional society that does not like novelty: when people do introduce new ideas, they claim that they are really very old! In the same way, the Israelites always tended to think of their religious ideas as having very ancient roots, even when in reality they were being quite innovative.

1. The covenant and the importance of the prophets

The earliest reliable evidence we have for how Israel's relationship to YHWH was understood is probably to be found in the work of the great prophets. The first of these was **Amos**, and from what he tells us it is clear that people in his day thought of the relationship between the nation and its God as a kind of natural relationship. YHWH was, as it were, automatically the God of Israel. People did not see this as based on any kind of contract between God and themselves, but as simply a matter of course: every nation had its national god, and Israel's was YHWH. Consequently, YHWH could be relied on to come to Israel's help whenever it was threatened by its enemies: that was his job.

However, Amos sharply attacked this idea of God's relationship to Israel. On the contrary, he maintained, the relationship with YHWH was totally dependent on Israel being loyal and obedient to YHWH, especially by maintaining what we would call 'social justice' — looking after the poor and making sure that the rich did not exploit them. YHWH's position as Israel's God depended on Israel maintaining its side of a contract with him: only if the Israelites kept their side of the bargain would YHWH continue to defend them. Interestingly, Amos says this as though it is something new, an idea that people at large had not had or at least had not understood. It was news to Amos's audience that YHWH's relationship with Israel was a conditional one: they thought of it as part of the natural order of things rather than a relationship based on a historical covenant. Amos never uses the word 'covenant' to describe Israel's relationship with its God, but it is clear that he has in mind something on the lines of the Mosaic covenant that we outlined above. However, this way of understanding the relationship of YHWH and Israel seems to be a new insight of his, not something that rested on older tradition.

Much the same can be said of his younger contemporary, **Hosea**, who is the first prophet actually to use the term 'covenant' (Hosea 8:1). He too seems to be confronted with people who do not at all see their relationship with God in covenantal terms, but think of it as a natural relationship — nothing to do with any free choice on YHWH's part, and certainly not dependent for its success on any response by Israel. Hosea and Amos both wanted people to see that in reality it was only on the basis of a proper response by Israel that the relationship with YHWH could endure. This idea is essentially what we mean by 'the (Mosaic) covenant', but Amos and Hosea may well have been the first to grasp it.

If that is true, then writers influenced by the prophets have read the covenant idea back into the time of Moses. Such a conclusion would mean that there was no covenant in the sense of a contract between YHWH and Israel before the eighth century and that all the texts concerning the earlier period were influenced by the thought of the prophets.

However, this does not necessarily mean that individual texts that became important for covenant thinking were in themselves later than the prophets. The old laws that form 'the Book of the Covenant' in Exodus 21–23 may well be

Amos was a native of the southern kingdom of Judah who described himself as a 'herdsman and dresser of sycamore trees' (Amos 7:14). He prophesied to the northern kingdom of Israel in the eighth century BCE. It was a time of relative peace and prosperity, but Amos registered God's displeasure that, in spite of this, the poor were oppressed and subject to injustice, that the rich squandered their wealth in immoral ways, and that their religion seemed to have become nothing more than empty rituals. His message was that being God's people meant that they had a responsibility to act with justice and righteousness and that, if they did not change their ways, God would punish them with destruction at the hands of their enemies. Thus, 'the day of the LORD' that the people were celebrating annually, looking forward to the glorious day when God would fulfil his promises and reward Israel, would actually be a day of judgement and destruction — a scenario he tried to convey through the reporting of a series of visions.

Amos's message is almost entirely threatening, and it is only in the final few verses (9:8b–15), which many believe are a later addition to the book, that there is the hint of a restoration from exile and the coming of a glorious Davidic messianic age.

For more about Amos and his message see 4.2 'Thus Says the Lord!' and 2.4 'How Should We Live?'

Hosea was a prophet of the northern kingdom of Israel who preached just after Amos in the eighth century BCE. Although the political threat of the Assyrians was mounting, it was still a relatively prosperous time, and Hosea, like Amos, was keen to point out the need for people to remember the covenant and what God had done for them in the past. Hosea tried to show how unfaithful they had become towards God and spoke about a forthcoming time of judgement when God would use the Assyrians to punish Israel. However, in contrast with Amos, love is the dominant feature of Hosea's message, and he uses the image of Israel as an unfaithful wife, whom God will divorce, but God's love for Israel is so great that he will forgive her and ask her to return to him so that the relationship can begin anew. In this, Hosea focuses on God's love for his sinning people and the fact that, after punishment, a time of hope and restoration will follow.

For more about Hosea and his message see 4.2 'Thus Says the Lord!' and 2.4 'How Should We Live?'

much older than the prophets, and the prophets often seem to appeal to them in their condemnations of the people of their day. Nevertheless, the link between these laws and the story of the making of the covenant with Moses may well be a later feature. Similarly, the Ten Commandments may be older than the prophets — though not all scholars think so — but could have originated as a summary of the moral law which was unconnected with Israel's special relationship with YHWH. After all, similar laws are found in other ancient cultures.

The fullest development of a covenant theology in the Old Testament is in the book of Deuteronomy, which is almost certainly very heavily influenced by the prophets. Here we find an emphasis on YHWH's free choice of Israel, and the fact that he had entered into a binding contract with them, from which their moral obligations flowed:

> *Although heaven and the heaven of heavens belong to the* LORD *your God, the earth with all that is in it, yet the* LORD *set his heart in love on your ancestors alone and chose you, their descendants after them, out of all the peoples, as it is today. . . . You shall fear the* LORD *your God; him alone you shall worship; to him you shall hold fast. . . .* (Deuteronomy 10:14–15, 20)

In Deuteronomy, all the individual laws are the working out of the special relationship with YHWH, so that this is the covenant text in the Old Testament par excellence. In turn, it seems likely that it has influenced the way some of the other books of the Pentateuch have been edited, so that the reader gets the impression that such a covenant theology had been around in Israel from the time of Moses. In reality it was a later, quite sophisticated way of thinking about a connection between God and Israel that had originally been conceived more in terms of a natural relationship, like that of a father and son.

Therefore, 'YHWH is the God of Israel and Israel is the people of YHWH' was in itself a very old idea. However, in reality it seems that the idea that it rested on some kind of contract between the two partners, freely entered into, may well have been the outcome of the preaching of the prophets.

2. The covenants with Noah and Abraham

In light of such a conclusion, we might ask where that leaves the covenants with Noah and Abraham. As we saw, the stories about these figures do not present the relationship between God and humans as a conditional one. For this reason, it seems probable that the use of the term 'covenant' to describe the relationship was a later import into the texts about these two characters from remote antiquity.

Originally, Noah was simply a good man who escaped the Flood, like other characters in Flood stories from all over the Middle East. Much later, he was then linked to the history of Israel through lists of his descendants in order to make the book of Genesis tell a story in a historical sequence. Thus, talk of his having been given a 'covenant' by God seems to derive from a time when the Hebrew Bible was being organized to present Israel's relationship with God as a series of covenants.

Abraham was also a traditional figure from the past, remembered as the original ancestor of the Israelites. Indeed, Second Isaiah, writing in the sixth century BCE, implies that everyone knew of him as the origin of Israel:

> *Look to the rock from which you were hewn,*
>   *and to the quarry from which you were dug.*
> *Look to Abraham your father,*
>   *and to Sarah who bore you;*
> *for he was but one when I called him,*
>   *but I blessed him and made him many.* (Isaiah 51:1–2)

However, the idea of the *covenant* with Abraham, with circumcision as its sign, implies a time, probably after the Exile, when Israelites were marked off from other races by their circumcision. This is because circumcision was common in Egypt and Palestine, and it was probably only when Israelites had to live among the peoples of Mesopotamia, after the Exile to Babylonia, that they began to insist on it as a mark of their religious identity. That means that the stories about God's covenant with Abraham may well be from much later than the time they claim to be about, even if Abraham himself really was an ancient figure.

3. The origins of covenant and treaty

At this point, it is worth considering where the term 'covenant' comes from anyway. Almost certainly it originally meant 'treaty' and you can still see it used in that way in 1 Kings 20:34, where King Ahab makes a *berith* with Benhadad, the Aramean king. Treaties, of course, are two-sided arrangements, imposing obligations on both parties, and this suggests that the idea of the covenant between YHWH and Israel as a *two-sided* contract is older than the idea of it as a pure promise on YHWH's part. If this is the case, it would support the suggestion that the covenantal presentation of YHWH's relationship with Noah and Abraham, which concentrates on promise rather than on mutual obligation, may well be later than the idea of the Mosaic covenant.

Unfortunately, since treaties were well known throughout the Middle East from very ancient times, we cannot use this approach alone to gauge how old the covenant idea is in Israel. However, they certainly became more familiar to Israelites in the eighth and seventh centuries BCE when they came into contact with the great Mesopotamian powers of Assyria and Babylon. Indeed, the image of YHWH as being like a **suzerain**, with Israel as his **vassal**, could well owe something to Israel's experience of domination by the Assyrians or Babylonians. Deuteronomy also has some sec-

Two major sources for our knowledge of the covenants of the ancient Near East are the Hittite Treaties (from 1400–1200 BCE) and the Assyrian Treaties (from the eighth and seventh centuries BCE). Evidence exists for parity treaties where two equal parties entered into an agreement, such as the treaty dating from around 1280 BCE between Rameses II and Hattusilis III discovered in the 1900s in both its Egyptian and its Hittite editions. However, the majority of treaties used in alliances in the ancient Near East suggest that dominant empires imposed them on weaker nations to gain obedience in return for some sort of protection. Such ancient suzerainty or vassal treaties are characterized by the following elements:

1. an introduction which sets out the credentials of both parties and of their previous relationship;
2. a section detailing the responsibilities of each party under the terms of the treaty;
3. the arrangements for the treaty to be recorded officially and read regularly;
4. a list of witnesses to the treaty, usually gods;
5. litanies of curses on those who break the terms of the treaty and of blessings on those who keep the terms of the treaty.

In addition, it seems that it was common to ratify such a treaty by sacrificing an animal and sharing a meal.

There are clearly points of comparison, in terms of both the form of the agreement and the ritual associated with it, between such treaties and the covenants of the Old Testament. In particular, the covenant between God and Israel as set out in Deuteronomy and in Joshua (Joshua 24) is stated in formal terms that display clear parallels to the treaties of the ancient Near East. Thus, at least at some level, the Israelites understood God as the dominant party who was choosing to offer status and protection to the people of Israel in return for their obedience to his laws.

Suzerain is a term for a great king or overlord.

Vassal is a term for a slave and can be applied to a powerless nation which, through being conquered or being under threat of being conquered, is forced to treat the dominant nation as its master.

'The term "covenant" is no longer a legal contract...but a device for explaining the meaning and nature of Israel's election.' (H.H. Rowley, *The Biblical Doctrine of Election*, Lutterworth Press, 1950)

tions that are very like those of one Assyrian treaty — the vassal treaty of Esarhaddon. For example, Deuteronomy concludes with a long list of curses that will come on Israel if it is disobedient, just as the Assyrian treaty curses the vassal who is disloyal, and the imagery used is strikingly similar:

> *The sky over your head shall be bronze, and the earth under you iron.* (Deuteronomy 28:23)

> *Just as rain does not fall from a copper sky, so may there come neither rain nor dew upon your fields, but let it rain burning coals on your land instead of dew.*
>
> (Vassal Treaties of Esarhaddon 64)

Of course, the interesting thing is that although covenants were a common institution in the ancient Near East, and there are clearly points of contact in terms of both composition and ritual, the Israelites in some ways appear to have made this idea their own. From their point of view, although God is the dominant party, he offers covenants with Israel as a *gift* of his loving kindness, a gift that is ultimately bound up with the necessity for fidelity and obedience in return for a special relationship with God.

4. The covenant with David

The covenant with David falls outside all this development. As we saw above, it is a separate issue and did not in any way 'replace' the Mosaic covenant. Indeed, in pre-exilic Judah there is no particular reason to think that the Mosaic covenant was a familiar idea even long after the time of David: the prophet Isaiah, in the eighth century, does not mention it at all.

So the question is whether the idea that God made a covenant with David really goes back to David's own time. It may well do so, as part of the ideology that David devised to justify his own reign and to legitimize his heirs. In 1 Kings 1 we read of the rival attempts of Solomon and Adonijah to succeed David. However, although there seems to have been no rule that would have decided which of them would win out, it is assumed by all the people involved that the kingdom would naturally pass to one or another of David's sons, not someone else altogether. This may mean that David had already established the belief that YHWH had chosen him and his line to rule the nation. Whether he actually used the word 'covenant' in this process we cannot tell, because we don't know whether Psalm 89 is really a psalm from his time — it could reflect the ideas of later kings who read back, into the time of their great ancestor David, their own sense of being protected by God's covenant. In any case, God's special relationship with the king was a very common idea in most nations in the Middle East at this time. In Egypt, the king was actually reckoned to be a god himself, but Israel's thinking seems closer to that in Mesopotamia, where the king, for all his majesty, was ultimately simply the gods' chief servant. However, it was normal to believe that the gods would underwrite the existing dynasty, and ensure a good succession of descendants. So, in this respect, Israel was not unusual among the nations of its day.

THE COVENANT AND THE VOCATION OF ISRAEL

To conclude, it is worth looking at some particular effects that Israel's covenant with God had on its understanding of its own special vocation. For example, there is hardly anywhere in the Old Testament that contemplates the possibility that Israel might *not* be special. Amos comes near to it:

> *Are you not like the Ethiopians to me,*
> *O people of Israel? says the* LORD.
> *Did I not bring Israel up from the land of*
> *Egypt,*
> *and the Philistines from Caphtor and the*
> *Arameans from Kir?* (Amos 9:7)

Such words, equating the exodus of Israel from Egypt with the movements of other peoples, should have made his listeners deeply uncomfortable. Yet, even here, Amos was perhaps exaggerating, in the interest of stressing just how angry YHWH had become with his people, rather than really denying that they had ever been special.

In some parts of the Old Testament the idea of Israel's 'election' is regarded as giving them the right to take over Canaan from its native inhabitants and to obliterate the very memory of the people they massacred. This is the impression given in places in Joshua and Judges particularly, and the **principle of herem** is laid down in Deuteronomy:

> *When the* LORD *your God brings you into the land that you are*
> *about to enter and occupy, and he clears away many nations*
> *before you ... and when the* LORD *your God gives them over to*
> *you and you defeat them, then you must utterly destroy them.*
> *Make no covenant [i.e. treaty] with them and show them no*
> *mercy.* (Deuteronomy 7:1–2)

Of course, this is one of the ideas that has given the Old Testament such a bad name among many people today, and there is no doubt that the idea of putting conquered peoples to the 'ban' is one of the least attractive features of ancient Israel — though it may not actually have happened very much in practice. However, there are other places where God's choice of Israel is presented in a more positive light.

In the first place, Israel is special, not because God is always on its side, but because it has special obligations

The Vassal Treaties of Esarhaddon are good examples of Assyrian vassal treaties. They were imposed by King Esarhaddon (680–669 BCE) on small nations he conquered and required that, on his death, these nations would not rebel against his son, Ashurbanipal. © Copyright The British Museum

Herem is the Hebrew word for 'utter destruction' and the principle of herem was that there should be a total destruction of the enemy and the enemy's property as a means of dedicating a victory to God.

towards God. This is one essential theme in Amos, who regards the specialness of Israel as implying greater obligation rather than a greater freedom to do as it likes. Deuteronomy stresses this too:

> *He brought you out of Egypt with his own presence, by his great power, driving out before you nations greater and mightier than yourselves. . . . So acknowledge today and take to heart that the Lord is God in heaven above and on the earth beneath; there is no other. Keep his statutes and his commandments, which I am commanding you today for your own well-being. . . .* (Deuteronomy 4:37–40)

Secondly, Israel is meant to be a 'light to the nations' (Isaiah 42:6) because, since it has a unique experience of God and his love for his chosen ones, Israel can witness to other nations that God is good and great. In fact, there is not much of this 'missionary' theme in the Old Testament, but it is worth looking at some of the passages in the book of Isaiah (19:18–25; 42:1–4; 56:3–8; 60:1–7). However, the image is clearest in Zechariah, a text from soon after the Exile in the late sixth century BCE, in which it is said that other nations will come to worship YHWH through Israel:

> *Many peoples and strong nations shall come to seek the Lord of hosts in Jerusalem, and to entreat the favour of the Lord. Thus says the Lord of hosts: In those days ten men from nations of every language shall take hold of a Jew, grasping his garment and saying, 'Let us go with you, for we have heard that God is with you.'* (Zechariah 8:22–23)

Thus, Israel's covenant with God was at the root of the sense of its own identity as a nation. Through it its people enjoyed the protection and privileges of being God's special nation but, as the story of the Old Testament makes clear, they often forgot that such God-given rights also entailed special responsibilities.

2.3 Who Am I?
THE OLD TESTAMENT VIEW OF THE HUMAN CONDITION

T H E   B A S I C S

- On the upside, according to the Old Testament, being human means being made in the image of God and involves a high level of dignity and responsibility as God's representative on earth.
- On the downside, according to the Old Testament, being human involves frailty, toil, a good deal of inequality between the sexes, and no hope of life after death or immortality.

HUMAN DIGNITY

[W]hat are human beings that you are mindful of them,
   mortals that you care for them?
Yet you have made them a little lower than God,
   and crowned them with glory and honour. (Psalm 8:4–5)

ON THE WHOLE, THE Old Testament has an optimistic view of the human condition. It sees human beings as created by God for positive reasons, to have partners with whom he can work, rather than — as often in the ancient world — as slaves. It recognizes human weakness and failure, but sees humans as having a certain God-given dignity that makes them worthy of respect. This attitude is in many ways summed up in Genesis 1:27, where we read that

God created humankind in his image,
   in the image of God he created them;
   male and female he created them.

The Sabbath

Such an attitude to human dignity is also evident in the **Sabbath** law, one of the Ten Commandments:

Remember the sabbath day, and keep it holy. For six days you shall labour and do all your work. But the seventh day is a sab-

In Judaism, the **Sabbath** is a day of complete rest, following God's example of resting on the seventh day after the work of creation. The Sabbath is observed from sunset on Friday until sunset on Saturday, and its observance is laid down in the Ten Commandments.

bath to the LORD your God; you shall not do any work — you, your son or your daughter, your male or female slave, your livestock, or the alien resident in your towns. (Exodus 20:8–10; cf. Deuteronomy 5:12–14)

A commandment such as this is, in many ways, extraordinary because leisure was a characteristic only of the *gods* in the ancient world. A number of mythical texts from Mesopotamia describe how the great gods, burdened with the labour of governing the world, created lesser gods to help them. Then, when even that did not completely relieve them of their work and when the lesser gods in turn began to complain that they were overloaded, human beings were created to take on the more tiring jobs.

> *[Marduk said,] Blood I will mass and cause bones to be.*
> *I will establish a savage, 'man' shall be his name.*
> *Verily, savage-man will I create.*
> *He shall be charged with the service of the gods*
> *That they might be at ease!*
> (The Babylonian Creation Epic, tablet 6)

> *Let the birth-goddess create offspring,*
> *And let man bear the toil of the gods.*
> *They summoned and asked the goddess,*
> *The midwife of the gods, wise Mami,*
> *'You are the birth-goddess, creatress of mankind,*
> *Create Lullâ that he may bear the yoke,*
> *Let him bear the yoke assigned by Enlil,*
> *Let man carry the toil of the gods.'* (Atra-Hasis, tablet 5)

'In the Babylonian creation stories people were made last of all, almost as an afterthought on the part of the gods, and always for menial duties. But the Old Testament will have none of this: women and men are the pinnacle and crowning glory of the world and all its affairs.' (John Drane, *Introducing the Old Testament*, Lion, 2000)

Thus, in ancient texts such as these, the destiny of the human race is to act as slaves for the gods. There is no question of the gods granting leisure time to their human slaves, for that would have been to recognize something godlike in them, which would have gone completely against the reason for creating them in the first place.

However, the Old Testament sees the status of the human race in a radically different way. Whatever may have been believed by ordinary Israelites, there are no 'gods' for the biblical writers, only the one God who is the creator of everything. Moreover, as Second Isaiah put it, this God 'does not faint or grow weary' (Isaiah 40:28) and, therefore, does not need an army of helpers to take the load from his shoulders. Rather than making human slaves so that he himself can rest, this God wishes the human beings he has made to share in the benefits of rest themselves. For this reason, they are to work six days a week but have the seventh off — a law that is to apply not only to free men and women, but also to slaves and foreigners living with the Israelites. Indeed, even livestock is included! In this sense, the animals that work for humankind take on a kind of semi-human status, and are allowed to share in the rest granted to their owners.

The Sabbath law is thus a remarkably humane and far-sighted recognition of human dignity. It recognizes that human beings were not created only for work, but also so that they might enjoy leisure — the prerogative of the gods and, to some extent, the ruling classes elsewhere in the ancient world. For the writers of the Old Testament, the entitlement to leisure is extended to *all* members of the human race. You do not have to have a special position in society to qualify for weekly rest: you simply have to be human.

God's representatives

All this implies a very high view of the human race, and is one of the Old Testament's most distinctive contributions to an understanding of what it means to be human. In comparison with other ancient views about human beings, the Old Testament highlights a remarkable attitude — an attitude summed up in the psalm quoted at the beginning of this chapter, which we will now present in full:

> *O LORD, our Sovereign,*
> > *how majestic is your name in all the earth!*
>
> *You have set your glory above the heavens.*
> > *Out of the mouths of babes and infants*
> *you have founded a bulwark because of your foes,*
> > *to silence the enemy and the avenger.*
>
> *When I look at your heavens, the work of your fingers,*
> > *the moon and the stars that you have established;*
> *what are human beings that you are mindful of them,*
> > *mortals that you care for them?*
>
> *Yet you have made them a little lower than God,*
> > *and crowned them with glory and honour.*
> *You have given them dominion over the works of your hands;*
> > *you have put all things under their feet,*
> *all sheep and oxen,*
> > *and also the beasts of the field,*
> *the birds of the air, and the fish of the sea,*
> > *whatever passes along the paths of the seas.*
>
> *O LORD, our Sovereign,*
> > *how majestic is your name in all the earth!* (Psalm 8)

The idea that human beings are so nearly 'God-like' that they even have 'dominion over the works of your hands' (verse 6) is picked up in Genesis 1:28:

> *God said to them, 'Be fruitful and multiply, and fill the earth and subdue it; and have dominion over the fish of the sea and over the birds of the air and over every living thing that moves upon the earth.'*

 Compared with the rather negative view of kings of other peoples given in I Samuel 8:10–18, Psalm 72 gives an interesting description of how Israel's kings should rule the people. The psalmist asks God to enable the king to judge the people with righteousness and with justice:

May he defend the cause of the poor of the people, give deliverance to the needy, and crush the oppressor. (Psalm 72:4)

Furthermore, the king is expected to value and protect all his subjects: 'precious is their blood in his sight' (Psalm 72:14).

For more information about kingship in Israel see 1.2 'The Story So Far', 3.3 'Give Us a King!' and 4.1 'The Social Scene'.

In this picture the god stands behind the king. The god and the king have an identical appearance, except that the god is slightly taller and has wings. He also carries symbols of his divine status: a flask of oil, with which he is anointing the king, and a bucket for sacred flowers.

It is not clear which of these passages depends on which, but together they give a clear message: human beings are to be God's deputies or representatives on earth, and are to share in his rule over the natural world. Human beings are rulers, not slaves.

Sometimes these texts have been used to justify the human race in exploiting the natural world, and ecologists and those who favour 'animal rights' at times blame the Bible for appearing to justify an attitude to the environment that encourages exploitation. While agreeing that this has sometimes been so, we do not think the biblical text really justifies such an attitude to the environment and much depends on how we interpret 'dominion'. The Old Testament ideal of how kings should 'have dominion' over their subjects, for example, is that they should do so not with harshness and in an exploitative way, but with care and concern for people's needs and rights. Similarly, human 'dominion' over the natural world is not meant to be exercised without care. In Genesis 2:15 God places Adam, the first human being, in the Garden of Eden 'to till it and keep it' — as a gardener, not a tyrant. This gives us a much more benign picture of the human vocation than the word 'dominion' may conjure up when we first meet it: it is not the same as 'domination'.

Made in the image of God

One way of expressing the high status of human beings in the Old Testament is to emphasize the idea that they are made 'in the image of God'. In Genesis 1, when God is about to create the human race to 'have dominion' over the natural world, he says, 'Let us make humankind in our image, according to our likeness' (v. 26). So, it is true that there could be a link between the divine 'image' and the idea of dominion: just as God has dominion over all the earth, so human beings are to share in his rule, and in that sense will be made 'in his image', that is, will be like him. However, the idea of the divine image may be more complicated than that.

The words translated 'image' and 'likeness', in Hebrew *tselem* and *demuth*, are more or less synonyms as both of them literally mean 'physical shape or form'. Thus Genesis 1:26 is an example of Hebrew **parallelism**. In the first instance, then, the writer of Genesis, in common with many other Old Testament writers, may be conveying the idea that human beings look like God. Or, to put it the other way round, if you saw God, you would see something that looked like a human being. Indeed, even though many religious believers today have much more sophisticated ideas about what God is like, the picture of God in human terms as 'an old man on a cloud' is not dead yet!

Of course, it was not uncommon in the ancient world to think that the gods had human forms. For example, the Greek and Roman gods, and gods in the cultures of Mesopotamia and the Middle East generally, were thought of as living a kind of exaggerated human life, with feasting and sex high on the agenda. Yet, the idea that humans were made in the image of gods was not at all a common way of thinking in ancient times, and the difference between gods and humans was stressed more than their (taken-for-granted) similarity. Thus, from a human point of view, whilst Zeus, the chief Greek god, or Marduk, the god of Babylon, had some very human features such as anger, lust, and greed, that did not make them approachably human! On the contrary, their power set them off sharply from the human world.

An exception, though, is to be found in the person of the king. Mesopotamian kings did not present themselves as literally divine: they were the gods' chief servants or slaves, not their equals. In practice, however, the king shared in a good deal of the prestige and authority of the god he served. You cannot look at an Assyrian palace as reconstructed by archaeologists without being intensely aware that an ordinary person, approaching the king in his throne room through various outer and inner rooms, would be overawed by his majesty. Indeed, that was the intention, and the graphic illustrations on palace walls emphasizing the likeness of the king to the god are quite obvious attempts to show that the king is made 'in the image/likeness' of the god. Such an idea contributed to his awe-inspiring quality: when you saw the king, you might almost as well be looking at the god himself — a realization which may well have made the king's subjects rather anxious as they approached him.

Against this background, the Old Testament's idea that human beings, both male and female, are made in the likeness of God is very remarkable. We could almost call it a **democratic** idea of the human person. Not only kings, but even ordinary people are seen as being 'like God', simply 'a little lower', as Psalm 8 puts it (v. 5). As with the Sabbath law, so here, characteristics that elsewhere in the ancient world were the prerogative of the few are extended to everybody. All

Parallelism in Hebrew poetry is where one line either repeats the idea of the previous line with variations, or else draws a contrast with it.

A **democratic** view is one that favours social equality.

Reconstruction of an Assyrian palace. © Copyright The British Museum

human beings are 'Godlike', not merely those of high rank.

We do not know how people in Israel worked out this idea of human dignity in practice. Kings were no doubt often just as oppressive as those in other cultures, and had just as little respect for their subjects; and people cheated and defrauded each other with little respect for the 'divine image' in which all were believed to share. The ideals of Genesis 1 or Psalm 8 are just that: ideals. Nevertheless, Israel preserved these ideal pictures of what it is to be human, and they stand as a witness to a way of approaching the human condition that was very unusual in the world Israel inhabited.

HUMAN FRAILTY

A life without hope?

However, human dignity is by no means the whole story in the Old Testament. Its writers were as aware as we are of how much can go wrong in human life, and of how weak and inadequate human beings can be. Nowhere is this clearer than in the book of Job, which was probably written in the early post-exilic period, when Israel was governed by the Persians. However, although it was probably not far removed in time from either Genesis 1 or Psalm 8, it presents a very different picture of the human condition:

> 'Do not human beings have a hard service on earth,
>   and are not their days like the days of a labourer?
> Like a slave who longs for the shadow,
>   and like labourers who long for their wages,
> so I am allotted months of emptiness,
>   and nights of misery are apportioned to me.
> When I lie down I say, "When shall I rise?"
>   But the night is long,
>   and I am full of tossing until dawn. . . .
> My days are swifter than a weaver's shuttle,
>   and come to their end without hope.

> 'Remember that my life is a breath;
>   my eye will never again see good.
> The eye that beholds me will see me no more;
>   while your eyes are upon me, I shall be gone.
> As the cloud fades and vanishes,
>   so those who go down to Sheol do not come up;
> they return no more to their houses,
>   nor do their places know them any more.' (Job 7:1–4, 6–10)

This lament for human existence is uttered by someone suffering great hardship. Job is ill and in pain, having lost all his possessions. However, that does not mean his lament is specific only to himself: it is deliberately worded as though it applies to humanity in general. Whereas the Sabbath law, as we have seen, regards human beings as far more than the slaves of the gods, Job puts the other side of the argument. Much human life is, as he says, like hard labour followed by no rest at all. What is more, some people suffer in such a way that even the literal rest they get — in bed at night — is not refreshing to them. As it says in one of the curses in Deuteronomy, 'In the morning you shall say, "If only it were evening!" and at evening you shall say, "If only it were morning!" — because of the dread that your heart shall feel' (Deuteronomy 28:67).

A life without immortality?
Other ancient cultures, like Egypt, had a vivid idea of life after death, but in Israel, and older forms of Greek culture, a belief in a worthwhile afterlife was lacking, and it is not until the very latest books in the Old Testament and **Apocrypha** that we encounter a hope of life beyond death. For the majority of the Old Testament writers, there is no long-term hope for humankind, because 'those who go down to Sheol do not come up'. Thus, human life, for all its promise, ends in death. As Job says:

> '... there is hope for a tree,
>   if it is cut down, that it will sprout again,
>   and that its shoots will not cease. ...
> But mortals die, and are laid low;
>   humans expire, and where are they?
> As waters fail from a lake,
>   and as a river wastes and dries up,
> so mortals lie down and do not rise again;
>   until the heavens are no more, they will not awake,
>   or be roused out of their sleep.' (Job 14:7, 10–12)

For the most part the Old Testament writers agree with Job that there is no hope beyond this life. The dead were dead, and there was little more to be said. However, this does not generally depress them: it is simply treated as a given, and as a reason for celebrating and enjoying life while it lasts:

Apocrypha is the name given to the collection of books which are included in the Greek version of the Old Testament (the Septuagint) but not in the Hebrew Scriptures. These books are often also called 'deuterocanonical' books.

Sheol is the land of the dead, and the general consensus of the Old Testament is that, though it is not 'hell', a place of torment, it is a sad and dark place where there is no life worth having. This idea is, in many ways, similar to the ancient Greek idea of Hades — a place where the dead survived only as shadowy figures with no real existence worth a name.

> *. . . Sheol cannot thank you,*
> *death cannot praise you;*
> *those who go down to the Pit cannot hope*
> *for your faithfulness.*
> *The living, the living, they thank you,*
> *as I do this day;*
> *fathers make known to children*
> *your faithfulness.* (Isaiah 38:18–19)

Of course, in times of sickness or depression the thought that there is nothing beyond this life is bound to make the suffering worse, as it does for Job. The psalmists sometimes speak as though when they are ill they are already as good as dead: 'one foot in the grave' is not a biblical quotation, but it easily could be:

> *I am counted among those who go down to the Pit;*
> *I am like those who have no help,*
> *like those forsaken among the dead,*
> *like the slain that lie in the grave,*
> *like those whom you remember no more,*
> *for they are cut off from your hand.* (Psalm 88:4–5)

Similar stories which explain why humans do not live for ever can be found in the literature of the ancient world, and usually the reason has to do with a trick played on humans by the gods. For example, in the Mesopotamian story of Adapa a god offers the hero 'bread of life and water of life' — which would have ensured his immortality. However, he has previously been warned that he will be offered 'bread of death and water of death', and so he suspects a trick, refuses the gift he is offered, and thus he loses the chance to become immortal. In the story of Gilgamesh, the hero finds a plant that confers immortality; but before he can eat it a snake snatches it away. Genesis 3 fits well into the context of these stories, which all see the possibility of immortality as something that was once, tantalizingly, on offer, but which the human race failed to achieve. It is unusual, however, in seeing this as due to a fault or sin on the part of the humans involved. What God does in forbidding Adam and Eve to eat from the tree of the knowledge of good and evil is a motif we find in other folktales: as soon as we hear that just one thing is forbidden, we know that the characters in the story are bound to do it! However, it is clear that the Old Testament does not present this as a trick on God's part, but as an aspect of human frailty and weakness.

What is clear is that, whatever might happen after death, death itself was an observable fact for everyone, and so the Old Testament, in common with other ancient cultures, faced a related but distinct question about human life. Why did people die in the first place? The Old Testament answer to this question of why human beings were not immortal is presented in the story of the Garden of Eden at the beginning of Genesis:

> *The LORD God took the man and put him in the garden of Eden to till it and keep it. And the LORD God commanded the man, 'You may freely eat of every tree of the garden; but of the tree of the knowledge of good and evil you shall not eat, for in the day that you eat of it you shall die.' . . .*
>
> *Now the serpent was more crafty than any other wild animal that the LORD God had made. He said to the woman, 'Did God say, "You shall not eat from any tree in the garden"?' The woman said to the serpent, 'We may eat of the fruit of the trees in the garden; but God said, "You shall not eat of the fruit of the tree that is in the middle of the garden, nor shall you touch it, or you shall die."' But the serpent said to the woman, 'You will not die; for God knows that when you eat of it your eyes will be opened, and you will be like God, knowing good and evil.' So when the woman saw that the tree was good for food, and that it was a delight to the eyes, and that the tree was to be desired to make one wise, she took of its fruit and ate; and she also gave some to her husband, who was with her, and he ate. Then the eyes of both were opened, and they knew that they were naked; and they sewed fig leaves together and made loincloths for themselves. . . .*

*Then the LORD God said, 'See, the man has become like one
of us, knowing good and evil; and now, he might reach out his
hand and take also from the tree of life, and eat, and live for
ever' — therefore the LORD God sent him forth from the garden
of Eden, to till the ground from which he was taken.*

(Genesis 2:15–17; 3:1–7, 22–23)

The story of the Garden of Eden is often described as 'The
Fall' because it is seen as primarily being about the way sin
and death entered the world. The writer of one of the books
from the Apocrypha called the Wisdom of Solomon clearly
interpreted it in this way:

*. . . God created us for incorruption,
and made us in the image of his own eternity,
but through the devil's envy death entered the world.*

(Wisdom 2:23–24)

The New Testament writer, Paul, follows this tradition of
interpretation in the Letter to the Romans: 'sin came into
the world through one man, and death came through sin,
and so death spread to all because all have sinned' (Romans
5:12). However, as it stands, the story in Genesis 3 actually
presupposes that human beings were created *mortal*. They
could have become *immortal* only if they had succeeded in
taking fruit from the tree of life, and it was to prevent them
from doing this that God expelled them from the garden.
Thus, immortality was not part of the human condition from
the beginning; it was, at most, a possibility that could have
arisen. In practice, it did not arise because disobedience to
God's command not to eat from the tree of the knowledge of
good and evil meant that Adam and Eve were expelled from
the garden, and, therefore, access to the tree of life, and immortality, was denied. In fact, although God told Adam and
Eve that if they ate from the tree of the knowledge of good
and evil they would die, God shows mercy and sends them
out into the wide world, where they will have to work hard
for a living instead of doing gentle gardening in a ready-made
orchard. Immortality is therefore denied them, but then they
never had it in the first place.

So the story of the Garden of Eden explains why life is hard
and burdensome: it is the result of human sin. However, the
Old Testament story takes it for granted that life is finite and
ends in death. Immortality is a sort of futile dream.

A life without point?

Job's unhappy thoughts about human life may easily lead us
to ask: Is there any point in life at all? This question has occurred to many thinkers in both religious and non-religious
traditions. Job curses the day of his birth:

*'Let the day perish in which I was born,
and the night that said, "A man-child is conceived."'* (Job 3:3)

He continues:

'Why did I not die at birth,
  come forth from the womb and expire? . . .
Now I would be lying down and quiet;
  I would be asleep; then I would be at rest. . . .
Or why was I not buried like a stillborn child,
  like an infant that never sees the light? . . .

'Why is light given to one in misery,
  and life to the bitter in soul,
who long for death, but it does not come,
  and dig for it more than for hidden treasures . . . ?'

(Job 3:11, 13, 16, 20–21)

Clearly, life is pointless, and one would be better off dead. No other book in the Old Testament is so negative about human life. Of course, in the case of Job's laments, we are dealing with speeches put into the mouth of a despairing character, not necessarily with the author's own sentiments; and the book turns out well in the end, with Job being restored to well-being. Nevertheless, the author could hardly make Job utter such heartfelt cries of misery if he had not confronted such dark thoughts himself. Thus, the fear that life might turn out to be pointless is not only a modern fear, but meets us in antiquity too.

One other book, however, is often thought to be like Job in its negative assessment of life, the book called Ecclesiastes. This probably comes from no earlier than the third century BCE, and reflects the influence of the Greek philosophical movement known as **Scepticism** on Jewish thought. Qoheleth seems to share this belief, arguing that we cannot know most of what we would like to know about life; for example, 'Who knows whether the human spirit goes upwards and the spirit of animals goes downwards to the earth?' (Ecclesiastes 3:21). All human activity, he says, is 'emptiness' (Hebrew *hebel*, pronounced he-vel, with the stress on the first syllable) — English translations usually render it 'vanity', which used to mean pointlessness (as in 'in vain'): 'I saw all the deeds that are done under the sun; and see, all is vanity and a chasing after wind' (Ecclesiastes 1:14).

However, unlike Job, the author does not conclude from this that we would be better off dead. On the contrary, he argues that since we stand absolutely no chance of understanding life, we should stop worrying our heads about such questions, and get on with enjoying it:

I know that there is nothing better for them than to be happy
and enjoy themselves as long as they live; moreover, it is God's
gift that all should eat and drink and take pleasure in all
their toil.   (Ecclesiastes 3:12–13)

The members of the movement called **Scepticism** taught that the answers to all the important questions of life were unknown and that all reasoning about them was always inconclusive. People are termed 'sceptics' today if they question or doubt the truth of a generally accepted idea.

This is what I have seen to be good: it is fitting to eat and drink and find enjoyment in all the toil with which one toils under the sun the few days of the life God gives us; for this is our lot. Likewise all to whom God gives wealth and possessions and whom he enables to enjoy them, and to accept their lot and find enjoyment in their toil — this is the gift of God. For they will scarcely brood over the days of their lives, because God keeps them occupied with the joy of their hearts.

(Ecclesiastes 5:18–20, our emphasis)

Scepticism about the possibility of ultimate knowledge is thus combined with practical advice to get on with life and make the most of it. Work hard and play hard, seems to be the message: avoid philosophy and theology! We might put Qoheleth's point more seriously like this: there is plenty of point to life, provided we do not bother our heads looking for *the* point. There is no 'meaning of life', or if there is, we cannot find it. But that does not mean life is meaningless: lived to the full, it is very satisfying.

Moreover, although this message is nowhere conveyed in so stark a form as in Ecclesiastes, a lot of the wisdom literature makes sense on rather similar assumptions. It is not the human task to be concerned with deep questions, but with practical wisdom — living well, doing good, 'maintaining the fabric of the world' as Jesus son of Sira puts it (Sirach 38:34), or, as the psalmist says:

O Lord, my heart is not lifted up,
my eyes are not raised too high;
I do not occupy myself with things
too great and too marvellous for me.
But I have calmed and quieted my soul,
like a weaned child with its mother. (Psalm 131:1–2)

Men and women in the Old Testament

As a final section in this chapter on the human condition, some mention must be made of the way the Old Testament views the roles of men and women. Firstly, the Old Testament comes from what is nowadays called a 'patriarchal' culture — Israelite society was run by men; only men had full legal rights and responsibilities; it was men who wrote the works that make up the Old Testament; and all its original readers were men. There is no point in denying this male bias, and a clear example of it is how the Law does not treat men and women equally. For example, men, married or unmarried, can have sexual relations with any woman provided she is not another man's wife, whereas married women are limited to sexual relations with their legal husband. Property law also assumes that it is men who usually inherit, and it is boys alone who receive education — note that in the book of Proverbs the words of wisdom are always addressed to 'my son', never 'my daughter'.

Furthermore there are stories in the Old Testament in

 Do not confuse the book of 'Ecclesiastes' with the book of 'Ecclesiasticus'. Both books are collections of wisdom teachings, but Ecclesiastes is in the canon of the Old Testament, whereas Ecclesiasticus is part of the Apocrypha. The book of Ecclesiastes is a collection of teachings in the Hebrew wisdom tradition on the theme of the vanity of human desires and achievements, and takes its name from the Greek translation of the Hebrew word *Qoheleth*. This word means 'preacher' and is sometimes used as a way of referring to the author of this book. On the other hand, Ecclesiasticus is a title that means 'used in the church'. At one time, such a descriptive title was applied to all the apocryphal books but only this one has retained it. It is a compilation of late wisdom teaching of a professional sage in Jerusalem called Jesus ben Sira — hence the book of Ecclesiasticus is also known as Sirach.

For more information about the wisdom tradition of the Old Testament, see 4.4 'Can We Cope?'

Examples of powerful women in the Old Testament include Rebekah, who masterminds the deception of her husband, Isaac, in order to secure the birthright for her favourite son, Jacob (Genesis 27). In Judges 4, it is Deborah who is the driving force behind the Israelites' defeat of the Canaanite commander, Sisera, and in the books of Esther and Judith, it is Jewish women who save their people from destruction. During the period of the divided monarchy, nearly all the mothers of the kings of Israel and Judah are listed in the books of Kings and given the title 'Queen Mother' (Hebrew *gebirah*, pronounced guh-vee-raa, with the stress on the last syllable). Characters such as Jezebel (I Kings 18–19 and 21, 2 Kings 9) and Athaliah (2 Kings II) evidently had considerable power, although it has to be conceded that the Old Testament does not exactly present them as role models!

To be **androgynous**, in this context, is to be both male and female at the same time.

which the characters (though probably not the story-teller) exhibit 'male chauvinist' attitudes to women: read, for example, the horrible stories in Genesis 19 and Judges 19 of rape and murder. There is no point whatever in trying to pretend that ancient Israelite society acknowledged equality between the sexes. It would fall outside all we know about traditional societies if it did. However, with all that said, there are some surprises.

Firstly, we noted that it is both male and female who are said to be made 'in the image' of God in Genesis 1:27 — a verse which shows that the 'image' cannot mean a merely physical resemblance to God, who was certainly not imagined as female or **androgynous**. Secondly, the Sabbath law requires rest for both male and female slaves, and one of the laws about slaves sets male and female on an equal footing (Deuteronomy 15:12–17 — probably a deliberate updating and improvement of Exodus 21:2–11). It is also interesting to note that the narrative books of the Old Testament contain a great many powerful female characters, some of whom easily get the better of the men in the story, and the historical books make it clear that the 'queen mother' held power and influence. Furthermore, in the book of Proverbs, people are told to honour and obey their mothers as well as their fathers, and the book ends with a poem in praise of the 'woman of worth'. Such a woman not only looks after her family, but also engages in trade, gives to the poor, and is a respected figure in her town:

> Strength and dignity are her clothing,
>   and she laughs at the time to come.
> She opens her mouth with wisdom,
>   and the teaching of kindness is on her tongue. . . .
> Give her a share in the fruit of her hands,
>   and let her works praise her in the city
>   gates. (Proverbs 31:25–26, 31)

Nevertheless, Israelite society was predominantly 'traditional' and, even where there is some degree of equality between men and women, there is no notion that they have similar roles. For the most part, there are men's tasks and women's tasks, and we do not normally find women fighting in the army or men cooking food in the home.

2.4 How Should We Live?
ETHICS AND THE OLD TESTAMENT

THE BASICS

- The ethical material in the Old Testament, which has some similarities with that of its ancient Near Eastern neighbours, is in the form of laws, wisdom and prophetic exhortation to live righteous lives in the eyes of God.
- The ethical material in the Old Testament cannot easily be classified as fitting one brand of ethical theory, but many believe it has something valuable to offer modern-day reflection on ethical issues.

ALL HUMAN SOCIETIES NEED some moral rules. These are expressed in many different ways. Laws lay down what is and is not allowed; teaching given by parents to their children, and by teachers to students, suggests ideals and helps to fashion a lifestyle; religious institutions motivate moral action, and impose special obligations of their own. Putting these all together, we can speak of the 'ethics' of the society in question. All three ethical resources were clearly present in ancient Israel. In this chapter we shall look at a number of specific areas of human conduct, trying to see in each case what contribution the three types of resource made to the total picture. Then we shall go on to ask some deeper questions about how people in Israel understood the basis of moral obligations.

God's law forbidding murder is one of the seven commandments given to Noah after the Flood. These laws are known as the Noahide Laws and specify that people should worship only God, should not blaspheme, murder, steal, commit adultery or be cruel to animals, and should establish a just rule of law to enable people to live in harmony with each other. Jews regard these laws as the basic framework for all people for a moral and spiritual life and view any religion that upholds these laws as an acceptable way for a non-Jew to serve God.

SIX ETHICAL SPHERES

Human life

One of the first requirements of any civilized society is that people are able to live without fear of personal attack. The Old Testament is like almost every source of ethical teaching, ancient or modern, in forbidding murder. It is well known that murder is forbidden in the Ten Commandments (Exodus 20:13; Deuteronomy 5:17), but it is also forbidden in what is probably the earliest law code, the 'Book of the Covenant' (Exodus 21–23): 'Whoever strikes a person mortally shall be put to death' (Exodus 21:12). In the very next few verses, Exodus 21:13–14, a distinction is drawn between deliberate murder and accidental homicide, but the Old Testament Law is clear that murder proper always calls for the death penalty. This is laid down in a narrative in Genesis, the story of Noah, where we read that after the Flood Noah is told, 'Whoever sheds the blood of a human, by a human shall that person's blood be shed' (Genesis 9:6). This rule does not apply to killing people in war or in self-defence, or to judicial execution, but where one person kills another without provocation he forfeits his own life — a harsh law by modern European standards, but one that seemed vital to ancient Israelites. Indeed, it is important to realize that this was unusual in the ancient world. Unless the person killed was an aristocrat and the murderer belonged to a lower class, the normal penalty for murder in the ancient world was to pay compensation to the victim's family. Perhaps the Israelite law about murder reflects the higher status of human beings in Israel's thought, where, whatever their class, a person had the basic right to life because humans are made in the image of God (Genesis 9:6).

In the prophets we find condemnations of the society of their day, and murder is occasionally mentioned as one of the crimes people were committing (see Hosea 4:2 and Jeremiah 7:6), though more often the prophets concentrated on less 'obvious' sins, such as injustice towards the poor. The wisdom literature, again, tends to focus on more subtle moral questions, but Proverbs 1:8–19 warns the reader against robbery with violence and condemns those who 'hurry to shed blood' (1:16).

The word **abortion** refers to the termination of a pregnancy.

Interestingly, whilst the basic right to life is clear in the Old Testament, and is often quoted by those who oppose **abortion** and euthanasia, it has little to say directly about such ethical matters. As a general principle in the Old Testament, no one has the right to cut short anybody's life except in cases of self-defence or war or punishments. However, in Jewish thought abortion is not viewed as murder at all because it is believed that a foetus does not become a full person until the moment of birth. This draws on the biblical story of creation where God creates Adam's body from the dust of the ground but the creation becomes a living person only when God breathes into it the breath of life (Genesis 2:7). On the other hand, Psalm 139:13–16 and Jeremiah 1:5 seem to indicate an understanding that the foetus inside the womb is a unique creation which can be known to God and for whom God can have a special plan. As a result, many Christians would wish to say that the Old Testament does provide evidence in support of the view that a unique life is created at the moment of conception and, therefore, that abortion is murder. In terms of euthanasia, the Old Testament's stance on a person's basic right to life is more relevant. Life is clearly viewed as a gift from God and, therefore, no human being has the right to terminate it. The giving and taking away of life is God's pre-

The word 'euthanasia' literally means 'a good death' and today refers to the practice of bringing about a painless death for the seriously ill. Voluntary or active euthanasia, sometimes also called 'assisted suicide', involves helping a person who wishes to die to do so. Involuntary euthanasia involves helping persons to die, although they are unable, or unwilling, to request this for themselves. This is usually done out of a desire to end the person's suffering and is, therefore, sometimes called 'mercy killing'. Where a person is allowed to die as a result of the deliberate withdrawal of treatment or nourishment, it is termed 'passive euthanasia'. The term 'indirect euthanasia', sometimes referred to as the 'double effect', is used where treatment provided with the primary intention of relieving pain has the effect of hastening death.

rogative alone. Ecclesiastes 3:1–4 states that human beings cannot choose when they die because such times as birth and death are ordained by God. Moreover, if such references are viewed in conjunction with the concern for the elderly and the weak it seems unlikely that a case for euthanasia can be made on the basis of the Old Testament texts.

Property

Respect for other people's property goes hand in hand with respect for their life in Old Testament thought. All the law codes that forbid murder also condemn theft in all its forms. The Ten Commandments sum this up in the terse formula 'You shall not steal' (Exodus 20:15; Deuteronomy 5:19). It is hard to imagine a society without some such basic law.

However, there are more ways than one of 'stealing'. One of the concerns of the Book of the Covenant is with people who agree to look after someone else's property but then embezzle it:

> *When someone delivers to a neighbour money or goods for safekeeping and they are stolen from the neighbour's house, then the thief, if caught, shall pay double. If the thief is not caught, the owner of the house shall be brought before God, to determine whether or not the owner had laid hands on the neighbour's goods.* (Exodus 22:7–8)

What is envisaged here is a sort of early form of banking. If the banker loses your money and alleges that someone else stole it, that will need to be proved; otherwise, the matter is settled 'before God', which may mean by the parties involved taking an oath before a priest, or maybe by some kind of trial by ordeal.

There is also a kind of theft involved in forcing people off their land, by violence or even by unjust forms of compulsory purchase. In Israel land was felt to be an ancestral possession which could not simply be bought and sold as it can with us, and dispossessing people of their land by shady means was repeatedly condemned by the prophets of the eighth and seventh centuries:

> *They covet fields, and seize them,*
> *   houses, and take them away;*
> *they oppress householder and house,*
> *   people and their inheritance.* (Micah 2:2)

The story of Naboth's vineyard in 1 Kings 21 shows how attached people were to their ancestral property. Naboth will not sell his land to King Ahab even at a good price. Then Ahab's wife Jezebel goes ahead and takes it from him by getting Naboth falsely accused of a capital crime and executed, so that his property comes to the state and thus becomes Ahab's anyway. God's punishment for such a crime is severe and involves total disaster for Ahab and his family. On the other hand, it needs to be remembered that Israel itself saw no problems with taking the land of Palestine from its native Canaanite inhabitants and using considerable force when it was under God's instructions:

> *When the LORD your God brings you into the land that you are about to enter and occupy, and he clears away many nations before you . . . you must utterly destroy them. Make no covenant with them and show them no mercy.*
>
> (Deuteronomy 7:1–2)

Commerce

As in most cultures of the ancient Near East, there were laws in Israel to regulate trading practices. A particular concern was that traders should have fair weights and scales because, with no Trading Standards Authority to check and regulate them, it was all too easy for an unscrupulous shopkeeper to make sure that his balances were weighted in his own favour. Amos tells us that this happened in the northern kingdom in the eighth century BCE, where there were traders who said,

> '*When will the new moon be over*
> 　　*so that we may sell grain,*
> *and the sabbath,*
> 　　*so that we may offer wheat for sale?*
> *We will make the ephah small and the shekel great,*
> 　　*and practise deceit with false balances . . .*
> 　　*selling the sweepings of the wheat.*' (Amos 8:5–6)

The ephah is a measure of volume, so a small ephah means that customers will get less wheat than they have paid for; the shekel is the weight of a coin, and by demanding that it weigh more than it should the traders exact a higher price than people think they are paying. In the Old Testament there are laws about weights and measures (see, for example, Deuteronomy 25:13–16), and commercial practices that resulted in defrauding the poor were in the minds of all the prophets, for whom social injustice was the great national sin that was calling down God's anger on the nation. However, it is in the wisdom literature that concerns for fair trade surface most clearly. God is said to take pleasure in just weights and measures:

The word 'abomination' is a strong term of disapproval. In Hebrew the word is to'ebah (pronounced toe-ay-vaa, with stress on the final syllable), and it indicates something that is not only against the Law, but horrible to any right-thinking person.

> *A false balance is an abomination to the LORD,*
> 　　*but an accurate weight is his delight.*
>
> (Proverbs 11:1; cf. 16:11, 20:10)

Moreover, Israel was not alone in holding such a view, and the same attitude towards falsity in weights and measures is reflected in the wisdom literature of other ancient cultures: thus the Egyptian Teaching of Amen-em-opet warns, 'Do not lean on the scales nor falsify the weights, nor damage the fractions of the measure' (chapter 16).

Legal practice

In ancient Israel, the local council of elders in a town or village administered law. This council met 'in the gate', that is, just inside the city gate where trading also took place — an area corresponding to the town square in a European town. Originally, it seems as though all adult males could take part in the activities of the court. In the course of time, there also came to be professional judges, perhaps to hear harder cases, or cases on appeal; and in the time of the monarchy the king constituted a supreme court. Even when Israel was subject to one of the great powers, as so often in its history, it is unlikely that these concerned themselves with the day-to-day administration of justice: it would have been left to the Israelites to operate their own system. However, what was important was that the law should be administered justly, and legal, wisdom, and prophetic books alike express strong judgements on those who take bribes or otherwise pervert the course of justice. Typical examples are:

> *You shall not pervert the justice due to your poor in their law-*
> *suits. Keep far from a false charge, and do not kill the innocent*
> *or those in the right, for I will not acquit the guilty. You shall*
> *take no bribe, for a bribe blinds the officials, and subverts the*
> *cause of those who are in the right.* (Exodus 23:6–8)

> *A faithful witness does not lie,*
>   *but a false witness breathes out lies.* (Proverbs 14:5)

> *One who justifies the wicked and one who condemns the*
>   *righteous*
>   *are both alike an abomination to the LORD.*
>   (Proverbs 17:15; cf. 17:23, 18:5, 19:9)

> *Your princes are rebels*
>   *and companions of thieves.*
> *Everyone loves a bribe*
>   *and runs after gifts.*
> *They do not defend the orphan,*
>   *and the widow's cause does not come before them.*
>   (Isaiah 1:23; cf. 5:23)

Sexual ethics

The basic model of sexual life in the Old Testament is that sexual desire should be expressed within marriage, although nowhere is it laid down that men should be **monogamous** and there are striking cases of men with two wives. For ex-

Amen-em-opet lived and taught in Egypt between 1250 and 1000 BCE, and two versions of his 'wise words' were discovered in the 1900s. One version, now in the British Museum in London, is written on papyrus sheets and the other, now in a museum in Turin in Italy, is on clay tablets. The Teaching of Amen-em-opet is interesting to biblical scholars because it contains a number of striking similarities to some of the wisdom in the Old Testament.

A man is **monogamous** if he is married to only one woman at any one time.

A man is practising **polygamy** if he is married to more than one woman at the same time.

ample, Jacob in Genesis 29–35, and Samuel's father, Elkanah, in 1 Samuel 1–2, both have two wives. The Law, however, warns against one of the dangers of **polygamy**, namely that one of a man's wives will be his favourite and he will tend to be unfair to the other, depriving her children of their rights of inheritance. Deuteronomy 21:15–17 explicitly deals with this problem, and may well hint that such marriages are less than ideal. In any case there is no symmetry between men and women, since women are strictly limited to one husband.

This lack of symmetry is seen also in the laws about adultery. A man and a woman commit adultery, according to the Old Testament, if they have sexual relations when the woman is married to someone else. A man is not reckoned to have committed adultery if he is unfaithful to his wife with an unmarried woman or a widow — indeed, the category of 'unfaithfulness' simply does not apply in this case. In addition, men are not forbidden from using prostitutes, though the practice is not encouraged; nor from taking female slaves as concubines — though if a man marries his slave, then she acquires the same rights as any other wife would have (see Deuteronomy 21:10–14). No such freedoms apply to women at all.

We may gain a little more insight into Israelite thinking about sexual matters from the stories in Genesis 19 and Judges 19, where the men of Israelite towns seek to have homosexual intercourse with male visitors. The main sin in these cases is probably seen as ill-treatment of guests, which is a heinous offence all over the ancient Near East. However, what is interesting in the present context is that the visitors' hosts offer the attackers their own daughters or female concubines in substitution — an offer that is taken up in Judges 19 with terrible consequences. The assumption seems to be that the townsmen are in the grip of a sexual lust which can be met by the offer of a male or female victim: in other words, they are not seen as having a homosexual orientation, but simply as over-sexed in an unfocused way. It is often pointed out that such stories of violence and rape offer no guidance on the question of consensual homosexual acts. However, although nothing is said anywhere in the Old Testament about sexual relations between women, all sexual relations between men appear to be illicit. Indeed, in Leviticus 20, homosexual acts are listed alongside incest and bestiality as 'abominations': 'If a man lies with a male as with a woman, both of them have committed an abomination; they shall be put to death; their blood is upon them' (v. 13). That said, some have suggested that there may be overtones of a homoerotic attachment in the story of David and Jonathan (1 Samuel 18:1–5), and it is striking that the prophets nowhere mention homosexuality, though they are vocal in condemning adultery:

> When I fed them to the full,
>   they committed adultery
>   and trooped to the houses of prostitutes.

They were well-fed lusty stallions,
*   each neighing for his neighbour's wife.* (Jeremiah 5:7–8)

The same is true of the wisdom literature in the Old Testament which is full of advice to young men about the dangers that come from contact with women. In particular, it counsels the reader against getting into compromising positions with other men's wives, and warns that,

. . .he who commits adultery has no sense;
*   he who does it destroys himself.*
He will get wounds and dishonour,
*   and his disgrace will not be wiped away.*
For jealousy arouses a husband's fury,
*   and he shows no restraint when he takes revenge.*
He will accept no compensation,
*   and refuses a bribe no matter how great.*

(Proverbs 6:32–35)

Indeed, the whole of Proverbs 5–7 is worth reading on this theme. However, the reader should note that this is advice based on prudence rather than on law or even morality: committing adultery puts a man in danger of his life, perhaps from the Law, which strictly speaking enjoins the death penalty (Deuteronomy 22:22 — but probably rarely enforced), or perhaps from the anger of the jealous husband. Yet, here again nothing is said about homosexuality. From this we could conclude either that it was not an issue that mattered, or that it was so obviously abhorrent that advice against it was not needed! The latter is perhaps more likely in the kind of society we can see Israel to have been.

Religious obligations

In all ancient societies religious observance was a natural part of the social fabric, and no one could decide to ignore it. Offering sacrifices was a necessary part of acknowledging the gods. The same is true of ancient Israel, where people were expected to attend the rites at their local sanctuary or, in later times, at the Temple. For example, the Law lays down three occasions in the year when all male Israelites must 'appear before **YHWH**' (see Exodus 23:14–17): the three main agricultural festivals.

However, Israel was unusual in incorporating into its law codes the rules about worship alongside rules about civil matters. This may have something to do with the fact that in other cultures the gods required worship but it was the king who laid down the law in civil matters, whereas in Israel both spheres were seen as deriving equally from the will of God. Therefore, all the Israelite law codes in the Old Testament mix civil and religious legislation together. In addition, the wisdom writers in the Old Testament acknowledge that religious observance is part of the national ethic:

YHWH is the primary way God's name appears in the Old Testament. It is simply four Hebrew consonants which many scholars believe may have been pronounced Yahweh. For a more detailed examination of this issue, see 2.1 'Watchmaker or Living God?'

Honour the LORD with your substance,
  and with the first fruits of all your produce;
then your barns will be filled with plenty,
  and your vats will be bursting with wine. (Proverbs 3:9–10)

However, at the same time they reckon that other forms of ethical behaviour are a higher priority:

To do righteousness and justice
  is more acceptable to the LORD than sacrifice.

(Proverbs 21:3)

For these writers, sacrifice is also no substitute for an upright life:

The sacrifice of the wicked is an abomination to the LORD,
  but the prayer of the upright is his delight. (Proverbs 15:8)

The pre-exilic prophets are those prophets who existed before the Exile in the sixth century BCE when many of Israel's people were taken captive and deported to Babylon. Important pre-exilic prophets were Amos, Hosea, Isaiah, and Micah.

This theme is developed in detail by the **pre-exilic prophets** who think that the people's assiduous sacrifices serve only to make their social sins worse. They seem to have believed that YHWH had not really commanded the sacrificial cult as it was practised in their day. This goes further than the wisdom writers' preference for acts of righteousness and actually makes sacrifice illicit when it is not accompanied by justice:

I hate, I despise your festivals,
  and I take no delight in your solemn assemblies.
Even though you offer me your burnt-offerings and
    grain-offerings,
  I will not accept them;
and the offerings of well-being of your fatted animals
  I will not look upon.
Take away from me the noise of your songs;
  I will not listen to the melody of your harps.
But let justice roll down like waters,
  and righteousness like an ever-flowing stream.

(Amos 5:21–24; cf. Isaiah 1:10–20)

In biblical studies, the **Exile** refers to the period in Israel's history in the sixth century BCE when many of its people were taken captive and deported from Israel to Babylon.

However, this extreme prophetic rejection of sacrifice and the system of festivals never became a mainstream attitude in Israel, and from the time of the **Exile** even prophets thought of the Temple and its rites as what God required for his people. We see this in Haggai and Zechariah, the prophets of the time of the return in the late sixth century, who think it is vital that the Temple should be rebuilt. We also find it a little later in the prophecies of Malachi, the last of the Old Testament prophets, who criticizes the people of his day not because they offer sacrifice, but because they sacrifice blemished animals (Malachi 1:6–14). Judaism never abandoned its belief that God required sacrifices, though during the Exile and once the Temple was destroyed by the Romans in 70 CE the idea grew up that prayer and fasting were an acceptable substitute for it.

LIFESTYLE AND ATTITUDE

Prophetic summaries of morality

In several places in the Old Testament there are summaries of what is required ethically of Israelites. The prophets occasionally list, not what the people should do, but what they have done wrong, and two of these lists are particularly important:

> *There is no faithfulness or loyalty,*
> *   and no knowledge of God in the land.*
> *Swearing, lying, and murder,*
> *   and stealing and adultery break out;*
> *   bloodshed follows bloodshed.* (Hosea 4:1–2)

Here Hosea, prophesying in the eighth century BCE, draws up a list reminiscent of the Ten Commandments. He sums up all the sins he identifies in his contemporaries as a lack of 'faithfulness', in Hebrew *emeth* (pronounced uh-meth, with stress on the second syllable), and 'loyalty', in Hebrew *chesed* (pronounced as written, with stress on the first syllable: 'ch' is the guttural sound in Scots 'loch'). These are rich terms, which together tell us that the Israelites have not simply committed certain specific sins, but have been far from the right way in their whole mode of conduct, lacking in reliability and failing to keep faith with God. Since they are not reliable in their attitude towards him and what he requires, he will prove 'false' to them, in the sense that he will not keep his side of the contract (covenant).

A similar point is made in the book of Jeremiah:

> *Will you steal, murder, commit adultery, swear falsely, make offerings to Baal, and go after other gods that you have not known, and then come and stand before me in this house, which is called by my name, and say, 'We are safe!' — only to go on doing all these abominations?* (Jeremiah 7:9–10)

For Jeremiah, the conduct of the people is symptomatic of a reckless and unfaithful approach to God: they do all the things he has forbidden, and then think he will keep them safe if they come into the Temple. Underlying this seems to be the same critical attitude towards the Temple and its rites that we saw in Amos and Isaiah. It is Isaiah who also includes another major list of sins, sometimes known as the 'Woes' ('Ahs' in the NRSV) of Isaiah 5:11–23. This list condemns those who get drunk (vv. 11–13), are proud of their status (vv. 14–17), are impatient with God (vv. 18–19), 'call evil good and good evil' (v. 20), are 'wise in [their] own eyes' (v. 21), and are 'heroes in drinking wine' but have no care for the innocent, whom they convict in return for bribes (vv. 22–23). This is a particularly interesting list because, apart from the accusation of bribery, there is nothing here that can be found in Israelite law. Rather, Isaiah appears to be concentrating on attitudes of mind as these express themselves in a certain lifestyle, rather than speaking in terms of an ethical code found in the Law.

Therefore, for the prophets, a list of sins is more than a mere list and is greater than the sum of its parts: it adds up to a complete indictment of the people as those who abandon God and his ways.

The Ten Commandments

The Ten Commandments are presented in the Old Testament as very old, going back to the time of Moses; although this may be a deliberate fiction to gain status for them, we should note the logic of the Commandments. Like the lists of sins in the prophets, they are an attempt not simply to list a number of important moral or legal rules, but to encapsulate the whole of a way of life. For the most part this is done negatively ('You shall not...'), though there are also positive commands ('Honour your father and your mother'; 'remember the Sabbath day'). However, as Jews and Christians have always insisted, the Commandments stake out large general areas of life and give us indications of how we are to live within them, rather than specifying detailed infringements as do many of the other laws in the **Pentateuch**.

Thus the law against murder can stand as a warning against every form of personal hostility to others, the law against theft as an encouragement to respect other people's property. Indeed, the final commandment is not even apparently directed against actual crime, but is concerned with the intentions of the heart: 'You shall not covet your neighbour's house; you shall not covet your neighbour's wife, or male or female slave, or ox, or donkey, or anything that belongs to your neighbour' (Exodus 20:17; cf. the different wording in Deuteronomy 5:21). Just as with many of the sins listed by Isaiah, there is no way of enforcing this commandment: it appeals to each person's knowledge of his own desires.

Wisdom and lifestyle

The lists of the prophets are in fact closer to some of the wisdom literature than they are to law — indeed, some might say that is even true of the Ten Commandments. For example, it is wisdom that supplies the Old Testament's major criticism of drunkenness and, incidentally, an answer to the accusation that there is no humour in the Bible:

> *Who has woe? Who has sorrow?*
> *Who has strife? Who has complaining?*
> *Who has wounds without cause?*
> *Who has redness of eyes?*
> *Those who linger late over wine,*

Pentateuch is a common collective term for the first five books of the Old Testament — Genesis, Exodus, Leviticus, Numbers, and Deuteronomy. It is derived from the Greek word *pente* meaning 'five'. In the Jewish tradition, these are sometimes referred to as the five books of Moses.

those who keep trying mixed wines.
Do not look at wine when it is red,
    when it sparkles in the cup
    and goes down smoothly.
At the last it bites like a serpent,
    and stings like an adder.
Your eyes will see strange things,
    and your mind utter perverse things.
You will be like one who lies down in the midst of the sea,
    like one who lies on the top of a mast.
'They struck me,' you will say, 'but I was not hurt;
    they beat me, but I did not feel it.
When shall I awake?
    I will seek another drink. (Proverbs 23:29–35)

True, this attacks drunkenness by way of ridicule rather than stern prophetic condemnation, but it shows very clearly that there were things permitted by the Law that the 'wise' in Israel did not approve of — just as they did not approve of (perfectly legal) prostitution. The issue is lifestyle, rather than obedience to the Law.

That, in fact, is what the wisdom literature is about: how we should live rather than how we are obliged to live. The prophets surely drew on this tradition, for they too do not always speak of ethical ideals that were also legal rules, but more often draw on an insight into how human beings should best live life together. They are of course concerned with detailed matters of conduct, but they are also — and chiefly — concerned with attitudes and character.

THE BASIS AND MOTIVATION OF ETHICS IN THE OLD TESTAMENT

Ethical theories

Ethicists ask questions not only about what types of conduct are good or bad, but also about the basis of ethics — what makes this or that course of action right or wrong. There are many ethical theories on the market, but there is no reason to think that people in ancient Israel, a 'pre-philosophical' society, thought consciously in such terms. For one thing, Biblical Hebrew does not have the sort of abstract terms needed for discussing them. At the same time, Old Testament literature is not unreflective, and at a more subconscious level there are at least analogies to some of the issues discussed by moral philosophers today.

The main way of thinking about ethics in the Old Testament bears some resemblance to what is now called a deontological system. In many of the texts this idea derives from a **theonomous** ethical belief. This is most obvious in the law codes, where it is made explicit that God is the Law-giver, who must be obeyed. The Ten Commandments begin, 'God spoke all these words. . . .' (Exodus 20:1), and then the detailed instructions follow. Sometimes the prophets, too, speak as though God has commanded certain things, and they are to

A **theonomous** ethic is one in which God is seen as the ultimate ethical authority. Thus moral rules are accepted as a collection of instructions issued by God.

Karl Barth (1886–1968) was a Swiss Protestant theologian who believed that God communicated with humankind principally through the word of God in the Scriptures and the revelation of Christ, rather than through human reason.

The term 'ethics' is used to describe the study of the moral value of human conduct and the rules and principles that should govern it. There are many ethical theories and, although there is no space in this book to examine them in detail, it is good to have a very basic knowledge of some of the main ideas when looking at the Old Testament. Deontological theories are concerned with absolute morality — the idea that actions are intrinsically right or wrong, irrespective of their consequences. Natural Law is the idea that everything created has a particular design and a particular purpose, and that an action is morally right and good if it fulfils that purpose. Teleological theories are concerned with relative morality — the idea that the rightness or wrongness of an act should be decided by consideration of the consequences and is relative to the society and age in which a person lives. Consequentialism is an ethical theory which assesses the consequences of an action when making a judgement about what is right and wrong. Situation Ethics says that a right action should always be the one which is the most loving thing to do in a particular circumstance, and Utilitarianism argues that a person should act based on whether the outcome will give the greatest happiness to the greatest number of people. Virtue Ethics is another theory that claims that being good requires the practice of a certain kind of behaviour so that a person habitually does what is right.

be done whatever the consequence. Amos, for example, in following his vocation to prophesy, is aware of obeying a direct divine command: 'the LORD took me from following the flock, and the LORD said to me, "Go, prophesy to my people Israel"' (Amos 7:15). So, of course, he did.

On the other hand, not all the ethical teaching in the Old Testament can be understood on the basis that, as the great theologian **Karl Barth** called him, God is the Commander. The wisdom literature seems more interested in what we might call the moral pattern of the world, a sort of natural order in things that has ethical consequences. When God created the world, he did it according to his 'wisdom', and this wisdom is a kind of order of nature. Terms such as 'justice' and 'righteousness' in Hebrew, like the word *ma'at* that occurs in Egyptian wisdom texts, seem to capture this sense that there is a moral order somehow inherent in the world. The wisdom writers do not tell us that God 'commanded' this or that, but more commonly speak as though certain courses of action will produce certain consequences automatically: they are 'naturally' good or bad. The prophets also sometimes pick up this way of speaking, saying, for example, that the natural world follows the right path but Israel all too often fails to do so:

> *Even the stork in the heavens*
>   *knows its times;*
> *and the turtle-dove, swallow, and crane*
>   *observe the time of their coming;*
> *but my people do not know*
>   *the ordinance of the LORD.* (Jeremiah 8:7)

At other times, we meet appeals to what is morally 'obvious', 'done' or 'not done'. When David's daughter Tamar is about to be raped by her brother Amnon she appeals to him,

> *'No, my brother, do not force me, for such a thing is not done in Israel; do not do anything so vile! As for me, where could I carry my shame? And as for you, you would be as one of the scoundrels in Israel.'* (2 Samuel 13:12–13)

Here we are not dealing with an appeal to God's Law, so much as with a sense within the culture that certain acts are 'vile', perpetrated only by 'scoundrels': these are things that anyone in that culture would immediately recognize as twisted and wrong. This might be called a 'conventional' kind of morality, based on human consensus rather than on divine decree.

Motives for conduct

The Old Testament is also more diverse than we might expect in the motivations it gives for human conduct. Sometimes, as in the last example, a sense that certain acts are outrageous is enough to justify not doing them; though even there, we should note, Tamar points out the consequences, in terms of shame for her and of a loss of reputation for Amnon. In fact, consequences are commonly mentioned as incentives to good actions and to dissuade people from bad ones. This represents a more teleological approach to ethics and is true even in the Law, where at one level God's command might be motive enough:

> *If you take your neighbour's cloak in pawn, you shall restore it before the sun goes down; for it may be your neighbour's only clothing to use as cover; in what else shall that person sleep? And if your neighbour cries out to me, I will listen, for I am compassionate.* (Exodus 22:26–27)

Alongside an appeal to the potential offender's better nature (how do you expect someone to sleep with no bedding?) there is also the threat that God will intervene to punish the individual who acts so heartlessly towards someone who has nothing left to pawn but the cloak that is his only outer clothing.

The wisdom tradition focuses to a great extent on incentive as a motive for conduct, with the reward of success for those who are 'wise' and the threat of disaster for those who are not.

> *Therefore, walk in the way of the good,*
> *and keep to the paths of the just.*
> *For the upright will abide in the land,*
> *and the innocent will remain in it;*
> *but the wicked will be cut off from the land,*
> *and the treacherous will be rooted out of it.*
>
> (Proverbs 2:20–22)

However, sometimes the motivation for good conduct is not a threat or a promise, but a recollection of God's past acts of kindness towards the individual or towards Israel as a whole. Thus, in the instructions given in Deuteronomy regarding proper provision for slaves when the time comes to release them from their service, the writer recalls Israel's experience after the **Exodus**: 'Remember that you were a slave in the land of Egypt, and the LORD your God redeemed you; for this reason I lay this command upon you today' (Deuteronomy 15:15). Gratitude for past goodness as well as anxiety about future success or failure can thus be a powerful motivating force leading to good behaviour.

The word **exodus** literally means 'way out' and refers to the departure of the Israelites from Egypt under the leadership of Moses. Exodus is also the name of the second book in the Old Testament in which these events are retold.

A WORD OF CAUTION . . .

On the one hand, we have seen that a variety of ethical viewpoints are evident in the Old Testament, and it is important to remember that the Old Testament presents ethical material that reflects only a selection of the changing practices of a nation through many hundreds of years. Therefore, individual examples from the Old Testament ought not to be quoted

'The best way to approach the Old Testament ethical system . . . is to remember that the purpose of the Old Testament is not primarily to give information about morality...but to provide materials that, when pondered and absorbed into the mind, will suggest the pattern or shape of a way of life lived in the presence of God.' (John Barton, 'Approaches to Ethics in the Old Testament', in *Beginning Old Testament Study*, ed. John Rogerson, SPCK, 1983)

out of context in modern ethical debates. Indeed, there are ethical topics, such as genetic engineering, about which the Old Testament says nothing, as well as proof texts which can be gathered from the Old Testament both in favour of and against a number of key ethical topics such as capital punishment, divorce, and war.

On the other hand, since the Old Testament holds the status of authoritative Scripture for Jews and Christians, it still makes sense to ask questions about what God may or may not be saying in general terms through these Scriptures about what his followers should or should not do when faced with any particular ethical dilemma. This is because there is, at least to some extent, a recognizable ethical style in the Old Testament that centres on respect for life and property, honesty and loyalty in relationships, and a concern for justice, especially for those who are vulnerable in society — ethical principles that can surely still be profitably used to inform ethical discussions today.

2.5 Why Me?

THE OLD TESTAMENT VIEW OF HUMAN SUFFERING

THE BASICS

- The search for an explanation for the sufferings of human beings, both as individuals and as a nation, is a major theme in the Old Testament.
- The idea that suffering is God's punishment for sin is the basis of the response of the biblical authors. However, this is not a satisfactory response for them all; the issues of why some wicked people prosper, whether suffering might be good for you, and whether God is just are also explored.

WHY DO BAD THINGS happen to good people? This question echoes down the ages and is the theme of much literature in many cultures, ancient and modern. It arises in a particularly acute form for anyone who believes in a good God, as Jews and Christians do. In theology and in the philosophy of religion, theoretical attempts to cope with this issue are usually called **theodicy**, and this is a major theme in the Old Testament.

In fact, the Hebrew language had no word for this kind of inquiry, but many Old Testament writers were deeply concerned with making sense of a world in which people do not get what they deserve — or asserted that they really do. Most people would think first of the book of Job but, although Job is centrally important, and will be discussed later in this chapter, there are many other parts of the Hebrew Bible where the issue is raised.

In modern discussions of theodicy it is common to draw a distinction between the natural evils that cause human suffering (earthquakes, famines) and the moral evil caused by human malice (torture, murder, theft). However, this distinction is not nearly so important in the Old Testament where a more significant distinction is probably that between the sufferings of the nation (Israel), and various groups within it, and the sufferings of the *individual*.

Coming from the Greek words for 'god' and 'just', **theodicy** literally means an inquiry into the justice of God. However, today it is used more generally for any attempt to make sense of the suffering in the world in the light of a belief in God.

NATIONAL SUFFERING

Suffering as punishment

The Old Testament is full of examples of nations suffering at the hands of their enemies or through natural disaster such as plague or drought. For the most part these are given a simple explanation as the judgement of God on a wicked people. The earliest case of such judgement recorded in the Old Testament is the overthrow of Sodom and Gomorrah in Genesis 19:24–25, where the means God uses to destroy these wicked cities are 'sulphur and fire from the LORD out of heaven'. More commonly in later stories it is enemy action that defeats nations that sin, and God is seen just as much as the cause of that action as of what we would think of as 'natural' disasters.

Sometimes it is not very clear what form the destruction willed by God takes. In the **oracles** against the nations in Amos 1–2, for example, it is repeatedly said that God will send 'fire' on Israel's enemies (1:4, 1:7, 1:10, 1:12, 1:14, 2:2, 2:5). This could mean a fire caused 'directly' by **YHWH** (probably lightning-strikes), or it could mean the 'firing' of the cities by troops attacking them (note how in 2:2 the fire is followed by 'shouting and the sound of the trumpet', implying an enemy army at work). It was generally believed in the ancient world that major battles were accompanied by signs and portents in heaven, and that the gods assisted armies whose side they were on by hurling thunderbolts or causing other disturbances in the natural order. Thus, in Judges 5:20, it is recorded that 'the stars fought from heaven' against the enemy of Israel. Therefore, when God punishes nations that sin he may do so by enemy action, by upsetting the natural order with meteorological disturbances, or both. Sometimes he also does it by sending sickness as in Numbers 21:4–9, where the people of Israel who disobey God in the wilderness are bitten by snakes, or 1 Samuel 5:6, where YHWH present in his sacred ark, known as the Ark of the Covenant, afflicts the Philistines with 'tumours'.

We sometimes think of God in the Old Testament as being on Israel's side against its enemies, and there is some truth in this. Nevertheless, it is important to realize that practically all the accounts of wars and battles in the Bible see God as controlling the destinies of all nations, and this means that he can fight against Israel just as much as on their behalf. If they deserve punishment, then it is he who 'sends' an enemy to defeat them. In several stories in the **Pentateuch** and in the historical books YHWH fights against Israel: see, for example, Numbers 14:39–45; Joshua 7:2–5; 1 Samuel 4:1–11. Amos is clear that the God who punishes Israel's enemies for their war crimes will also punish Israel, and will do so through the agency of an enemy army:

> *The city that marched out a thousand*
>   *shall have a hundred left,*

An **oracle**, in this sense, is a short saying given in the name of God.

YHWH is the primary way God's name appears in the Old Testament. It is simply four Hebrew consonants which many scholars believe may have been pronounced Yahweh. For a more detailed examination of this issue, see 2.1 'Watchmaker or Living God?'

The Ark of the Covenant (not to be confused with Noah's Ark which uses a different Hebrew word!) is an important part of Old Testament history. It was a large wooden box covered with gold which was constructed according to God's specific instructions (Exodus 25:10–22) and said to contain the two tablets on which God had written the Law. For more about this, see 3.6 'Digging Up the Old Testament'.

Pentateuch is a common collective term for the first five books of the Old Testament — Genesis, Exodus, Leviticus, Numbers, and Deuteronomy. It is derived from the Greek word *pente* meaning 'five'. In the Jewish tradition, these are sometimes referred to as the five books of Moses.

> *and that which marched out a hundred*
> > *shall have ten left.* (Amos 5:3)

This idea that a nation's own god could punish it through a foreign power is also seen very clearly in Isaiah, prophesying a little later than Amos:

> *Ah, Assyria, the rod of my anger —*
> > *the club in their hands is my fury!*
> *Against a godless nation I send him,*
> > *and against the people of my wrath I command him,*
> *to take spoil and seize plunder,*
> > *and to tread them down like the mire of the streets.*
> > > (Isaiah 10:5–6)

Isaiah thought, indeed, that YHWH would later punish the Assyrians in their turn because their defeat of Israel had been too harsh (10:7–19), but that is another story: there was no doubt in his mind that the Assyrians were YHWH's instrument to punish Israel.

This was by no means an unusual idea in the ancient world. On a monument found in the territory of the Moabites, the 'Moabite Stone', King Mesha of Moab (see 2 Kings 3:4) explains that the Israelite king Omri had invaded his country and subjugated it 'because Chemosh was angry with his land' (Chemosh was the god of Moab). This is exactly the same idea as Isaiah had about the Assyrians: Omri was being seen as a tool in the hand of Chemosh. On this subject we can therefore talk about a common ancient theology.

Undeserved suffering?
The normal response in the Old Testament to national suffering that did not seem to be the result of national sin was to maintain that there must really have been some sin, only it was not obvious. Thus in Joshua 7 the Israelites are defeated in battle at Ai, soon after the entry into the Promised Land. God tells Joshua that this is someone's fault: goods that should have been destroyed, under the rule that everything belonging to the enemy must be wiped out, have instead been hidden away. Joshua institutes an enquiry that involves casting lots (Joshua 7:16–18), until the fault is narrowed down to a man called Achan. He is executed (along with his family — this was evidently not felt to be unjust), and next time the Israelites go out to battle, they are successful (Joshua 8). Thus, in this instance the 'innocence' of Israel in its suffering is only apparent: there is a sin in the background which accounts for the disaster.

However, not all the writers in the Old Testament were satisfied with the idea that the sins of one man, or of a few people, could be used to explain the suffering of the whole nation. In Genesis 18:22–33 Abraham argues with God about the coming destruction of Sodom, maintaining that it would be unjust if God were to destroy the whole city if there were a core of good people in it. The passage is striking in the freedom with which Abraham haggles with God, beating him down from fifty righteous people for whose sake he would agree to spare the entire city to a mere handful, just ten. Tantalizingly, Abraham stops at ten, so we never learn whether God would have spared Sodom for the sake of just one righteous person — although the next chapter appears to give us our answer: only Lot and his family are righteous, and so the city is doomed.

This story, however, also shows how reluctant the writers are to concede that any really good person ever perishes even in a situation like that of the overthrow of Sodom, for Lot himself, with his family, is spared: the angels lead him out of the city. In one of the Bible's great comic scenes, they have to hurry him along, and even then he is so reluctant to go that they have to spare a small town nearby, which is as far as he is willing to flee (see Genesis 19:15–23).

Much later, when Ezekiel is foretelling the sack of Jerusalem by the Babylonians, he thinks of similar questions: would God really allow righteous people to die alongside the wicked? This does not seem to have worried earlier prophets such as Amos, for whom God would sweep away the whole nation, even though it is only its ruling classes who are really guilty. But Ezekiel concedes that if there were people in Jerusalem as righteous as Noah, Daniel, or Job, they would be spared (Ezekiel 14:12–20). However, contrary to God's agreement with Abraham, their righteousness would not save the city as a whole, and indeed would not even save their own families (Ezekiel 14:20), as happened with Lot. The impression we get is that Ezekiel did not think there really were any righteous people in the city anyway — certainly not as righteous as Noah, Daniel, and Job. He makes his point about them mainly in order to stress just how wicked the city is: even they would not be good enough to save it, though naturally they would not be killed themselves. As things stand, Jerusalem is far from having anyone that righteous in it anyway.

So in national disasters the Old Testament is very unwilling to grant that there really is any innocent suffering. Reading between the lines, however, we can tell that there were people in Israel who did think there was a problem here. The 'official' line in the historical books and the prophets is that nations never suffer unless they deserve it, but elsewhere we can see that people did agonize about these questions. Some of the psalms, which probably reflect more 'popular' ideas, show clearly that people complained to God about national suffering and did not accept that they were to blame:

> *In God we have boasted continually,*
> *   and we will give thanks to your name for ever.*
> *Yet you have rejected us and abased us,*
> *   and have not gone out with our armies.*

You made us turn back from the foe,
  and our enemies have taken spoil for themselves.
You have made us like sheep for slaughter,
  and have scattered us among the nations. . . .

All this has come upon us,
  yet we have not forgotten you,
  or been false to your covenant.
Our heart has not turned back,
  nor have our steps departed from your way,
yet you have broken us in the haunt of jackals,
  and covered us with deep darkness.
If we had forgotten the name of our God,
  or spread out our hands to a strange god,
would not God discover this?
  For he knows the secrets of the heart.
Because of you we are being killed all day long,
  and accounted as sheep for the slaughter.

(Psalm 44:8–11, 17–22)

The indications are that this psalm may come from a time of really major national disaster, perhaps the **Exile** ('you . . . have scattered us among the nations', v. 11). It was certainly the overthrow of Jerusalem by the Babylonians in 587 BCE, and the exile that followed, that seems to have provoked the most anguished heart-searchings about divine justice.

In biblical studies, the Exile refers to the period in Israel's history in the sixth century BCE when many of its people were taken captive and deported from Israel to Babylon.

We see it too in the book of Lamentations, almost certainly a text from this period. The problem for Lamentations is that God's destruction of Jerusalem seems to contradict his very own promises to protect it at all times. In Lamentations 2:15 the writer says that people who see Jerusalem in ruins are asking, 'Is this the city that was called the perfection of beauty, the joy of all the earth?' This description is a quotation from Psalm 48:1, one of the psalms of Zion in which God does indeed promise to keep Jerusalem safe against all attacks by foreign armies.

Lamentations was probably written to be recited or sung in the ruins of the Temple. It does at times think in terms of the disaster as God's punishment for the nation's sin, and as a fulfilment of the predictions of the prophets:

The LORD has done what he purposed,
  he has carried out his threat;
as he foreordained long ago,
  he has demolished without pity. . . . (Lamentations 2:17)

Why should any who draw breath complain
  about the punishment of their sins? (Lamentations 3:39)

Yet at the same time it also raises questions about God's justice and challenges the idea that all the terrible suffering that has come has been deserved:

Look, O LORD, and consider!
  To whom have you done this?
Should women eat their offspring,
  the children they have borne?
Should priest and prophet be killed
  in the sanctuary of the Lord? (Lamentations 2:20)

Why have you forgotten us completely?
  Why have you forsaken us these many days?
Restore us to yourself, O LORD, that we may be restored;
  renew our days as of old –
unless you have utterly rejected us,
  and are angry with us beyond measure.
                        (Lamentations 5:20–22 — the book's last words)

Thus, where the historical books operate with a definite theodicy — claiming that everything bad that has ever happened to Israel has been a justified punishment for its sins — Lamentations and some of the psalms are more ambivalent. They acknowledge that suffering is often, perhaps usually, punishment, but they also raise the question of whether the particular suffering the nation is enduring can really be accounted for on that basis. They seem to be open to the suggestion that God might be unjust in terms of the reason for and severity of the punishment of his people.

Another group that raised the same question were the exiles in Babylonia, to whom Ezekiel prophesied. We learn in Ezekiel 18:2 that they were using a proverb, 'The parents have eaten sour grapes, and the children's teeth are set on edge'. What they meant was that they were suffering — in exile — when it was their forebears who had done wrong. The suffering was punishment for sin, but it was the wrong people who were being punished, they claimed: hence, God was unjust. Ezekiel's answer is not to say that it is perfectly fair for people to suffer for the sins committed by their ancestors. He agrees that that would be unjust, with the comment, 'it is only the person who sins that shall die' (18:4). However, he says, that must mean that if you are suffering, it is for your own sins!

So Ezekiel turns the proverb back on his audience. It is not that God is so unjust as to punish people for what someone else has done; on the contrary, he is just, and that can only mean that the sufferers have deserved their suffering themselves. If, metaphorically speaking, their teeth are on edge, they must have themselves to blame for it — it must be they who have been eating the sour grapes (in other words, doing wrong). Ezekiel thus rejects the puzzlement of his audience, which is essentially the same as the puzzlement in Lamentations and the Psalms, and reasserts the justice of God. Nevertheless, the price is a high one because it means that anyone who suffers must have sinned — a harsh belief.

Other thinkers in Israel, including the authors of the historical books, tended in a different direction. They accepted the force of the proverb about the sour grapes, but thought the situation it portrayed was quite just: it was entirely reasonable that people should suffer for what their parents or grandparents had done. This seems to be the idea behind the Ten Commandments, too: 'I the Lord your God am a jealous God, punishing children for the iniquity of parents, to the third and the fourth generation of those who reject me' (Exodus 20:5).

Thus, most of the books of the Old Testament deny that there can really be undeserved suffering at the national level, though they have slightly different ideas about how apparently undeserved suffering is to be accounted for, and in particular whose sin it is a punishment for. Only at the edges of the Old Testament do we hear voices challenging this consensus, and asking the question 'Why?' Why has all this befallen us when we have not forsaken our God? The official answer is: you must have forsaken him! You should realize that you have, and repent.

INDIVIDUAL SUFFERING

Some 'individual' suffering in ancient Israel, of course, was part of the suffering of the nation. The mothers reduced to cannibalism in the siege of Jerusalem, mentioned in the quotation above from Lamentations 2:20, were individuals. However, for the most part the historical books, and writings connected to the national history such as Lamentations, see such people as symptomatic of the suffering of the entire nation rather than focusing on them individually. It is in the wisdom literature and Psalms that we find the most sustained concentration on individuals taken out of the national context. For this reason, the wisdom literature can appeal to people who do not have any sense of belonging to the traditions of Judaism or Christianity: it seems to speak to us simply as human beings.

The prosperity of the wicked

The commonest question in the realm of theodicy asked in the wisdom books and Psalms is not, 'Why do bad things happen to good people?' but its opposite, 'Why do good things happen to bad people?' The prosperity of the wicked is the great concern of many wisdom books both in Israel and elsewhere in the ancient world. This is very clear in the Psalms:

> . . . *I was envious of the arrogant;*
>   *I saw the prosperity of the wicked.*
> *For they have no pain;*
>   *their bodies are sound and sleek.*
> *They are not in trouble as others are;*
>   *they are not plagued like other people.* . . .
> *Such are the wicked;*
>   *always at ease, they increase in riches.* (Psalm 73:3–5, 12)

Job also complains about this:

> *Why do the wicked live on,*
>   *reach old age, and grow mighty in power?*
> *Their children are established in their presence,*
>   *and their offspring before their eyes.*
> *Their houses are safe from fear,*
>   *and no rod of God is upon them.*
> *Their bull breeds without fail;*
>   *their cow calves and never miscarries.*
> *They send out their little ones like a flock,*
>   *and their children dance around.*
> *They sing to the tambourine and the lyre,*
>   *and rejoice to the sound of the pipe.*
> *They spend their days in prosperity,*
>   *and in peace they go down to **Sheol**.* (Job 21:7–13)

Sheol is the land of the dead, and the general consensus of the Old Testament is that, though it is not 'hell', a place of torment, it is a sad and dark place where there is no life worth having.

The usual reply to this complaint in the Old Testament is that the prosperity of the wicked is only apparent, or only temporary. Most writers accept that they enjoy good things for a while, but deny Job's suggestion that 'in peace they go down to Sheol', that is, that their prosperity extends right to the day of their death. They seem lucky for a while, but they come to a sticky end:

> *Truly you set them in slippery places;*
>   *you make them fall to ruin.*
> *How they are destroyed in a moment,*
>   *swept away utterly by terrors!*
> *They are like a dream when one awakes. . . .*
>
> (Psalm 73:18–20)

However, Psalm 73 actually goes a little further than this, and suggests that the righteous person's sense of fellowship with God is so great that such a person can be indifferent to the earthly success of the wicked:

> *When my soul was embittered,*
>   *when I was pricked in heart,*
> *I was stupid and ignorant;*
>   *I was like a brute beast towards you.*
> *Nevertheless I am continually with you,*
>   *you hold my right hand.*
> *You guide me with your counsel,*
>   *and afterwards you will receive me with honour.*
>
> (Psalm 73:21–24)

This might — just might — suggest that good people enjoy a life beyond the grave. However, it at least argues that their closeness to God is a fair exchange for the success of the wicked. They suffer in seeing the wicked prosper only if they forget that the wicked do not enjoy God's friendship, as they do.

The suffering of the righteous

The suffering of the righteous is the subject of the book of Job. **Job** is a good man, who suffers various torments, and the initial chapters are concerned with the question of whether a good man will remain good if he is sorely tested. This is a slightly different question from that raised in the dialogues which form the core of the book (chapters 3–42), namely, why good people suffer. As the book stands, however, it is this question that soon comes to command the reader's interest.

Job begins with a quotation from Jeremiah, who had also suffered so much that he came to wish for death — or rather, to wish never to have been born:

> *'Let the day perish on which I was born,*
> *and the night that said, "A man-child is conceived."*
> *Let that day be darkness!*
> *May God above not seek it,*
> *or light shine upon it...*
> *because it did not shut the doors of my mother's womb,*
> *and hide trouble from my eyes.'*
>
> (Job 3:3–4, 10; cf. Jeremiah 20:14–18)

However, after this he starts to reflect rationally on his plight, and to seek answers from God to questions about why anyone should suffer so much. His friends Eliphaz, Bildad, and Zophar supply him with 'stock' answers.

The first of these answers, which is like the answer to the question of national suffering, is that anyone who suffers simply must have sinned: their 'righteousness' must be an illusion:

> *Eliphaz the Temanite answered:*
> *'... Think now, who that was innocent ever perished?*
> *Or where were the upright cut off?*
> *As I have seen, those who plough iniquity*
> *and sow trouble reap the same.'* (Job 4:1, 7–8)

Later Eliphaz amplifies this by going on to detail the sins Job 'must have' committed (see Job 22:6–11, and cf. 11:6)! The proper course of action for Job is to repent and return to God in humility: then all will be well with him again (see Job 5:8–16).

The second of these answers is that human beings are inherently sinful. Whether or not a given person has committed specific sins, all human beings as such inevitably fall short of God's standards. Eliphaz tries this argument too, saying that he has had a vision in which a spirit spoke to him as follows:

> *'Can mortals be righteous before God?*
> *Can human beings be pure before their Maker?*
> *Even in his servants he puts no trust,*
> *and his angels he charges with error;*

Job is the central character of the book of Job which tells the story of how a man who is righteous and blessed by God with a rich and happy life is struck down by a series of disasters — his animals are stolen, his family are killed, and he develops boils all over his body. At first Job refuses to blame God for his misfortunes; hence he became a legendary character such that the 'patience of Job' is mentioned in the New Testament in James 5:11. However, his three friends, Eliphaz, Bildad, and Zophar, try to comfort him in his despair with the explanation that Job must have done something to deserve such suffering. Job is unsatisfied with that explanation and angrily demands that God, who he feels is arbitrary (Job 9:16–24) and who he feels has attacked him like a savage beast (Job 16:7–13), answer his question. God finally responds with an explanation of how great and infinite a being he is and how Job, a lowly and finite creature, has no way of understanding or judging God's actions. In response, Job realizes that he has indeed no right to question God and that only faith can make suffering tolerable, and he says, 'therefore I despise myself and repent in dust and ashes' (Job 42:6). The story then ends with God restoring Job's fortunes and allowing him to live a long and happy life.

The exact nature of the origins and composition of the book of Job has been much debated. Many think the beginning and end of the book, which are written in prose, were originally a simple folktale, perhaps a version of a well-known tale common in the ancient Near East, which the author used as a setting for the dialogues between Job and his friends and between Job and God (chapters 3–42). Since nothing is said of him until he suddenly appears in chapter 32:2, many critics also believe that the speeches of a fourth friend, Elihu, are a later addition to the work. The book itself contains no clear references to the author or the date of writing, but most believe the author was Israelite and that the book was written between the fifth and third centuries BCE.

For more about the book of Job, see 4.4 'Can We Cope?'

how much more those who live in houses of clay. . . .'
(Job 4:17–19; cf. 15:14–16)

Bildad makes the same point in 25:4–6: mortals are maggots, and less than worms, so how could they be pleasing to God? This seems to imply that whatever happens to you, you have it coming to you.

A third answer involves the idea that suffering can be good for you and may be discipline rather than punishment — an idea that was made more plausible in the ancient world by the fact that education usually involved corporal punishment. Eliphaz, never at a loss for ideas, gives this argument an inning too:

'How happy is the one whom God reproves;
therefore do not despise the discipline of the Almighty.
For he wounds, but he binds up;
he strikes, but his hands heal.' (Job 5:17–18)

The other friends also promise that a properly chastened Job will be restored to God's favour:

'He will yet fill your mouth with laughter,
and your lips with shouts of joy.' (Job 8:21)

Fourthly, the friends insist that Job should not compare his own suffering with the prosperity of the wicked, for the wicked do not prosper for long — an argument we have already reviewed in this chapter (see Job 15:17–35 for the details).

Finally, there is a late intervention in the dialogue by a further character, Elihu, who adds a new argument: that God is unknowable anyway, so that attempts to find out what he does about issues of justice and suffering are pointless:

'Surely God is great, and we do not know him;
the number of his years is unsearchable. . . .
The Almighty — we cannot find him;
he is great in power and justice. . . . (Job 36:26; 37:23)

God is simply not available for interrogation:

'Who has prescribed for him his way,
or who can say, "You have done wrong"?' (Job 36:23)

However, Job either demolishes, or gives a wry twist, to every one of these friends' arguments. He emphasizes the full extent of his own suffering and humiliation, which he does not believe they are taking nearly seriously enough: their theories lead them to overlook the facts. Chapter 29 gives a particularly poignant idea of how Job's previous prosperity has now turned into misery and darkness. Job says he will believe that he has sinned if the friends can tell him how he has done so:

> '*Teach me, and I will be silent;*
>> *make me understand how I have gone wrong.*
> *How forceful are honest words!*
>> *But your reproof, what does it reprove?...*
> *Is there any wrong on my tongue?*' (Job 6:24–25, 30)

In fact, they are quite unable to do this. We, the readers, know that this is bound to be so, since we have already been told in the first chapter that Job is 'a blameless and upright man who fears God and turns away from evil' (1:8; cf. 2:3).

As for the suggestion that human beings are sinful by nature, Job twists this and throws it back in the friends' faces, arguing that if human beings are weak and morally corrupt, then it is God himself who made them that way and so he is to blame. Job asks why, if God dislikes humans so much, he bothers with them, or takes the trouble to torment them. In a kind of parody of Psalm 8, which itself highlights the dignity of humankind, Job asks:

> '*What are human beings, that you make so much of them,*
>> *that you set your mind on them,*
> *visit them every morning,*
>> *test them every moment?*
> *Will you not look away from me a while,*
>> *let me alone until I swallow my spittle?*
> *If I sin, what do I do to you, you watcher of humanity?*
>> *Why have you made me your target?*
>> *Why have I become a burden to you?*
> *Why do you not pardon my transgression,*
>> *and take away my iniquity?*' (Job 7:17–21)

In response to the idea that suffering is good for you and makes you a better person, Job points out that this is valid only if those who are being improved have a future. If they are suffering from an incurable disease which will kill them — as Job believes himself to be doing — then, given that there is no possibility of a future life, the argument is entirely empty. Moreover, if this is the case, then not only Job but humankind in general is doomed to death without hope:

> '*If mortals die, will they live again?*
>> *All the days of my service I would wait*
>> *until my release should come.*
> *You would call, and I would answer you;*
>> *you would long for the work of your hands.*
> *For then you would not number my steps,*
>> *you would not keep watch over my sin;*
> *my transgression would be sealed up in a bag,*
>> *and you would cover over my iniquity.*
> *But the mountain falls and crumbles away,*
>> *and the rock is removed from its place;*

> *the waters wear away the stones;*
>> *the torrents wash away the soil of the earth;*
>> *so you destroy the hope of mortals. . . .*
> *Their children come to honour, and they do not know it;*
>> *they are brought low, and it goes unnoticed.*
> *They feel only the pain of their own bodies,*
>> *and mourn only for themselves.'* (Job 14:14–19, 21–22)

Job also argues against his friends' explanation that the wicked do not really prosper, or that their prosperity is only short-lived. Job maintains that such an explanation is entirely false:

> 'The wicked remove landmarks,*
>> *they seize flocks and pasture them.*
> *They drive away the donkey of the orphan;*
>> *they take the widow's ox for a pledge.*
> *They thrust the needy off the road;*
>> *the poor of the earth all hide themselves. . . .*

> 'Yet God prolongs the life of the mighty by his power;*
>> *they rise up when they despair of life.*
> *He gives them security, and they are supported;*
>> *his eyes are upon their ways.'* (Job 24:2–4, 22–23)

Job says that the idea that the wicked come to a bad end is purely wishful thinking and he asks, 'How often is the lamp of the wicked put out?' (21:17), implying the answer 'seldom or never':

> 'the wicked are spared on the day of calamity,*
>> *and are rescued on the day of wrath. . . .*
> *When they are carried to the grave,*
>> *a watch is kept over their tomb.'* (Job 21:30, 32)

Finally, Job addresses the explanation that God is greater than we are, and so cannot be interrogated, and he concludes that this is precisely the problem! It is because God is all-powerful that human beings cannot bring him into court, and even if they could, they would find that he was judge and jury in his own cause. So, Job concludes that God is also radically unjust and if humans could ever get him tried, he would be convicted:

> 'Though I am innocent, I cannot answer him;*
>> *I must appeal for mercy to my accuser.*
> *If I summoned him and he answered me,*
>> *I do not believe that he would listen to my voice. . . .*

> 'If it is a contest of strength, he is the strong one!*
>> *If it is a matter of justice, who can summon him?*
> *Though I am innocent, my own mouth would condemn me;*
>> *though I am blameless, he would prove me perverse. . . .*

'It is all one; therefore I say,
he destroys both the blameless and the wicked.
When disaster brings sudden death,
he mocks at the calamity of the innocent.
The earth is given into the hand of the wicked;
he covers the eyes of its judges –
if it is not he, who then is it?' (Job 9:15–16, 19–20, 22–24)

The last line is probably the most important line Job ever utters. It takes the hypothesis that God is all-powerful, which Elihu uses as a stick with which to beat Job, and turns it back on God himself. Job concludes that if there are faults in the world, who is to blame but the one who made it? At that point, Job believes there seems little left to be said.

However, God does appear to Job, against all his expectations, and talks to him (or at him) for four chapters (38–41). Yet what he says is more or less what Elihu has already said: that God is greater than Job, and cannot be called to account by someone so puny. In the end, Job submits, as we and he knew he would have to. He never gets any of the explanations he had sought. He does get all his possessions restored, and doubled, and he has ten new children to replace the ones who were killed by Satan in chapter 1. Within the fairy-tale setting of the story, this is satisfactory; but in real life one might wonder whether it would really feel like a good outcome, leaving as it does all his complaints unanswered. At least it does not sweep them away, but they are allowed to stand; and most

'I read the book of Job last night — I don't think God comes well out of it.' (Virginia Woolf, *The Letters of Virginia Woolf: Vol. II, 1912–1922*, 1975)

Does evil come from God? Job's taunt to God — 'if it is not he, who then is it?' — confronts us with the possibility that evil in the world derives from God himself. Judaism and Christianity, as they have developed over the years, have tended to deny this, saying that God created the world good but it is through the actions of created beings (the devil, or human beings) that evil has entered it. In the earlier parts of the Old Testament, however, there is little idea of 'anti-God' forces in the world, and the idea of a devil has not yet developed. Consequently, some Old Testament writers are prepared to tolerate the thought that evil as well as good comes from God. Second Isaiah says that God 'makes peace and creates evil' (Isaiah 45:7 — NRSV renders 'peace' and 'evil' as 'weal' and 'woe' respectively), and there is a similar line in Amos (Amos 3:6). Whether God really is the source of evil in such passages may be debated, and the NRSV uses alternatives for the word 'evil', but we certainly find

this idea in the story of Moses and Pharaoh in the book of Exodus. Here, the answer to why Pharaoh refused to let the Israelites leave Egypt is that 'the LORD hardened Pharaoh's heart' (Exodus 10:27). This seems to suggest that if Pharaoh set his heart against releasing the Israelites, this was because YHWH caused him to do so. The explanation for why this was the case is that God wanted to be able to punish Pharaoh justly, so he made him sin in a way that would justify the punishment (Exodus 10:1–2). This may seem very strange to our ideas of justice. Partly it undoubtedly reflects an understanding in which God is the source of all that happens, and hence is ultimately responsible even for evil, and partly it describes a distinctive way of understanding punishment for sin. When humans are wicked, then God may punish them by forcing them to continue in their sin so that they may receive an even greater punishment than would otherwise have been theirs! It is not that God chooses to harden the heart

of someone who was previously innocent. Rather, because Pharaoh is guilty, God makes him sin all the more as part of his punishment.

Such a view is also the explanation of a terrifying statement, made by the prophet Ezekiel (Ezekiel 20:25–26), that God actually caused the Israelites to sacrifice their own children. However, it should be noted that this punishment does not come out of the blue but after a long history of disobedience on the people's part. This statement, therefore, marks the moment when, in a sense, God's patience snaps, and he makes them sin so horribly that the justice of his punishment of them becomes manifest — and also, perhaps, that they come to see the enormity of what they are doing, and so at last repent. In some strange way, then, God is viewed as 'being cruel to be kind', although his actions surely push the boundaries of what most modern believers in God would be prepared to regard as actions of a good God.

Satan is a Hebrew word meaning 'adversary'. In the book of Job, Satan is simply a heavenly being in God's heavenly court who becomes the adversary of Job by challenging God to take away Job's blessings to see if he would still remain righteous. However, in Judeo-Christian tradition, Satan came to be viewed as an angel who was expelled from heaven for leading a rebellion against God. In this role he has come to represent the supreme embodiment of evil and is sometimes referred to as the 'devil'.

mysteriously, God himself seems to acknowledge the accusations of Job that, since he is so great, any faults in the world are his responsibility, that he is radically unjust, and that the explanations of the friends are inadequate. Thus, he says to the friends, 'you have not spoken of me what is right, as my servant Job has' (42:7). It seems as though God prefers his arrogant accuser to his obsequious defenders.

'One fate comes to all alike'

However, there is another approach to individual suffering that is mentioned, though not focused on at length, in the book of Job. This is the argument that righteousness and wickedness, prosperity and suffering, all make no difference in the end, since everyone dies one day and all differences are then obliterated. This rather bleak thought is certainly mentioned by Job:

> '. . . mortals die, and are laid low;
>> humans expire, and where are they?
> As waters fail from a lake,
>> and a river wastes away and dries up,
> so mortals lie down and do not rise again;
>> until the heavens are no more, they will not awake
>> or be roused out of their sleep.' (Job 14:10–12)

This point is developed further in Psalm 49 where the psalmist urges the reader not to be worried by the prosperity of the wicked, not on the grounds that the wicked will die sooner than the righteous, but on the grounds that everyone ends up dead anyway, so why worry?

> When we look at the wise, they die;
>> fool and dolt perish together,
>> and leave their wealth to others. . . .
> Mortals cannot abide in their pomp;
>> they are like the animals that perish. (Psalm 49:10, 12)

The fullest discussion of this aspect of theodicy is found in Ecclesiastes, with its pronouncement:

> the same fate comes to all, to the righteous and the wicked, to the good and the evil, to the clean and the unclean, to those who sacrifice and those who do not sacrifice. As are the good, so are the sinners; those who swear are like those who shun an oath. This is an evil in all that happens under the sun, that the same fate comes to everyone. . . . The living know that they will die, but the dead know nothing; they have no more reward, and even the memory of them is lost. Their love and their hate and their envy have already perished; never again will they have any share in all that happens under the sun. (Ecclesiastes 9:2–6)

Such a view does not make **Qoheleth** pessimistic in his

attitude to daily life, where according to him the thing to do in the face of inevitable death is to enjoy what one can while one can. However, it is a powerful argument against any theodicy that depends on distinguishing the fate of righteous and wicked. With this theory, if God is to be just it would have to be in apportioning good and evil in this life; and this is just what Qoheleth denies that he does:

> *There is a vanity that takes place on earth, that there are righteous people who are treated according to the conduct of the wicked, and there are wicked people who are treated according to the conduct of the righteous. I said that this also is vanity.* (Ecclesiastes 8:14)

As Qoheleth himself puts it in his closing words, 'The end of the matter; all has been heard' (Ecclesiastes 12:13). More or less all available options for theodicy are discussed somewhere in the Old Testament — but it is true to say that a solution is not found!

Qoheleth is the alternative name for the book of Ecclesiastes. 'Ecclesiastes' is the Greek translation of the Hebrew word *qoheleth,* which means 'preacher'.

2.6 Can We Know God?
RELIGIOUS EXPERIENCE IN THE OLD TESTAMENT

THE BASICS

- A variety of individual religious experiences is mentioned in the Old Testament, including divine appearances, dreams, visions, and the inspiration of the word of God.
- According to the Old Testament, people were also able to encounter God through personal prayer and to discover his will through the use of mechanical techniques such as casting lots.

AT THE BEGINNING OF this book we described the Old Testament as the record of an encounter between Israel and God. On the national level, this was seen primarily in the way the God **YHWH** was felt to have guided his people, entering into various **covenants** with them and intervening from time to time in human affairs. However, it is also evident in the Old Testament that some individuals experience encounters with God in a variety of ways.

EXPERIENCING GOD THROUGH DIVINE APPEARANCES, DREAMS, AND VISIONS

In the 'historical' books of the Old Testament, we often come across stories of how certain special individuals experience their own personal **theophany**. Many such encounters with God share similar characteristics:

- God may be dangerous, yet ultimately beneficial;
- God brings a promise or an instruction and in some way blesses the people he visits;
- God speaks to people in a language they can understand.

On such occasions, for all his mystery, God is portrayed as a character in the story like the human characters. He meets people on earth, and they do not have to be in a special spiritual state: they are simply going about their business in an

YHWH is the primary way God's name appears in the Old Testament. It is simply four Hebrew consonants which many scholars believe may have been pronounced Yahweh. For a more detailed examination of this issue, see 2.1 'Watchmaker or Living God?'

A **covenant** is a solemn, binding, mutual agreement between two parties; the covenants between God and his people are an important feature of the Old Testament. For more information about these various covenants, see 2.2 'The Chosen People?'

A **theophany** is a visible manifestation of God to a person.

The account of Moses' life in the Old Testament includes numerous references to him experiencing God. Perhaps the most famous of these incidents is when he encounters God in a bush that is burning, yet is not being consumed (Exodus 3:1–6). God speaks to Moses, reveals himself as YHWH, and calls Moses to lead his people out of slavery in Egypt. This incident is a crucial turning point in Moses' life. As a result of this encounter, Moses begins a personal relationship with God, and throughout his life he continues to experience God in a variety of ways which give him the strength and conviction to be a great leader of God's people. For example, in further conversations with God, Moses experiences God as thunder (Exodus 19:19), as lightning (Exodus 20:18), as fire and smoke (Exodus 19:18 and 24:17), and as dazzling glory (Exodus 24:16 and 33:18–23).

An **angel** is a messenger of God. In the Bible, angels are depicted as heavenly beings who are with God in his heavenly court and carry out his commands. The Hebrew word for angel is *mal'ak* (pronounced mal-ak, with stress on the second syllable).

ordinary way when God arrives in their lives. We see this in the opening chapters of the Old Testament, in the story of the Garden of Eden in Genesis 3. It is not said there that Adam and Eve saw God, but they certainly heard him, and the fact that, for example, he makes them leather aprons after they have discovered their own nakedness presumably means that he is physically present in their world and can interact with it. In the same way, Moses experiences God in a divine appearance on Mount Sinai where we are told, 'The LORD descended in the cloud and stood with him there' (Exodus 34:5). Another, perhaps more mysterious, appearance of God involves Jacob wrestling all night with a mysterious 'man' at the ford of the River Jabbok (Genesis 32:22–32). In the story the 'man' refuses to give his own name but renames Jacob 'Israel' and blesses him. After this wrestling bout — which Jacob wins! — Jacob reflects, 'I have seen God face to face, and yet my life is preserved' (Genesis 32:30). Underlying this story may be an old tale about a troll-like being who lurks by the ford and kills passing travellers, but it has been turned into an account of how the great Israelite ancestor came by his famous name — by 'defeating' God himself. On another occasion, Jacob encounters God in a dream featuring a ladder reaching from earth to heaven on which **angels** are ascending and descending. We are told, 'the LORD stood beside him and said, "I am the LORD. . . ."' (Genesis 28:10–17), and delivered a message of blessing. Likewise, God appears to Solomon in a dream and grants him wisdom, wealth, and power (1 Kings 3:5–14).

In some stories, encounters with God appear to be through the divine appearance of 'the angel of YHWH'. For example, Abraham has such an encounter when he is about to sacrifice his son Isaac (Genesis 22:11–18), and it is an angel who leads Israel through the Red Sea (Exodus 14:19) and who kills the Assyrian army besieging Jerusalem (2 Kings 19:35). However, on other occasions 'the angel of YHWH' is not clearly distinguished from YHWH himself. For example, Joshua encounters near Jericho a 'man' who is described as 'commander of the army of the LORD' but who instructs him to remove his sandals because, just as if God himself is present, 'the place where you stand is holy' (Joshua 5:13–15).

Another example where there is similar ambiguity is the encounter of Samson's parents with 'the angel of the LORD' in Judges 13. Samson's mother meets 'a man', who gives her a prediction of the birth of Samson. When she describes him to her husband, Manoah, she says his appearance was 'like that of an angel of God, most awe-inspiring; I did not ask him where he came from, and he did not tell me his name' (v. 6). Both of them clearly feel that this is a messenger from God, but they do not yet suspect that he really is 'an angel of God'. When he appears again to the couple, they again treat him as an important but essentially human visitor — Manoah asks him, 'Are you the man who spoke to this woman?' (v. 11). After the angel has confirmed his earlier message, they offer him a

Angel playing the Lute, detail from Angels Window, William Morris / Church of St Michael, Berkshire /
Martyn O'Kelly Photography / Bridgeman

Angels of one sort or another appear hundreds of times in the Bible and are ascribed various titles. For example, there are the seraphim who guard the throne of God and are mentioned in Isaiah's vision of God (Isaiah 6:1-8), and the cherubim who guarded the Garden of Eden with flaming swords (Genesis 3:24) and who are also described in a vision of Ezekiel as multi-faced, winged, and sparkling 'like burnished bronze' (Ezekiel 1:7). Much later, students of the many scriptural references to angels attempted to classify them. The classification set out in a work by Dionysius the Areopagite in around 500 CE divided them into seraphim, cherubim, thrones, dominions (or dominations), virtues, powers, principalities (or princedoms), archangels, and angels. Early Christian art began a tradition of depicting angels in the style of the winged messengers of the Greek and Roman gods, but later artists often distinguished between different classifications of angels, and their images were influenced by the biblical descriptions of angels by people such as Isaiah and Ezekiel. Artistic representations of angels also reflect the belief that they are extremely beautiful and are constantly engaged in praising God. For more about angels in the apocalyptic works, see 4.7 'The Number of the Beast'.

meal, and it is then that his divine status becomes clear:

> *Manoah said to the angel of the LORD, 'Allow us to detain you, and prepare a kid for you.' The angel of the LORD said to Manoah, 'If you detain me, I will not eat your food; but if you want to prepare a burnt-offering, then offer it to the LORD' (For Manoah did not know that he was the angel of the LORD.) Then Manoah said to the angel of the LORD, 'What is your name, so that we may honour you when your words come true?' But the angel of the LORD said to him, 'Why do you ask my name? It is too wonderful.'* (Judges 13:15–18)

By now Manoah and his wife must be getting suspicious: the stranger refuses a meal, and also refuses to give his name, which he describes as 'wonderful' — neither things that most human visitors, however exalted, would do. The final revelation comes when they offer the sacrifice:

> *When the flame went up towards heaven from the altar, the angel of the LORD ascended in the flame of the altar while Manoah and his wife looked on; and they fell on their faces to the ground. The angel of the LORD did not appear again to Manoah and his wife. Then Manoah realized that it was the angel of the LORD.* (Judges 13:20–21)

At this point it is clear that the 'angel of YHWH' and YHWH himself are hard to distinguish; for Manoah goes on to say, 'We shall surely die, for we have seen God' (v. 22)

Exactly how a human being can describe a God whom one believes to be eternal and infinite is an issue that has occupied the minds of many great theologians. Some, like St Augustine (354–430) and St Anselm (1033–1109), stated that it is possible to speak intelligibly and truthfully about God since God gave us the gifts of speech and reason. St Thomas Aquinas (1225–74) developed the idea that one can use human words like 'wisdom' or 'goodness' to describe God because, whilst such words can be applied to earthly things, it is when they are applied to God that they have their truest meanings. However, later scholars, like Karl Barth (1886–1968), suggested that, since sin affects human reason, humans have no capacity for thought or speech about God except through God's gifts of faith and revelation. On the other hand, some, like Rudolf Otto (1869–1937), have concluded that the nature of God can never be fully expressible in words.

When God is described in anthropomorphic terms, God is ascribed human characteristics. Such an attempt to make God seem like a human being is often part of an effort to make God more understandable.

When applied to God, the term transcendent means that God is greater than the world and in some sense is beyond it and outside human experience.

— not merely 'an angel', then. God has appeared in person, though taking on human characteristics — so effectively that although Manoah's wife is already struck by the awe-inspiring qualities of the 'man' even at first acquaintance, neither of them recognizes the full truth until the 'angel' ascends into heaven. Incidentally, they do not die: as his wife sensibly points out to Manoah, God would hardly have accepted the sacrifice if he then intended to kill them (v. 23).

Of course, in other places God and angels are clearly distinguished. For example, when God appears to Abraham to tell him and Sarah that they will have a child, he is accompanied by two angels (Genesis 18). The account says that three men come to Abraham's tent in the heat of the day and, until verse 22, the impression is almost that they speak as one person. However, the two angels then go on their way while YHWH stays with Abraham, and it is only these two who arrive in Sodom in the first verse of chapter 19. Nevertheless, it is noteworthy that YHWH cannot initially be distinguished from the angels — all of them simply appear to be 'men'. For this reason, the author of the Letter to the Hebrews in the New Testament is right to comment that 'some have entertained angels without knowing it' (Hebrews 13:2). So, whilst God appears to people in the Old Testament in human form, the boundaries between God and his angels are a bit indistinct, and to meet 'the angel of YHWH' is clearly tantamount to encountering God himself.

In other parts of the Old Testament, visions of God are much less **anthropomorphic**, and the **transcendent** and glorious nature of God is emphasized. In the vision of God in the Temple recounted by Isaiah, it is God's glory that is highlighted (Isaiah 6:1–8). Isaiah sees God, 'sitting on a throne, high and lofty' with angels calling out, 'Holy, holy, holy is the LORD of hosts; the whole earth is full of his glory!' and he is struck by the contrast between God's infinite holiness and the sinfulness of humanity. Similarly, the prophet Ezekiel describes a vision of God in which he sees God's glory and 'splendour all around' (Ezekiel 1:4–28). However, Ezekiel's description that 'there was something like a throne, in appearance like sapphire; and seated above the likeness of a throne was something that seemed like a human form' appears to indicate that God's majesty is so awesome that Ezekiel does not really have the language to describe his experience adequately.

EXPERIENCING GOD THROUGH HIS WORD

The second major way in which people experience God in the Old Testament is illustrated in God's communication with prophets. In their case, the manner of communication does not often seem to have been through a divine appearance in person, as it were, but through 'the word of the LORD'. However, exactly what that phrase means is obscure, and the story of one of the earliest prophets, Elijah, demonstrates this problem.

After his victory over the prophets of Baal on Mount Carmel, Elijah arrives exhausted at a cave, where he has an overwhelming experience of God, and talks to God. Yet, God is not in any recognizable form:

> *Now there was a great wind, so strong that it was splitting mountains and breaking rocks in pieces before the LORD, but the LORD was not in the wind; and after the wind an earthquake, but the LORD was not in the earthquake; and after the earthquake a fire, but the LORD was not in the fire; and after the fire a sound of sheer silence.* (1 Kings 19:11–12)

The 'sound of sheer silence' here was translated in the Authorized Version as 'a still small voice', and it is in that form that it became a well-known quotation, perhaps as a result of its use in the final verse of the popular hymn 'Dear Lord and Father of Mankind' (John Whittier, 1807–92). Exactly what the phrase 'sound of silence' means is obscure, but the New Revised Standard Version is probably right to think it is deliberately paradoxical. It is obviously contrasted with the noise and turmoil of wind, earthquake, and fire, and perhaps stresses that God's 'speech' is not like our speech. Be that as it may, Elijah then has a conversation with God using ordinary words, and God replies in an audible voice (1 Kings 19:13–18).

However, according to the books of the prophets, the prophetic experience of being addressed by 'the word of the LORD' does not seem to suggest that they actually heard physical sounds, in the sense that they were in a trance-like condition and heard mysterious voices speaking to them, as some people suffering from schizophrenia do. Amos, for example, tells us that 'I am no prophet, nor a prophet's son; but I am a herdsman, and a dresser of sycamore trees, and the LORD took me from following the flock, and the LORD said to me, "Go, prophesy to my people Israel"' (Amos 7:14–15). This sounds like the expression of an inner sense of vocation rather than the record of hearing voices, though that cannot be ruled out.

In general, when the prophets say, 'Hear the word of the LORD', they are expressing what they are sure is the will of God, but they are probably not reporting words they had actually heard uttered in Hebrew by a divine voice. On occasions when they had heard a voice, that is stated explicitly, as for example in Isaiah's vision in the Temple:

> *Then I heard the voice of the Lord saying, 'Whom shall I send, and who will go for us?' And I said, 'Here am I; send me.' And he said, 'Go . . .'* (Isaiah 6:8–9)

Samuel, too, is recorded as hearing God calling to him as he lay at night in the temple at Shiloh. It is not until the voice is repeated several times that his mentor, the priest Eli, realizes it must be God who is calling to him (1 Samuel 3:1–10).

This is rather like the inability of Manoah and his wife to recognize that they are speaking to the angel of YHWH.

Another way the prophets of the Old Testament expressed a sense of knowing the will of God was to say that one had 'stood in the council of YHWH'. Just as human kings had a court, in which counsellors would give advice and the king would then make an informed decision about matters of state, so YHWH was believed to have a heavenly court. It consisted of various superhuman or semi-divine beings, more or less what we might call angels or spirits, whom he assembled from time to time to get advice. It is hard to say whether people believed this was literally true, but some probably did. For prophets to say that they had 'stood in the council of YHWH' was one way in which they could express their sense of knowing about God's plans. Jeremiah, for example, talking about false prophets says:

> *I did not send the prophets,*
> *   yet they ran;*
> *I did not speak to them,*
> *   yet they prophesied.*
> *But if they had stood in my council,*
> *   then they would have proclaimed my words to my people,*
> *and they would have turned them from their evil way,*
> *   and from the evil of their doings.'*
>
> (Jeremiah 23:21–22, our emphasis)

The way such a divine council was thought to operate can be seen from two passages. One is Isaiah's Temple vision (see above) in which he sees God asking for volunteers to take his message to Israel, and Isaiah — rather than one of the angels in the divine council — volunteers. The other is the prophecy of Micaiah son of Imlah, a prophet in the ninth century BCE, in the time of Ahab:

> *'I saw the LORD sitting on his throne, with all the host of*
> *heaven standing beside him to the right and to the left of him.*
> *And the LORD said, "Who will entice Ahab, so that he may go*
> *up and fall at Ramoth-gilead?" Then one said one thing, and*
> *another said another, until a spirit came forward and said, "I*
> *will entice him." "How?" the LORD asked him. He replied, "I will*
> *go out and be a lying spirit in the mouth of all his prophets."*
> *Then the LORD said, "You are to entice him, and you shall suc-*
> *ceed; go out and do it."'* (1 Kings 22:19–22)

According to this, the prophet has privileged access to the divine council, and so knows much more about God's plans than ordinary people do. This particular description again suggests a visionary experience within which the prophet had heard the voice not only of God but of other spirits too. However, this does not necessarily mean that all the prophets' words uttered in God's name had been 'heard' in this way.

On other occasions in the Old Testament, God's word

seems to come to prophets in a dream or vision at night. For example, when David's court prophet, Nathan, tells David that he should build a temple for YHWH, his instruction is almost immediately countermanded by God as a result of 'the word of the Lord' coming to Nathan 'by night' (2 Samuel 7:4) and saying that it will not be until the reign of Solomon that the Temple will be built. Though it is not made explicit, the detail 'by night' suggests that this information was revealed by God to Nathan in his sleep.

In later times, it was generally believed that the prophets had received their inspiration through dreams or visions. The post-exilic prophet Zechariah received 'the word of God' in the night (Zechariah 1:8ff.), and some of the prophetic knowledge that Daniel acquired is presented as having come through visions by night (see Daniel 2:19, 7:1). Indeed, by the time the book of Daniel was written, in the second century BCE, this appears to have been seen as the normal way for God to communicate with a prophet. However, such an idea may well be a matter of reading back later ideas of prophecy into the imaginary past time in which Daniel is set.

In fact, in pre-exilic times there is no definite evidence to indicate that prophets really got their information through dreams; and some later prophets, like Jeremiah, express scepticism about 'revelations' obtained through dreams and contrast them with receiving God's word:

> *I have heard what the prophets have said who prophesy lies in my name, saying, 'I have dreamed, I have dreamed!' How long? Will the hearts of the prophets ever turn back — those who prophesy lies, and who prophesy the deceit of their own heart? They plan to make my people forget my name by their dreams that they tell one another, just as their ancestors forgot my name for Baal. Let the prophet who has a dream tell the dream, but let the one who has my word speak my word faithfully.* (Jeremiah 23:25–28)

Finally, we should mention that there are occasions in the Old Testament when prophets seem to experience the word of God as the result of ecstatic, trance-like states. A story involving the early career of Saul offers an example of **theolepsy**, perhaps induced by music, in which Saul meets a band of prophets. Samuel tells Saul,

Theolepsy describes the possession or seizure of a person by the spirit of God.

> *'As you come to the town, you will meet a band of prophets coming down from the shrine with harp, tambourine, flute, and lyre playing in front of them; they will be in a prophetic frenzy. Then the spirit of the Lord will possess you, and you will be in a prophetic frenzy along with them and be turned into a different person. . . .'* (1 Samuel 10:5–6)

True enough, a band of prophets met him, 'and the spirit of God possessed him, and he fell into a prophetic frenzy along with them' (1 Samuel 10:9–10). Indeed, prophets in

In *The Varieties of Religious Experience* (1902), William James (1842–1910) noted four basic features of mystical religious experiences. He said that they were ineffable (they defy adequate description), noetic (they are believed to reveal special knowledge), transient (they may have lasting effects but the actual experience is not sustained for long), and passive (the person senses they are controlled by God). Such features can be identified in some of the religious experiences of the prophets of the Old Testament, and the ecstatic nature of some of the experiences is similar to more modern religious phenomena such as the Toronto Blessing where worshipping Christians feel 'seized' by the spirit of God and experience a variety of uncontrollable emotional states. However, religious experiences — whether modern or recorded in ancient scriptures — are almost impossible to verify because a believer will rarely be swayed by explanations which deny God's involvement, and sceptics will argue that a believer is an unreliable witness!

Indeed, sceptics try to explain so-called 'religious experiences' in a variety of other ways. Some, following the ideas of people like Sigmund Freud (1856–1939) and Carl Jung (1875–1961), offer psychological explanations based on the view that religion is an invention of the human mind. Others, like Émile Durkheim (1858–1917) and Hjalmar Sunden (1908–98), say that such experiences are the result of sociological and cultural conditioning. Moreover, as our understanding grows of how the human brain functions, it can be argued that such experiences are scientifically explicable in terms of unusual, temporary electrical activity in certain areas of the brain, similar to those which cause epilepsy or which can be induced by a person taking mood-altering or hallucinatory types of drugs.

Israel appear to have experienced a range of odd forms of consciousness in which they received visions or found themselves engaged in prophetic actions designed to communicate the word of God they had received. For example, Ezekiel had a number of visions, experienced himself as eating a prophetic scroll (3:1–3), and was struck dumb (3:26). He also felt constrained by God to act in many strange ways — cutting off his hair as a symbol of the destruction of Jerusalem, for example (5:1–4), and weighing out his food as a symbol of the coming famine in the besieged city (4:9–17).

Such examples make it clear that God was thought to communicate his word to people in a variety of ways and not simply through audible speech. Undoubtedly, the 'word of God' was an important feature of the prophets' experience of God, but exactly how they thought they had come by their message is quite obscure. They were certain that in some way it had come from beyond themselves and that they had not simply made it up out of their own heads. They might also have said that God had given them the words of their message, but that is not the same as saying that he dictated them orally in a literal sense and that they took them down. The prophets' words are, therefore, perhaps best viewed as human elaborations of messages that in essence had been revealed as a result of a real experience of God.

EXPERIENCING GOD THROUGH PERSONAL PRAYER

So far we have thought about how God gets in touch with human beings and, according to the Old Testament, this is often through channels we would regard as miraculous: through theophanies and the appearances of angels, through visions and revelations. However, even though they might not receive miraculous visitations or see wonderful visions, ordinary people in Israel believed they could also be in touch with God through prayer. It was normal for people to pray aloud in temples and shrines and, although we do not have many prayers of particular named individuals in the Old Testament, the variety of the psalms suggests that individuals offered prayers to God in all circumstances. In times of trouble, God was asked to protect a person from enemies (Psalm 64:1–4); in times of joy, God was praised and thanked for his kindness (Psalm 116:1–6). The psalms also indicate that people prayed to God for forgiveness of their sins (Psalm 51:1).

TECHNIQUES FOR CONTACTING GOD

Alongside these expressions of personal piety and divine inspiration there existed other techniques for getting in touch with God and discerning his will. Divination was common in the ancient world, and the Old Testament accounts indicate that the Israelites were not wholly opposed to the idea that mechanical techniques could reveal the will of God.

One example of such techniques is the use of the sacred lot. According to 1 Samuel 14:24–46, this is used to discover who has violated a sacred prohibition on eating until the outcome of a battle has been decided. In verse 41, Saul asks that God will 'give Urim' if the guilt lies with him or Jonathan, and 'give Thummim' if it lies with the people. The meaning of these terms is unknown, but presumably they correspond to 'yes' and 'no', or 'A' and 'B'. According to Exodus 28:30, the high priest wore 'Urim and Thummim' on his breastplate, suggesting instruments for casting the lot; this in turn probably means that supervising the lot was a priestly task.

It is also clear that Israelites consulted the spirits of the dead, though various reformers tried to prohibit the practice. The prophet Isaiah condemns those who say, 'Consult the ghosts and the familiar spirits that chirp and mutter' (Isaiah 8:19), and in 1 Samuel 28:3 we read that Saul had expelled 'mediums and wizards' from the land. However, in time of need Saul is still able to find a woman at Endor who can conjure up for him the spirit of the dead Samuel and extract from him information about the outcome of the coming battle with the Philistines (1 Samuel 28:6–20). Of course, we might not regard these practices as a matter of contacting 'God', but the average pre-exilic Israelites probably regarded their dead ancestors as at least semi-divine. Indeed, the people presented as speaking in Isaiah regard the dead as 'gods' who can rightly be consulted by the living (Isaiah 8:19–20), and when the woman at Endor sees the spirit of Samuel she describes him as 'a divine being'. In fact, the Hebrew uses the word *elohim,* which means 'god' or 'gods'.

The ephod and teraphim probably also belong to this world of divination. Hosea threatens that 'the Israelites shall remain many days . . . without sacrifice or pillar, without ephod or teraphim' (Hosea 3:4). In some passages an ephod is a sacred vestment — David wears one in 2 Samuel 6:14 — but elsewhere it is evidently the name of an object used in a sanctuary, and seems to have a divinatory function. Important passages for this include Judges 17:5, where a man called Micah makes an ephod for his own house, and 1 Samuel 23:9, where David consults God by getting a priest to bring him the ephod. What it looked like we cannot even guess. On the other hand, we know that teraphim were objects in human shape, because one is put in David's bed to give the impression he was there himself when in fact he had fled (1 Samuel 19:11–17). In Genesis 31 teraphim is translated in the New Revised Standard Version as 'household gods', and that is probably what they were: images of lesser gods thought to protect the household. Such objects remind us that by no means all Israelites were strict **monotheists**, at least not until after the time of the monarchy.

This chapter demonstrates that the Old Testament presents examples of a variety of religious experiences and, whatever explanation you may wish to offer for what was happening in specific cases, it is true to say that such experiences were clearly enormously important for the individuals involved. Indeed, for the leaders and the prophets of Israel,

Divination is the word used to describe the practice of gaining insight into the future. It might seem strange to our minds that, for example, the entrails of animals could contain coded messages about fate and luck, but in Mesopotamia, a whole 'science' developed of inspecting the insides of animals. In fact, divination in the ancient world encompassed a variety of methods including studying the entrails of sacrificial victims, especially the liver (hepatoscopy), contacting the dead (necromancy), the reading of palms (cheiromancy), and interpreting the configurations of flames (empyromancy) or the flight of birds (ornithomancy) — an idea which survives in our own culture in popular superstitions about magpies! Interestingly, there is little direct evidence of such practices in Israel and, although a number of references to divination do appear in the Old Testament, Hebrew Law actually forbade it under penalty of death (Leviticus 19:31, 20:6 and Deuteronomy 18:10–11).

 The word 'teraphim', probably referring to images of gods thought to protect a household, should not be confused with the word 'seraphim' which describes the angels who guard the throne of God. Neither should it be confused with 'terrapin', a type of freshwater turtle!

A **monotheist** is someone who believes in only one God.

Speaking of religious experiences recorded in the Bible, F.W. Dillistone says, 'The dominant feature of the experiences recorded is that they were vouchsafed to those destined to share actively in God's ongoing purpose for mankind. The experience was never self-enclosed: the enjoyment of a secret revelation or the excitement of a state of exaltation. Those who were granted visions were called to engage in the great conflicts between right and wrong in the world at large and to become agents in the working out of God's redeeming purpose. A searching criterion of whether an experience is truly religious is whether it issues in sacrificial service.' (F.W. Dillistone in *The New Dictionary of Christian Theology*, ed. John Bowden and Alan Richardson, SCM Press, 1983)

it was their individual religious experiences of God that compelled them to give up their ordinary lives and do as God wanted. This usually involved great personal sacrifice and often meant risking not only the ridicule of their peers but also their lives. It is, therefore, perhaps worth reflecting that religious philosophers and psychologists often look to the consequences of a religious experience in order to begin to assess its validity, believing that a genuine religious experience must result in a changed life. Thus, whilst some may hold that religious experiences are solely psychological, sociological or physiological in nature, the evidence of the Old Testament seems to suggest that such experiences are rather just one particular way in which God very powerfully communicates the nature of his being and his will to his people.

Section 3

History and the Old Testament

3.1 Tall Stories?
WRITING THE HISTORY OF ISRAEL

THE BASICS

- The question of how much of the Old Testament might be fact and how much might be fiction is a lot more complicated than some people might believe.
- Just how much of the history of ancient Israel can be known with any certainty from the Old Testament is one of the most hotly debated topics of current Old Testament scholarship.

MANY PEOPLE TODAY THINK of the Old Testament's account of history as no more than myths and legends. People tend to think of the stories in the Old Testament as all very much the same kind of thing. 'Bible stories' are still vaguely known in western culture, and many people have heard of Adam and Eve, Noah and his ark, David and Goliath, Daniel in the lions' den, and Jonah being swallowed by a whale. If they think that some of these stories are obviously just folk tales or fictions — as most people think the story of Jonah and the whale is — then they generally reckon that *all* the stories in the Bible are the same. They regard it all as a complete fiction: tall stories.

At the other extreme, some religious believers (Christians or Jews) think that everything the Bible tells us must be completely correct. They think that if, for religious reasons, they believe the central stories of the Bible are essentially true, then they are committed to believing that all of them are true — even the story of Jonah. Furthermore, critics of religion nearly always assume that all believers take all the stories 'literally', meaning by this that they think the stories are historically and factually true in every detail. If you say that one of them *isn't* true — for example, that Jonah is just a fable about a fictional prophet — then you are assumed to think that none of them is true. However, the **historicity** of the Old Testament is really more complex than either of these positions, and we need to remember that the Bible is made up

The question of **historicity** in the Old Testament is the question of how much is fact and how much is fiction.

In common usage a myth has come to mean a fictitious story. However, in the ancient world it is worth remembering that people created myths as a response to reflection on the key areas of their life such as the purpose of life, suffering, death, fertility, nature, and evil forces. Thus, myths dealing with creation, the cycle of the seasons, etc., were common in the ancient Near East, and it is interesting to note the similarities in themes across different cultures. In some cases, a myth was simply a story that explained the causes of something, like the nature of a particular god or the reason for a particular custom, but often a myth was the spoken part of a religious ceremony and was accompanied by appropriate ritual (the actions in a religious ceremony). For example, the Babylonian new year festival included a dramatic re-enactment featuring the recitation of their creation myth in which the god Marduk — played by the king — overcame Tiamat, the evil monster. Such a scenario signalled that the evil forces had been overcome again and it was safe to begin a new year. Thus, myths were used to help explain important truths about life that were largely unrelated to historical or scientific concerns. In this sense, the term 'myth' is sometimes applied to the stories in Genesis 1–2 as, for example, the creation story is more concerned with people understanding God's creative power and intimate relationship with humankind than with a record of exactly how the world was created in accurate historical and scientific terms.

So, ancient myths may not offer much in the way of historical or scientific explanations for the modern reader, but they certainly serve to illustrate how certain groups of people viewed the world around them.

of different types of literature, each of which may assume a different idea of truth.

IS THERE ANY TRUTH IN THE OLD TESTAMENT STORIES?

People today are quite used to understanding the differences implicit in a variety of types of stories they encounter. We distinguish, without any difficulty, between reports in newspapers, novels, anecdotes, and fairy tales. All of these can be true — but in different ways. A newspaper report can be true if things happened more or less as it describes them (though we know that the reporter could be biased). An anecdote can be true because it really conveys the character of the person it is about, even though things may not have happened exactly as it describes. A novel can be true in the sense that it reflects the nature and complexity of human life, but of course it is not true in the sense that the events described ever actually took place. In addition, a fairy tale may be true by revealing some general insight into life — for example, that the person who is apparently least important can really be the one that matters most. These are all types of truth, but it is only really in the case of a news report that we mean *historical* truth. Of course, any of these types of narrative can also be false. The reporter may be lying; the anecdote may falsify the character of its subject; the novelist may not have much understanding of human beings, and so may have written a shallow novel; the fairy tale may not be true to our experience of the world.

Nevertheless, the point is that we do not judge the 'truth' of each of these types of narrative by standards appropriate to the others. We would not fault a novel because it described events that never happened — on the contrary, we would be very surprised if it did. In the same way, we would not criticize a newspaper report because it did not show a deep understanding of human nature. That is not what matters in a newspaper report: we want factual accuracy there, not depth of insight.

For these reasons, we need to know what kinds of story we are dealing with before we can say anything sensible about the relationship of biblical stories to historical truth. In some cases, we find something that looks like reporting. Of course, there is nothing in the Bible like a modern newspaper report, but there are texts that seem to record sober fact, such as the following:

> *In the fourteenth year of King Hezekiah, King Sennacherib of Assyria came up against all the fortified cities of Judah and captured them. The king of Assyria sent the Rabshakeh from Lachish to King Hezekiah at Jerusalem, with a great army. He stood by the conduit of the upper pool on the highway to the Fuller's Field. And there came out to him Eliakim son of Hilkiah, who was in charge of the palace, and Shebna the secretary, and Joah son of Asaph, the recorder.* (Isaiah 36:1–3)

This might be true or false, but it makes a straightforward historical claim about certain events that took place on a specific date. A historian will want to try to discover whether it is true or not, but if it is true it will be in the sense that it describes events that actually occurred.

Compare with this the following:

The LORD God said to the serpent,
'Because you have done this,
cursed are you among all animals
and among all wild creatures;
upon your belly you shall go,
and dust you shall eat
all the days of your life.' (Genesis 3:14)

This is part of a story that explains why snakes crawl on the ground instead of walking on legs like other animals — it seems to imply, in fact, that before this they did have legs. It is what Old Testament scholars call an **aetiological** story. This is a story that explains how things came to be as they are in the world, but we do not normally treat stories of this kind as historical reporting, any more than we believe that presents appear on 25 December because Santa Claus has come down the chimney. It would seem odd to ask on what date God spoke in this way to the snake, or whether an archaeologist might one day find the remains of the snake in question. Whatever truth the story may have, it is surely not that kind of truth.

Now a big question is just what kind of stories are contained in the Old Testament narrative. Most people can probably see that the story about Hezekiah makes a straightforward historical claim, and that the story about God talking to the serpent does not. However, what of stories like Noah and the ark or Daniel in the lions' den? To many people it seems that these stories might or might not be historical reporting, and that they might or might not be true. Different readers vary in how much 'historicity' they think such stories contain.

For example, some people believe that the story of Noah is completely historical — it is just like the account of Hezekiah — while others think it is a legend, like the story of how snakes came to crawl on the ground. In addition, there are those in between who think that the story is *partly* true. They believe that there really was a major flood at some point and that this is an essentially accurate account of it. However, they think the details of the story cannot necessarily be known and are happy to accept that there might not really have been two animals of every kind in the ark, that the waters did not literally cover the whole earth, and that the flood did not literally wipe out every single person on earth. Others might say, more minimally still, that the story arose because there was a lot of experience of flooding in the area where the story originated, but it is not an account of *the*

An **aetiological** story, based on the Greek word *aitia* which means 'cause', is a story which contains an explanation of the origins of something.

In the 1920s, the archaeologist Sir Leonard Woolley thought he had found evidence of the Flood near Ur when shafts dug deep into the ground revealed a layer of clay that could be dated to around 4000 BCE and that could only have been deposited by water. By digging similar shafts in other places and measuring the thickness of this layer of clay, Woolley established the extent of a large flood in the Persian Gulf and was confident enough of his findings to send a telegram from Mesopotamia which caused a sensation as it read 'We have found the Flood!' However, whilst no one doubts that the evidence Woolley found proves that ancient Mesopotamia experienced severe floods, most scholars are more cautious about proclaiming that we have clear evidence of the flood which inspired the biblical story.

Stories of a huge flood are common in many different cultures around the world, and one of the longest and best preserved of them comes from Babylon and has significant similarities to the biblical story. The Babylonian flood story forms part of a longer narrative, called The Epic of Gilgamesh, and was discovered in 1872 when a scholar working in the British Museum in London recognized a flood story on a clay tablet which had been unearthed at an archaeological dig in Nineveh in the 1850s. In this story, the Babylonian gods decreed a flood to destroy humankind, but the god Ea decided to warn Utnapishtim of the plan in a dream. As a result, Utnapishtim built a huge boat and took on board his family, craftsmen and all kinds of animals, and they survived a flood that lasted six days. The boat came to rest on Mount Nisir, and Utnapishtim sent out a dove, then a swallow, and finally a raven to check if the waters had receded enough to leave the boat. Utnapishtim then offered sacrifice on Mount Nisir and the gods gathered round. The goddess Ishtar gave Utnapishtim her necklace of lapis lazuli as a reminder of the event, and the god Enlil conferred immortality on Utnapishtim and his wife. This story contains obvious similarities to the story of Noah in Genesis 6–9, and many think, therefore, that the biblical account is simply part of a common tradition in the ancient Near East, perhaps based on some universal memory of a huge flood in the area.

However, a close examination of the Genesis account reveals that the biblical writers are clearly more interested in theological rather than historical truth. Indeed, for many scholars it is the differences in the stories that are of most importance because they show 'how the Hebrews took a piece of ancient tradition and retold it in order to make it a vehicle of their own distinctive religious beliefs, in particular their conception of divine justice and providence' (John McKenzie, *Dictionary of the Bible*, Macmillan Publishing, 1965).

one great Flood. Such a view may be supported by the fact that many ancient cultures had flood stories similar to that of Noah and that, whilst they are not really accounts of a historical flood of worldwide proportions, such stories surely would not have arisen if there had never been any floods. Others again might say that, whether or not there is any historical foundation to it, the story expresses truths about God and humanity — for example, God's disapproval of human sin and the calamitous consequences sin can have. That is its 'truth', rather than any correspondence to historical events.

How can we decide questions like these? There is no easy answer. But a general consensus has emerged in biblical studies that there is certainly some narrative in the Old Testament that can claim to be historically rooted. This includes, at a minimum, many of the stories about the kings of Israel and Judah in the books of Kings, and the stories about post-exilic times in Ezra and Nehemiah. Most scholars also think that the books of Samuel rest on real historical records and memories. At the other end of the scale, there is a widespread agreement that the stories in Genesis 1–11, which deal with the very early history of the human race, should be seen more as legends or myths. In addition, it is generally agreed that a number of the tales in later books, such as Jonah, Esther, and Ruth, are probably fictional — never even intended to be read as though they were historical. However, that leaves room for great disagreement over many, perhaps most, Old Testament narrative texts. Writing a *History of Israel* is thus a difficult task, and no two people are likely to approach it in quite the same way.

THE MINIMALIST DEBATE

In recent years, much has been made in Old Testament study of the arguments of the so-called 'minimalists'. This term, together with the terms 'biblical revisionists' and 'biblical nihilists', has been used to describe those scholars, such as Thomas Thompson and Niels Peter Lemche from the University of Copenhagen, and Philip Davies and Keith Whitelam from the University of Sheffield. These scholars share a certain scepticism regarding the value of the biblical books of the Old Testament in reconstructing a history of Israel. They say that such accounts make little use of earlier sources and contain no reliable historical information at all. Indeed, the minimalists categorize the biblical account of the history of Israel as fiction, the product of religious propaganda from a much later date.

Of course, many scholars might agree with this basic idea where the stories of Genesis are concerned, and they may even accept that the biblical record of the Exodus and the conquest and settlement of Canaan is historically dubious. However, they would hold that the biblical record of the Israelite monarchy is relatively reliable as it was written in the eighth or ninth century BCE, close to the events being described. For this reason, the assertion by the minimalists that the biblical account of the Israelite monarchy was written in Persian times (sixth to fourth century BCE) or even Hellenistic times (fourth to second century BCE) and contains no reliable history is at the core of the debate. The minimalists contend that previous attempts to verify the historicity of the biblical record of the Israelite monarchy were based on archaeological discoveries made and interpreted by those with a theological bias. They highlight events for which no biblical evidence has been found outside the Bible and view any clear correlations between the biblical record and extra-biblical evidence as incidental, claiming that, like all good works of historical fiction, the later writers ensured that their stories were placed in a relatively realistic and accurate setting.

Such an analysis of the biblical account of the Israelite monarchy results in the denial of the existence of an Israelite state or a kingship in Jerusalem. In particular, it casts David and the Davidic state as a fictional story created as a result of the **Exile** to encourage a sense of national identity and to support a claim to the land. Of course, such a position has wide-ranging implications for the Jewish people and for the politics of the Middle East today and has even led to the minimalists being accused of **anti-Semitism** — a charge they fervently deny.

Undoubtedly, there is room for further debate about the historicity of the biblical record. Few would argue that the biblical history of Israel is history as modern scholars might define it in terms of a critical and research-based reconstruction of the past. However, many would accept that with careful, scholarly analysis of the text and of relevant archaeological data, it is possible to verify a good deal of the biblical history of Israel in its broad outlines if not in its detail. For the time being, then, the minimalists are in the minority.

Philip Davies describes the narratives of the Old Testament as 'literary constructions, serving the ideological interests of a period centuries later than the time in which they were set' and says that it is 'in their literary, philosophical, even theological character that their original purpose lay and their contemporary value should be primarily sought' (P. Davies, 'Erasing History: What Separates a Minimalist from a Maximalist?' in *Biblical Archaeology Review,* March/April 2000).

In biblical studies, the **Exile** refers to the period in Israel's history in the sixth century BCE when many of its people were taken captive and deported from Israel to Babylon.

The term **anti-Semitism** is used to describe a view that is hostile to and prejudiced against Jewish people.

3.2 Meet the Ancestors
WHAT CAN WE KNOW ABOUT THE EARLY HISTORY OF ISRAEL?

THE BASICS

- How much reliable information can be known about the early history of Israel, from Abraham to Saul, depends to a large extent on how old these stories in the Old Testament actually are, and there is no clear answer to that.
- Scholarly opinion is divided as to the age of these stories. At one end of the scale, some believe they are as old as they seem and date from the second millennium BCE, thus offering some 'historical' information. At the other extreme, others believe they date from the sixth century BCE, or indeed even later, and are little more than created fictitious stories about the past intended to promote a sense of national identity.

ACCORDING TO THE BIBLE, Israel's history before the rise of the kings consisted of several stages. First came the **patriarchs**. Abraham had come from Mesopotamia and had settled in Palestine, but Jacob's sons went down to Egypt because of a famine. There the nation became so large that the Egyptians felt threatened by it and enslaved the Israelites. They were brought out of Egypt under the leadership of Moses, crossed the Red Sea, received the Law on Mount Sinai, wandered for forty years in the desert, and then entered the Promised Land with Joshua as their leader. They conquered many of the Canaanite cities and settled in the land, being ruled by a series of 'judges'. Eventually, when the Philistines became a threat, the scattered tribes united under Saul, and with him the monarchy began. All of this amounts to what we may call the 'early history of Israel'.

But what really happened? This is a difficult question to answer since the Old Testament is far from supplying straightforward historical reporting of events. This is especially clear where these early episodes are concerned. Many of the stories in the **Pentateuch**, Joshua, and Judges, which cover these early times, are legendary in character and sometimes confused in detail. Hardly any of them can be dated accurately. Nevertheless, in the twentieth century many scholars argued that we could know more about these periods than might be expected of such remote times, though others were deeply sceptical. The matter is hotly debated

Patriarchs is a term used in biblical studies to describe the key ancestors or father figures of the Israelites, specifically Abraham, Isaac, Jacob, and Jacob's twelve sons after whom the later tribes of Israel were named.

Pentateuch is a common collective term for the first five books of the Old Testament — Genesis, Exodus, Leviticus, Numbers, and Deuteronomy. It is derived from the Greek word *pente* meaning 'five'. In the Jewish tradition, these are sometimes referred to as the five books of Moses, or the Chumash (from the Hebrew word meaning 'five').

and there is no consensus, but everything hinges on how old these stories really are.

ARE THE STORIES AS OLD AS THEY SEEM?

During the second half of the twentieth century, many biblical scholars came to think that the stories of early Israel really did go back to the times they appear to describe. This was not a 'fundamentalist' belief that any story in the Bible must be true. It rested chiefly on the painstaking work of archaeologists in the Middle East, and it was especially influential among the 'Albright school', forming the basis for John Bright's *History of Israel*. This conservative attitude to the stories of early Israel focused on the evidence relating to population movements, social customs, and names.

The evidence relating to population movements makes a fairly general point in that the movements of the early ancestors of Israel according to the Old Testament appear to be consistent with what we now know of extensive migrations of people from one country to another during the second millennium BCE. People did, indeed, move from Mesopotamia into Syria-Palestine as Abraham is said to have done: examples are the Hurrians (the biblical Horites) and the 'Amorites', the biblical term for what we would now call 'North-West Semites', whose movements can partly be charted in the seventeenth and sixteenth centuries BCE. In terms of the early Israelites journeying into Egypt, we also have evidence that in several periods there were foreigners working in Egypt, and one group of these, the Hyksos, even ruled Egypt for a time, also in the seventeenth and sixteenth centuries BCE. In the Tell El-Amarna Letters, we also read of people in Egypt called *habiru,* which may be related to the term 'Hebrew'. When we first encounter the name 'Israel' it is on the Merneptah **Stele**. The reign of Pharaoh Merneptah in the thirteenth century BCE is regarded by many as a plausible date for the settlement of the Promised Land under Joshua. Some cities in Palestine also show evidence of dramatic destruction during the same general period, and this could have been due to incomers attacking them. These incomers may have been the Israelite tribes.

A second, and more specific, point that supports the idea that these stories are as old as they seem relates to the fact that the stories in Genesis about the patriarchs contain a number of social customs that do not appear to have been common in later times. For example, in three stories in Genesis (12:10–20, 20:1–18, and 26:1–11) one of the patriarchs passes off his wife as his sister to avoid the risk that he will be killed by a king who would like the woman for himself. In the second case, we are explicitly told that this is not a complete lie, because Sarah is, indeed, Abraham's half-sister (Genesis 20:12). Such stories do not occur in any later books, where for a man to marry his half-sister is regarded as illicit.

In addition, some of these customs appear to have direct parallels in other societies of the second millennium BCE.

A **stele** (sometimes written as stela) is an upright stone monument with an inscription, often to commemorate a military victory.

The Merneptah Stele tells of the victorious exploits of Merneptah, Pharaoh of Egypt (1211–1202 BCE), and was discovered in Egypt at Thebes in 1896. The stele has twenty-eight lines of hieroglyphic text and, on the second line from the bottom, it mentions 'Israel' as being destroyed in an attack on Palestine. Although scholars are undecided as to whether this refers to a people or a territory, this is arguably the oldest evidence outside the Bible for the existence of Israel as early as the thirteenth century BCE. The Merneptah Stele is in the Cairo Museum in Egypt.

For example, the biblical story presents Abraham first as adopting one of his servants as his heir (Genesis 15:2–3) and then as engaging in a kind of surrogacy to get over the fact that he and his wife Sarah have no children. According to the story, Abraham has intercourse with one of his wife's slaves, Hagar, and the son born to her is treated as if he were Sarah's (Genesis 16:1–6). Neither of these customs occurs in the later books of the Old Testament, but legal documents relating to adoption found at Nuzi provide evidence of such practices in the second millennium BCE. Cases such as these suggest that the stories are quite old — older than the time of the kings of Israel, in whose days the Old Testament does not report any of these customs as current. Since they were not known in these latter times, they cannot very well have been 'read back' into earlier periods; instead they look like survivals from an earlier time. The time of these texts thus provides what is sometimes called a 'unique congenial context' for the stories of the patriarchs, and makes it likely that they are as old as they claim to be.

A further final point that may corroborate this is that the names of the patriarchs are not found elsewhere in the Old Testament. No one in 'historical' times was ever called Abraham, Isaac, or Jacob — at least, not until a very much later period, by which time these were 'biblical' names and used for that reason. But in Jeremiah, for example, where there are dozens of personal names, no one is called by any of these. Yet such names are found in texts from the second

The Nuzi Texts is the name given to several thousand cuneiform tablets that were found in the 1920s and 1930s at Nuzi, in present-day Iraq, on the River Tigris. These legal and cultural texts reflect the laws and customs of the Hurrian population in the fifteenth century BCE, and there are clear parallels between these and some of the customs of the Patriarchal period. For example, a Nuzi text that states that a child born of a slave cannot be expelled if a natural son is born may help explain Abraham's reluctance to agree to Sarah's request to send his son Ishmael and his mother away when Isaac is born (Genesis 21:10–11). Another Nuzi text stresses that a word or blessing spoken on a death-bed has legal weight, and this may help our understanding of the story of Jacob, who tricks his father into giving the death-bed blessing that is rightfully his older brother's (Genesis 27:41). The Nuzi archives were held by the Iraq Museum in Baghdad.

Mari, on the borders of present-day Iraq and Syria, was a prosperous centre of commerce in ancient times. It stood on the banks of the River Euphrates on the main trade route from Palestine to Babylon. A stone statue dug up here by a group of Arabs in 1933 led to a proper excavation by André Parrot, and this unearthed a huge palace belonging to Zimri-Lim, King of Mesopotamia (1730–1697 BCE). More than twenty thousand cuneiform tablets were found and they included legal, administrative, and religious texts. What is interesting is the many similarities between the practices and language of Mari and ancient Israel. Many of the names in the Mari Texts are similar to ones found in Genesis, such as Abram, Ishmael, Turaki (Terah), and Nahur (Nahor), and the name Benjamin appears as the name of a group of tribes. Certain words like *nawum* (Akkadian) and *naweh* (Hebrew) meaning 'pasturage' have so far appeared only in the Mari texts and the Bible, and evidence of altars, the sacrifice of animals, and the establishment of diplomatic covenants seems to tie

in with what can be known from the Bible of certain traditions in the Patriarchal period. The Mari Texts are preserved in the Louvre Museum in Paris and the Damascus Museum in Syria.

Although the site of Tell Mardikh (Ebla) in Syria has been the subject of archaeological excavations since 1964, the site's most valuable find did not occur until 1975 when thousands of cuneiform tablets were uncovered. These tablets include legal and administrative documents that feature familiar biblical names such as Ishmael, Adam, and David. In addition, some names appear to end in *el* (the word for 'god') and *ya* (the shortened form of Yahweh) — a fact some scholars originally equated with evidence of a knowledge of Israel's god. The Italian scholar who first worked on these tablets even went so far as to suggest King Ebrium of Ebla might be the Eber listed as one of Abraham's ancestors in Genesis 10:21 — a claim that is clearly impossible to prove!

'Silence about the patriarchs from all sources except the Bible leads some writers to conclude that the patriarchs never existed . . . those who use archaeology as a platform for such a conclusion are, however, failing to look at the evidence properly. . . . Archaeology can shed light on their background. It cannot bring proof that they are true. Neither can it prove that they are baseless legends.' (Alan Millard, *Treasures from Bible Times,* Lion Publishing, 1985)

millennium found at Mari in Mesopotamia, and also in texts found at Ebla from an even earlier period. Thus again the 'unique congenial context' for the names found in Genesis may be the very period from which the stories purport to come — before the first millennium BCE.

Similarly, the names of those who are supposed to have been in Egypt — Moses, Aaron, Hophni, Phineas — are genuinely Egyptian names. (Moses is a common element in the names of Egyptian kings such as Tutmoses and Ahmoses.) Again, no one in historical times is ever called by these names. This makes it unlikely that they have been 'read back', and likely that they really do go back to the time from which they appear to come. This in turn means that the stories could be true. Notice that it does not prove they are true, and no one who took this line of interpretation ever said that. However, it does mean that the stories really could give us genuine information about very early Israel, rather than being later fictions.

DO THE STORIES COME FROM THE TIME OF THE JUDGES OR EARLY MONARCHY?

On the other hand, we must be careful not to fall into the trap of making the text and the archaeology fit together without first studying each in its own right. The archaeologists who first discovered the customs and the names that seem to correspond with those in the Bible sometimes couldn't resist a 'eureka!' feeling, and may have jumped to conclusions rather prematurely. They tended to argue that the distinctive customs in Genesis were paralleled in Mari or Nuzi, and, therefore, the texts must be that early. When the third-millennium Ebla texts were discovered in Syria some immediately concluded that, since they contained the name Abram, Genesis must be even older than the second millennium.

Nevertheless, dating a text should be done on the merits of the text itself before noticing parallels. If, for example, we could actually prove that the text of Genesis cannot be earlier than (say) the ninth century, then the parallels (though still interesting) could not possibly show that the text was really older. The parallels would have to have some other explanation. One possibility might be coincidence — different societies do sometimes have similar customs even though one has not influenced another; another might be that the stories reflect memory of the customs, even though the stories themselves are later.

'We attain to no historical knowledge of the patriarchs, but only of the time when the stories about them arose in the Israelite people; this later age is here unconsciously projected, in its inner and outward features, into hoar antiquity, and is reflected there like a glorified mirage.' (Julius Wellhausen)

Biblical scholars from the German-speaking world tended to be sceptical about the claims of the biblical archaeologists, because they thought the texts simply could not be so early as was being suggested. When, they asked, would people have been interested in the remote ancestors of Israel? Presumably it would have been in the period when an Israelite state was beginning to form, in what the Old Testament calls 'the days of the judges'. The interest Genesis shows in the twelve 'sons of Jacob' is surely linked to the fact that they have the names of the twelve tribes of Israel. For such reasons, these scholars held that the stories about the patriarchs do not really reflect the world of the second millennium BCE, but that of the time just after the settlement, when the tribes were all coming together to form a nation. Indeed, they felt that stories about the patriarchs, who are thought of as the ancestors of the tribes, were probably in reality stories about incidents during that early settlement period. So, although as the Bible is now arranged they precede the stories of Moses and the Exodus, in reality they are probably later tales which have been artificially projected back in time to a legendary past.

For those who hold such a view, like the great nineteenth-century Old Testament scholar Julius Wellhausen (1844–1918), it means that we do not learn anything real about the very early history of the Israelites from the Pentateuch. Moreover, the discoveries of the texts at Mari and Nuzi and Ebla, which happened long after Wellhausen, do not undermine this conclusion, because we know that the texts of the Pentateuch are really later than the second millennium BCE on other grounds.

What are those grounds? Although the stories in Genesis do not mention events later than the 'patriarchal age', they do reflect a sense of national identity for the Israelites which many say makes sense only from the time of the judges onwards. The stories even in the oldest source, J, come from the tenth century at the earliest, since J assumes the leading role of Judah among the tribes (see especially Genesis 37:26–27 and 49:8–12), which was not the case until the kingdom of David. Of course, some of the tales may rest on older oral tradition, but stories are not passed down accurately by word of mouth for more than a generation or two, and they could not possibly have survived all the way from the mid-second millennium. Maybe the names are genuinely old, but the stories that have clustered round those names must be later inventions. Thus, the view that the patriarchal stories come from the time of the judges and the early monarchy has been the prevailing view in German scholarship.

What about the stories of Moses and Joshua? Most biblical scholars think that there is some truth in the idea that some, but not all, of the ancestors of the later Israelites had, indeed, been in Egypt. Probably a small group settled in Palestine from the west, and their folk memory of deliverance from Egypt and the giving of the Law at Sinai was gradually adopted by all the tribes. This would be like the way in which all Americans celebrate Thanksgiving, which commemorates the arrival of the Pilgrim Fathers on the east coast, even though they are not really the ancestors of, for example, Californians or Texans. A national myth is often the tradition of a small group which has been generalized and extended to cover the whole nation. Some people think that the giving of the Law has been spliced into the story of the Exodus, wanderings, and settlement. Originally, perhaps, it was a separate tradition belonging to a group of tribes in the south of Palestine who venerated a desert sanctuary where YHWH was believed to have spoken to them. Only later was it incorporated into the story of the Exodus. Speculation like this can never come to any firm conclusions, but it does undermine one's confidence that in reading the Pentateuch we are dealing with historical narrative. More likely these are the founding legends or myths of the nation. Their ultimate origins are lost to us, but they are unlikely to go back into a remote enough period for the parallels with Mari and Nuzi, let alone Ebla, to be relevant.

ARE THE STORIES LATE FICTIONS?

In recent biblical scholarship a more extreme possibility has emerged. This is that the stories in the Pentateuch were simply created in much later times, perhaps as late as the **Exile** in the sixth century BCE or even later. It is a striking fact that the earliest references to the patriarchs or to Moses outside the Pentateuch itself are in the eighth-century prophets, and even there only in a very brief form. Amos calls Israel the 'house of Isaac' (Amos 7:16, and see also 7:9). Hosea refers briefly to the **Exodus**:

> *When Israel was a child, I loved him,*
> *   and out of Egypt I called my son.* (Hosea 11:1)

> *By a prophet the LORD brought Israel up from Egypt,*
> *   and by a prophet he was guarded.* (Hosea 12:13)

On the other hand, Isaiah does not mention any historical events earlier than David, and it is not until Second Isaiah, as late as the sixth century BCE, that we encounter references to Abraham:

> *Look to the rock from which you were hewn,*
> *   and to the quarry from which you were dug.*
> *Look to Abraham your father,*
> *   and to Sarah who bore you. . . .* (Isaiah 51:1–2)

So, some scholars have suggested that it was not until after the prophets that Israel really began to develop its traditions about the early times. Perhaps the Exile was the matrix for this. The nation had lost its identity, and had to forge a new one. There could be little hope that the future would involve a restoration of the monarchy, but some looked back to a time before the kings and believed that Israel's identity and unity rested on older foundations. So they began to spin stories about those earlier times, and to create a national myth that would form a basis for a new nation if or when the Exile ended. Once it did, and some Jews were restored to their homeland, the work began of writing stories to justify the nation's unity by looking back to remote times and weaving tales that would give substance to hope. The 'glorified mirage' Wellhausen spoke of was thus 'projected' from an

In biblical studies, the **Exile** refers to the period in Israel's history in the sixth century BCE when many of its people were taken captive and deported from Israel to Babylon.

The word **exodus** literally means 'way out' and refers to the departure of the Israelites from Egypt under the leadership of Moses.

even later period than he realized, from the sixth or even fifth century BCE.

Whilst many may feel that this is too harsh a reading of the evidence, this theory of a very late origin for the stories about the early history of Israel does account for a couple of odd features. For example, Abraham is promised dominion 'from the river of Egypt to the great river, the river Euphrates' (Genesis 15:18). Israel never commanded anything like this extent of land, so probably this is a utopian hope coming from a period when hopes were unreal, rather than from the pre-exilic period when people knew what was a realistic extent for Israel. Furthermore, Moses is presented in the stories of Exodus as a prophet, speaking the 'word of the LORD' and called to this vocation through a series of visions and signs (Exodus 3–4). It is hard to see how this story can be earlier than the existence of the 'classical prophets' of Israel, such as Amos, Isaiah, and Jeremiah, who all experienced a similar 'call'. Moses is being made in the image of much later prophets, so these stories about him surely cannot be as early as they seem.

In general, however, most scholars feel it is unlikely that the stories of early Israel can be quite so late as this. What emerges from the points made above about 'archaic' features of the patriarchal narratives is that there is a great deal in the stories no one in later times could have invented. If the names of the patriarchs were remembered down the years — and they cannot have been invented, because they are names that were not current then at all — then why should some of the stories about these people not also be quite early? There may also be many reasons why the stories are not referred to much in subsequent books. When the prophets do refer to them, they seem to think that people will immediately pick up what they are talking about. Even though no one before Second Isaiah mentions Abraham, when he does mention him it does not sound as though he is a new character, but much more as though everyone would know enough to make sense of such a brief reference.

SO, WHAT CAN WE REALLY KNOW ABOUT THE EARLY ANCESTORS OF ISRAEL?

Despite its weaknesses, the theory that the stories are late fictions is a useful reminder of how little we can really be sure of where the early history of Israel is concerned. We certainly cannot write a biography of Abraham, or talk of Moses as though he were someone like Julius Caesar, for whom there is a lot of historical material from his own time. These people are figures of legend. The legends may be old legends, but they are not historical records. The most anyone can show is that they *could* be true in essence: there is no possibility at all of knowing that they *are* true. What we have in the Pentateuch is the collected memories and impressions of the founding of the nation from a later time. Mixed up in it may be genuine features, such as unusual names, or customs that

Did the Exodus really happen?

The minimalists dismiss the story of the Exodus as a fictitious creation from the sixth century BCE or later and will point out that there is no clear evidence of the Exodus in Egyptian records and no conclusive archaeological evidence of a large number of people wandering around the Sinai Peninsula — evidence you might expect if the story were true. However, the Exodus is usually viewed as one of the most important events in the Old Testament, and the image of the liberation by God of a people from their oppressors is one that is central to Jewish and Christian theology. Many have said that without the experience of the Exodus there would have been no nation of Israel at all, and it is so fundamental to the Jewish understanding of God and how he acts in history that the story forms the centrepiece of the annual festival of Passover. As a result, many scholars would agree with Bernhard Anderson when he says, 'Every reader of the bible has to make up his or her own mind about the historical nucleus which lies at the heart of the tradition that has been elaborated and coloured by Israel's faith over a period of generations. . . . Nevertheless, Israel's ancient faith undoubtedly was based on the experience of actual events which facilitated the escape of slaves from Egypt, events in which they perceived in moments of faith the work of God' (*The Living World of the Old Testament*, 4th edn., Longman, 1988). Others have made specific attempts to prove the historical fact of the Exodus by searching out archaeological evidence. Most recently, Larry Williams and Bob Cornuke claim to have discovered the real mountain of Sinai at Jabal Al Lawz in Saudi Arabia, complete with an image carved in stone of the golden calf and evidence of the twelve pillars mentioned in Exodus 24:4.

Whatever the origins of the Exodus story, it is worth remembering that as a tale of God's deliverance it is central to the Judaeo-Christian story and continues to have an impact in modern times, for example, providing an important model for the Liberation Theology movement. For more information about Liberation Theology, see 5.4 'A Good Read?'

no one was familiar with any longer — but the Pentateuch is not a work of history.

An analogy may help. No one imagines the fairy-tale character Cinderella ever existed; the story of Cinderella is no more than a story. Those who take the minimalist approach to the early history of Israel are more or less saying that the ancestors, Abraham, Isaac, Jacob, Joseph, Moses, and so on, are fictional characters like Cinderella — people who exist only in a story. Yet most biblical scholars think this goes one stage too far. Better analogies might be King Arthur or Robin Hood. These people are equally surrounded by legend and romance, and no one imagines that you could write their biography. However, nearly all who have studied them think that there is some underlying foundation of fact. Arthur may have been a Romano-British prince towards the end of the Roman Empire; Robin Hood may be a kind of composite figure, woven from the memory of many local heroes, but still there is some factual basis — there really were such local heroes. His story is located in the Nottingham area, just as Arthur's is in the old Celtic domains of Wales and Cornwall and Brittany, and this is not pure fiction. However much these tales have grown in the telling, they are not made up from scratch: they rest on tradition. The second approach described above, which has been typical of German scholarship, seems in many ways to capture best this sense of characters who straddle the border between legend and history.

3.3 Give Us a King!
WHAT CAN WE KNOW ABOUT THE MONARCHY IN ANCIENT ISRAEL?

T H E   B A S I C S

- The importance of characters like David and Solomon has undoubtedly been exaggerated for religious purposes by the biblical authors, and some scholars have more recently questioned their existence at all. However, many scholars still believe that both the style of parts of the stories and archaeological evidence seem to suggest that the Old Testament accounts of the monarchy are rooted more in actual historical events than in myth and legend.
- The biblical accounts, as well as the words of eighth-century prophets, indicate that political life during the time of the monarchy was relatively unstable. The turbulent fortunes of the various kings and their attempts at alliances eventually delivered Israel into the hands of the Assyrians and Judah into the hands of the Babylonians.

ACCORDING TO THE OLD Testament, monarchy began in Israel with Saul. At the end of the time of the judges, threats from the Ammonites and the Philistines made it essential for all the northern tribes to collaborate, and they came together under Saul's leadership. In due time he became their king; some texts suggest that this was through **YHWH**'s choice, others that it was a strictly political decision of which YHWH disapproved. On his death, his most successful general, David — who was swiftly recognized as king by the southern tribe of Judah — soon came to be seen as a natural successor, and he supplanted Saul's own son to take control of the whole of Israel, north and south alike. Under David and his son Solomon the Israelites, with a new capital city at Jerusalem, established a considerable empire, gaining control of the surrounding nations and even making alliances with the great powers such as Egypt. When Solomon died, the kingdom fell apart, and the other lands he and David had ruled over were gradually lost. The 'divided monarchy' of the separate northern and southern states, Israel and Judah, slowly declined, until both kingdoms were eventually captured, by the Assyrians and Babylonians respectively. Israel ceased to exist in the late eighth century, Judah in the early sixth.

Modern biblical study has called much of this into question. It is highly doubtful whether David and Solomon ever reigned over an 'empire', and it is not clear that we are deal-

YHWH is the primary way God's name appears in the Old Testament. For a more detailed examination of this issue see 2.1 'Watchmaker or Living God?'

ing with genuine historical information in the Old Testament until the times of the prophets in the eighth century. Just as 'early Israel' was the subject of much legend and embroidery, so the exploits of Saul, David, and Solomon owe a lot to the story-teller's art. Nevertheless, it is at some point during the history of the monarchy that many scholars feel we can be reasonably confident that we are talking about actual historical events, rather than simply about folklore.

SOURCES FOR THE AGE OF THE KINGS

(a) Information from outside the Bible

Archaeology itself cannot prove or disprove the detailed stories in the Old Testament, but it can illuminate their

---

THE KINGS OF ISRAEL AND JUDAH

The United Monarchy

Saul (1030–1010 BCE)
David (1010–970 BCE)
Solomon (970–931 BCE)

The Divided Monarchy

Israel *(the northern kingdom)*	*Judah* *(the southern kingdom)*
Jeroboam I (932/931–911/910 BCE)	Rehoboam (932/931–916/915 BCE)
	Abijam (916/915–914/913 BCE)
	Asa (914/913–874/873 BCE)
Nadab (910–909 BCE)	
Baasha (910/909–887/886 BCE)	
Elah (887/886–886/885 BCE)	
Zimri (7 days 886/885 BCE)	
Omri (886/885–875/874 BCE)	
Ahab (875/874–854/853 BCE)	Jehoshaphat (874/873–850/849 BCE)
Ahaziah (854/853–853/852 BCE)	Joram (850/849–843/842 BCE)
Joram (853/852–842/841 BCE)	Ahaziah (843/842–842/841 BCE)
Jehu (842/841–815/814 BCE)	Athaliah (842/841–837/836 BCE)
Jehoahaz (815/814–799/798 BCE)	Joash (836/835–797/796 BCE)
Joash (799/798–784/783 BCE)	Amaziah (797/796–769/768 BCE)
Jeroboam II (784/783–753/752 BCE)	Uzziah (769/768–741/740 BCE)
Zechariah (753/752–752/751 BCE)	
Shallum (752/751–751/750 BCE)	
Menahem (751/750–742/741 BCE)	Jotham (741/740–734/733 BCE)
Pekahiah (742/741–741/740 BCE)	Ahaz (734/733–715/714 BCE)
Pekah (741/740–730/729 BCE)	Hezekiah (715/714–697/696 BCE)
Hoshea (732–721 BCE)	Manasseh (697/696–642/641 BCE)
The fall of the northern kingdom	Amon (642/641–640/639 BCE)
	Josiah (640/639–609/608 BCE)
	Jehoahaz (609/608 BCE)
	Jehoiakim (609/608–598/597 BCE)
	Jehoiachin (598/597 BCE)
	Zedekiah (598/597–587/586 BCE)
	The fall of the southern kingdom

Note that it is very difficult to be certain of the dates of the reigns of these kings. These dates follow those in Siegfried Herrmann's *A History of Israel in Old Testament Times* (translated by John Bowden, 1983). The double dates offered reflect the fact that the Hebrew year did not begin on 1 January, but in either the autumn or the spring.

background and so make them more or less likely. For the period from about 1000 BCE there is extensive evidence from many excavations. These show that there was a considerable expansion of population which resulted in the formation of many new villages and small settlements over a period of about two hundred years, and then from the eighth century onwards a growth in city life, with Israelite towns — including Jerusalem — expanding and prospering. The population growth of the early years may have something to do with incomers to Palestine, including early Israelites, but there is little evidence of a change in culture, so this must remain speculation.

What is clear is that Syria-Palestine in the early first millennium was no longer subject to control by the great powers in Egypt and Mesopotamia, and so there was scope for it to develop its own political life. This meant that local leaders — scarcely 'kings', with the grand overtones that word has for us — were able to operate fairly freely, and little rudimentary states could start to form. It is among these that Judah and Israel are to be found, alongside the kingdoms of Moab, Ammon, Edom, various small Syrian (Aramaean) states, and the city-states of the Philistines. The stories of Saul, David, and Solomon have undoubtedly grown in the telling. However, the biblical record probably rests on a foundation of fact in claiming that 'Israel' (both in the sense of the northern tribes and as a name for the whole people, including Judah) organized itself much more centrally at this time. It no longer depended on occasional charismatic figures (the 'judges') but came to have kings who at least tried to establish dynasties. This attempt was much more successful in the small southern state of Judah than in the north, where the Old Testament tells a plausible story of continual coups and assassinations.

What is also clear is that this time of relative independence for the small states of Syria and Palestine did not last. They entered a period of relative prosperity in the ninth and eighth centuries. However, by the middle of the eighth century Mesopotamia was again a united force under the Assyrian king Tiglath-pileser III (who came to the throne in 745 BCE). Whereas Ahab, in the previous century, had been part of a coalition that had defeated the Assyrians at the battle of Qarqar, under his successors the northern kingdom suffered invasion, and eventually (in 722 BCE) destruction. Many people were deported to Assyria, and the area of Israel was turned into an Assyrian province. Judah became more or less a **vassal** of the Assyrians, though it retained control over its internal affairs for more than another century. In due course the Babylonians took over the Assyrian Empire and they captured Judah, which had unwisely sought to resist their king, Nebuchadnezzar. In 587 BCE there ceased to be an independent Judean state with its own king. Opinions differ as to how large a section of the population Nebuchadnezzar deported, but Judean independence was lost irrevocably. All this can

Vassal is a term for a slave and can be applied to a powerless nation which, through being conquered or being under threat of being conquered, is forced to treat the dominant nation as its master.

be confirmed from Assyrian and Babylonian sources, such as the Annals of Sennacherib and Esarhaddon, the Babylonian Chronicle, and the Chronicles of Nebuchadnezzar.

(b) Information from the Old Testament

The story of the monarchic period in Israel and Judah can be found in the books of Samuel and Kings, with some parallel accounts in the later books of Chronicles. In their present form, these books are probably no older than the period of the **Exile**. In other words, they were written to tell the story of how Israel had gone from a position of prominence, even dominance, in the Promised Land to the abject condition it found itself in by the middle of the sixth century, with those who survived in the land deprived of all independence, and their leaders in exile in Babylonia. Only a few biblical scholars think that the authors of these books simply made the story up, and so it is with the monarchy — especially the later monarchy — that many feel we can begin to speak of 'history' in the Old Testament.

Almost certainly there were underlying historical sources which the authors drew on. Of course, some of these sources may themselves have been legendary in character. Examples might be the tales of Elijah and Elisha, which can be found from 1 Kings 17 to 2 Kings 9, or famous episodes like the visit of the 'Queen of Sheba' to Solomon (1 Kings 10:1–10). However, the compilers of Kings draw attention to earlier documents, the 'Book of the Acts of Solomon' (see 1 Kings 11:41), the 'Book of the Annals of the Kings of Judah' (see 1 Kings 14:29), and the 'Book of the Annals of the Kings of Israel' (see 1 Kings 15:31). They do not say in so many words that they themselves have used these sources, but it seems likely that they did.

One of the striking features of the biblical records about the monarchy is the complex dating system that the authors of Samuel and Kings used. Every king is dated by reference to his contemporary kings in the other kingdom: 'In the nth year of King X of Israel, King Y of Judah began to reign, and he reigned z years over Israel' (for one example of many, see 1 Kings 16:8). There is in fact a chronological scheme running through the whole Old Testament, and it has different details in the original Hebrew version and in later translations, such as the Greek **Septuagint**. In many places the dates have a symbolic significance and are probably round numbers rather than an attempt to present real historical memory. However, the years of the kings are not round numbers, but very specific and mostly non-symbolic, and from them it is possible to build up a realistic chronology for Israel in the monarchic period and correlate it with what is known from Mesopotamian sources. Indeed, the Old Testament itself makes correlations. For example, in 2 Kings 25:8 we learn that the sack of Jerusalem by the Babylonian army happened in 'the nineteenth year of King Nebuchadnezzar', the Babylonian king.

Apart from these features that suggest genuine historical

In biblical studies, the **Exile** refers to the period in Israel's history in the sixth century BCE when many of its people were taken captive and deported from Israel to Babylon.

'We have at our disposal, fortunately, sources that are both exceedingly full and of the highest historical value, much of the material being contemporaneous, or nearly so, with the events described...information regarding David, and the bulk of that regarding Solomon, comes to us in the form of excerpts from official annals, or a digest of them, and is exceptionally valuable. We are, in short, better informed about this period than any comparable one in Israel's history.' (John Bright, *A History of Israel*, SCM, 1960)

According to an ancient account, seventy scholars were originally involved in translating the Hebrew Scriptures into Greek. For this reason, based on the Latin word for seventy, **Septuagint** is the name given to the Greek version of the Old Testament. It is sometimes abbreviated to LXX (the Roman numerals for seventy).

sources, the books of Samuel and Kings also contain detailed stories that are more novel-like in character. Whereas in the earlier books of the Bible we find short tales, told in a few chapters at most, and reminiscent of folktales (think of the stories about Samson in Judges 14–16), 1 and 2 Samuel on the other hand contain lengthy accounts with a wealth of circumstantial detail. The longest of these is the story of David's court in 2 Samuel 9–20, probably completed in 1 Kings 1–2. This is often known in modern scholarship as 'The Succession Narrative', because it is concerned principally with the question of who is to be David's heir on the throne of Judah.

The author of this narrative uses flashback techniques, and is able to tell two parallel stories at once ('Meanwhile, back at the palace . . .': see 2 Samuel 16:15). This suggests literary skill, and may undermine our confidence in his historical accuracy — we don't expect a historical novelist to report exact history. Yet, on the other hand, his story is so damaging to the reputation of David that it is hard to think it can be a mere invention. It was unwise to make up stories detrimental to the greatest of Israel's kings, as David was seen in later years. Because of this, most scholars think the Succession Narrative must rest on a bedrock of fact about the intrigues at David's court. The Narrative tells a plausible tale explaining how it came about that Solomon succeeded David, even though he was not David's eldest son and was actually born from his father's very dubious marriage to Bathsheba (whose husband David had had killed to get him out of the way, according to 2 Samuel 11).

David was probably not a great king ruling over an empire stretching from Egypt to Mesopotamia. He was a local leader, who had been a bandit (see 1 Samuel 22:1–2), and who prospered only because of a temporary power vacuum in the Middle East. Nevertheless, most scholars believe he is not purely a figure of legend, but someone about whom there are historical records. The same is probably true of Solomon. He is depicted in 1 Kings 3–10 as an even more splendid figure than David, and over the years archaeologists have hunted for his stables, his mines, and his fleet, though never successfully. Most scholars would now agree that his reign has been written up with a wealth of legendary features. However, the stories did not come from thin air, and the Old Testament records not only his splendour but also the ease with which his kingdom fell apart on his death, as a result of the harshness of his rule (see 1 Kings 12) — features no more likely to be invented than David's misdemeanours.

None of this means that the biblical record suddenly becomes hard, factual reporting when we get to the monarchy. However, neither is it pure fiction, nor traditional folklore; and it starts to connect with history we can reconstruct from other ancient records. Therefore, at least where the monarchy is concerned, there is some hope of gaining historical information from the biblical account. However, in presenting

 There are some numbers in the Old Testament which appear to be wholly symbolic. For example, the number seven is associated with completeness and perfection — the Sabbath or 'rest' day of creation is the seventh, and the walls of Jericho collapse on the seventh day of marching when seven priests blowing seven trumpets lead the Israelites seven times around the city walls. The number forty also appears simply to represent 'a long time' with the flood lasting for forty days and forty nights and with the Israelites wandering in the desert for forty years. For more about the Old Testament and numbers, see 4.7 'The Number of the Beast'.

 The books of I and 2 Chronicles seem to be little more than a version of the stories about David in 2 Samuel and I Kings with the more disagreeable aspects of his reign omitted. The adultery, the murder, and the family troubles are all missing in this later account; such a selection of the material gives some insight into what the writers perceived, in retrospect, were the successes and the failures of David's reign. For more about the reign of David see I.2 'The Story So Far'. For more about the writer of the books of Chronicles, see 4.5 'The Plot Thickens'.

Israel as though it were the centre of the world the biblical authors undoubtedly vastly exaggerate the importance of this little state or pair of states, which were never really to be compared with the empires of Egypt or Mesopotamia.

POLITICAL HISTORY IN THE TIME OF THE KINGS

There seems to be justification for the Old Testament's claim that the decision to have a 'king' — a ruler who would have a permanent tenure, rather than a military leader to deal with a crisis — began with Saul, at around the beginning of the first millennium BCE. The stories that portray the appeal 'Give us a king to govern us, like other nations' (e.g. 1 Samuel 8:5) as showing disrespect for YHWH may reflect later, bitter experience of the damage kings can do. But they may also go back to a genuine memory that Israel had not traditionally been governed in this way, but had relied on 'the spirit of YHWH' to raise up a leader when needed. Early Israel may have distinguished its more rudimentary kind of government from the sophisticated monarchies of Egypt and Mesopotamia, and may have had an ideal picture of itself as ruled only by God. If so, this might be a little like the much later Roman idea that kings are detrimental to the freedom of a people. This idea is certainly reflected in Samuel's speech as recorded in 1 Samuel 8:11–17:

> 'These will be the ways of the king who will reign over you: he will take your sons and appoint them to his chariots and to be his horsemen, and to run before his chariots; and he will appoint for himself commanders of thousands and commanders of fifties, and some to plough his ground and reap his harvest, and to make his implements of war and the equipment of his chariots. He will take your daughters to be perfumers and cooks and bakers. He will take the best of your fields and vineyards and olive orchards and give them to his courtiers. He will take one-tenth of your grain and of your vineyards and give it to his officers and his courtiers. He will take your male and female slaves, and the best of your cattle and donkeys, and put them to his work. He will take one-tenth of your flocks, and you shall be his slaves.'

The threat from enemies was, however, so overwhelming that the people thought it worth taking this risk, and so Saul became king, but only over the northern tribes, and without much of a settled 'court'. In any case, war with the Philistines lasted throughout his reign, and he eventually fell in battle with them (1 Samuel 31).

If our sources are to be believed, David and Solomon lived in a time when Israelite power had become more substantial. David defeated the Philistines, and then began aggressive wars to take over some of the small surrounding nations. Solomon was in general able to hold on to these gains, though he is said to have lost Edom and some part of Aram (1 Kings 11:14–25).

However, once Solomon died, all claims to an Israelite 'empire' quickly disappeared. We are not well informed about the history of the ninth century BCE, the century that followed the death of Solomon. The Old Testament writers portray the kings of the northern kingdom, such as Omri and Ahab, as 'evil' because they allowed Canaanite elements to creep into their religion; but that is the perspective of a later age. Omri, as we know from the Moabite Stone, was a powerful king who made incursions into Moabite territory:

> *As for Omri, king of Israel, he humbled Moab many years, for Chemosh was angry at his land. . . . Omri had occupied the land of Medeba, and (Israel) had dwelt there in his time and half the time of his son Ahab, forty years.*

Under Ahab, there were both coalitions with various Aramaean kingdoms in opposition to expansionist moves by the Assyrians, and also defeats at the hand of Aram. The picture we get from 1 and 2 Kings is of constantly shifting allegiances. In 2 Kings 5 the king of Aram sends his top general to be cured of leprosy by Elisha; in 2 Kings 6:23 the Aramaeans invade Israel but are thwarted and 'no longer came raiding into the land of Israel'; yet in the very next verse 'King Ben-hadad of Aram mustered his entire army; he marched against Samaria and laid siege to it' (2 Kings 6:24).

Leprosy is a bacterial skin disease which can lead to loss of limbs and death if left untreated. It flourishes in hot and humid climates and still exists today. Scholars are unsure whether all the references to leprosy in the Bible refer to this disease or whether the Hebrew word traditionally translated 'leprosy' was a term used simply to describe any kind of infectious skin disease.

Victory stele for King Mesha of Moab,
Louvre, Paris / Bridgeman

The Moabite Stone (or Mesha Stele)
This black basalt stele can be dated to c. 830 BCE and is about 1 metre high and 0.6 metres wide with thirty-four lines of writing. It was first discovered in 1868 in Dhiban (ancient Dibon), in present-day Jordan, but was subsequently shattered into pieces by local people. A French scholar named Clermont-Ganneau recovered most of the fragments, and from these, and a paper impression he had taken when he had first seen it, it was possible to reconstruct the stone. It is now in the Louvre Museum in Paris. The inscription on the stele preserves a text from ninth-century Moab, an area just across the River Jordan from Israel. It records that Moab had been subject to Israel during the reigns of Israel's King Omri and his son but that Mesha, king of Moab, had eventually defeated Israel. It also records how Mesha took vessels connected with the worship of Yahweh and presented them to his own god, Chemosh. The inscription confirms the biblical record of the northern kingdom of Israel's wars against Moab recorded in 2 Kings 3:4-27 and is particularly interesting from the point of view that each side's account tends to emphasize its own successes and gloss over its defeats in the course of these wars.

Like neighbouring states the world over, the little nations of Syria and Palestine formed and broke alliances as the balance of power and advantage shifted.

The prophets Elijah and Elisha belong somewhere in the ninth century BCE, but the stories about them often do not make it clear just which king's reign they were active in. Often we read simply of 'the king of Israel' (see, for example, 2 Kings 5, the story of Naaman, where the king makes several appearances but is never named).

In the next (eighth) century, when for the first time we have really contemporary evidence in the words of the prophets Amos, Hosea, Micah, and Isaiah, the Aramaean threat has clearly begun to fade. Amos reports that people are rejoicing at having recaptured two cities from the Aramaeans, Qarnaim and Lo-debar across the Jordan (Amos 6:13). However, the joy faded mainly because of the growing power of Assyria in the east. Until the middle of the eighth century BCE the Assyrians had been largely preoccupied with the state of Urartu, to their north (biblical 'Ararat', now the south of Turkey), but as the threat from Urartu ended they turned their attention westwards. From this point on, the fate of the little states of Syria and Palestine was sealed.

The northern kingdom went through a period of general chaos, with a succession of military coups. Hosea is a witness to the condition of the nation in the later years of the century:

> I will destroy you, O Israel;
>   who can help you?
> Where now is your king, that he may save you?
>   Where in all your cities are your rulers,
> of whom you said,
>   'Give me a king and rulers'?
> I gave you a king in my anger,
>   and I took him away in my wrath. (Hosea 13:9–11)

Finally an Assyrian invasion put an end to its independence, and it became an Assyrian province.

Although it was more or less an Assyrian vassal, Judah struggled on for more than a century, with two strong rulers, Hezekiah and Josiah. In 701 BCE the Assyrians, provoked by Hezekiah's withholding of tribute, besieged Jerusalem, but evidently did not capture it. The story of this 'Assyrian crisis' is one of the most heavily discussed events in the history of Judah. It is told in 2 Kings 18:13–19:37, with a parallel but not identical account in Isaiah 36–37. The overall impression given by both biblical accounts is that a miraculous plague defeated the Assyrians, but the Assyrian king Sennacherib's own annals suggest rather that Hezekiah bought him off. Certainly the city's escape came to be seen as implying its 'inviolability', which is celebrated in some of the psalms (see especially Psalms 46–48 and 76). Escape from being sacked did not mean independence, however, as Isaiah pointed out

Sennacherib's Prism (Taylor's Prism)
This hollow clay prism, about 37 centimetres high, was acquired by Colonel Taylor in Nineveh in 1830. The six sides of cuneiform writing record the attack of the Assyrian king Sennacherib (704–681 BCE) on King Hezekiah of the southern kingdom of Judah (716–687 BCE). It explains how Sennacherib conquered forty-six of Hezekiah's towns and besieged the king himself in Jerusalem 'like a bird in a cage'. This confirms the biblical record in 2 Kings 18 and Isaiah 36–37, but once again the two accounts differ in emphasizing their own successes and glossing over their defeats. The Assyrian account does not mention that Sennacherib failed to capture Jerusalem in the end while the biblical record makes much of the divine intervention by 'an angel of the Lord' who one night miraculously killed thousands of the Assyrian army camped outside Jerusalem, causing Sennacherib to end the siege and go back to Nineveh (2 Kings 19:35–36). This prism is in the British Museum in London.

(see Isaiah 22). The nation attempted various alliances with Egypt to try to secure itself against the power of Assyria; but Egypt was by now a spent force:

> *Alas for those who go down to Egypt for help*
> *and who rely on horses,*
> *who trust in chariots because they are many*
> *and in horsemen because they are very strong. . . .*
> *The Egyptians are human, and not God;*
> *their horses are flesh, and not spirit.* (Isaiah 31:1, 3)

The last years of Judah saw political decline and infighting, as the Assyrian threat was replaced by the growing power of Babylon. By the beginning of the sixth century BCE it was ripe for the picking, and the Babylonians had little difficulty in capturing Jerusalem and putting an end, for the time being, to the history of anything that could be called 'Israel'.

3.4 Refugee Status
WHAT CAN WE KNOW ABOUT THE EXILE AND RETURN?

T H E   B A S I C S

- The exact nature and scale of the deportation of the Jewish people from their land to Babylon in the sixth century BCE is debatable and was probably not the virtually complete depopulation portrayed in the biblical accounts.
- The experience of Exile was an important one for the nation as it produced a large amount of literature and was the catalyst for significant developments in religious thought and practice.

B Y THE END OF the seventh century BCE Judah had escaped the fate of the northern kingdom of Israel for more than a century, continuing to enjoy a limited but real independence first under the Assyrians, and then under the Babylonians. However, after the death of the reforming King Josiah (see 2 Kings 22–23), Judah began an inexorable decline and 'went into exile out of its land' (2 Kings 25:21).

The kings who succeeded Josiah refused to accept that the nation could hope to exist only as a **vassal** of the Babylonians, and declined to pay the Babylonians the tribute-money they demanded in return for leaving Judah alone. In 598/597 BCE the Babylonians deposed the young King Jehoiachin after only a few months on the throne, and imposed a ruler chosen by themselves, his uncle Mattaniah, whom they renamed Zedekiah (2 Kings 24:8–17). At the same time, they took many leading Judeans into captivity in Babylonia. Zedekiah, however, did not heed the warning and, egged on by unwise counsellors, he in turn withheld tribute. In 587/586 BCE the Babylonian army came and besieged Jerusalem. Zedekiah tried to escape by night, but was captured. His sons were killed before his eyes, then he himself was blinded, many of his officials executed, and he and many other Judeans followed Jehoiachin into exile (2 Kings 25:1–21).

The Babylonians left the remaining population under the command of a civil servant, Gedaliah, moving his head-

Vassal is a term for a slave and can be applied to a powerless nation which, through being conquered or being under threat of being conquered, is forced to treat the dominant nation as its master.

In 721 BCE, the Assyrians captured the northern capital of Samaria and took the people from the northern kingdom of Israel into exile in Assyria. This is recorded in 2 Kings 17:6 as well as in reports of the Assyrian king Sargon II's campaigns in Syria and Palestine found at Khorsabad, near Nineveh. Those deported are never heard of again in the biblical record and they are sometimes referred to as the 'ten lost tribes of Israel'. It seems likely that they were simply assimilated into Assyrian society, but this has not stopped their whereabouts being the subject of much fantastic speculation over the years, including suggestions that they may have been the ancestors of, among others, the Native Americans or the British!

quarters north from Jerusalem to Mizpah. But that was not the end of the story: a member of the royal family, Ishmael, who apparently wanted the throne of Judah for himself — though it can hardly have seemed a very attractive prospect! — assassinated Gedaliah, and Gedaliah's entourage fled to Egypt (2 Kings 25:22–26).

We next hear of the victims of the deportations some fifty years later. In 539 BCE the Babylonian Empire passed, by an almost bloodless coup, into the hands of Cyrus, king of Persia. According to the Old Testament, he decreed that those of the Jews in exile who wished to do so could return and rebuild the Temple in Jerusalem. This is recorded in Ezra 1–6. Progress was slow, and we learn from the books of Haggai and Zechariah that many of the people who returned were reluctant to get on with building the Temple, though they settled back comfortably into life in Judah. There was no question of their enjoying full political independence, but the Persians appointed as their 'governor' a fellow-Judean, Zerubbabel — perhaps a descendant of the royal line — who ruled them apparently alongside the high priest, Joshua. Thus, by the end of the fifth century there was once again a Jewish presence in the land, living in an area even smaller than Judah had been, in a Persian province named in Aramaic (the official language of the Persian Empire) *Yehud*.

WHAT WAS THE SCALE OF THE EXILE?

The impression we get from the biblical account is that Judah was virtually depopulated during the 'exilic period', from about 587 to about 515 BCE. However, the figures that the Old Testament itself records for the deportations do not really tally with this impression. At the time of Jehoiachin's capture, according to 2 Kings 24:13–16, the Babylonians took away mainly those who could be effective in aiding a further rebellion, 'all the men of valour . . . the artisans and the smiths', as well as Jehoiachin's administrative officials and the royal family. The text gives two slightly varying sums for the people exiled, 10,000 (v. 14) or 8,000 (v. 16). Estimates of the population of Judah at this time are in the region of 200,000, though this is only a 'best guess' based on the archaeology of towns and cities and some extrapolation from the figures Assyrians and Babylonians claimed to have deported on other occasions. Even if this is an overestimate, the text's claim that 'no one remained, except the poorest people of the land' is surely an exaggeration.

When Zedekiah's rebellion came to nothing eleven years later, 2 Kings gives no figures for those deported, but says,

Nebuzaradan the captain of the guard carried into exile the rest of the people who were left in the city and the deserters who had defected to the king of Babylon — all the rest of the population. But the captain of the guard left some of the poorest people of the land to be vinedressers and tillers of the soil.

(2 Kings 25:11–12)

Yet there was still a large enough population for some government to be needed: hence the appointment of Gedaliah. Still, the impression is that more or less all Judeans ended up as exiles in Babylonia.

However, there is a short passage in the book of Jeremiah which gives a quite different picture:

This is the number of the people whom Nebuchadrezzar took into exile: in the seventh year, three thousand and twenty-three Judeans; in the eighteenth year of Nebuchadrezzar he took into exile from Jerusalem eight hundred and thirty-two persons; in the twenty-third year of Nebuchadrezzar, Nebuzaradan the captain of the guard took into exile of the Judeans seven hundred and forty-five persons; all the people were four thousand six hundred. (52:28–30)

These three deportations correspond to the exile of Jehoiachin, the exile of Zedekiah, and reprisals for the assassination of Gedaliah. They are astonishingly low, and they also reverse the impression given in the book of 2 Kings that it was the second deportation that was the main one and that constituted 'the Exile': no more than 832 people are said to have been deported at that time, whereas 3,023 left Judah with Jehoiachin. Partly because these figures are not round numbers, scholars have tended to think that the book of Jeremiah here preserves a more reliable record than 2 Kings. If that is true, then by far the greater number of Judeans did not go into exile at all, but continued to live in their ancestral homeland. What changed for them would have been not the place they lived, but the loss of their leaders and the transfer of power to Babylonian officials, the end of Jerusalem as a capital city, and the changes in their religious life following the destruction of the Temple.

However, some people, including the leaders, did go into exile, although it appears that their living conditions in Babylon were not harsh. King Jehoiachin was kept under guard, but in appropriately regal surroundings in the royal palace, and others were allowed to live in groups and run their own settlements provided they did not attempt to return to Judah. Indeed, Jeremiah encourages the exiles to 'Build houses . . . plant gardens. . . . Take wives and have sons and daughters' (Jeremiah 29:5–6). In later times, the group who went into exile viewed itself as the 'true' Judah — indeed, the true 'Israel', heirs to the promises made to Abraham, Isaac, and Jacob. However, in terms of sheer physical reality, almost all those who lived in Judah after 'the Exile' were descendants of those who had always lived there — they had never gone away. But a kind of **ideology** of exile grew up, which taught that Israel's life in the land had suffered a huge break at the beginning of the sixth century — just as the prophets had said it would, if the people did not abandon their disloyalty to **YHWH**.

 Nebuchadnezzar is the common Old Testament spelling for the king of Babylon from 605 to 562 BCE. However, the book of Jeremiah consistently spells the Babylonian king's name 'Nebuchadrezzar', which is actually closer to the spelling in Akkadian.

There is some archaeological evidence relating to the life of the Jewish exiles in Babylon. In the 1930s four tablets from the royal palace in Babylon, dated between 594 and 569 BCE, were discovered. The entry for the years of Nebuchadnezzar's reign includes a list of rations for 'Jehoiachin, King of Judah' and his sons. In addition, a number of apparently prominent Jewish families appear as clients of a Babylonian banking firm, whose business records were discovered in great clay jars in Nippur — suggesting that there were opportunities for the exiles to settle down and engage in successful business ventures with the local population.

Ideology is a term for any system of ideas relating to a particular theme.

YHWH is the primary way God's name appears in the Old Testament. It is simply four Hebrew consonants which many scholars believe may have been pronounced Yahweh.

OLD TESTAMENT LITERATURE FROM THE EXILIC AGE

There is no continuous account in the Bible of what happened to the Jews in the exilic age. However, information about life, both for those in Babylon and for those who remained in Judah, can be gleaned from some of the Old Testament literature relating to the period.

(a) Lamentations

Bearing in mind that the great bulk of the population remained in Judah, we should not make the mistake of assuming that only those who were exiled could have written the literature of this period. One outstanding work that seems far more likely to have been produced in Judah is the book of Lamentations. Later tradition ascribed this work to Jeremiah, but it is really anonymous, probably the work of a Temple singer who laments the piteous condition to which the Babylonian invasion has reduced Judah, and the end of the worship of the Temple in Jerusalem:

> *Is it nothing to you, all you who pass by?*
>   *Look and see*
> *if there is any sorrow like my sorrow,*
>   *which was brought upon me,*
> *which the LORD inflicted*
>   *on the day of his fierce anger.* (Lamentations 1:12)

> *He has broken down his booth like a garden,*
>   *he has destroyed his tabernacle;*
> *the LORD has abolished in Zion*
>   *festival and sabbath,*
> *and in his fierce indignation has spurned*
>   *king and priest.* (Lamentations 2:6)

Even if not many Judeans were deported, the sufferings of those caught in the siege of Jerusalem and then in the capture of the city can certainly not be exaggerated:

> *Our skin is black as an oven*
>   *from the scorching heat of famine.*
> *Women are raped in Zion,*
>   *virgins in the towns of Judah.*
> *Princes are hung up by their hands;*
>   *no respect is shown to the elders....*

> *Because of this our hearts are sick,*
>   *because of these things our eyes have grown dim:*
> *because of Mount Zion, which lies desolate;*
>   *jackals prowl over it.* (Lamentations 5:10–12, 17–18)

But even in the midst of such disaster they cannot bring themselves to believe that God has abandoned them forever:

A lament is a song or poem of mourning for a dead person; the author of Lamentations has chosen to express himself in the form of a funeral lament to heighten the effect of the words on the reader. The form expresses heartfelt grief for what the author views as the 'death' of Jerusalem, of the Temple, of the king, and of his nation's way of life.

> But this I call to mind,
> and therefore I have hope:
> *The steadfast love of the* LORD *never ceases,*
> *his mercies never come to an end.* . . .

(Lamentations 3:21–22)

However, Lamentations follows in the steps of the prophets in seeing what has happened to Judah as a just punishment from God for repeated sins.

(b) Jeremiah

This is also the message of Jeremiah, whose prophetic activity began under King Josiah, but who was still speaking out when the two successive Babylonian invasions destroyed his nation. For most of his career, Jeremiah spent his time warning the people of Judah that their evils would result in God's destruction of Jerusalem; and the chapters of Jeremiah that describe the last days of the kingdom of Judah are highly informative as well as very poignant (see especially Jeremiah 32–34 and 37–44). Jeremiah himself urged Zedekiah to surrender to the Babylonians because he believed that it was part of God's punishment and that Babylonian rule would be limited once the people turned away from their sins. For his pains, he was treated as a traitor, suspected of being in the pay of Nebuchadnezzar. He was imprisoned and ill treated. However, once the destruction of Jerusalem had taken place he also addressed words of hope and consolation to the people in exile, reassuring them that they would be the new Israel of the future. Jeremiah tells those in exile of God's plans 'for your welfare and not for harm, to give you a future with hope' (Jeremiah 29:11) and speaks of a time when God will renew his covenant with the people by writing it in their hearts (Jeremiah 31:31–34).

(c) Ezekiel

A younger contemporary of Jeremiah was the prophet Ezekiel, who was deported with Jehoiachin in 598 BCE. In his book we see the small community of the exiles trying to come to terms with what has happened, and continuing to worship YHWH in Babylonia. Ezekiel reacts angrily to the feeling of some of them that they were not to blame for their exile, but that responsibility lay with their ancestors, or with the community back in Judah (see Ezekiel 18, where these ideas are rejected). His message is that the exiles must repent, and repent as individuals, choosing to obey the Law no matter what the community as a whole are doing (Ezekiel 18:26–28). Ezekiel also looks forward to a time when YHWH will heed their repentance and will put 'a new heart' and 'a new spirit' inside his people (Ezekiel 36:24–28). This idea is supported by his famous vision, in which God orders him to preach to a valley full of dry human bones which promptly come back to life, presenting the message that one day God would breathe new life into the Jewish nation (Ezekiel 37:1–14). At that stage,

We are not sure how the book of Jeremiah came to be written or survive, but it contains some passages that probably reflect more the end of the exilic period, when Babylon was about to fall (see especially chapters 50 and 51), and so it may have been finally compiled forty years or so after the siege of Jerusalem. Jeremiah's secretary, Baruch, may have had a hand in this, though almost certainly some later editors added to his work. Again, this book may come from Judah itself rather than from the exiles in Babylonia; it might even derive from the Judean community in Egypt, for the people who fled there after Gedaliah was assassinated apparently took Jeremiah with them (see Jeremiah 43–44).

The word **exodus** literally means 'way out' and refers to the departure of the Israelites from Egypt under the leadership of Moses.

Ezekiel says, YHWH will bring those who are faithful among them (purged of disloyal elements) back to their land in a kind of new **Exodus**:

> *As I live, says the Lord GOD, surely with a mighty hand and an outstretched arm, and with wrath poured out, I will be king over you. I will bring you out from the peoples and gather you out of the countries where you are scattered...and I will bring you into the wilderness of the peoples, and there I will enter into judgement with you face to face. As I entered into judgement with your ancestors in the wilderness of the land of Egypt, so I will enter into judgement with you, says the Lord GOD. I will make you pass under the staff, and will bring you within the bond of the covenant. I will purge out the rebels from among you, and those who transgress against me; I will bring them out of the land where they reside as aliens, but they shall not enter the land of Israel.* (Ezekiel 20:33–38)

Two things are worth highlighting here. Firstly, Ezekiel refers not only to those in Babylon, but to 'the countries where you are scattered' — this will include those in Egypt, and perhaps others who have fled to other places. Secondly, the coming restoration will include elements of judgement, and not every single individual will form part of the new 'Israel', but only those who are loyal to YHWH.

(d) Second Isaiah

The name Isaiah, appropriately enough for the message of Second Isaiah, means 'Yahweh is Salvation', but we do not really know who Second Isaiah was. The Old Testament book of Isaiah is actually a compilation of different types of prophecy that span quite a period of time. Most scholars agree that chapters 1–39 relate to a prophet called Isaiah who lived in Jerusalem and engaged in prophetic activity from 742 to 701 BCE. The next section of the book, however, has a distinct literary and theological style and clearly relates to a later period towards the end of the Exile, from 550 to 540 BCE, since it includes the idea of Cyrus as a liberator of Israel in exile in Babylon. As these chapters come second, the prophet is referred to as Second or Deutero-Isaiah. In addition, some scholars argue that there is a distinct third section to the book in chapters 56–66 and refer to the author of these chapters as Third or Trito-Isaiah.

Similar themes occur in the third great prophet of the exilic age, whom we know as the 'Second Isaiah'. Second Isaiah reflects the period when Cyrus was already becoming a force to be reckoned with. He actually mentions him by name as one who will be responsible for restoring Israel to its land (see Isaiah 44:28, 45:1). For Second Isaiah, too, the coming deliverance will be like the Exodus:

> *Go out from Babylon, flee from Chaldea,*
>   *declare this with a shout of joy, proclaim it,*
> *send it forth to the end of the earth;*
>   *say, 'The LORD has redeemed his servant Jacob!'*
> *They did not thirst when he led them through the deserts;*
>   *he made water flow for them from the rock;*
>   *he split open the rock and the water gushed out.*
>   (Isaiah 48:20–21)

What we have here is a prophecy that in effect the history of Israel is going to begin all over again, just as it began in the days of Moses when the people were led through the desert and into the Promised Land. These hopes may have been alive both in Judah and in Babylonia as news of Cyrus's conquests began to spread. Consequently, it is not possible to be sure where Second Isaiah lived, though most scholars think that, like Ezekiel, he was in Babylonia. One notable difference between Second Isaiah and Jeremiah and Ezekiel is that his message is full of confident hope and does not include any judgement or condemnation of Israel. His message is one of comfort, enshrined in his opening verses — Israel has 'served her term' and 'her penalty is paid' (Isaiah 40:1–2). Second Isaiah sees Israel's future as being even greater than the past and as one in which God will re-create his people and restore them to their land. Of course, the rise of Cyrus may have provided a political basis for his message but the theological basis for his message of hope comes from his fundamental belief that God is an active, present God who not only did great things in the past but also continues to do them now.

> *Do not remember the former things,*
> *or consider the things of old.*
> *I am about to do a new thing.* . . . (Isaiah 43:18–19)

Thus, he constantly refers to God as saviour, holy one, king, creator and lord, and no one in the Old Testament applies the term 'redeemer' to God as often as Second Isaiah.

(e) Psalms

Dating the Psalms is generally almost impossible: they could come from many different periods in Israel's history. However, one of the most recognizable psalms that refers to the anguish of exile in Babylon is Psalm 137. It is a psalm of lament, and its opening lines clearly convey the genuine distress of the Jews who found themselves in Babylon with no heart even to sing the songs of **Zion**:

> *By the rivers of Babylon —*
> *there we sat down and there we wept*
> *when we remembered Zion.* . . .
> *How could we sing the LORD's song*
> *in a foreign land?* (Psalm 137:1, 4)

Two psalms, 74 and 79, also refer explicitly to the destruction of YHWH's sanctuary, and are very likely to come from the same setting as Lamentations — the early years after the destruction of the Temple:

> *Your foes have roared within your holy place;*
> *they set up their emblems there.*
> *At the upper entrance they hacked*
> *the wooden trellis with axes.*
> *And then, with hatchets and hammers,*
> *they smashed all its carved work.*
> *They set your sanctuary on fire;*
> *they desecrated the dwelling-place of your name,*
> *bringing it to the ground.* (Psalm 74:4–7)

> *O God, the nations have come into your inheritance;*
> *they have defiled your holy temple;*
> *they have laid Jerusalem in ruins.* (Psalm 79:1)

'From beginning to end, the prophecy of Second Isaiah is an exultant proclamation of good news. The people who dwell in darkness hear that a new day is dawning. Captives are told that deliverance is on the way. The broken-hearted are comforted. Every poem is filled with the excitement and expectancy of great events about to come to pass.' (Bernhard W. Anderson, *The Living World of the Old Testament*, 4th edn., Longman, 1988)

Zion is the name of the principal hill of Jerusalem but it is used poetically in the Old Testament to refer to the whole city of Jerusalem. Later generations referred to the entire nation of Israel as Zion, and the Jewish nationalist movement, whose aim was to establish a Jewish state in the land of Israel, attached the name Zionism to its cause.

From these texts we can form some idea of the grief caused by the destruction of the Temple. Yet both already show signs of hope. In Psalm 74, the psalmist recalls that God is the creator, who in the beginning showed that he could overcome the forces of chaos:

> *Yet God my King is from of old,*
>   *working salvation in the earth.*
> *You divided the sea by your might;*
>   *you broke the heads of the dragons in the waters. . . .*
> *Yours is the day, yours also the night;*
>   *you established the luminaries and the sun.*
> *You have fixed all the bounds of the earth;*
>   *you made summer and winter.* (Psalm 74:12–13, 16–17)

On this basis it is possible to hope that he will once again step in to undo the 'havoc' wreaked by the enemies of Israel.

(f) The 'Deuteronomistic History'

One final work deserves to be mentioned. It consists of the historical books from Joshua to 2 Kings. In the Hebrew Bible these books are called, rather confusingly, 'The Former Prophets', but in modern scholarship they are often referred to as the 'Deuteronomistic History', because they apply criteria taken from the book of Deuteronomy in judging the actions of the characters in the story, especially the kings of Israel and Judah.

The majority view is that this continuous history of Israel was finally compiled at some point during the exilic age to explain why the kingdoms of Israel and Judah had failed and why, in spite of God's covenant promises, the Temple had been destroyed and the people exiled. It was a time when people began to look back not just at particular periods and incidents in the history of Israel, but at the whole sweep of that history from its beginnings to its dark conclusion in the events associated with the Babylonian invasion. It was, in a sense, a history that had come to an end, and the whole story was compiled to illustrate that the Exile was the result of, and the deserved punishment for, Israel's sin — rather than God's powerlessness in the face of the enemy.

These historical books contain much material that comes from older sources, and hardly anyone would suggest that they were actually written from scratch in the exilic age. Moreover, since as a finished whole they tell the story of Israel from its settlement in the land to its exile from it, they can hardly date from a later period, when there had been a return and a re-establishment of the national life. Similarly, they cannot be earlier, since they relate the Babylonian capture of Jerusalem. We should probably date the finished history to around 540 BCE, shortly before it became clear that Israel might, after all, be going to have a further lease of life. The last recorded incident is the release from prison

The interpretation of history by the Deuteronomists centres on the idea that Israel has constantly been unfaithful to God, who has, on the other hand, been completely faithful to his promises. The people are presented as having been given a clear choice by God, 'See, I have set before you today life and prosperity, death and adversity. If you obey the commandments of the LORD your God . . . then you shall live and become numerous, and the LORD your God will bless you in the land that you are entering to possess. But if your heart turns away and you do not hear, but are led astray to bow down to other gods and serve them, I declare to you today that you shall perish; you shall not live long in the land . . .' (Deuteronomy 30:15–18).

For more information about the style and authorship of the Deuteronomistic History, see 4.5 'The Plot Thickens'.

of Jehoiachin by Evil-merodach (the Hebrew version of his Akkadian name, Amel-Marduk), a Babylonian king who came to the throne in 562 BCE and reigned for only two years. Perhaps the historian saw in this the first hints of some hope for his people even though its history seemed to have come to a full stop: we cannot be sure.

THE 'RESTORATION' UNDER CYRUS

Cyrus began his career as the king of a small Persian state, but developed a vision of establishing the greatest empire the world had ever known. In that, he succeeded. The last king of Babylon, Nabunaid (usually the Greek/Latin form 'Nabonidus' is used now), had left his capital city and gone to live in what is now Saudi Arabia, leaving his son Belshazzar to act as regent in Babylon. Nabonidus was unpopular because he dethroned many of the traditional Babylonian gods, promoting instead the worship of the moon-god, Sin, of whom his mother had been a priestess. Cyrus moved swiftly to capture Babylon and, according to his own record on what is called the Cyrus Cylinder, he was welcomed into Babylon without the need to draw a sword. He quickly restored the gods to their shrines, and took over the entire Babylonian Empire, which he and his successors extended even further. It would be two hundred years until that empire fell to the armies of Alexander the Great.

The restoration of the Temple of YHWH in Jerusalem could plausibly have followed from Cyrus's policy of religious tolerance, and it is credible that he might have allowed some Judeans to return and work on rebuilding it. It is also credible that he would have restored some proper local government to the territory of Judah. Since Gedaliah was assassinated, it had lacked any proper government. The books of Haggai and Zechariah make it clear that by their day (520 BCE or so) there was again political life in Jerusalem in the form of the curious joint rule of governor and high priest.

The Cyrus Cylinder
This clay cylinder is 23 cm long and is covered in cuneiform writing. The Babylonian text records the capture of Babylon in 539 BCE by Cyrus, king of Persia (549–530 BCE), and his policy of returning exiled people to their own countries. This appears to confirm the biblical records in 2 Chronicles 36:22–23 and Ezra 1:1–4 which report that it was Cyrus who issued an edict allowing the Jews to return to Jerusalem and rebuild their Temple. Cyrus is also mentioned in Isaiah 44:28–45:4 as the one God has chosen to free his people to return to Jerusalem, although whilst this biblical record accredits Yahweh as the power behind Cyrus's victories, the Cyrus Cylinder claims that they have been achieved by the power of the Babylonian god Marduk! The cylinder is on display in the British Museum in London. © Copyright Ancient Art and Architecture Collection Ltd

It is less certain that the Old Testament's records of Cyrus's decrees permitting the return are authentic. One version of the decree can be found in Ezra 1:2–4 (a shorter form appears in 2 Chronicles 36:23):

> 'Thus says King Cyrus of Persia: The LORD, the God of heaven, has given me all the kingdoms of the earth, and he has charged me to build him a house at Jerusalem in Judah. Any

> *of those among you who are of his people — may their God*
> *be with them! — are now permitted to go up to Jerusalem in*
> *Judah, and rebuild the house of the* LORD, *the God of Israel*
> *— he is the God who is in Jerusalem; and let all survivors, in*
> *whatever place they reside, be assisted by the people of their*
> *place with silver and gold, with goods and with animals, be-*
> *sides freewill-offerings for the house of God in Jerusalem.'*

The decree is in Hebrew, which means it would have to be a translation of the original as Cyrus would have written either in Persian or in Aramaic, the common international language of the Middle East by this time. It ascribes Cyrus's conquests to YHWH, which he himself is unlikely to have claimed; and it requires people who live alongside exiled Jews to provide them with what they need for the task of rebuilding. Altogether, it seems to be the kind of decree Jews would have liked Cyrus to issue, rather than one he is likely to have produced himself in so many words.

However, there is another version of the decree in the book of Ezra. In a later time, according to Ezra 6 — in fact, in the days of Haggai and Zechariah — there was a dispute about whether Jews really had been authorized to work on the Temple. A record was found in the archives of the Persian kings which did indeed authorize the work. This document appears in Aramaic in Ezra 6:2–5, and is followed by a detailed decree by the later king, Darius, that the work must now be allowed to go forward. Cyrus's decree reads here as follows:

> *A record. In the first year of his reign, King Cyrus issued a*
> *decree: Concerning the house of God at Jerusalem, let the house*
> *be rebuilt, the place where sacrifices are offered and burnt-*
> *offerings are brought; its height shall be sixty cubits and its*
> *width sixty cubits, with three courses of hewn stones and one*
> *course of timber; let the cost be paid from the royal treasury.*
> *Moreover, let the gold and silver vessels of the house of God,*
> *which Nebuchadnezzar took out of the temple in Jerusalem and*
> *brought to Babylon, be restored and brought back to the temple*
> *in Jerusalem, each to its place; you shall put them in the house*
> *of God.* (Ezra 6:2–5)

This version does not imply that Cyrus is a worshipper of YHWH, and it is a much more business-like document, limiting the size of the restored Temple. The restoration of the Temple vessels would have corresponded in Cyrus's mind to restoring gods to their shrines — of course, there was no image of YHWH that could be replaced in the Temple, but all the paraphernalia of the old customs of worship roughly fitted the bill.

Even if Cyrus did authorize the rebuilding in something like these words, that does not mean that huge numbers of exiled Judeans actually returned. In the books of Ezra and Nehemiah we have lists that purport to include all those who did (see Ezra 2 and Nehemiah 7), though these may be later concoctions — the books named after Ezra and Nehemiah may have been written more than a century after the return. Just as the population of Judah contained many people who had never left for Babylonia, so the population of Babylonia from the time of the Exile onwards contained many Judeans who never returned, and Babylonia was a flourishing centre of Jewish life throughout all the following centuries.

THE IMPACT OF THE EXILE

Julius Wellhausen described the Exile as a 'critical watershed' for Israel and, even if we need to be careful about talking as though all Jews were 'in exile' in the sixth century BCE, most scholars would agree that the exilic experience marked a vital stage in the development of Israel's religion, history, and literature. Broadly speaking, it was in this time that Judaism became a religion that could be practised anywhere, not only in 'the land'. In religious terms, the development of worship in synagogues is often credited as being the result of the Exile and the loss of the Temple. With no temple and no altar on which to offer animal sacrifice, a new emphasis was laid on the spiritual offerings of prayer and fasting. In addition, although they may have their roots in pre-exilic Judaism, many believe that adherence to food laws, circumcision, and Sabbath observance assumed a new importance at this time as they served as distinguishing features for a people who were foreigners in a strange land. Although for the great pre-exilic prophets YHWH had already been the one God of all the world, it was also in the exilic period that such an idea of God became more **transcendent** and more general, and a theoretical **monotheism** was first articulated.

The Exile was also a highly creative phase in terms of the amount of literature produced, and most scholars believe that it was at this time that much work was done on the collection and editing of the sacred books and traditions of the early history of Israel. This was a natural response to such a national crisis, and those who reviewed the stories of Israel's past took hope from the fact that God's covenant with his people originated from a time when Israel was not a nation and had no king, except God himself. Therefore, the situation in which the people now found themselves seemed to provide a clear opportunity to recover that special relationship with God. As a result, the stories of Israel's past were collected and presented in a way which reminded people what God had done for them and which, therefore, provided hope for the future. God was their creator and could be expected to bring order out of chaos again. God was also their redeemer. Just as he had rescued his people from Egypt in the Exodus, he could be expected once again to free his people and restore them to their land. Thus, the people in exile were encouraged to focus their hopes on a God who was consistent — God had not failed them in the past and would not abandon them now. Such a vision enabled the people to see the meaning of

When applied to God, the term **transcendent** means that God is greater than the world and in some sense is beyond it and outside human experience. For more information, see 2.1 "Watchmaker or Living God?"

The term **monotheism** refers to the belief in only one God.

'These centuries were an incredibly creative time as the lessons of the past were assessed and their spiritual power was harnessed to a new cause'. (John Drane, *Introducing the Old Testament,* Lion, 2000)

what they had experienced an d provided the basis for a new hope.

So this period, so bleak in many ways for the people of Judah, was rich in writings and ideas. In the midst of the apparent utter failure of Israel's life there were those who had the depth of insight and the drive to make sense of what had happened. In the process, new ideas were forged that would come to dominate Jewish thought in the post-exilic period: the oneness of God, the interpretation of history as the arena in which divine justice was to be seen, the ultimate hope that God would be true to his people. It was a time in which people felt that the teachings of the prophets had been vindicated, and that their version of the religion of Israel was consequently proved to be correct. Thus, the exilic age is important whatever the political realities may have been, and however much the Old Testament exaggerates the sheer physical reality of exile.

3.5 Loyal Subjects?
WHAT CAN WE KNOW ABOUT THE 'SECOND TEMPLE' PERIOD?

THE BASICS

- In post-exilic times Palestine existed as a relatively minor area, first of the Persian Empire (sixth to late fourth century BCE), then of the Greek Empire of Alexander the Great and his descendants (late fourth to first century BCE), and finally becoming part of the Roman Empire in 63 BCE.
- With the exception of some information about attempts to rebuild the Temple and restore Jewish religious life in Jerusalem, there is little clear information in the Old Testament about this post-exilic age.

YOU MIGHT THINK THAT the history of Israel would be clearer, the nearer it is to today; and there is some truth in that. The real history of the **patriarchs** or Moses is veiled in obscurity, whereas for the period of the divided **monarchy** we have evidence that is more solid. Unfortunately, after the **Exile** there are, once again, few historical sources on which we can rely.

However, the history of the Mediterranean world in general in this period is not obscure. After **Cyrus**, the Persian Empire expanded to control the whole of Mesopotamia, Syria–Palestine, and even Egypt, and it continued in a very stable form for around two hundred years until the rise of **Alexander the Great** in the late fourth century BCE. Alexander first defeated the Persians at the battle of Issus in 333 BCE, and the last Persian king (Darius III) lost his throne

Patriarchs is a term used in biblical studies to describe the key ancestors or father figures of the Israelites, specifically Abraham, Isaac, Jacob, and Jacob's twelve sons after whom the later tribes of Israel were named. For more information about them see 3.2 'Meet the Ancestors.'

A **monarchy** is a form of government with a king (or queen) as its head. In biblical terms, the period of the divided monarchy refers to the time when there were separate kings for the northern and the southern parts of what was once the united kingdom of Israel. Israel was a divided monarchy from about 931 BCE until the collapse of the northern kingdom in 721 BCE. The southern kingdom remained in existence a few hundred years more until 587 BCE when it was defeated by the Babylonians. For more information about this period, see 3.3 'Give Us a King!'

In biblical studies, the Exile refers to the period in Israel's history in the sixth century BCE when many of its people were taken captive and deported from Israel to Babylon. For more information about this period see 3.4 'Refugee Status'.

Coming from 'Hellenes', which is the Greek word for 'Greeks', the **Hellenistic Age** refers to the period in which the whole Middle East came under intensive influence of Greek history, language, and culture. This term is particularly used to refer to the period following the death of Alexander the Great (fourth century BCE) until the time of Augustus (first century BCE).

A **satrapy** is an administrative area in the ancient Persian Empire, ruled over by a provincial governor — a satrap.

 The post-exilic period is sometimes known as the Second Temple period because the Temple built in the years of the return to replace Solomon's original one was standing throughout this time. For more about the Jewish Temples in Jerusalem, see 4.3 'Hallelujah!'

Mentioned by name in Isaiah 44 and 45, 2 Chronicles and the books of Ezra and Daniel, the **Cyrus** of the Bible was Cyrus II the Great, founder of the Persian Empire. Having completed his conquest of Asia Minor in 547 BCE, Cyrus began a successful campaign against Babylonia and in 538 BCE permitted Jews in exile in Babylon to return to Jerusalem and rebuild their Temple. For more about Cyrus' liberation of these exiles see 3.4 'Refugee Status'.

Alexander the Great (356–323 BCE) was from Macedon in northern Greece. Having become king in 336 BCE and united Greece, he began a campaign to remove the domination of the Persians in the Mediterranean and Asia Minor, eventually taking his troops as far as India. He proved himself an excellent military commander but died in Babylon of a fever aged only thirty-two. His body was taken to Alexandria in Egypt to be buried and his vast empire was divided up among his successors. However, the extent of his conquests ensured that Greek culture had a profound and lasting effect across the ancient Near East.

Josephus was a Jewish historian who lived in the first century CE. He was governor of Galilee during the Jewish revolt of 66 CE against the Roman Emperor Nero and was captured by the Romans. However, they spared his life and, after the fall of Jerusalem in 70 CE, he went to live in Rome and eventually became a Roman citizen. Josephus's works include his *Jewish Antiquities,* which tells the story of the Jewish people from creation up to his own time, and the *History of the Jewish War,* which provides a summary of Jewish history from 168 BCE to 66 CE. These writings were an important source for later Christian writers and commentators on the New Testament period.

only two years later. Alexander took control of the whole of what had been the Persian Empire, and the so-called **Hellenistic Age** began. For the next two hundred years or so the Eastern Mediterranean world was ruled by descendants of Alexander's three generals (known as the Diadochoi in Greek, meaning 'successors'). This period ended only with the rise of Rome to world prominence in the middle of the second century BCE.

The fate of the Jews in all this is far from clear. In the Persian period Palestine was a minor province within the Persian **satrapy** that covered all the land west of the River Euphrates (known in the Bible as 'Beyond the River' or Transeuphrates). Under Alexander's successors, it was fought over by rulers in Egypt and in Syria, rather as it had been back in the second millennium. Only for brief periods does it emerge into the spotlight, when we happen to have biblical evidence. For the later years, the Jewish historian **Josephus** has preserved a little historical information but, in general, the whole post-exilic age or 'Second Temple' period is quite obscure.

THE PERSIAN PERIOD

Although some Jews were allowed by Cyrus to return in about 538 BCE, probably under a leader called Sheshbazzar, and to begin work on rebuilding the Temple, the work was completed only in the days of the prophets **Haggai** and **Zechariah**, around 520 BCE. By then the governor of Judah was Zerubbabel, evidently a descendant of the pre-exilic Judean kings. After the rebuilding of the Temple the screen goes dark for seventy years or so, and we do not know what happened to Zerubbabel and his colleague, Joshua (or Jeshua) the high priest.

Just possibly the book of Malachi comes from this unknown time, but it does not help us to fill in the history. It is simply a series of complaints about bad practices in worship (offering diseased animals, for example), though it concludes with prophecies that better days will one day come, in which the righteous will be rewarded and the wicked punished. We learn from it that the Jews were still ruled by a 'governor' (Hebrew *pechah,* Malachi 1:8), but are not told his name.

In the middle of the fifth century there was another 'return' to Jerusalem, this time by a new governor called Nehemiah. This man, who had apparently risen to a high position at the Persian court, has left us his memoirs, which can be found in Nehemiah 1–6 and some of chapter 13. His mission seems to have been to mend the walls of Jerusalem. This would have had a practical purpose, to protect the people from marauders, but also a symbolic value, re-establishing Jerusalem as a proper city again. It makes us realize that, despite the rebuilding of the Temple, the city as a whole was still not repaired.

Nehemiah encountered a lot of opposition, much of it from the governor of Samaria, Sanballat: it is as though the pre-exilic rivalries between the northern and southern king-dom were being re-enacted in a later time. Opposition also came from Tobiah, evidently the head of an old Israelite fam-ily from east of the River Jordan. Behind this we can probably sense the opposition of those Jews who had never been in exile towards people like Nehemiah, who saw themselves as the 'true' Israelites, descended from the ruling classes who had been exiled with Jehoiachin or Zedekiah. Sanballat and Nehemiah were both minor officials compared with the sa-trap of Transeuphrates, both ruling over comparatively small areas in Palestine — indeed, in Nehemiah's case we do not know whether his territory even extended much beyond the city of Jerusalem itself.

As well as repairing the walls, which Nehemiah seems to have carried out quickly and with widespread support (see Nehemiah 3–4), he embarked on a programme of religious 'purification'. We put the word in inverted commas because in some ways it looks like what we might now call ethnic cleansing. Nehemiah forced those men who had married foreign wives to divorce them (Nehemiah 13:23–27) and was particularly opposed to a Jew who had married the daugh-ter of Sanballat (Nehemiah 13:28–29). In general, Nehemiah seems to have wanted to turn the community in Jerusalem into a very religious community, focused on the Law of Moses — though we do not know what form this Law took in his day. He tried to enforce the Sabbath regulations (Nehemiah 13:15–22), and ejected foreigners (or people he thought were foreigners) from the Temple (Nehemiah 13:4–9). He also re-instituted the distribution of offerings to the **Levites** in the Temple, who had become so impoverished they had had to return to farming their land instead of maintaining Temple worship (Nehemiah 13:10–14).

It is probably in the context of this rigorous restoration of ritual and national 'purity' that we should understand the work of Ezra. In Jewish tradition Ezra became more famous than Nehemiah, and a whole set of writings grew up attrib-uted to him including 1 and 2 Esdras (Greek for Ezra) in the **Apocrypha**, but who Ezra really was is highly obscure. He appears to have been both a priest and a 'scribe' (a kind of Secretary of State), yet he became neither high priest nor governor when he returned to Jerusalem. The book of Ezra reports that he too returned to Jerusalem from Persia (Ezra 7) to re-establish true worship at the Temple. This happened,

TABLE OF THE PERSIAN KINGS

Cyrus	559–530 BCE
Cambyses	530–522 BCE
Darius I	522–486 BCE
Xerxes	486–464 BCE
Artaxerxes I	464–423 BCE
Darius II	423–404 BCE
Artaxerxes II	404–358 BCE
Artaxerxes III	358–336 BCE
Darius III	336–330 BCE
Conquest of Alexander the Great	

The prophets **Haggai** and **Zechariah** spoke to the people who returned from exile. The book of Haggai contains a small collection of prophecies that appear to have been delivered in Jerusalem around 520 BCE. The thrust of Haggai's message was that the people should get on with build-ing the Temple. As he says in Haggai 1:4, 'Is it a time for you yourselves to live in your panelled houses, while this house lies in ruins?' Zechariah also urged the people to complete the Temple, encouraging them with accounts of his night visions from God that suggested that the rebuild-ing of the Temple was the sign that the time of messianic salvation was approaching.

Apocrypha is the name given to the collection of books which are included in the Greek ver-sion of the Old Testament (the Septuagint) but not in the He-brew Scriptures. These books are often also called 'deuterocanoni-cal' books.

The **Levites** were one of the twelve tribes of Israel and, although there are a num-ber of inconsistencies in the informa-tion about them in the Old Testament, they are generally recognized as the tribe associated with the priesthood. By the period of the Second Temple, the term 'Levites' refers to those who assist the Temple priests. In the book of Chronicles King David is presented as stating their role as, 'for the service of the house of the LORD, having the care of the courts and the chambers, the cleansing of all that is holy, and any work for the service of the house of God' (I Chronicles 23:28).

'Any conclusions about the relationship of the work of these two men [Ezra and Nehemiah] and the historical con-texts to which they belonged must remain highly uncertain and rely on intuitive speculation.' (J. Maxwell Miller and John H. Hayes, *A History of Ancient Israel and Judah*, SCM, 1986)

according to Ezra 7:8, in the seventh year of King Artaxerxes. If this is Artaxerxes I, then the year in question would be 458 BCE, and that would mean that Ezra arrived in Jerusalem thirteen years before Nehemiah, whose mission is dated to the twentieth year of Artaxerxes (445 BCE) in Nehemiah 2:1. However, Ezra is said to have instituted marriage reforms not unlike Nehemiah's (Ezra 9–10), yet Nehemiah later seems unaware of this. On the other hand, if Ezra came back in the seventh year of Artaxerxes II (398 BCE), then his mission would actually have followed Nehemiah's but, if Ezra is the later figure, he seems unaware of the marriage reforms of Nehemiah. Another solution proposed is that there was some overlap in their time in Jerusalem and that Ezra was a much more minor player than the books of Ezra and Nehemiah suggest, since the only time they appear together, in one verse (Nehemiah 8:9), Nehemiah seems to play no part in the ceremonies described there.

Thus, there has been a lot of discussion among biblical scholars about the true relative dates of Ezra and Nehemiah, and little progress can really be made on this issue without more information than the Bible provides. In fact, given that Ezra's major activity seems to be to read 'the Law' to the people and, confusingly, this activity is reported not in the book of Ezra itself but in Nehemiah 8–9, many scholars have come to the conclusion that Ezra is actually a fictitious character, a kind of personification of 'the Law'. Indeed, it is interesting that when Jesus son of Sira later lists the great men of the history of Israel (Sirach 44–49), he does not mention Ezra at all, but only Nehemiah (Sirach 49:13).

Apart from the activities of Nehemiah, and of Ezra if he is really a historical figure, we know nothing about the life

Esther is the heroine of the book of Esther that tells the story of how the Jews in the Persian Empire were saved from destruction. It is set at the time when Xerxes (called Ahasuerus in the Old Testament) was king of Persia (486–464 BCE) and features Esther, a beautiful young Jewish woman married to the king, and her uncle Mordecai. The story goes that Mordecai uncovered a plot by Haman, the Persian Prime Minister, in which he had tricked the king into ordering the slaughter of all the Jews in the Persian Empire on a certain day. At the risk of her life, Esther reported this to the king and persuaded him to help save her people. As a result, the king had Haman executed and issued a decree allowing the Jews to defend themselves. After two days of fighting, the Jews had overpowered their enemies and celebrated their deliverance with feasting and prayers of thanksgiving. Today, this story forms the basis for the Jewish festival of Purim — *purim* being the Assyrian for 'lots' as it was by casting lots that Haman decided the day on which to order the Jewish slaughter. Interestingly, God is not mentioned once in the book of Esther, but Jews view the story as an excellent example of God's providence in guiding the events of history for his people, even though his presence is not obvious. However, it should also be noted that, whilst Xerxes is a historical character and the author displays some knowledge of Persian life and customs, most modern scholars consider the book a historical romance rather than a historical account. Some have even suggested that it was simply a story concocted for the feast of Purim, which originally had a different origin.

Ruth is a Moabite woman who, although she would be a foreigner in Israel, agreed to accompany her mother-in-law, Naomi, who wished to return to Bethlehem after the death of her husband and her sons. In Bethlehem, Ruth falls in love with Boaz, a rich relative of Naomi. At the end of the story, it turns out that Ruth was the great-grandmother of the great King David! Ruth is, therefore, an important example of a Gentile who displays great faith and trust in God and who is blessed by God. She is also a reminder that God is the God of all people, not just the Jews. The story is set during the period of the judges, but most modern scholars place the composition of the book after the Exile. Most also regard it as fictitious, perhaps composed to explain the presence of a Moabite in the genealogy of David or perhaps written as a protest against the attempts of Ezra and Nehemiah to force Jews to divorce their Gentile wives. For more about the book of Ruth see 5.4 'A Good Read?'

of the Jews under Persian rule. Some of the narrative books of the Old Testament, such as **Esther**, Jonah, and **Ruth**, may come from this time, as the book of Job probably does (at least in the form we have it today). However, as all these little tales are set in an imaginary past age they do not give us any certain picture of what Jewish life was like at the time. It is interesting, though, that both Ruth and Jonah show a receptive attitude towards foreigners that is not at all like Nehemiah's **xenophobia** — hinting that not everyone saw things as he did. It is also just possible that Malachi's opposition to divorce (Malachi 2:13–16) may have in mind the forced divorces that Nehemiah caused, rather than divorce as such.

Xenophobia is the deep mistrust and fear of foreigners.

THE HELLENISTIC AGE

After the death of Alexander the Great in 323 BCE, his successors divided his empire among themselves, but their hold on their territories tended to be unstable. The descendants of Ptolemy ruled from Egypt, and those of Seleucus from Syria, and both claimed the right to control Palestine. In 301 BCE a treaty assigned it to Seleucus, but Ptolemy seized it and he and his heirs ruled it as part of Egypt. But the heirs of Seleucus kept trying to get it back, and after a series of wars lasting through the third century they eventually succeeded in getting rid of Ptolemaic rule about 200 BCE. From then on, the Jews were ruled from Syria until a series of revolts gave them a brief spell of renewed independence.

It is important to realize that there was nothing very new in Palestine being fought over: it had always been a bone of contention between the powers of Egypt and of Asia. It is also important to see that, though in the third century the Jews were largely governed from Egypt and in the second from Syria, this did not mean that cultural influences changed much during the Hellenistic period.

In an important sense the whole Eastern Mediterranean after Alexander was a single cultural area. The different peoples spoke their own languages and lived by their own customs, both political and religious, but their culture was a mixture of local Middle Eastern traditions and the culture of Greece, forming a mix nowadays referred to as 'Hellenism'. The administrative language under both Ptolemies and Seleucids was Greek, which had supplanted Aramaic, the international language during the Persian Empire. People in Palestine spoke Aramaic to each other, but Greek to officials and other representatives of the government, and Greek was the language in which different peoples could communicate with each other. The best comparison is with American culture today. Throughout the western world, each nation has its own language, its own traditions, its own foods and customs. Yet when people communicate across national divides they increasingly do so in English, and they all eat hamburgers, listen to American pop songs, and watch American soap operas. Hellenism was like that: a vague, formless force that conditioned the way everyone in the Eastern Mediterranean

TABLE OF THE PTOLEMAIC AND SELEUCID KINGS

Ptolemy I	323–285 BCE	Seleucus I	312–280 BCE
Ptolemy II	285–246 BCE	Antiochus I	280–261 BCE
		Antiochus II	261–246 BCE
Ptolemy III	246–221 BCE	Seleucus II	246–226 BCE
Ptolemy IV	221–203 BCE	Seleucus III	226–223 BCE
Ptolemy V	203–181 BCE	Antiochus III	223–187 BCE
Ptolemy VI	181–146 BCE	Seleucus IV	187–175 BCE
		Antiochus IV	175–163 BCE
		Antiochus V	163–162 BCE
		Demetrius I	162–150 BCE
		Alexander Balas	150–145 BCE
		Demetrius II	145–138 BCE
Ptolemy VII	146–145 BCE	Antiochus VI	145–141 BCE
Ptolemy VIII	145–116 BCE	Antiochus VII	138–129 BCE
		Demetrius II	129–125 BCE

thought and acted, even when they did not realize it.

Furthermore, Jews did not live only in Palestine. Some, as we have seen, continued to live in Mesopotamia as descendants of those exiled in the sixth century. Others had settled in Egypt, where there was a flourishing Jewish colony on Elephantine Island (Jeb) near where the present Aswan Dam is located. We know of their life from many fragments of papyrus containing letters and other documents in Aramaic found in 1906–8. In later years, there was a large Jewish population in the great coastal city of Alexandria, among whom the author of the Wisdom of Solomon (in the Apocrypha) lived, as did the Jewish philosopher Philo (c. 20 BCE – 50 CE), a contemporary of St Paul.

> The word 'Diaspora' is used to denote Jews living outside Palestine. By the first century CE they greatly outnumbered those living in Palestine.

There is little in the Old Testament that definitely comes from the Ptolemaic period, that is, from the third century. Probably the books of Chronicles were written during this time. They are a reworking of the books of Samuel and Kings, with a nine-chapter preface — mostly made up of genealogical lists — taking the story back to Adam in a very brief way. Chronicles may occasionally draw on genuine historical tradition, but for the most part it is an account of the history of Israel as it should have happened. Stories in the older history books that are damaging to great reputations, such as David's adultery with Bathsheba, are omitted, and whole incidents are invented out of thin air, for example, Hezekiah's great Passover celebration in 2 Chronicles 30. Interestingly, there is no contemporary history produced in this period: the Chronicler retells the story up to the end of the Exile, but does not go on into the Second Temple period itself. It is possible that the books of Ezra and Nehemiah also received their final form in the Ptolemaic age.

In 200 BCE the Seleucid king Antiochus III defeated Ptolemy V, and took control of Palestine at last. Many Jews, especially the influential family called the Tobiads, had supported Antiochus, and were rewarded with tax concessions when he took over. There was no question of forbidding Jewish religious customs. Like almost all ancient conquerors, the Seleucids had no interest in what religious practices their subjects followed. All the time, however, Hellenism was making inroads into traditional faith and practice. Sophisticated Jews had begun to imitate Greek ways, and this led some of them to be less than wholehearted in their devotion to their religious traditions.

The book of Ecclesiastes or **Qoheleth** may come from the early second century BCE and, if so, it probably bears out the sceptical and reserved attitude towards traditional religious beliefs that Hellenism encouraged. For example, Qoheleth was doubtful about discerning God's hand in daily events even though he encouraged traditional religious customs with comments such as, 'Guard your steps when you go to the house of God' (Ecclesiastes 5:1) and 'When you make a vow to God, do not delay fulfilling it' (Ecclesiastes 5:4). In general, he was sceptical about theological speculation and concluded, 'for God is in heaven, and you upon earth; therefore let your words be few' (Ecclesiastes 5:2). In this period, Jews also began to enjoy the cultural and social habits that the Greeks had given to the world: music, art, competitive sport, fine dining. These things were not necessarily incompatible with Jewish faith, but they had not been characteristic of it, and a new Jewish upper class became, in the view of those who held to the old ways, more like Greeks than Jews.

Under Antiochus III's successor, Antiochus IV (175–163 BCE), this clash of cultures resulted in much bloodshed and eventually in significant political change. Antiochus IV was approached by Jason, the brother of the high priest, and asked to develop Jerusalem into a polis, the technical Greek term for a city organized along Greek lines, with institutions such as a gymnasium — a sports and social centre. Other parts of the package were that Jason would become high priest and that he would pay a large sum into Antiochus' funds. The offer proved irresistible, and so Jerusalem became essentially a Hellenistic city with a ruling high priest who was extremely friendly towards the Seleucid dynasty. However, after only a few years, Menelaus, who was a relative of Jason, paid even more to gain the high priesthood. He ousted Jason, exiled him, and tried to reverse the Hellenization process.

In 168 BCE these complex events took a new twist. Jason heard a mistaken report that Antiochus IV was dead; he had, in fact, been fighting a successful war in Egypt, but had been stopped by the Romans from taking control over the Ptolemaic kingdom. Jason attacked Jerusalem and made a failed attempt to oust Menelaus. Antiochus intervened and, with widespread slaughter, drove Jason out again. After this he seems to have decided, and no one really knows why, to suppress Judaism and to make sure that the Jews would be so humiliated and disheartened that they would never revolt again.

It was very unusual, even unprecedented, in the ancient world to suppress a religious culture: people were entirely tolerant of each other's religions, and even conquerors often

Qoheleth is the alternative name for the book of Ecclesiastes. 'Ecclesiastes' is the Greek translation of the Hebrew word *qoheleth,* which means 'preacher'.

The book called 2 Maccabees in the Apocrypha gives some gruesome descriptions of the martyrdom of people who broke the new laws of Antiochus IV declaring Jewish laws and customs illegal. Women who circumcised their children were paraded around the city with their children hanging round their necks before being thrown from the city wall. One man who refused to eat pork had his tongue cut out, his head scalped, and his hands and feet cut off, before being fried in a huge pan, all whilst his mother and brothers looked on!

The story of this Maccabean revolt forms the basis for the annual eight-day Jewish festival of Hanukkah. According to this, the Temple was in a shocking state of repair when the Jews finally drove Antiochus' soldiers out of the land. Whilst clearing up they found a small bottle of oil for the Temple oil lamp that was still pure and had the high priest's seal on it. There was only enough oil to keep the lamp burning for one day, but in fact it kept burning for eight days until new oil could be found. This was declared a miracle, and Jews today remind themselves of it by using a special candlestick, called a hanukkiah, during the festival of Hanukkah. Foods like doughnuts and potato-cakes, fried in oil, are also eaten to remind people of the miracle of the oil, and children play a game with a spinning top, called a dreidel, to remind them of the time when Antiochus IV tried to stop the Jews studying the Torah — the Hebrew letters on the spinning top stand for the phrase 'a great miracle happened there'. The festival reminds Jews not only of the heroic sacrifices made by those who accepted torture and death rather than break God's commandments, but also of the fact that God was faithful to his covenant and helped them overthrow their enemies so that Jewish religion and culture could be preserved.

TABLE OF THE HASMONEAN RULERS

Judas Maccabeus	166–160 BCE
Jonathan	160–142 BCE
Simon	142–134 BCE
John Hyrcanus	134–104 BCE
Aristobulus I	104–103 BCE
Alexander Jannaeus	103–76 BCE
Salome Alexandra	76–67 BCE
Aristobulus II	67–63 BCE
Hyrcanus II	63–40 BCE
Antigonus Mattathias	40–37 BCE

offered sacrifice to the gods of those they conquered to keep them favorable. In 167, however, Antiochus IV apparently declared Jewish customs illegal. Circumcising male babies, possessing scrolls of the Law, and even refusing to eat pork or to work on the Sabbath became criminal acts, punishable by the death penalty. Worst of all for the Jews, a pagan altar was established in the Temple and pigs offered in sacrifice on it to Antiochus' own Syrian god, Baal Shamem. Jews described this event as 'the abomination of desolation' (see Daniel 8:13, where NRSV translates 'the transgression that makes desolate').

If this was an attempt to crush the Jews, it misfired badly. Faced with this challenge to their ancestral traditions, a group of Jews led by a family called the Maccabees revolted. Their story is told in the book of the Apocrypha called 1 Maccabees, which is probably a nearly contemporary document — not free of bias, but reliable on the essential facts. Within three years they had reclaimed and purified the Temple. The Syrian army remained in Jerusalem, however, and battles continued from time to time: Judas Maccabeus, the first great leader, was killed in one of these, and replaced by his brother Jonathan.

By 140 BCE, with Antiochus long dead, a third Maccabean brother, Simon (Simeon), took over the high priesthood, and with him began a period of genuine Jewish independence — perhaps the first since some time in the seventh century. Simon issued a decree establishing that the high priest was also to be the political leader of the nation. He began what is called the Hasmonean dynasty (from Hasmon, an ancestor of the Maccabees). From 104 BCE, when Aristobulus I was high priest, even the title of 'king' once again began to be used. Despite much internal strife and bloodshed, the Hasmoneans managed to rule Judah for eighty years or so. However, in 63 BCE the Romans, who had been interfering in Judean affairs for some time, found a pretext to invade and besieged Jerusalem. The Roman general Pompey entered the Temple, though he did not destroy it, and he put an end to Judean independence. From this point on Judah became part of the emerging Roman Empire.

From the Seleucid and Maccabean periods the main writing in the Old Testament is the book of Daniel. The first six chapters of Daniel are stories about Jews at the court of a pagan king — Nebuchadnezzar or Darius, figures of legend by the second century BCE. Some of these stories may reflect conditions of life for THE Jews under Persian or Ptolemaic rule, but others definitely reflect the problems of the time of Antiochus. An example is the story of the 'burning fiery furnace' in Daniel 3, where Jews are to be punished by death for refusing to give up their religion and adopt that of their conqueror. In this case, of course, God miraculously delivers them. The rest of the book records visions which Daniel is supposed to have had in the sixth century, while in exile in Babylon, but which in fact present in a coded form the events of the Maccabean age and what preceded it. This is why nearly all scholars agree that Daniel in its present form must be a work from the second century BCE.

There are also two books in the Apocrypha from the later part of the Second Temple period: Sirach and the Wisdom of Solomon. The grandson of Jesus son of Sira, who translated his book and wrote a preface to it, tells us that he did this in the thirty-eighth year of the reign of Euergetes in Egypt — one of the Ptolemies, whose full name was Ptolemy VIII Physkon Euergetes. This would be 132 BCE, and the book itself must have been written soon after 180 BCE, since its long section on the praises of the ancestors concludes with a passage in praise of the high priest Simon (219–196), whom Jesus had evidently seen (Sirach 50:1–24). The Wisdom of Solomon almost certainly comes from the first century, and was written within the Jewish colony in Egypt. Such literature contains a great deal of evidence for the Hellenistic themes that were commonplace in Judaism at the close of what might be regarded as the Old Testament era.

 'From the time of the Maccabees through to the Christian era, Jewish history was dominated by the issues that emerged in the course of these early struggles with Hellenism. The twin issues of politics and religion were to become inextricably interwoven as the Jewish people tried to reconcile their aspirations for a society in which God would be all-important with the plain fact that their world was dominated by rulers with a different world-view and spirituality.' (John Drane, *Introducing the Old Testament*, Lion Publishing, 2000)

3.6 Digging Up the Old Testament
THE CONTRIBUTION OF ARCHAEOLOGY TO STUDY OF THE OLD TESTAMENT

THE BASICS

- The discovery, excavation, and interpretation of the many finds of the so-called 'biblical archaeologists' over the last few centuries have captured the imagination of readers of the Old Testament and informed their understanding of the text.
- Archaeology has a great deal to contribute to the debate about how much of the Old Testament might be fact and how much might be fiction, but any claims that archaeological evidence proves the Bible is true ought to be treated with caution.

ARCHAEOLOGY HAS UNEARTHED A wealth of information from excavations across the Bible lands of the ancient Near East, and it appears to have an endless fascination for people when linked to the Bible. Early expeditions to the Bible lands resulted in the discovery of certain treasures, but it was the late nineteenth century and the middle years of the twentieth century that saw the rise of a style of archaeology that called itself specifically 'biblical archaeology'. This was a natural title because those involved were concerned especially with what archaeology could contribute to a better understanding of the Bible, especially the Old Testament. However, the title 'biblical archaeology' seems to some people to suggest that its practitioners are primarily involved in an attempt to prove the accuracy of the Bible using archaeology and, for this reason, many scholars today prefer to use alternatives such as Near Eastern Archaeology. Whatever term is used, the past century has seen massive developments in the archaeological study of the Bible lands, and archaeological discoveries have the potential to enhance our knowledge and understanding of the Old Testament.

Archaeology is the study of the human past through the excavation and analysis of physical remains.

A **tell** (or tel) is an artificial mound that has been formed from the debris accumulated as a result of ancient cities being built on top of the remains of previous ones. 'Tel' comes from the Arabic word for 'hillock' and is often incorporated into place names in the Middle East.

WHERE AND HOW TO DIG?
It is often said that the eyes are the archaeologist's best tool. A **tell** can be an obvious indication of a potential site, but accurate observation of even the smallest detail of the appearance

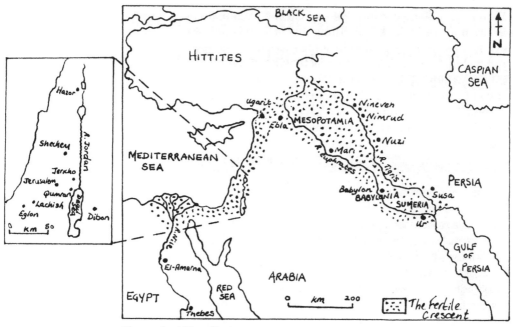

The ancient Near East

of the landscape can give clues as to where there may be a structure buried. For example, earth above a buried wall may appear lighter than the surrounding earth or the crops above it may grow less well than others in the same area. This is typically because the soil above a buried structure contains less moisture and dries out quicker than the surrounding soil. Today, techniques such as aerial photography and the use of a **magnetometer** or **resistivity survey** serve to help an archaeologist decide where to dig, but the early pioneers of biblical archaeology, such as **Austen Henry Layard** (1817–94) had much less to go on. Many simply chose sites based on careful observation of the landscape and on place names, often attempting to identify the Hebrew name of a place in the Bible with reference to its traditional, local name.

Once a place is chosen, the excavation needs to be carefully carried out — earth needs to be dug away and sifted

A **magnetometer** measures variations in the earth's magnetism and is able to record evidence of where humans may have disturbed the soil. **Resistivity surveys** measure variations in the electrical resistance of the earth's surface and record evidence of human disturbance. Surveys of this type can give an archaeologist an idea of the basic layout of a whole site.

Austen Henry Layard (1817–94) was not a professional archaeologist but a British adventurer who discovered and excavated the ruins of Nimrud, from 1845 to 1851. His excavations produced thousands of clay tablets with cuneiform writing from the library of Ashurbanipal (king of Assyria 668–629 BCE) and included the Black Obelisk of Shalmaneser III (king of Assyria 858–824 BCE), which shows the Israelite king Jehu bringing tribute to Shalmaneser III. In addition, he discovered nearly three kilometres of stone carvings from the palace of Sennacherib (king of Assyria 704–681 BCE), including images of the siege of Lachish in the time of King Hezekiah of Judah. Much of what Layard discovered he managed to ship back to his patrons at the British Museum where it is today. His discoveries provided important information about Assyrian history, religion, and society and made a key contribution to people's understanding of the biblical world of the Old Testament.

with infinite care to be certain that objects and fragments of objects are not overlooked. Everything that is found ought to be recorded and preserved, and in some cases it is as important to be alert to what is not there as to what is. When the British archaeologist Sir Leonard Woolley (1880–1960) was working at Ur in the 1920s and 1930s, he spotted an unusually shaped hole in the ground as he was excavating some tombs. He poured plaster-of-paris into the void and thereby created a complete plaster cast of a wooden harp whose substance had long since decayed. When he excavated the plaster cast he even discovered that the original bull's head made of copper and the shell plaque which decorated the front of the harp had stuck to the plaster, and this eventually enabled the whole piece to be reconstructed.

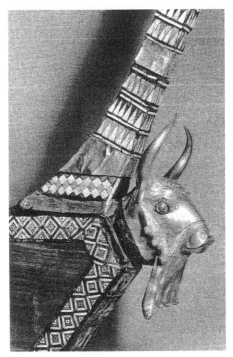

A reconstruction of the wooden harp discovered by Leonard Woolley at Ur in the 1920s

DATING THE FINDS

The basic classification of archaeological eras in Palestine and their relation to Old Testament chronology are set out in the accompanying table, and it can be easy to identify and date quite accurately some of the items discovered by archaeologists. For example, many coins, **bullae** or inscriptions include clear dates or references to people or events that can be verified and dated from other sources. However, whilst whatever an archaeologist finds may have an architectural or artistic value in itself, ruined buildings, **potsherds**, and jewellery, etc., can contribute much more to our understanding if their origin and date can be identified.

The most basic way of dating an item is related to the manner in which a site is excavated, with archaeologists digging trenches on their site to reveal the different layers (strata) in the earth, similar to cutting a slice of sponge cake and revealing its layers. Working on the basic idea that each layer is deposited after the one below it, it is possible to work out at least the relative ages of the layers and, therefore, any items found in them. However, the usefulness of **stratigraphy** is highly dependent on careful digging and meticulous observation and record keeping — for once an item is removed

Bullae (the singular is 'bulla') are pieces of clay used as seals for papyrus documents. The seal often has an impression that may include the title or name of the owner.

A **potsherd** (pronounced potsherd) is a broken piece of pottery.

Stratigraphy is the study of the relative position of strata (layers) in the ground as a means of establishing their dates.

Flinders Petrie (1853–1942) was a British archaeologist who specialized in Egyptology. However, on a visit to Palestine in 1890 he worked on the excavation of Tell el-Hesi (believed by nineteenth-century scholars to be ancient Lachish but now thought rather to be Eglon) and began work on classifying pottery by age and style according to the different layers of earth in which it was found. Later, by comparing pottery from different excavation sites, he catalogued typical types of pottery that could be accurately dated and created a 'ceramic index'. In the 1960s, W. F. Albright (see below) described him as 'the greatest single excavating genius of modern times'.

Kathleen Kenyon (1906–78) was a British archaeologist who is particularly famous for her excavations at Jericho and the old city of Jerusalem in the 1950s and 1960s. Following claims by an earlier excavator (John Garstang) that he had unearthed the original walls of Jericho that had collapsed for Joshua (Joshua 6) she excavated the area in 1952. By careful analysis of the layers and of the pottery finds, she concluded that Jericho had been destroyed a number of decades before 1500 BCE and not at the time traditionally ascribed to Joshua.

from the soil and the layer of soil dug away, the evidence is gone for good. As early as 1890, during his excavations of Tell el-Hesi, **Flinders Petrie** (1853–1942) identified the importance of the relationship of the finds, mainly pottery, to the different layers of earth in which they were found. Later, the renowned archaeologist **Kathleen Kenyon** (1906–78) came to be referred to as 'the mistress of stratigraphy' for her use and development of this method in her excavations in Jericho and Jerusalem. Of course, modern archaeologists also have the benefits of laboratory tests, such as Radiocarbon/Carbon-14 dating and Thermoluminescence dating, in order to help them establish the age of the items they excavate. Any item that can be dated, in whatever way, can then be used to help establish a date for a particular layer of an excavation.

CRACKING THE CODES

One result of the efforts of archaeologists working in the Bible lands has been the discovery of hundreds and thousands of ancient texts in different languages. Being able to date these finds is important, but being able to decipher what these texts say is perhaps the real key to unlocking the world of the Old Testament. Some texts are preserved on clay, some on **papyrus**, and some carved into stone, but they are not always clear or intact, and the majority of the languages in which they are written are unknown to those who unearth them. Cracking the codes of these languages is obviously an extremely important task, but it is also an extremely difficult task, not least of all because a single language can be written in more than one script and one script can be used to write more than one language! So, a text is usually described in terms of its script and its language. For example, a text might be described as '**cuneiform** Babylonian' or 'alphabetic Phoenician'.

A TABLE OF BASIC ARCHAEOLOGICAL ERAS IN PALESTINE

Archaeological Era		Dates	Old Testament Periods/Key Events *
Paleolithic		before c. 8000 BCE	
Neolithic		c. 8000–4000 BCE	
Chalcolithic		c. 4000–3200 BCE	
Bronze Age	Early	c. 3200–2150 BCE	
	Middle	c. 2150–1550 BCE	The Patriarchal Era?
	Late	c. 1550–1200 BCE	The Exodus
Iron Age	I	c. 1200–1000 BCE	The Settlement (Joshua & Judges) and Rise of the Monarchy
	II	c. 1000–800 BCE	The Monarchy
	III	c. 800–587 BCE	
Babylonian Period		c. 587–539 BCE	The Exile
Persian Period		c. 539–332 BCE	The Return to Jerusalem & Building of the Second Temple
Hellenistic Period		c. 332–63 BCE	The Maccabean Revolt
Roman Period		c. 63 BCE–324 CE	

*Although you will find variations, this represents the general views of many biblical scholars.

In simple terms, the main scripts used in the texts from the Bible lands can divided into three categories:

Pictographic — in which pictorial symbols represent objects, words or phrases, for example in the hieroglyphs of Egypt.

Sa Rā (son of the god Ra)

(Egyptian)

ānkh djet (Who lives eternally)

Cuneiform — in which wedge-shaped marks represent syllables or word-signs, for example in Sumerian, Babylonian, and Assyrian.

god
heaven   (Assyrian)

man   (Assyrian)

Alphabetic — in which a set of symbols is used to represent individual sounds which are combined to form words, for example in Moabite, Phoenician, and Hebrew.

arrowhead of
ʾAda'
son of   (Phoenician)
Ba'la'

The understanding of such ancient languages is an on-going process, but, thanks to the pioneering work of the likes of Jean-François Champollion (1790–1832) and Henry Rawlinson (1810–95), the deciphering of hieroglyphs from Egypt and cuneiform Babylonian remains one of the great achievements of nineteenth-century scholarship.

IMPORTANT FINDS FOR BIBLICAL ARCHAEOLOGY

Over the years, archaeology in the Bible lands has produced a huge amount of evidence relevant to biblical studies, and much is on public display in museums around the world today. Excavating sites that are associated with particular biblical stories, like Shechem, Lachish, Jericho, and Jerusalem itself, reveal much about ancient times and the way people lived in these places. However, much of what is excavated — city walls, houses, statues, pottery, etc. — might be termed 'mute' archaeology when compared with those finds which incorporate texts. These texts can be classed as some of the most interesting finds for students of the Old Testament as they allow people from the past to come alive and tell their story in their own words. Such finds can throw a great deal of light on the world of the Old Testament and, tantaliz-

Papyrus (plural papyri) is a writing material used in ancient Egypt made from the stem of the papyrus plant native to the River Nile. The stalks of the plant, which are three to five metres high, were dried and split along their length before being cut to size and glued together to form sheets of paper.

Cuneiform writing is formed by using a series of wedge-shaped impressions in clay.

Radiocarbon dating/Carbon-14 dating is a laboratory test based on the principle that all organic materials absorb from the atmosphere the radioactive isotope carbon-14 (fourteen being the atomic weight of this particular carbon atom). Since carbon-14 decays at a known rate, a sample of an object can be tested to determine how much carbon-14 is left and, therefore, roughly how many years it has been since the sample was living. This method has proved a useful tool in biblical archaeology but is not possible or appropriate in every case as the test destroys the sample. There is also always a margin of error with this method, sometimes considerable with extremely ancient samples, and this is why a ± symbol is used to express a radiocarbon date.

Thermoluminescence dating is a laboratory test based on the principle that certain elements in clay store energy over time in the form of electrons which, when heated to very high temperatures, are released and cause the emission of light. The greater the intensity of the luminescence (light), the greater the age of the item. This is a useful test for pottery or clay items that have been fired; the results are generally accurate to ± 10 to 15 per cent.

Excavation of walls at Jericho
(Photo: J. Bowden)

ingly, some appear to contain direct references to biblical characters and events. Some of the most important finds are already detailed elsewhere in this book but the following are also worth mentioning.

Execration Texts

The Execration Texts is a name given to a group of texts discovered in Egypt which appear on potsherds and clay figurines and date from the twentieth to the eighteenth centuries BCE. On each of these is written a curse (or 'execration') against a ruler, place, or peoples. It was believed that damaging these items and giving them a ritual burial would bring ill-fortune on the ruler, place, or peoples named; and this may well have been done before military campaigns to ensure the victory of the Pharaoh over his opponents. The texts are of interest to biblical scholars because they include many names of biblical places and their rulers.

The Ras Shamra Tablets

Excavations in Ras Shamra, in present-day Syria, unearthed the ruins of the ancient city of Ugarit. A farmer ploughing his field discovered the site accidentally in 1928. When he tried to move a large stone out of his way, he revealed a passage leading to an underground room which turned out to be a tomb. When the site was more fully investigated, hundreds of cuneiform texts were found. They revealed not only information about the day-to-day business of government but also many stories about the gods the people worshipped, their religious prayers and rituals. Such a find has enabled us to gain a better understanding of the myths that were native to the area and to compare them with the mythological stories of the Mesopotamians.

The Tell El-Amarna Letters

More than four hundred cuneiform tablets were discovered in Tell El-Amarna in Egypt in 1887 as a result of an Egyptian woman digging for earth to take away to enrich her own field for farming. These tablets include diplomatic letters

The storm-god Baal with a thunder-bolt, from Ugarit (Ras Shamra), Assyrian School / Louvre / Bridgeman

sent to the kings of Egypt in the fourteenth century from the kings of small city-states in Palestine. They complain to the king of Egypt about the problem of groups of foreigners — whom the letter writers call Habiru — who were roaming the land and attacking towns. Although most scholars no longer believe a clear connection can be made between these Habiru and the Hebrews of the Old Testament, the letters give us an interesting insight into Egyptian administration in the unsettled conditions of Palestine in the fourteenth century BCE. The Tell El-Amarna tablets are preserved in the Vorderasiatisches Museum in Berlin, the Cairo Museum in Egypt, the Louvre Museum in Paris, and the British Museum in London.

Detail from the Black Obelisk found at Nimrud, Iraq, Assyrian
British Museum

The Sheshonq Inscription

On the walls of the Amun Temple in Karnak, Egypt, there is a list of cities, including Jerusalem, which Pharaoh Sheshonq I (935–914 BCE) attacked during his military campaigns in 918 BCE aimed at returning Israel and Judah to Egyptian control. These attacks appear in the biblical record in 1 Kings 14:25 and 2 Chronicles 12:1–9; this is perhaps the earliest incident in Israel's history which is reflected in an extrabiblical source.

The Black Obelisk of Shalmaneser III

Discovered by Austen Henry Layard in 1845 during excavation of Nimrud, this black basalt, two-metre-high **obelisk** is covered with relief sculptures and cuneiform inscriptions which celebrate the military successes of Shalmaneser III, king of Assyria (858–824 BCE). The caption above the second series of relief sculptures identifies the scene as Jehu, king of the northern kingdom of Israel (841–814 BCE), bringing **tribute** to Shalmaneser III. Although this particular incident is not mentioned in the Old Testament record of Jehu's reign in 2 Kings 9–10, the inscription is particularly interesting because it refers to Jehu as 'son of the house of Omri'. This indicates that Omri, king of Israel (885–874 BCE), had been such a prominent king that the Assyrians referred to Israel as 'the house of Omri' — an interesting point given that the biblical record of Omri's reign warrants only six verses! The Black Obelisk is on display in the British Museum in London.

An **obelisk** is a pillar of stone set up as a monument. It usually has four sides and tapers to a point at the top.

In the ancient world, one ruler often made offerings of gold, silver, or other valuable items to another ruler in recognition of his superiority. Such an offering is called a **tribute.**

The Samaria Ostraca

Around 1910, a group of **ostraca** were found in the store rooms of the royal palace in Samaria. They probably come from the late eighth century BCE, the later period of the northern kingdom of Israel, and are mainly commercial texts dealing with the payment of taxes in kind and noting the receipt of various deliveries of oil and wine. One interesting

Ostraca (the singular is 'ostracon') are pieces of pottery with writing on them, usually a letter or memo.

The II September 2003 edition of the science journal Nature included a report on the Carbon-I4 analysis of wood, coal, and ash found in the plaster walls of the Siloam tunnel in Jerusalem, and on the tests on the uranium and thorium present in stalactites on the tunnel's ceiling. The tests showed that the tunnel was dug around 700 BCE, a date consistent with the biblical record.

feature is that they include many names which contain the divine name Baal, helping to confirm that Baal-worship was common, as the prophets tell us.

The Siloam Inscription (Hezekiah's Tunnel)

In 1838, archaeologists first surveyed a 534-metre-long tunnel built to bring water from a spring outside Jerusalem into the 'pool of Siloam' in the city. However, it was not until 1880 that an inscription was found just inside the tunnel leading from the pool. It describes how the two work parties, who had begun digging the tunnel from opposite ends, met in the middle. The tunnel and the inscription are dated to the time of Hezekiah, king of the southern kingdom of Judah (715/714–697/696 BCE), and appear to relate to the deeds of Hezekiah recorded in 2 Kings 20:20. The inscription is now in the Istanbul Museum in Turkey.

The Lachish Letters

In the 1930s a British team discovered a collection of letters written in black ink on potsherds in the ruins of ancient Lachish. They date from the late seventh and early sixth centuries BCE, the era of the prophet Jeremiah. These letters are part of the correspondence between military outposts and the military commander at Lachish. They give an insight into the Babylonian advance on the city which is also described in 2 Kings 24–25 and Jeremiah 37–39. Examples of these ostraca are preserved in the British Museum in London.

The Dead Sea Scrolls

The Dead Sea Scrolls is the collective name given to a large number of manuscripts traditionally thought to have been discovered by a Bedouin herdsman in caves at Qumran near the northwestern edge of the Dead Sea in 1947. Until their discovery there were no manuscripts of any of our Old Testament texts older than the late first millennium CE, but this collection includes some copies dating back more than two thousand years. This makes them some of the earliest manuscripts of the Old Testament and, since there are so few differences in the text from the later copies, they are an important find in terms of showing the accuracy with which Hebrew scribes copied their holy Scriptures. A scroll of seventeen leather sheets that contains all sixty-six chapters of Isaiah is among the manuscripts and, with others, is on display today in the Shrine of the Book in Jerusalem.

INTERPRETING THE FINDS

Two prominent figures in the original development of a systematic approach to archaeology in the Bible lands were **William Foxwell Albright** (1891–1971) and **George Ernest Wright** (1909–74). Together, they can be seen as the founders of a largely American school of biblical archaeology, and many of their findings were presented in an accessible form in the *History of Israel* written in 1960 by John Bright. (There

William Foxwell Albright (1891–1971) was an American archaeologist whose influence in the excavation of the Bible lands was so huge that he is sometimes called the father of modern biblical archaeology. He went to Palestine in the 1920s and championed the importance of the integration of the disciplines of biblical and Near Eastern historical, geographical, and literary studies into archaeology. Building on the earlier work of others, Albright also established a new standard for archaeological publications, and refined and promoted the study of pottery and archaeological strata by comparing the results from a wide range of sites both inside and outside Palestine. His great pupil was **George Ernest Wright** (1909–74), who became the founding editor of the magazine *Biblical Archaeologist* (still published today under the title *Near Eastern Archaeology*) and who is noted for his excavations of Shechem in the 1950s and 1960s. Together, they emphasized the wide-scale exposure of complete architectural units in archaeological excavations — a method that became known as the Albright-Wright method.

Ron Wyatt (1933–99) was an American nurse anaesthetist with a passion for biblical archaeology. He was a member of the Seventh Day Adventist Church and believed that God had called him to find certain biblical treasures. He is particularly famous for his claims to have located Noah's Ark, the sites of Sodom and Gomorrah, complete with brimstones, the point at which the Israelites crossed the Red Sea during the Exodus, the true site of Mount Sinai, and the Ark of the Covenant. Many have called him a charlatan and a liar, and his discoveries have been denounced as frauds, but he also has a huge popular following.

were further editions in 1972 and 1981.) This essentially retells the biblical story, but illustrates it from the findings of archaeology.

Biblical archaeologists in this tradition did not claim, as various more maverick characters, such as **Ron Wyatt** (1933–99), still do claim from time to time, to have discovered the remains of Noah's Ark or the original Ark of the Covenant. However, they did claim that archaeology could strongly illuminate the world revealed by the biblical text, and that in general terms archaeological findings showed that many biblical stories rested on a historical foundation. As Dr Werner Keller claimed in the subtitle of the classic book *The Bible as History*, written in 1956, *Archaeology confirms the Book of Books*!

According to Genesis 7:1–8:19, God ordered Noah to build a huge boat (roughly 133 metres long by 22 metres wide and 13 metres high) large enough to take on board his wife, his three sons and their wives, and two of every living creature. This boat has traditionally been called an ark — from Latin translation (*arca*) of the Hebrew word *tebah* — and those who have tried to find its remains are sometimes rather irreverently called 'arkologists'! The majority of expeditions to find it have been centred on Mount Ararat in Turkey, and as recently as 1997 it was claimed that American satellites and spy planes had taken photographs which showed a boat-shaped mark under the ice at the summit of the mountain. However, most serious scholars would say that, even if the biblical account is a historical account of a factual event, there is, as yet, no credible evidence that Noah's Ark has survived to the present day. For more information about the biblical story of the flood see 3.1 'Tall Stories?'

The Ark of the Covenant (not to be confused with Noah's Ark which uses a different Hebrew word!) is an important part of Old Testament history. It was a large wooden box covered with gold which was constructed according to God's specific instructions (Exodus 25:10–22) and said to contain the two tablets on which God had written the Law. Before the Temple was built in Jerusalem and it was placed in the inner part, the people of Israel carried the Ark with them as a sign of God's presence with them. Tradition has it that the Ark was lost when the Babylonians attacked Jerusalem in 586 BCE; the majority of scholars have yet to be convinced by any of the alternative theories. However, the Ark has a certain mystery and fascination as a biblical artifact; some have tried to locate it, and there has been much speculation about whether, in fact, it still exists. Some believe it is hidden in secret chambers under the Temple Mount in Jerusalem, although the Muslims who control this area have forbidden excavations there. Another idea, taken from the second book of Maccabees (2:4–6), is that the prophet Jeremiah saved the Ark from the Babylonians by hiding it in a cave in a mountain — possibly Mount Nebo. Ron Wyatt even claimed to have found it, together with other items from the Temple, underneath the hill in Jerusalem on which some believe Jesus was crucified. The whereabouts of the Ark even inspired the adventure film *Raiders of the Lost Ark* (1981), which has the Ark hidden in a government warehouse in the USA!

Yigael Yadin (1917–84) was an archaeologist who combined his scholarly career with an active role in politics and was for a time Deputy Prime Minister of Israel. He led many major archaeological expeditions in Israel, including at Hazor, where, in line with the biblical record of I Kings 9:15, he assigned the gates excavated to the time of King Solomon. He was also noted for his work on the Dead Sea Scrolls.

Patriarchs is a term used in biblical studies to describe the key ancestors or father figures of the Israelites, specifically Abraham, Isaac, Jacob, and Jacob's twelve sons after whom the later tribes of Israel were named.

Of course, archaeology is extremely unlikely ever to prove the historical truth of individual incidents mentioned in the biblical text — for example, that David really did kill Goliath. Moreover, it can never verify crucial issues of belief — for example, it might prove that a temple once stood in Jerusalem but it cannot prove that God dwelt there! However, the 'Albright School' argued that archaeology can illuminate the periods in which incidents are said to have taken place, and can show whether or not the Old Testament's account is plausible. Such an approach continued in much early Israeli archaeology with archaeologists, such as **Yigael Yadin** (1917–84), who understandably had an interest especially in those sites which showed evidence of early Israelite settlement in the land. Like the American school, such archaeologists also tended to argue that archaeological findings often supported the biblical text. As a result, they were relatively optimistic about the historicity of the biblical accounts and their reconstructions of the history of Israel stick quite closely to them.

This contrasts sharply with a considerable scepticism about the historicity of biblical stories in much German-speaking scholarship in the twentieth century. To put it in a very simple form, German scholars tended to think that you could study how the stories of a particular period in the history of Israel developed and that you might be able to recover their oldest forms, but that you could not really decide how historically accurate those stories are. In some cases, German reconstructions of the history of Israel were quite at odds with the story the Old Testament itself tells. For example, the stories of the **patriarchs** were viewed by some as fictitious tales projected back in time to a legendary past and were described as no more than a 'glorified mirage'.

These issues continue to be relevant today and are part of the ongoing debate over the historicity of the Old Testament. The impact of such issues on archaeology are clearly highlighted in the reaction to two relatively recent discoveries, the so-called 'House of David' and King Jehoash inscriptions.

In 1993–94 excavations at Tel Dan, in the Golan Heights of northern Israel, revealed a monument made of basalt which referred to Judah as 'the house of David' (*bytdwd* in Aramaic consonants). Some scholars have concluded that this is an ancient reference to the biblical King David, and that it confirms his importance. But others argue that we cannot be sure *dwd* means the biblical David — it could be some other ruler of that name, or it might not even be a proper name at all (there are no capital letters in Hebrew and Aramaic) but a common noun meaning 'beloved'. In previous years biblical archaeologists might well have argued straightaway that the Tel Dan inscription confirms the biblical stories about David, the first king of Judah. Nowadays, however, many are more conservative in their evaluations of such a find — the monument could be a forgery and, even if it is genuine, it is possible to hold the position that all the biblical stories about 'David' are later than this monument, and are made up to create a history for an otherwise unknown king.

The Jehoash inscription is a piece of black sandstone, 27 centimetres long, 22 centimetres wide and 7 centimetres thick, which was allegedly found near the walls of the Temple Mount in Jerusalem and was first shown to an expert in 2001. The fifteen lines of Hebrew text record contributions of silver for repairs to the Temple by Jehoash, king of the southern kingdom of Judah (835–796 BCE), and this very closely parallels the biblical records in 2 Kings 12:4–16 and 2 Chronicles 24:4–14. On the surface, this is an amazing find — it is the first royal inscription of an Israelite king ever found, it supports the historicity of 2 Kings, and it may even have modern political implications for Jewish claims to the Temple Mount! However, it is also a very controversial find, principally because its **provenance** is unclear and because its owner wishes to remain anonymous. **Geologists** who have examined it say that it is authentic and that the chemical composition and coverage of the patina are convincing. Some even explain the tiny globules of gold and carbon particles found in the **patina** as the result of the burning down of the Temple in 586 BCE. On the other hand, eminent **palaeographers** and **epigraphers** say that the shape of some of the letters and the style of the language suggest it is a forgery!

Such archaeological finds always seem to capture the imagination of the public and the media, and support can still be found for the views of the 'Albright School' which predominated in the last century. However, in recent years, there has been a marked swing in scholarly opinion. There has tended to be more caution about the role archaeology can play and, consequently, histories of Israel such as Bright's are now rather dated and are viewed as probably being more optimistic about how much we can know of Israel's history than is really justified. As a result, a number of scholars have argued that study of the archaeology and of the text ought not to be undertaken with an assumption that they will be mutually supportive. Instead, what can be known from archaeology should be laid out entirely without reference to the biblical data; the biblical texts ought to be studied entirely without reference to the archaeology; and then — and only then — may one be compared with the other. Otherwise, it is argued, the text creates prejudices which the archaeology is brought in to confirm. Thus, when evidence for massive destruction is discovered, it must be dated purely by archaeological methods; it must not be dated by looking for a period in which the biblical record says that a destruction occurred, for example, as the result of an attack by the invading Israelites under Joshua. Equally, we must ask about the date of the texts that speak of such invasions, and check whether they are real historical records or legends. After all, the story could be a later attempt to explain a ruined site which already existed — in other words, it could be an **aetiology** rather than a real historical record. Only if the

The **provenance** of an archaeological item refers to the details relating to its excavation and subsequent ownership. There is generally no issue of provenance for items from legal archaeological excavations because detailed site records exist and items eventually pass into the hands of authorized museums which catalogue them accurately. However, items which simply appear on the antiquities market or surface in private collections, and which may have been looted or scavenged from excavations, often have their provenance, and therefore their authenticity, questioned.

A **geologist** is someone who specializes in the study of the composition, structure, and origin of rocks.

The **patina** is a thin film caused by age that covers the surface of ancient objects. It is often analysed in order to help determine the age of an object.

A **palaeographer** is someone who specializes in the study of writing from the past, particularly in the shape and form of the letters.

An **epigrapher** is someone who specializes in the study of the language and form of ancient inscriptions.

An **aetiology**, based on the Greek word *aitia* which means 'cause', is an explanation of the origins of something.

independently studied archaeological and textual material both point to the same period can we begin to say that the archaeology 'supports' the text.

Nevertheless, many people may still feel that there is currently some undue scepticism about the value of archaeological finds in some quarters. However, it is a caution against being too quick to jump from archaeology into the biblical text and back again without looking before you leap. Imagine that in many centuries' time someone unearths a document referring to a London theatre as 'the home of Cinderella'. Scholars at that time might then say that this confirms that Cinderella, about whom (we can imagine) the stories are still known, must have been a real person who lived in the period from which the document came. The archaeology 'confirms' the stories — yet we know that this would really be a false conclusion, because the stories are obviously fictitious! The existence of a historical document referring to these stories would not make them any more factual; it would only confirm that they (or some other stories about the person of that name) were known about. The parallel is not exact, but it does warn us to be on our guard.

Interpreting archaeological evidence and relating it to the Old Testament is, therefore, no easy task, and it is perhaps also wise to remember that what archaeology has so far unearthed is surely no more than an accidentally discovered sample of what once existed. New discoveries and new technologies may yet allow archaeology to provide us with new insights into the world of the Old Testament.

Section 4

The Institutions of the Old Testament

4.1 The Social Scene
THE SOCIAL LIFE OF ANCIENT ISRAEL

THE BASICS

- Although information about the social life of ancient Israel comes mostly from the Old Testament, and is very sketchy in places, there is information to be gleaned about the structure of Israelite society.
- The role of kings, civil servants, wise men, priests, prophets, and the status of women and children can also be inferred from various Old Testament texts.

T O UNDERSTAND THE LITERATURE of any nation it is important to have some idea of the social setting behind it. For example, we should miss a lot in reading the plays and poetry of William Shakespeare (1554–1616) if we knew nothing about ordinary life for people like him during the reign of Elizabeth I of England (1558–1603). Where the Old Testament is concerned most of our evidence for the social setting comes from within the text, though there is some material from other cultures of the Middle East that can throw light on how Israel is likely to have organized its life.

So, we need to ask questions such as these:

- How were the people organized and governed?
- What was the role of different people in society — the wise, priests, prophets?
- What was ordinary family life like?

Since the Old Testament covers a period of perhaps 1,000 years, it is only to be expected that there will have been changes in all these areas. However, although evidence is often skimpy, answers to such questions can at least be sketched for some periods.

The word **exodus** literally means 'way out' and refers to the departure of the Israelites from Egypt under the leadership of Moses.

An **amphictyony** is a confederation of neighbouring tribes or states focused on worship at a central sacred shrine and primarily formed for the purpose of self-defence. Such a formation was used by the Greek city-states centuries later.

A **covenant** is a solemn, binding, mutual agreement between two parties; the covenants between God and his people are an important feature of the Old Testament. For more information on this, see 2.2 'The Chosen People'.

The **Ark of the Covenant** was a large wooden box covered with gold which was constructed according to God's specific instructions (Exodus 25:10–22) and said to contain the two tablets on which God had written the Law. For more about this, see 3.6 'Digging Up the Old Testament'.

 'Not only does the Old Testament provide no support, but the cultural and chronological separation of Israel from the Greek and Italian amphyctionies argues against the use of the analogy.' (John H. Hayes in *Israelite and Judaean History*, ed. J.H. Hayes and J. Maxwell-Miller, SCM, 1977)

 'Early Israel was neither a racial nor a national unit, but a confederation of tribes united in covenant with Yahweh.' (John Bright, *A History of Israel*, SCM, 1960)

The Old Testament says that there were twelve tribes, each descended from the twelve sons of Jacob — Asher, Benjamin, Gad, Issachar, Joseph, Judah, Levi, Naphtali, Reuben, Simeon, and Zebulun (Genesis 49; Deuteronomy 33). However, in some places in the Old Testament, the tribe of Levi is excluded from the list because it had a special status as priests in the Temple and no ancestral land, and the tribe of Joseph is divided into two tribes, named after Joseph's sons, Ephraim and Manasseh (e.g. Numbers 1:5–16).

HOW WERE THE PEOPLE ORGANIZED AND GOVERNED?

Tribes, clans, and families

Before Solomon and subsequent kings organized Israel and Judah into nation-states, the people of Israel were apparently divided into 'tribes'. When they entered the land after the **Exodus**, the book of Joshua recounts that each tribe was given a specific section of the new land in which to settle. The way these tribes then related to one another is a matter of debate, but some scholars, following the work of Martin Noth (1902–68), have suggested that at the time of the settlement these tribes existed as an **amphictyony**, bound together by the **covenant** and with the **Ark of the Covenant** as their focal point. Such a 'tribal league' arrangement was a rather loose form of government but meant that the tribes were united under God and would unite against a common enemy. However, other scholarship holds that the evidence for an amphictyony in ancient Israel is rather slim. They point out that the tribes, if indeed they existed in such a structured way, were too geographically scattered for such a confederation, and they point to textual evidence, for example in Judges 12:1–6, that highlights inter-tribal rivalry and the fact that it was not always easy to get tribes to act together. After the reign of Solomon, such friction contributed to the division between the tribes into the southern kingdom of Judah (formed with the tribes Judah and Benjamin) and the northern kingdom of Israel (formed by the other ten tribes).

However, whatever the exact nature of the organization of these tribes, the sense of belonging to a particular tribe seems to have been important and continued long after this had stopped being the way the nation was organized: Paul, in the first century CE, can still refer to himself as a member of the tribe of Benjamin (Philippians 3:5). Tribes were divided into clans and clans were divided into families, and we can see this structure clearly in some of the stories about early Israel. For example, in Joshua 7 there is a story about a man, Achan, who stole some goods that should have been destroyed after the capture of Jericho. Joshua uses the sacred lot to discover who is to blame:

So Joshua rose early in the morning, and brought Israel near tribe by tribe, and the tribe of Judah was taken. He brought near the clans of Judah, and the clan of the Zerahites was taken; and he brought near the clan of the Zerahites, family by family, and Zabdi was taken. And he brought near his household one by one, and Achan son of Carmi son of Zabdi son of Zerah, of the tribe of Judah, was taken.

(Joshua 7:16–18)

Similarly, when Saul is chosen as king by Samuel, he protests, 'I am only a Benjaminite, from the least of the tribes of Israel, and my family is the humblest of all the families of the tribe of Benjamin' (1 Samuel 9:21). In this case, the clan is not mentioned but it is clear that families were seen as a subdivision of the tribe.

After the **Exile**, the tribal structure seems to have no longer operated in any functional way, but the main division of the nation was still by family, literally by 'fathers' houses'. We see this when, in seeking to establish the truth about the foreign wives of Jews, 'Ezra the priest selected men, heads of families, according to their families, each of them designated by name' (Ezra 10:16).

ADMINISTRATION AND JUSTICE — THE ROLE OF THE ELDERS

In the pre-exilic period, being the head of a house was probably the qualification for taking a full part in the administration of towns and cities. The 'elders' who met inside the gate of the town, both to constitute a local council and to hear legal cases, would have been chosen from among these adult men — the kind of people envisaged in the Ten Commandments, who have a wife, children, slaves, livestock, and elderly parents who must be looked after. However, although the Old Testament provides little evidence about the administrative processes, the book of Job may give us some idea of what a council of elders was like:

> 'When I went out to the gate of the city,
>   when I took my seat in the square,
> the young men saw me and withdrew,
>   and the aged rose up and stood;
> the nobles refrained from talking,
>   and laid their hands on their mouths;
> the voices of princes were hushed,
>   and their tongues stuck to the roof of their mouths.
> When the ear heard, it commended me,
>   and when the eye saw, it approved;
> because I delivered the poor who cried,
>   and the orphan who had no helper.
> The blessing of the wretched came upon me,
>   and I caused the widow's heart to sing for joy.
> I put on righteousness, and it clothed me;
>   my justice was like a robe and a turban.
> I was eyes to the blind,
>   and feet to the lame.
> I was a father to the needy,
>   and I championed the cause of the stranger.
> I broke the fangs of the unrighteous,
>   and made them drop their prey from their teeth.'
>
> (Job 29:7–17)

This rich passage, describing the life of an honoured citizen (Job before his humiliation) shows us the Israelite council/law court in action, with pleas being heard from those being persecuted by others. Note particularly the importance placed upon giving justice to those with no one

In biblical studies, the **Exile** refers to the period in Israel's history in the sixth century BCE when many of its people were taken captive and deported from Israel to Babylon.

In Hebrew, the word for a tribe is *shebet* or *matteh* and the word for a clan is *mishpachah*. The word for a family in Hebrew is *bet 'ab* (pronounced bate aav) and literally means 'father's house'. For more about the Hebrew language, see 0.0 'Before We Start. . .'.

to plead for them — orphans, widows, foreigners. Note also the apparently 'democratic' character of the gathering: Job has an honourable place, as a leading citizen, even among 'princes' and 'nobles'. Israelite society clearly recognized these categories of upper-class people of noble birth, yet in the court they did not have any exclusive rights.

ADMINISTRATION AND JUSTICE — THE ROLE OF THE KING

It is probable that, during the time of the monarchy, there was a system of higher courts to deal with matters beyond the competence of the elders 'in the gate' — indeed, even before the kings we hear of Samuel and his sons acting as judges, and going on circuit to hear difficult cases (1 Samuel 7:15–8:3). From the Book of the Covenant in Exodus we also get the impression that local priests sometimes had a judicial function, perhaps in cases where the evidence was insufficient and a trial by ordeal or a decision by sacred lot was required. This is probably the meaning in this passage:

> *When someone delivers to a neighbour money or goods for safekeeping, and they are stolen from the neighbour's house, then the thief, if caught, shall pay double. If the thief is not caught, the owner of the house shall be brought before God, to determine whether or not the owner had laid hands on the neighbour's goods.* (Exodus 22:7–8, our emphasis)

A **monarchy** is a form of government with a king (or queen) as its head.

Under the **monarchy**, the king himself acted as a final court of appeal. When Absalom was preparing his revolt against David, he exploited this royal function by intercepting people with legal petitions to the king and dealing with their cases more quickly than the king himself might have done:

> *Absalom used to rise early and stand beside the road into the gate; and when anyone brought a suit before the king for judgement, Absalom would call out and say, 'From what city are you?' When the person said, 'Your servant is of such and such a tribe in Israel', Absalom would say, 'See, your claims are good and right; but there is no one deputed by the king to hear you.' Absalom said moreover, 'If only I were judge in the land! Then all who had a suit or a cause might come to me, and I would give them justice.'* (2 Samuel 15:2–4)

Interestingly, such a system rests on a clear belief that it is the duty of the king to guarantee justice; we can see this ideal in one of the royal psalms:

> *May he [the king] judge your people with righteousness,*
> *   and your poor with justice. . . .*
> *May he defend the cause of the poor of the people,*
> *   give deliverance to the needy,*
> *   and crush the oppressor.* (Psalm 72:2, 4)

Of course, kings in Israel and Judah no doubt behaved much like kings in other countries of the ancient Near East. Some were good leaders, living up to standards of a psalm such as Psalm 72; others were tyrants. For example, from the stories about Solomon, and about the complaints made to his successor Rehoboam, we can deduce that even under this most prosperous king the conditions of the average person were not very comfortable (1 Kings 12). In addition, Samuel's description of what living under a king was like (1 Samuel 8:11–17) makes it clear that there were inequalities of wealth in the kingdom; and in times of political crisis, especially during sieges, people's condition might become extremely dire — 2 Kings 6:28–29 speaks of people being reduced to cannibalism, and even eating their own children. However, for the most part, the Old Testament does not distinguish between 'good' and 'bad' kings in terms of their treatment of their subjects or the administration of justice. Rather, the books of Kings focus on questions about the religious activities of the kings — did they serve **YHWH** faithfully, or worship Baal? — and leave us in the dark about their other qualities.

> **YHWH** is the primary way God's name appears in the Old Testament. It is simply four Hebrew consonants which many scholars believe may have been pronounced Yahweh. For a more detailed examination of this issue, see 2.1 "Watchmaker or Living God?'

In the ancient Near East, generally kings were thought of as closer to the world of the gods than ordinary mortals. In Egypt, indeed, the king ('Pharaoh') was supposed to be a god (which did not prevent people from assassinating kings from time to time), and in Mesopotamia, where the king was officially simply the god's chief representative on earth, he was still held in great awe. This is obvious from the construction of palaces, with their enormous throne-rooms, and from their art, where the king is sometimes depicted as looking almost exactly like one of the gods. In the two Hebrew kingdoms the king seems never to have arrived at quite this status. Solomon is portrayed in glorious terms, with his elaborate carved throne (1 Kings 10:18–20), yet even he was not seen as semi-divine. Moreover, subsequent kings seem to be treated primarily as human leaders, full of faults and subject to frequent rebellions. In the kingdom of Judah at least there was what we may call an **ideology** of the monarchy as guaranteed permanently by God. We see this in Psalm 89:

> An **ideology** is a term for any system of ideas relating to a particular theme.

> *I will make him the firstborn,*
> *the highest of the kings of the earth.*
> *For ever I will keep my steadfast love for him,*
> *and my covenant with him will stand firm.* (Psalm 89:27–28)

However, even here the king's personal weaknesses are mentioned, and it is expected that God will punish him if necessary:

> *If his [i.e. David's] children forsake my law*
> *and do not walk according to my ordinances,*
> *if they violate my statutes*
> *and do not keep my commandments,*

> then I will punish their transgression with the rod
> and their iniquity with scourges.... (Psalm 89:30–32)

ADMINISTRATION AND JUSTICE — THE ROLE OF THE KING'S COURT AND CIVIL SERVANTS

At the time of the monarchy all the kings, again like their counterparts in other countries, had a 'court' of advisers, nobles, and officials who worked for them and assisted in the administration of the nation. What a royal court could be like can be seen from the story of David's court in 2 Samuel 9–20 and 1 Kings 1–2. Families that had had several generations in the king's employment acquired status as a result, and could be referred to as made up of 'princes' or 'nobles'. The prophets thought these people sometimes got above themselves, and Isaiah comments on Shebna, King Hezekiah's steward (called 'the one who is over the house' in Hebrew), who he thought had ideas above his station in making himself a rock-hewn tomb:

> *'Thus says the Lord GOD of hosts: Come, go to this steward, to Shebna, who is master of the household, and say to him: What right do you have here? Who are your relatives here, that you have cut out a tomb here for yourself, cutting a tomb on the height, and carving a habitation for yourself in the rock?'*
> (Isaiah 22:15–16)

A civil servant in modern Britain is an official who does not carry responsibility for government decisions, but acts as an adviser to those who do. Such a person also runs the government's offices and departments, and has to be highly literate and good at keeping reliable records. This job needs training as well as certain personal characteristics, such as reliability, discretion, and loyalty, and the ability to avoid the limelight.

As well as the steward, the kings had other officials, such as the royal Remembrancer and, naturally, the military Chief of Staff, and the Secretary: there are lists of such people in 2 Samuel 8:15–18 and 1 Kings 4:2–6. Exactly what they all did is not very clear, but some of them are evidently what we should call civil servants rather than nobles. This may strike us as a very modern idea, but one of the surprises in studying the ancient world is the realization that the cultures of Egypt and Mesopotamia had highly developed administrative structures staffed by people who corresponded closely to what we mean by civil servants. There were schools and colleges to train them, and they had a high status in society, partly because of their contact with the king's court. You could make a good living working in the royal chancellery.

There is a scene in the second book of Kings where royal officials make a rare public appearance. The Assyrian king, Sennacherib, is besieging Jerusalem in 701 BCE, in the days of Hezekiah, and sends his own royal officials (the Tartan, the Rabsaris, and the Rabshakeh) to negotiate: 'When they called for the king, there came out to them Eliakim son of Hilkiah, who was in charge of the palace, and Shebnah the secretary, and Joah son of Asaph the recorder' (2 Kings 18:18). The Rabshakeh proposes terms for surrender. Then the officials reply: 'Please speak to your servants in the Aramaic language, for we understand it; do not speak to us in the language of Judah within the hearing of the people who are on the wall' (2 Kings 18:26). The Assyrian refuses, in coarse terms (18:27), but we see from this that such men were trained in foreign languages, and particularly in Aramaic, the international language of the day. They were diplomats, who could deal with the representatives of foreign powers. From a much later period we read of the skills of such a person:

> He serves among the great
>   and appears before rulers;
> he travels in foreign lands
>   and learns what is good and evil in the human lot.
>
> (Sirach 39:4)

THE ROLE OF DIFFERENT PEOPLE IN SOCIETY

The wise

There seems to be some overlap between such trained civil servants and the people the Old Testament calls 'the wise'. At times, this term seems to be a technical term for a particular kind of person, parallel with other officially recognized groups: 'Then they said, "Come, let us make plots against Jeremiah — for instruction shall not perish from the priest, nor counsel from the wise, nor the word from the prophet"' (Jeremiah 18:18). This gives the impression that there were three groups of people in Judean society in the seventh century BCE (when Jeremiah was at work) who could claim to give reliable advice: priests, wise men, and prophets. The wise are said to give 'counsel' (Hebrew *etsah*, pronounced eight-sah), and though this could be a general term for advice, the parallel with the priest's 'instruction' and the prophet's 'word' suggests that it, too, may be a technical term. This may mean that there was a definite group in society called 'the wise', and it is possible that they should be identified with the civil servants who clearly existed. However, this is not certain, because 'wise' can of course also be an everyday word simply describing someone as astute or clever or, indeed, what we too would call wise. So, although there were definitely civil servants in the Hebrew kingdoms, it is not clear that these people were the same as 'the wise' referred to in the Old Testament.

Priests and other Temple officials

Ancient Israelite priesthood is surprising to anyone who approaches it with modern ideas of clergy as people with a special vocation to minister, and as outside the **secular** structures of society. A priest in Israel was primarily an official — senior clergy could be listed alongside other royal officials, as in the lists mentioned above (2 Samuel 8:15–18 and 1 Kings 4:2–6). The job was also hereditary, just like more or less all other occupations in ancient societies. Priests were members of a priestly family.

In early Israel it seems that anyone could undertake the

The word **secular** suggests a view of the world which rejects religion, or considers it as of little importance.

duties of a priest provided a competent person, primarily the head of a household, had appointed him. Thus in the story of Micah in Judges 17–18 we find that Micah is looking out for a priest and could in principle appoint anyone he liked. However, he is delighted when a young 'Levite' turns up (Judges 17:7–13), since Levites apparently made particularly good priests — Micah says, 'Now I know that the LORD will prosper me, because the Levite has become my priest' (17:13).

We do not know what 'Levite' meant in this early period. There may be some connection with the tribe of Levi, and certainly later Old Testament writers thought of Levi as the priestly tribe. However, during the period of the monarchy the connection between Levites and the priesthood certainly became very close. In the book of Deuteronomy, all Levites are qualified to act as priests and indeed are described as 'the levitical priests' (in Hebrew, 'the priests the Levites': see Deuteronomy 18:1). Deuteronomy, possibly written in the seventh century BCE, ruled that this priesthood could be exercised only at the central altar, the one in the Temple at Jerusalem, but before that time local Levites certainly carried out sacrifices all over the country. At least from the days of David there was also a chief or 'high' priest who was an official serving under first the kings, and then, after the Exile, under the governors appointed by the Persians.

After the Exile, there were much tighter rules about who might minister as a priest. Only the descendants of the priests who had served in the pre-exilic Temple — described as 'sons of Zadok' — were allowed full priestly rights: their family descent was traced back to Moses' brother Aaron, who was now seen as the first 'high priest' of Israel (Zadok was high priest under David). In this period 'Levite' came to be a term applied to a more junior kind of clergy, people who were allowed to assist in the Second Temple but not to offer the sacrifices. How and why this happened is much discussed by biblical scholars, but no one knows for sure. It may have had something to do with tensions between priests who had returned from exile and those who had never been deported, the latter (or rather their descendants) being 'demoted' by the powerful group that returned and took the lead in national reconstruction. Late in this post-exilic period — probably during Hellenistic times — the high priest took over the role of ruling the nation.

Of course, most people think of the priests in Israel as offering sacrifice, but many Old Testament texts make it clear that this was only one of their functions, and not always the most important. As we can see from the following two passages, according to the prophets the primary task of priests was to teach, to give 'instruction' (Hebrew *torah*):

> *My people are destroyed for lack of knowledge;*
> *because you have rejected knowledge,*
> *I reject you from being a priest to me.*

And since you have forgotten the law [torah] of your God,
I also will forget your children. (Hosea 4:6)

For the lips of a priest should guard knowledge, and people
should seek instruction from his mouth, for he is the messenger
of the LORD of hosts. But you have turned aside from the way;
you have caused many to stumble by your instruction; you have
corrupted the covenant of Levi, says the LORD of hosts, and so I
make you despised and abased before all the people, inasmuch
as you have not kept my ways but have shown partiality in your
instruction. (Malachi 2:7–9)

In this sense, priests were primarily consultants: you went to them when you wanted to know what God required, especially but not exclusively in terms of the sacrifices that should be offered. In early times, people actually offered the sacrifice (i.e. killed and burnt the animal) themselves, and the priest's job was to check that they were doing it right. After the Exile, sacrifice became a priestly prerogative, but the priest still had a teaching function as well as a sacrificial one.

Prophets

Prophecy was perhaps the only occupation in Israel that was not hereditary. It depended on a call from God — that is, an experience of a supernatural kind that conferred strange powers of clairvoyance and perhaps also the ability to work miracles. No one could be trained to do this: it was felt to come directly from God, and it might fall upon anyone, regardless of background. Saul, the first king of Israel, was a prophet, as was his predecessor, the great judge Samuel.

Prophets had unusual psychic experiences, ecstasy and trance, and some at least could foretell the future. They had no official position, though at times kings would take them on to the payroll as consultants, often to direct national events (1 Kings 1:32–40) or to give advice on battles they intended to fight (1 Kings 22). Some prophets also lived in small communities, such as those that gathered around Elisha (see 2 Kings 2:15–17, 4:38–41, 6:1–7), and were known collectively as 'the sons of the prophets'. However, by no means all prophets lived corporately, and Amos explicitly denies that he is 'one of the sons of the prophets', saying that his prophetic vocation came on him out of the blue, as he was working as a shepherd (Amos 7:14). The spirit of God might choose anyone to be a prophet, and official recognition was neither here nor there. Even though Nathan the prophet advised David, we do not find him in the lists of David's officials; he seems to have been an independent figure outside any such listing. The same was clearly true of most of the prophets whose books we have. They were outsiders, who could not be coerced into saying what the establishment wanted to hear.

 The term 'sons of the prophets' does not mean people whose fathers were literally prophets. Rather it means that such people were members of a prophetic guild. This is because the term 'son of' in Hebrew has a wide range of uses, one of them being the sense 'member of a group'.

ORDINARY FAMILY LIFE — MEN, WOMEN, AND CHILDREN

The family in Israel was, as in most pre-modern societies, **patriarchal** in structure. Whatever we may think about that, the fact of it is undeniable. Indeed, the people we have mentioned in this chapter so far were all men: the king, the priests, the civil servants, royal counsellors, judges, members of town councils. Men were the heads of their households and were in charge of their wives, their children, and their slaves. The ideal Israelite family was a large one, in response to God's instruction to Adam and Eve to 'be fruitful and multiply, and fill the earth' (Genesis 1:28). In addition, the psalmist describes the happy home of the faithful in these terms:

> *Your wife will be like a fruitful vine*
> *within your house,*
> *your children will be like olive shoots*
> *around your table.* (Psalm 128:3)

Therefore, children were viewed as a blessing from God, and women who were unable to have children suffered greatly as the experiences of characters like Sarah (Genesis 16:1–6) and Hannah (1 Samuel 1:1–7) demonstrate. Children were expected to obey their parents in all things under threat of death (Exodus 21:15) and were also expected to help their parents in the home and, especially, in their old age. Formal education appears to have been a possibility for a few, select boys, but children in general were educated in the home by their parents, with stories of their ancestors and explanations of the special relationship between God and Israel. Of course, a son, who would strengthen the family, was viewed as more important than a daughter, who would simply need to be married off when the time came.

Thus, for the whole of their lives, women existed mostly in relation to men, as their wives, their concubines, their daughters, their sisters, their widows, and their mothers; not as free and independent people in their own right. If the Old Testament contains references to the importance of protecting the rights of widows and orphans, it is precisely because these people had no legal standing and could, therefore, very easily be exploited. But it is an exaggeration to say that ancient Israelites regarded women merely as possessions — they were seen as persons with human rights, and husbands and fathers could not do just as they liked with the women under their authority. A man who married a woman he had captured in battle could not then treat her as a slave: if he no longer wanted to be married to her, he must give her a proper divorce (Deuteronomy 21:10–14). In the laws of Deuteronomy, male and female slaves had equal rights to freedom after serving for six years (Deuteronomy 15:12–17). Nevertheless, women were in something of the same position as children: they had rights, but no independent sphere of action.

The role of women was, of course, centred on the home. A woman was expected to be a faithful and reliable wife and would

A **patriarchal** structure is one dominated by men.

have been responsible for doing the majority of the household chores and for looking after the children. One reference in the Old Testament indicates that life could be very different for upper-class women who, according to the prophet Amos, could easily become rich and idle at the expense of the poor.

> *Hear this word, you cows of Bashan*
>   *who are on mount Samaria,*
> *who oppress the poor, who crush the needy,*
>   *who say to their husbands, 'Bring something to drink!'*
>
> (Amos 4:1)

However, the 'woman of worth' in Proverbs 31 is clearly the ideal wife, and she appears to exercise a good deal of independent action in the interests of her family:

> *She is like the ships of the merchant,*
>   *she brings her food from far away.*
> *She rises while it is still night*
>   *and provides food for her household*
>   *and tasks for her servant girls. . . .*
> *She perceives that her merchandise is profitable.*
>   *Her lamp does not go out at night. . . .*
> *She opens her hand to the poor,*
>   *and reaches out her hands to the needy.*
> *She is not afraid for her household when it snows,*
>   *for all her household are clothed in crimson.*
> *She makes herself coverings;*
>   *her clothing is fine linen and purple.*
> *Her husband is known in the city gates,*
>   *taking his seat among the elders of the land.*
>
> (Proverbs 31:14–15, 18, 20–23)

But, in general terms, Proverbs and other wisdom literature present women mainly as seductresses, tempting young men to leave the straight and narrow (e.g. Proverbs 2:16–19, 5:1–14, 7:6–27), and the writer of Ecclesiastes is positively **misogynistic** when he talks about his search for people with wisdom: 'One man among a thousand I found, but a woman among all these I have not found' (Ecclesiastes 7:28). Moreover, Jesus son of Sira goes about as far as anyone could go down this road:

> *For from garments comes the moth,*
>   *and from a woman comes woman's wickedness.*
> *Better is the wickedness of a man than a woman who does*
>   *good;*
>   *it is woman who brings shame and disgrace.*
>
> (Sirach 42:13–14)

Yet, it must be mentioned that the Old Testament also has a large gallery of female characters who somewhat belie the stereotypical picture of women in ancient Israelite society.

 It might seem rather shocking to a modern reader that the prophet Amos calls these rich and idle women 'cows'. In fact, cows of Bashan, the present Golan Heights, were apparently known for their sleekness and beauty, and the women may even have enjoyed the compliment! They would, of course, have minded that Amos was telling them that they were under a curse from God.

To be **misogynistic** is to display a hatred of women.

Indeed, there are a number of powerful women mentioned, such as Sarah (the wife of Abraham), Rebekah (the wife of Isaac), and Rachel (the wife of Jacob), Abigail and Michal (wives of David), Deborah (a judge who engineers the defeat of the Canaanite commander, Sisera), and Esther and Judith (women who save their people from destruction). In addition, Judean history also mentions a number of queen mothers who seem to have had an official role, and lists one queen, Athaliah, alongside the kings (see 2 Kings 11). However, she came to a bad end, and there were plenty of men, Isaiah included, who thought no good would ever come of a female ruler:

> *My people — children are their oppressors,*
>   *and women rule over them.*
> *O my people, your leaders mislead you,*
>   *and confuse the course of your paths.*

(Isaiah 3:12, our emphasis)

ANCIENT ISRAELITE SOCIETY — A QUESTION OF EVIDENCE

In the end, it has to be admitted that we have only patchy information when it comes to the social setting of the Old Testament, and it is important not to be misled — for example, by pictures in old-fashioned Bibles — into thinking that the ancient Israelites were basically Bedouin, living on the edge of the desert in tents. After the conquest of the land, there were many people whose jobs were not directly related to farming, who lived in stone buildings in towns and cities and had decorated utensils bought in shops. Such folk might have lacked many country skills, and many would have had servants or slaves to care for their needs. Indeed, the books of the Old Testament as we have them presuppose an active city life and are surely the product of the upper strata of society. This is because literature such as the Hebrew Bible does not come into existence except from a nation with enough surplus resources to allow the growth of a literate class, with time to spare for writing works that are not purely utilitarian. Archaeology can offer some help in filling in the detail of how ordinary people lived, but the fact

0 & 0 These two rooms sometimes had only partial walls separating them from the central room.

0 The central room was often left without a roof to form a courtyard .

0 0 & 0 These rooms were often subdivided further.

A floor plan of a typical Israelite house. From the excavation of Israelite houses from the time of the settlement and the monarchy, we learn that the typical Israelite family lived in a flat-roofed house consisting of rooms built around a central courtyard which housed a hearth and oven. The walls of these houses appear to have been built of stone and mud bricks, covered in a mud plaster, and the houses would have included rooms for communal sleeping and eating areas as well as space for animals to be housed at night. Utensils and storage vessels unearthed at these sites also suggest that basic supplies of grain, oil, and water were stored in each house and that baking, spinning, and weaving were all standard household tasks. However, such homes would have belonged to those whose work made them an adequate living; little trace remains of the small hovels inhabited by the very poor in Israel.

For more about what archaeology can contribute to our understanding of the Old Testament, see 3.6 'Digging Up the Old Testament'.

remains that much of the writing concerns the doings of the great and powerful in the religious history of Israel, and there is very little about ordinary people and their ordinary lives.

4.2 Thus Says the Lord!
PROPHECY IN ANCIENT ISRAEL

T H E   B A S I C S

- The prophets of the Old Testament are characters who claimed direct experience of God and conveyed messages of God's will to his people.
- Prophecy in the Old Testament ranges from bands of people relaying divine messages born out of prophetic frenzy in pre-exilic times, to individual characters of post-exilic times who, by use of words and symbolic actions, had a major role in shaping Israel's understanding of God and the people's relationship with God.

T HE BOOKS OF THE prophets make up a large portion of the Hebrew Bible, and they have been extremely important in Old Testament study. The prophets have been seen as highly original and creative figures. They acted as the nation's conscience, and predicted both coming disasters and coming deliverance for Israel. In both Judaism and Christianity they have been hailed as great moral teachers, yet also as people who saw into the distant future — among Christians there has traditionally been a great emphasis on their **messianic prophecies**. Their books are intricate

Messianic prophecies is the term used to describe prophecies in the Old Testament that relate to the future appearance of a Messiah — a person specially chosen by God who will signal the beginning of a great age of peace and prosperity for all people. The Jewish people are still awaiting the fulfilment of these prophecies whereas Christians have traditionally interpreted such prophecies as having been fulfilled in the person of Jesus.

The term 'prophet' is commonly used by people today to mean a person who can foretell future events, but that is not the prime meaning in the Old Testament. Abraham is the first person to be called a prophet in the Bible (Genesis 20:7), but it is Moses who is regarded by many as representing the classic image of a great prophet in the Old Testament because he was a man of authority who was able to perform wonders and who spoke to God face to face. Thus, prophets are people chosen personally by God to act as intercessors between God and his people and to communicate to them his messages of religious and ethical

importance. However, prophets in the Old Testament appear in many forms. For example, there are references to *cultic prophets*, who were particularly skilled in the rituals of worship and prayer and who lived and worked at the holy places. There is also mention of *ecstatic prophets* who received their messages as a result of the spirit of God seizing and inspiring them, as well as prophets who worked in the royal court, influencing the decisions of kings in a range of political, religious and ethical matters.

Individual prophets are often referred to in the Old Testament as 'men' or 'servants' of God, indicating their

special relationship to him, but there are three specific Hebrew words used for prophets in the Old Testament. The first is *nabi* (pronounced nah-vi, with the stress on the second syllable) which is simply translated 'prophet', but the other two, *roeh* (pronounced row-ay, with the stress on the second syllable) and *hozeh* (pronounced ho-zay, with the stress on the second syllable), are translated 'seer' because they are derived from the verbs meaning 'to see'. In general terms, the word *nabi* was used from earliest times for people who worked as prophets in a group, whereas individuals who had close personal encounters with God were referred to as 'seers'.

The prophets of the Old Testament have been categorized by scholars in a number of different ways. The term *classical prophets* is used to denote those prophets after whom books in the Bible are named; sometimes these prophets are also referred to as the *literary prophets* or *writing prophets* — although this prejudges the question of whether they, rather than their disciples, actually wrote their messages down themselves. Among these prophets, three (or four, if Daniel is included along with Isaiah, Jeremiah, and Ezekiel) are sometimes known as the *major prophets,* and the other twelve the *minor prophets.* However, in these categories, 'major' and 'minor' mean no more than 'large' and 'small', and the divisions are based purely on the relative length of their books and are not a value judgement on their content. At least three of the 'minor' prophets — Amos, Hosea, and Micah — are regarded in Old Testament scholarship as extremely 'major' in terms of their importance in the development of prophecy and, indeed, of Israelite thought.

Note also that the term *latter prophets* is also applied to these prophets after whom books in the Bible are named. This is to contrast them with the books of the Bible (Joshua, Judges, Samuel, and Kings) that are sometimes called the books of the former prophets. This is not because they are about prophets, although they do, of course, include stories about prophets and prophecy, but because they are books that are believed by some to present a *prophetic view of the history of Israel for the period they describe.*

and complex, and almost certainly came into being over a lengthy period, supplemented by followers and later scribes. The prophets contributed major insights to the biblical understanding of God.

THE DEVELOPMENT OF PROPHECY

In the early days of prophecy in the Old Testament there were groups of people, sometimes called 'sons of the prophets', as well as individuals such as Elijah and Samuel, who fulfilled the function of prophet in Israel, receiving inspiration from God and conveying his message to the people concerned. However, from the middle of the eighth century BCE we find a new breed of prophets, people whose words were preserved for posterity not primarily by story-tellers, as with Elijah and Elisha, but in books that bear the names of individual prophets. These classical prophets shared the main features of all prophets in Israel in that they were mediators, delivering God's message and praying for his people, and they had paranormal experiences in which they were called to do unusual things in order to convey God's message. Yet, they had a specific impact on the development of religion in Israel because (as we shall see) their message had a particular ethical and religious content. With this in mind, some development of the prophetic tradition can be traced, although it must be remembered that material in the Old Testament need not always come from the time it is describing!

The earliest forms of prophecy, ecstatic and cultic prophecy, were probably influenced by the prophets of the Canaanite religion and were common in the pre-exilic period. However, classical prophecy — with its emphasis on the prophet's divine call, its use of a variety of prophetic forms of speech, its message to the people of the need for obedience

The name Isaiah means 'Yahweh is Salvation', but we do not really know who **Second Isaiah** is. The Old Testament book of Isaiah is actually a compilation of different types of prophecy that span quite a period of time. Most scholars agree that chapters I–39 relate to a prophet, called Isaiah, who lived in Jerusalem and engaged in prophetic activity from 742 to 701 BCE. The next section of the book, however, has a distinct literary and theological style and clearly relates to a later period towards the end of the Exile, from 550 to 540 BCE, since it includes the idea of Cyrus as a liberator of Israel in exile in Babylon. As these chapters come second, the prophet is referred to as Second or Deutero-Isaiah. In addition, some scholars argue that there is a distinct third section to the book in chapters 56–66 written around 530 to 500 BCE. This section follows many of the ideas apparent in the first and second sections of the book of Isaiah but demonstrates a particular concern for the need for sincere worship. As this section comes third, the author of these chapters is referred to as Third or Trito-Isaiah.

The book of **Malachi** is, in fact, anonymous, but takes its name from the words 'my messenger' in Malachi 3:I. In Hebrew, 'my messenger' is *malachi*, hence the name given to the prophet whose words are featured in this book. The majority of the book is made up of six addresses which attribute the troubles of the post-exilic community to the failure of the priests and the people to observe the ritual of the cult. Malachi foresees a time when God will again judge his people for their empty worship, and he sets out a vision of a time when the whole world will recognize God and offer him acceptable sacrifice. The book ends with a reminder to observe the teachings of Moses and with a promise that God will send the prophet Elijah to earth again before the day of God's judgement.

to the one God, **YHWH**, and its rejection of idol worship and the oppression of the poor — dates from the period of Israel's domination by the great powers, Assyria, Babylon, and Persia. The first classical prophet was Amos, who worked during the reign of Jeroboam II, probably in the 760s BCE, just as the Assyrians began to loom over the horizon. Hosea was probably a younger contemporary. Both these prophets worked in the northern kingdom, though Amos was himself a Judean. By the end of the eighth century, Isaiah and Micah had also appeared in Judah, foretelling the decline of both kingdoms under Assyrian power.

In the seventh century, as Assyrian dominion was supplanted by Babylonian, the major prophetic figure is Jeremiah, who is said to have begun his prophetic career under Josiah in about 621 BCE, but who lived to see the destruction of Jerusalem by the Babylonians in 587 BCE. Habakkuk may have been his contemporary, and a little earlier Nahum foresaw the downfall of Assyria. During the **Exile** itself, Ezekiel, exiled to Babylonia with the king Jehoiachin in 598 BCE, spoke to the exiled community, and seems to have lived on long enough to see the first signs of hope as Babylonian power waned.

At the end of the exilic age, in the 530s BCE, the prophet we call **Second Isaiah** (the author of Isaiah 40–55) sounded a new note of hope for the restoration of Israel. Once a first return to Judah had occurred, slightly later prophetic figures probably produced 'Third Isaiah' (Isaiah 56–66), at the same time as Haggai and Zechariah called the people to get on with rebuilding the Temple. **Malachi** appears to come from a slightly later period, perhaps reflecting the age of Nehemiah (mid-fifth century BCE), while prophets such as **Joel** and **Obadiah** cannot be earlier than the late Persian or even early Hellenistic age.

What complicates the picture is that during the times of later prophets the books of the earlier ones were still undergoing editing and expansion. Thus there are passages in

YHWH is the primary way God's name appears in the Old Testament. It is simply four Hebrew consonants which many scholars believe may have been pronounced Yahweh. For a more detailed examination of this issue see 2.1 'Watchmaker or Living God?'

In biblical studies, the **Exile** refers to the period in Israel's history in the sixth century BCE when many of its people were taken captive and deported from Israel to Babylon.

The prophet **Joel**, for whom no personal data are recorded in the Old Testament, portrays the day of God's judgement on the earth as a huge plague of locusts that turns the land into a desert, and he urges the people to repentance and fasting. However, Joel also looks further ahead to a time when God will give his spirit to all people (Joel 2:28). Christian interpretations of this prophecy have often seen it fulfilled in the story, told in the New Testament book of Acts (Acts 2:I4–2I), of Jesus' disciples receiving the Holy Spirit.

The book of **Obadiah** is the shortest book in the Old Testament and contains the prophecies of the prophet Obadiah concerning the destruction of Edom, a kingdom to the south of Judah, and the restoration of Judah.

An oracle, in this sense, is a short saying given in the name of God.

Isaiah 1–39, which contain the words of the eighth-century prophet Isaiah, that can hardly come from earlier than the work of Second or Third Isaiah, and could even be as late as the material in Joel (for example, the **oracles** about Egypt and Assyria in Isaiah 19:16–25). All the prophetic books underwent this kind of development over the course of time; even a book as short as Obadiah, the shortest book in the Old Testament, probably contains material from two different periods. How far this kind of rewriting of the books is the work of disciples of the prophets, and how far it results from wider scribal activity on Israelite literature in general, it is difficult, if not impossible, to say.

We should also not forget that the stories of the earlier prophets — Samuel, Elijah, Elisha, Micaiah son of Imlah, Amaziah, and many others — do not come to us from books that go back as far as those prophets themselves. The stories are to be found in the historical books nowadays referred to as the 'Deuteronomistic History', which in their present form are no older than the exilic period. Obviously they rest on older sources, but the way the stories are told may well reflect the concerns of later ages. For example, the stories of Elijah focus strongly on the contest between YHWH and Baal, the God of the Canaanites. However, this issue may have been more important in the years leading up to the Exile when, for example, Jeremiah talks a lot about the supremacy of YHWH, than it really was in the ninth century, when Elijah is supposed to have lived. In that case, the stories may well have been embellished and perhaps given a new emphasis a long time after the days of Elijah himself, and we cannot necessarily rely on them to provide accurate data about prophecy before Amos.

This statue of Elijah is situated on Mount Carmel. In 1 Kings 18, Elijah engages in a competition with four hundred and fifty prophets of Baal. The challenge took place on Mount Carmel in front of 'all the people of Israel' and was won by Elijah. The story is that, after the prophets of Baal had spent hours invoking their god to send a fire to consume the sacrifice on the altar, Elijah ordered water to be poured over the altar and then, at the first attempt, successfully invoked Yahweh to send fire to consume the sacrifice. As a result, the people turned back to the worship of Yahweh. (Photo: J. Bowden)

THE NATURE OF PROPHECY — MEDIATION AND THE PARANORMAL

Most ancient societies had figures whose job was to mediate between the divine and human worlds. Human wishes and desires needed to be presented to God or the gods; and divine decisions and instructions had to be brought down to humankind. Among the people who acted as mediators in ancient Israel we might think first of the priests. In offering sacrifices they were putting ordinary Israelites in touch with God, and in teaching the Law they were communicating his messages to them. Prophets, however, were also important as mediators, and for an additional reason. The priests were technically qualified to offer sacrifices and inherited traditions of teaching which they could pass on to the people, but they were simply carrying out an official function. No one expected a priest to have any special personal contact with God. Prophets, on the other hand, were people who had direct experience of God. It might be said that they had 'stood in the council of YHWH', or that the 'spirit of YHWH' had come upon them. They had experiences which today might be called **paranormal**, experiences ordinary people (including priests) did not have. They heard voices, saw visions, even (like Moses) spoke to God 'face to face'. This made them crucially important people, respected yet also feared.

In one of the earliest stories about prophets in the Old Testament we read of Saul, after his anointing as king by Samuel, joining himself to a group of prophets. Samuel tells him:

> 'as you come to the town, you will meet a band of prophets coming down from the shrine with harp, tambourine, flute, and lyre playing in front of them; they will be in a prophetic frenzy. Then the spirit of the LORD will possess you, and you will be in a prophetic frenzy along with them and be turned into a different person.' (1 Samuel 10:5–6)

In itself, this kind of frenzy may not sound as though it had anything to do with mediation. From other passages, however, it is clear that what the prophets experienced in their frenzy often had implications for what God was about to do. They received messages from him and in more sober moments they could pass these on to the people or to kings and rulers, telling them what God had decided would happen.

In the so-called **classical prophets** we often find records of special visions. Sometimes these are like what we might call hallucinations — that is, the prophet sees something that is not objectively there, something other people would not have seen. This may in fact be God himself. Amos tells us, 'I saw the LORD standing beside the altar' (Amos 9:1). But Zechariah sees four horsemen, who turn out really to be angelic beings seen in a vision, rather than horsemen who were literally present (Zechariah 1:8–11); Ezekiel sees angels with swords patrolling the streets of Jerusalem (Ezekiel 9); Isaiah sees seraphim, fiery flying creatures, in the Temple at Jerusalem (Isaiah 6:2).

On the other hand, sometimes the prophet sees something that was there for all to see, but understands it as having a deeper meaning. Amos, for example, saw a basket of summer fruit but understood it as meaning that 'the end' was coming on Israel. This meaning was conveyed through a pun: 'summer fruit' is *qayits* (pronounced kites) in Hebrew, and sounds very similar to 'end' (*qets,* pronounced kates). In a similar way, Jeremiah understood an almond branch (*shaqed*) to imply that God was 'watching' (*shoqed*) over his word and would carry it out. However, both sorts of vision were seen as coming from God. Even where what was seen was objectively real, it was God who gave the prophet its distinctive interpretation.

In these ways, the prophets mediated God's decisions to their contemporaries, but mediation could also work in the

A **paranormal** experience is one that is regarded as being beyond the scope of normal objective investigation or explanation.

The term **classical prophets** is used to denote those prophets after whom books in the Bible are named. This is to distinguish them from prophets appearing in other books, like Elijah and Elisha who are mentioned in 1 and 2 Kings.

∵ The prophet Elisha should not be confused with the prophet Elijah (see above and chapter I.2 'The Story So Far'). Elisha is the prophet who was called by Elijah to accompany him and take over his prophetic spirit. He witnessed Elijah being taken up into heaven in a chariot of fire and took on his role. The collection of stories about Elisha can be found in 2 Kings 2:19–8:15 and includes a number of miracles, such as the multiplication of oil to enable a widow to pay her debts (2 Kings 4:1–7), the multiplication of loaves to feed a hundred people (2 Kings 4:42–44), and the curing of Naaman's leprosy (2 Kings 5:1–15).

opposite direction. Prophets had a role in bringing human petitions before God as when Amos pleads for Israel to be spared (Amos 7:2 and 7:5). We see this function most clearly with Moses, whom the Old Testament presents as a prophet. He prays for Israel, sometimes successfully, for example when God gives the people pure water in the desert (Exodus 15:24–25), sometimes not, for example when Moses fails to secure the people's forgiveness (Exodus 32:30–34). He, like Samuel, was remembered in later times as a great intercessor for Israel. In Jeremiah 15:1 we read, 'Though Moses and Samuel stood before me, yet my heart would not turn towards this people' — clearly implying that under normal circumstances you would expect the opposite, since Moses and Samuel had great power to influence God.

The prophets' power made some of them, in effect, what we might call magicians. Elijah was able to raise a dead boy to life again (1 Kings 17:17–24); he had previously caused his mother's meagre supply of flour and oil to multiply miraculously (17:8–16). He received from YHWH the message that there would be a great drought in Israel, but the way he described the message implies that he himself had been given the power to withhold the rain: 'As the LORD the God of Israel lives, before whom I stand, there shall be neither dew nor rain these years, *except by my word*' (1 Kings 17:1, our emphasis). His follower Elisha similarly raised a dead boy (2 Kings 4:17–37) and, when mocked for his baldness, caused a group of bears to kill the boys who had derided him (2 Kings 2:23–25). In fact, this may not have been quite so trivial a reason as it sounds — the 'baldness' may have been a mark of his prophetic status, a 'tonsure', so the boys were in effect mocking the God who called him to be a prophet.

People who have such supernatural powers are likely to be feared, as Elijah was by Ahab, king of Israel (875/874–854/853 BCE), but they are not likely to be loved. Prophets were useful, but also regarded as odd and eccentric, even mad. When a young prophet is sent to anoint Jehu as king of Israel (2 Kings 9:1–13), his anointing is regarded as effective and incontrovertible: if a prophet has anointed Jehu as king, then king he is. Yet when Jehu's colleagues ask him why the prophet came to him, they use these words, 'Why did that madman come to you?' (2 Kings 9:11), and he replies in a perhaps embarrassed way, 'You know the sort and how they babble'. Hosea similarly reports that people said, 'The prophet is a fool, the man of the spirit is mad!' (Hosea 9:7).

However, that the prophets were called 'mad' is perhaps understandable in the light of some of the strange and bewildering things they did. For example, Hosea thought God had told him to go and marry a prostitute, not a 'respectable' thing to do, as a symbol of YHWH's 'marriage' to sinful Israel (Hosea 1:2), and Isaiah walked naked and barefoot through Jerusalem (Isaiah 20) to represent the fate of the Egyptians and Ethiopians with whom Judah was trying to make an alliance. The prophet Jeremiah smashed an earthenware jug in public to symbolize the forthcoming destruction of Israel (Jeremiah 19:1–13) and, on another occasion, went around with a yoke on his neck to symbolize the future conquests of the Babylonian king, Nebuchadnezzar (606–562 BCE). Ezekiel also went in for symbolic actions (sometimes referred to as 'acted parables'), and on one occasion cut his hair off and divided it into three parts, burning a third, slicing a third up with his sword, and scattering a third in the wind (Ezekiel 5:1–4). This was to symbolize the fate of different groups in Israel who were to be captured by the Babylonians — some would die in the destruction of Jerusalem by fire when the siege was broken, some would be killed by the Babylonian troops, and others would flee. Such symbolism may be very effective, but such behaviour does nothing to dispel the image of the prophet as someone rather odd and to be feared.

THE NATURE OF PROPHECY — PROPHETIC FORMS OF SPEECH

The prophets used a variety of speech-forms in their oracles, and most of them are borrowed from other spheres of Israelite life. This is true even of the best known, the formula 'Thus says the LORD', which occurs hundreds of times in the prophetic books. This is in origin the formula by which ambassadors and other messengers announced the messages with which they were charged. It can be seen in a secular use in 2 Kings 18:19: 'The Rabshakeh said to them, "Say to Hezekiah: Thus says the great king, the king of Assyria. . .".'. In using this phrase, therefore, the prophets presented themselves as the ambassadors — trusted messengers, with the authority of the one who sent them — not of a human king, but of YHWH. They had 'stood in his council', as human ambassadors would have stood in the court of the king, and they believed that their message had his approval.

Amos is particularly rich in non-prophetic forms of speech which he takes and refashions for his own purposes. One is the **dirge**, marked out in Hebrew by its distinctive metre, which cannot be captured in translation:

> Hear this word that I take up over you in lamentation,
> O house of Israel:
> Fallen, no more to rise
> is maiden Israel;
> forsaken on her land,
> with none to raise her up. (Amos 5:1–2)

The implication, which an Israelite hearing this little snippet would at once have registered, is that Israel is already dead! This is a highly striking way of conveying the prophet's sense of the fate in store for his people, like publishing someone's obituary while he is still alive.

Another form of speech that Amos twists to his own purposes is the priestly torah or instruction:

A **dirge** is technically a lament over the dead but can refer to any mournful song or lament. In Hebrew poetry, the characteristic metre (poetic rhythm) of a lamentation consists of three stressed syllables in the first half of each pair of lines, followed by two in the second. The book of Lamentations contains five laments for the city of Jerusalem after its destruction by the Babylonians in 587 BCE, and a personal lament by David for Saul and Jonathan is recorded in 2 Samuel 1:17–27.

Come to Bethel — and transgress;
*   to Gilgal — and multiply transgression;*
bring your sacrifices every morning,
*   your tithes every three days. . . .* (Amos 4:4)

A priest, calling the people to worship, would have said something like this: 'Come to Bethel, and bring your sacrifices, to Gilgal, and multiply your offerings; bring your sacrifices tomorrow morning, and offer your tithes'. Amos deliberately turns the torah into a call to do evil, since that is what he thinks offering sacrifices at the sanctuaries actually amounts to, given the people's general moral condition. At the same time he ludicrously inflates the amount of offerings required, saying, in effect: since you so much enjoy this empty ritual, why not indulge in much more of it? Without realizing that the priestly torah is at the back of this oracle, we would not appreciate the sarcasm in it.

The prophets were thus people of considerable intellect, who could take up forms of speech at home in other settings and use them to make their own points. Amos may have been a simple 'herdsman and dresser of sycamore trees' (Amos 7:14), but he was schooled in literary techniques and used them to good effect. We have come a long way here from the wordless frenzy of the group of prophets encountered by Saul, and yet we are still dealing with prophets: mediators between God and humanity who have had an experience that is out of the ordinary, and who claim to be in touch with the living God.

THE NATURE OF PROPHECY — FORETELLING THE FUTURE

In traditional Christianity the main importance of the prophets was seen as consisting in their prediction of certain events that lay in the distant future for them — the birth, life, and death of Jesus Christ. In the nineteenth century scholars studying the prophets began to stress that they had not intended to predict these things: their books had been read as 'messianic' prediction from the New Testament period onwards, but they themselves had really been concerned for what was happening in their own day. This view has largely established itself in biblical scholarship, but many Christians still give credence to the idea that such prophetic predictions relate to Jesus.

It is important, however, not to throw out the baby with the bath water. The fact that the prophets were mainly concerned with their own times does not mean they were uninterested in 'the future' in every sense. On the contrary, the *immediate* future was very much at the centre of their concerns. As the threat from the Assyrians or, later, the Babylonians gathered strength, the prophets' role was to convey to the nation's leaders the outcome that God (as they saw it) intended to bring about.

This is consistent with the phenomenon of prophecy that we find in other Middle Eastern cultures. Indeed, from

'The Hebrew Prophets . . . occupy a position in the thought and faith of mankind unmatched by any other single group. They belong to their own times, but are not confined by them;...they address themselves to the needs and crises of the ancient world of men in which they lived, but their words continue to stir the conscience of men, to call them to responsibility, to assert the claims of the divine imperative.' (J. Muilenburg, 'Old Testament Prophecy', in Peake's *Commentary on the Bible,* Van Nostrand Reinhold, 1962) the land of Israel itself, from Deir Alla in the Jordan Valley — halfway between the Sea of Galilee and the Dead Sea — we have sayings attributed to a prophet called Balaam, who makes an appearance in Numbers 22–24. These, like other ancient prophecies, are all concerned with what will happen in the near future. The same is true of Egyptian and Mesopotamian prophecy, as can be seen from texts such as the second-millennium *Admonitions of Ipuwer* and the *Prophecy of Neferti* from Egypt, and from Mesopotamia in the oracles concerning Esarhaddon, and oracles and dreams about Ashurbanipal.

There is a general consensus that the message of the prophets, down to and including Jeremiah, was primarily one of coming disaster. In Amos, this is very clear, 'The end has come upon my people Israel; I will never again pass them by' (Amos 8:2). Amos vaguely suggests ways in which this disaster could still be averted ('Seek me, and live', Amos 5:4, cf. also 5:6 and 14), but seems unconvinced that 'repentance' will be forthcoming. Hosea and Isaiah both present a more complex picture, sometimes suggesting that the outcome is uncertain and can still be decided by the nation's response to YHWH, but at other times seeming as bleakly pessimistic as Amos. Both of them, however, include passages that seem to imply a restoration beyond the inevitable disaster — for example,

> *I will heal their disloyalty;*
> *I will love them freely,*
> *for my anger has turned from them.*
> *I will be like the dew to Israel;*
> *he shall blossom like the lily,*
> *he shall strike root like the forests of Lebanon.*
>
> (Hosea 14:4–5)

By the time we reach Ezekiel we find ourselves in an age when what the earlier prophets had predicted seemed to have occurred: the Exile was seen as the great disaster which all along had been waiting for YHWH's rebellious people, but now it was over, and better times could be expected. In Ezekiel the turn comes at 33:22, when the prophet is told of the fall of Jerusalem and he is freed from his divinely imposed dumbness, now to speak of a coming restoration of Israel. The worst that could happen has happened, and is now in the past. At this point, we begin to find optimistic prophecies:

> *I will make a covenant of peace and banish wild animals from the land, so that they may live in the wild and sleep in the woods securely. I will make them and the region around my hill a blessing; and I will send down the showers in their season; they shall be showers of blessing. . . . They shall know that I, the* LORD *their God, am with them, and that they, the house of Israel, are my people, says the Lord* GOD.
>
> (Ezekiel 34:25–26, 30)

Mentioned by name in Isaiah 44 and 45, 2 Chronicles, and the books of Ezra and Daniel, the **Cyrus** of the Bible was Cyrus II the Great, founder of the Persian Empire. Having completed his conquest of Asia Minor in 547 BCE, Cyrus began a successful campaign against Babylonia and in 538 BCE permitted Jews in exile in Babylon to return to Jerusalem and rebuild their Temple. For more about Cyrus' liberation of these exiles see 3.4 'Refugee Status'.

This theme is continued extensively in Second Isaiah, which contains almost entirely oracles of restoration and hope, hailing the Persian king **Cyrus** as the one who will give Israel back its land and its Temple (Isaiah 44:24–45:8).

Therefore, to a great extent, post-exilic prophecy focuses on the good future that Israel can hope to enjoy. Whereas the pre-exilic prophets had often seen foreign nations as God's instruments to punish Israel, now the post-exilic prophets thought that the future held only blessings for Israel and doom for its enemies:

> For the day of the LORD is near against all the nations.
> As you have done, it shall be done to you;
>   your deeds shall return on your own head. . . .
> But on Mount Zion there shall be those that escape,
>   and it shall be holy;
> and the house of Jacob shall take
>   possession of those who dispossessed them. (Obadiah 15, 17)

THE PROPHETS AND ETHICS

So far prophecy may have sounded like a rather irrational phenomenon: strange people hearing voices and seeing visions and behaving oddly. There is much truth in that. However, one of the new features in the classical prophets is their great concern to make rational sense of the message of doom that they often felt constrained to proclaim. The great prophets were in the business of producing a **theodicy**, explaining the disaster that was going to engulf Israel as expressing the will of a just God.

The term **theodicy** literally means an inquiry into the justice of God. However, today it is used more generally for any attempt to make sense of the suffering in the world in the light of a belief in God. For more information about this topic in the Old Testament, see 2.5 'Why Me?'

In order to do this, the prophets lay out an indictment against Israel for all sorts of national sins. Usually in the ancient world the anger of the gods was attributed to the nation's having omitted some sacrifice or other, or having neglected the gods in some other way. It is striking that the prophets of Israel in pre-exilic times never make this complaint. Indeed, both Amos and Isaiah say that, on the contrary, the people have been all too keen to offer sacrifices, while neglecting obligations of social justice and basic morality:

> I hate, I despise your festivals,
>   and I take no delight in your solemn assemblies.
> Even though you offer me your burnt-offerings and
>   grain-offerings,
>   I will not accept them;
> and the offerings of well-being of your fatted animals
>   I will not look upon.
> Take away from me the noise of your songs;
>   I will not listen to the melody of your harps.
> But let justice roll down like waters,
>   and righteousness like an ever-flowing stream.
>   (Amos 5:21–24)

Your new moons and your appointed festivals
    my soul hates;
they have become a burden to me,
    I am weary of bearing them.
When you stretch out your hands,
    I will hide my eyes from you;
even though you make many prayers,
    I will not listen;
        your hands are full of blood. (Isaiah 1:14–15, our emphasis)

Of course our hands are full of blood, people might have said — we're offering sacrifices! However, Isaiah had in mind more ethical concerns...to his mind they had blood on their hands because they were oppressing (and even murdering?) the poor and the needy. They had neglected what Amos calls 'justice' (Hebrew *mishpat*, pronounced mishpaat) and 'righteousness' (Hebrew *tsedaqah*, pronounced tsedaakaa, in each case with the stress on the last syllable), a common pair of terms used by the prophets for what we would call 'social justice', avoiding exploitation and oppression of the helpless and ensuring that everyone gets what is due to them.

In this way, the prophets are a major source of information about the ethical codes of ancient Israel. This is because their messages appear to draw on Israelite law and wisdom, as well as on what we might call international custom — their skill and originality, of course, being that they wove such ideas into a wholesale vision for a society of God's people. On the whole it is the rulers they condemn, and probably no one in the ancient world would have thought of the fate of the nation as depending on the sins of 'small' people, the ordinary folk: it was the leaders who held the fate of the nation in their hands. The paradox is that God's punishment of these people can come about only if he destroys the nation, and in the process those they were oppressing (according to the prophets) would be bound to suffer just as much. In a way, the guilt of the leaders is precisely that they have the power to bring everyone else down with them when they fall.

However, from about the time of the Exile onwards some prophets begin to address this problem. Ezekiel envisages that God will discriminate in his judgement between the guilty and the innocent. In chapter 9 the prophet sees the destroying angels going about Jerusalem, but among them he also sees an angelic scribe, whose job is to mark a Hebrew letter tau (a cross in the old Hebrew alphabet) on the foreheads of 'those who sigh and groan over all the abominations that are committed' (Ezekiel 9:4). Ezekiel also foretells that in the restoration of Judah sinners will be rooted out before the nation is resettled in its land — thereby avoiding the danger that history will repeat itself (Ezekiel 20:38).

Apart from social injustice, the pre-exilic prophets also condemn the kings of Israel and Judah for their foreign policy, particularly for thinking that they can escape the Assyrians or Babylonians by making alliances with other weak nations.

Isaiah is particularly scornful of the idea that the Egyptians can be of any help (Isaiah 30:1–5, 31:1–3), and Jeremiah spent much of his career as a prophet trying to convince the leadership of Judah that the best course was to surrender to the Babylonians, not to go in for fruitless resistance. However, on the whole, the prophets were not heeded, and it was not until their warnings were proved to have been accurate that people started to respect them retrospectively. Indeed, that may be how their words came to be preserved over such a long period.

THE PROPHETIC IDEA OF GOD

The prophets' insistence on linking divine judgement with human ethics had an important effect on the Israelite idea of God. As in all attempts to produce a theodicy, it resulted in a belief that God was to some extent predictable. He did not react angrily because of some minor cultic infringement, such as the wrong kind of goat offered or blood thrown against the altar in the wrong way. Rather, what angered him and what deserved punishment was human injustice. Thus, the prophets interpreted suffering that could have seemed mere random disaster, or the result of capricious divine anger, as the action of a just and purposeful God who cared deeply about human conduct. An old way of putting this was to say that the prophets discovered **ethical monotheism** — a phrase not used much nowadays, but which remains a good and helpful expression.

As to the element of **monotheism** in it, it is clear that all the prophets believed there was only one effective God over all the world. It does not matter whether he is called by a proper name ('YHWH') or is simply designated 'God': he is far more than the national God of Israel. In Amos he is simply assumed to be sovereign over all the nations, who are denounced in chapters 1–2 for their atrocities in war, irrespective of whether they knew YHWH as God of Israel. For Isaiah, similarly, all other 'gods' are 'the work of their [human beings'] hands, what their own fingers have made' (Isaiah 2:8). As his successor Second Isaiah will spell out in more detail, the other supposed gods are simply lumps of wood (Isaiah 44:9–20).

Since the prophets could not have spoken like this if their belief was so totally original that people would not have understood them, it would seem that Israelite religion must have had some monotheistic tendencies from an early period. Nevertheless, we know well that many Israelites before the Exile were in practice **polytheists** or **henotheists**. Thus, we know that the prophets moved the religion of Israel on considerably. They developed its monotheistic features so strongly that, after the Exile, other gods seem no longer to have been an issue, and the Jews began to acquire the name they had throughout the ancient world as the one nation that acknowledged only one

'The Prophets saw God as a Person, and ever in that light interpreted His attitude to man. Hence their task included — and this was perhaps its supreme function — the exposition of the character of God. His righteousness, His holiness and His love were the high themes of their investigation. Above all they had to insist on the practical application of these qualities to the life of the nation.' (T.H. Robinson, *Prophecy and the Prophets*, Duckworth, 1923)

TECHNICAL WORDS USED TO DESCRIBE BELIEF IN GOD

The term **monotheism** refers to the belief in only one God.

The term **polytheism** refers to the belief in many gods.

The term **henotheism** refers to the belief in one god, whilst acknowledging that there are others.

The term **ethical monotheism** refers to the belief that there is only one God, and that God is just and also requires justice.

God. Moreover, they established that this one God was a good being, bent on justice and righteousness, kind to Israel yet never overlooking their sins, and requiring good behaviour from all humanity. It was a remarkable achievement.

4.3 Hallelujah!
WORSHIP IN ANCIENT ISRAEL

T H E   B A S I C S

- In common with most religions, religion in the Old Testament involved sacred words and actions at specific sacred times and in specific sacred places.
- It is not always clear how ancient or distinctive particular elements of Old Testament religion are, but it seems likely that it became more complex and regulated as it developed and incorporated important changes as a result of key moments in national history, such as the Exile.

T HE WORSHIP OF GOD or the gods was a central part of all ancient religions, as it is of most modern ones, because recognizing the existence of a divine being or beings has little importance if there is no way of being in touch with them. Thus, people in ancient times tended to have a vivid sense that the divine had an impact on their daily lives, and they wanted to honour and, sometimes, to placate the gods they believed in, to ensure that the gods would do them good and not harm. The great prophets of Israel claimed that the God of Israel required above all social justice from his people, and that without that no amount of public worship would avail. However, most Israelites, like their counterparts in other countries, believed that God would help them if they turned to him through these appointed means, and they believed that God required and delighted in their praise, their prayers, and their sacrifices — especially at certain regular festivals. Therefore, we may divide the elements of their religion into four categories: sacred actions, sacred words, sacred times, and sacred places.

SACRED ACTIONS

Sacrifice
The main type of action that constituted religious practice in the ancient world was **sacrifice**. Indeed, offering sacrifice is such a universal feature of religion that it is hard to imag-

Sacrifice, in general, refers to the practice of offering to a divine being something of personal value in recognition of his greatness. In the ancient world, sacrifice usually involved the ritual slaughter of animals and, in some ancient cultures, humans.

Pentateuch is a common collective term for the first five books of the Old Testament — Genesis, Exodus, Leviticus, Numbers, and Deuteronomy. It is derived from the Greek word *pente* meaning 'five'. In the Jewish tradition, these are sometimes referred to as the five books of Moses.

The term **post-exilic** is used to denote the period in Israel's history after the Exile in the sixth century BCE when many of its people were taken captive and deported to Babylon.

ine there was a time when it was wholly unknown to the Israelites. However, it is uncertain whether the Israelites offered sacrifices before they settled in the Promised Land. The prophet Amos (5:25) seems to imply that they did not, but the **Pentateuch** assumes that the sacrificial system was put into place during Israel's time in the wilderness, and the Yahwist source (J) in Genesis takes it for granted that sacrifice goes right back to the time of Noah (Genesis 8:20–22). What is likely is that the system developed over time, from simple beginnings that may well belong in the period before Israel settled in the Promised Land, to a complex and intricate set of rules that applied in the **post-exilic** Temple, and which we find in the Priestly source (P).

Sacrifices, at least by post-exilic times, fell into many categories, but there is a basic twofold distinction which can be seen throughout the development of the system. This is between sacrifices that were wholly consumed in fire on the altar (like the *'olah*), and sacrifices in which the worshippers ate part of the animal and burned the rest (like the shelamim). The first type, the 'whole burnt-offering', is given entirely to God and thus the worshipper gives up claims on it: this makes it especially suitable as a way of expressing penitence or sorrow. Like a fine, it is something valuable which the worshipper gives up. The second type, the 'sacrifice of well-being' as the New Revised Standard Version calls it, is more like a meal, in which both the worshipper and God share. This does not necessarily mean that people had the crude idea that God actually ate the food burnt on the altar — any more than modern worshippers at a Harvest Festival think of God as consuming the food that is brought into church. Such sacrifices may go back ultimately to a belief that the gods literally shared in the meal, but by the time the Old Testament describes the sacrifices such ideas had been rejected as too unsophisticated. Nevertheless, the emphasis falls on the eating, and there is at any rate a sense that the meal is eaten in the presence of God, and that God shares in the rejoicing.

The association of sacrifice with a shared meal or feast is probably not the element that most modern people think of when they hear the word 'sacrifice', because in modern speech it almost always contains the element of giving something up, and implies some pain or suffering on the part of the person who offers it. So, it is important to see that in ancient Israel a sacrifice was often a happy event. When the prophets condemn sacrifice, they are at least in part condemning people's love of feasting and celebration in a time when they think mourning and weeping would be more appropriate. It is not necessarily that they think people are trying to buy God's favour through their sacrifices; rather, they think that feasting is out of place given the national crises during which they spoke.

In early Israel, it seems that all meat eating was seen as sacrificial. When people wanted to eat meat — which most could not afford to do very often — they took the animal to the local sanctuary and killed it on the altar. This meant that its blood could run down as an offering to YHWH and he could be given the portions of the animal that were his due, and then they could cook and eat the rest of the animal. When the book of Deuteronomy centralized worship at the Jerusalem Temple, one of the things it had to do was to legislate that henceforth killing animals was no longer to be seen as sacrificial in itself:

> Take care that you do not offer your burnt-offerings at any place you happen to see. But only at the place that the LORD will choose in one of your tribes — there you shall offer your burnt-offerings and there you shall do everything I command you. Yet whenever you desire you may slaughter and eat meat within any of your towns, *according to the blessing that the LORD your God has given you.* . . .
>
> (Deuteronomy 12:13–15, our emphasis)

TYPES OF SACRIFICES IN THE OLD TESTAMENT

The Old Testament is rich in sacrificial terminology, but it is notoriously difficult to determine the exact significance of each of these terms. Sacrifice was not a unique feature of Israelite religion, but this table offers a very general guide to the various types of sacrifices known to us from the text of the Old Testament.

Name	General Type	Ritual Detail (where known)
'issah	An offering by fire.	
minhah	A cereal offering.	
korban	A gift.	
zebah	Literally meaning 'slaughter', this term is a common designation for sacrifice in the Old Testament and is often used in conjunction with one of the other terms.	
'olah (pronounced oh-lah)	Whole burnt offerings — the commonest of all sacrifices in the Old Testament — probably used in order to make atonement for sin in a general way, not intended to remove the sin, but rather to express sorrow and to mitigate God's anger.	The animal — which must be in perfect condition — is slaughtered, the blood is thrown against the base of the altar, and the animal is then cut into pieces and burned on the altar.
shelamim (pronounced she-laa-meem, with stress on the last syllable)	A peace offering or offering of well-being (NRSV) — a symbol of good relations between God and humankind — often used in celebration of a victory or joyful event.	The animal — which must be in perfect condition — is slaughtered, the blood is thrown against the base of the altar, the fat of the entrails is burned on the altar for God; the breast and the right thigh are for the priests to eat, and the rest of the animal forms a sacrificial banquet for those who are ritually clean.
'asam*	A guilt offering — a symbol of the repairing of a broken relationship between God and humankind — often used in cases where some sort of material damage might have been caused, for example in the case of swearing or concealing evidence.	The animal — which must be in perfect condition — is slaughtered, the blood is smeared on the horns of the altar and poured on the ground in front of the altar, the fat of the entrails is burned on the altar for God. What is not given to the priests to eat is burned.
hattat*	A sin offering — a symbol of the repairing of a broken relationship between God and humankind — often used in cases of moral misdeeds or to remove ritual impurity following childbirth or leprosy.	

* Note that the distinction between these two sacrificial offerings is extremely unclear.

If such a rule had not been set out, then eating meat would have become impossible for most people.

The centralization of worship that Deuteronomy required was evidently carried out only partially in the seventh century, which is the time when most scholars think the book was written; see the description of King Josiah's reforms in 2 Kings 23:4–19. However, it seems that after the destruction of the Temple by the Babylonians in 587 BCE neither the community left in Judah nor those who had been exiled practised sacrifice any longer, until the Temple was restored in the 520s BCE. In fact, after that date there seems to have been little sacrifice anywhere in Judah except at the Temple, though we know that the Jewish settlers in Egypt, at Elephantine near the present site of the Aswan Dam, had a temple of their own and offered sacrifices there during the Persian period. By New Testament times the custom of sacrificing anywhere except at the Temple had certainly fallen away, and with the destruction of the Temple by the Romans in 70 CE all sacrifice ceased in Judaism, and the service of the synagogue wholly replaced the sacrificial system.

Fasting and lamentation

Just as much of the sacrificial practice of Israel expressed rejoicing and celebration, so there were also ceremonies to express sorrow and penitence. As we have seen, there were sacrifices that could be used to express repentance, and after the Exile these grew in importance until the whole sacrificial system was tinged with a concern for the removal of sin, rather than with rejoicing. But even in pre-exilic times people found ritualized ways of giving expression to their sorrow, especially in times of national or local disaster.

Many religions use **fasting** to express penitence and to persuade the gods to pardon, and so it was in Israel. It had a public dimension, being accompanied by lamentation, and a visible expression in customs such as putting dust on one's head, sitting on the ground, and wearing 'sackcloth' — a coarse and uncomfortable piece of cloth tied around the waist beneath clothing that had been torn. At times, it also seems to have included beating the breast, and perhaps, since there are laws against it (e.g. Deuteronomy 14:1), self-laceration. In modern Judaism, fasting survives as part of the ritual of the Day of Atonement (Yom Kippur) — an annual event at which people recall their sins over the past year and pray for forgiveness. Other customs can also be seen in Jewish mourning rites, where bereaved families still observe a period of sitting on the floor and eating only meals prepared for them by others.

The clearest case of a public fast in the Old Testament is to be found in the post-exilic book of the prophet Joel where the ravages caused by a plague of locusts cause sacrifice to cease (there are no animals or crops left to sacrifice), and the people are called to public lamentation:

Fasting is a term used to describe the practice of deliberately abstaining from some or all kinds of food and drink, traditionally for a religious purpose.

Yet even now, says the LORD,
  return to me with all your heart,
with fasting, with weeping, and with mourning;
  rend your hearts and not your clothing.
Return to the LORD, your God,
  for he is gracious and merciful,
slow to anger, and abounding in steadfast love,
  and relents from punishing.
Who knows whether he will not turn and relent,
  and leave a blessing behind him,
a grain-offering and a drink-offering
  for the LORD, your God?
Blow the trumpet in Zion,
  sanctify a fast;
call a solemn assembly;
  gather the people.
Sanctify the congregation;
  assemble the aged;
gather the children,
  even infants at the breast.
Let the bridegroom leave his room,
  and the bride her canopy.
Between the vestibule and the altar
  let the priests, the ministers of the LORD, weep.

(Joel 2:12–17)

Individuals could also use similar gestures in times of personal grief, as we see in Job. After the loss of his family and possessions, 'Job arose, tore his robe, shaved his head, and fell on the ground, and worshipped' (Job 1:20). His friends, sharing in his sorrow, 'raised their voices and wept aloud; they tore their robes and threw dust in the air upon their heads' (Job 2:12). Job, of course, is only a story, but it presumably reflects what people would actually have done under such circumstances.

Processions

In celebrating the festivals we shall be considering later in this chapter, Israelites seem to have taken part in solemn processions. We can read an account of such a procession in the story of David bringing up the Ark of the Covenant to Jerusalem. On this occasion, the Ark was borne on a cart drawn by oxen, and 'David and all the house of Israel were dancing before the LORD with all their might, with songs and lyres and harps and tambourines and castanets and cymbals' (2 Samuel 6:5). Sacrifices were offered to accompany the procession (2 Samuel 6:13).

At least one of the psalms also probably reflects a form of worship involving a procession, Psalm 118. In verse 19 the worshippers say, 'Open to me the gates of righteousness', and the reply comes in verse 20, 'This is the gate of the LORD; the righteous shall enter through it'. It is easy to imagine that this is a little dialogue between the people in the proces-

The Ark of the Covenant (not to be confused with Noah's Ark which uses a different Hebrew word!) is an important part of Old Testament history. It was a large wooden box covered with gold, which was constructed according to God's specific instructions (Exodus 25:10–22) and was said to contain the two tablets on which God had written the Law. For more about this see 3.6 'Digging Up the Old Testament'.

sion, who have just reached the doors of the Temple, and the priests inside it who lay down the conditions for entry. Verse 27 may actually mention the 'festal procession', though the Hebrew of this verse is obscure.

It was certainly normal in the ancient world for religious festivals to involve processions, and Israel was no exception. Even when describing the progress of the people through the wilderness, the Pentateuch sometimes describes their march in a highly ritualized way, implying that it too was a kind of procession:

> *So they set out from the mount of the LORD on three days' journey with the ark of the covenant of the LORD going before them for three days' journey, to seek out a resting-place for them, the cloud of the LORD being over them by day when they set out from the camp.*
>
> *Whenever the ark set out, Moses would say,*
> *'Arise, O LORD, let your enemies be scattered,*
> *　　and your foes flee before you.'*
> *And whenever it came to rest, he would say,*
> *　　'Return, O LORD of the ten thousand thousands of Israel.'*
> 　　　　　　　　　　　　　　　　　　　(Numbers 10:33–36)

The same is true of the Israelites' march around the walls of Jericho recounted in Joshua 6.

SACRED WORDS

A great deal of sacrificial worship was probably silent. There may have been special words that were always spoken as an animal was slaughtered or grain-offerings placed on the altar but, if so, we do not know what they were. Only Deuteronomy tells us of a formula used at the offering of the first-fruits of the harvest. When the priest takes the offering from the worshipper, the latter is told to recite an account of how Israel came to settle in the land (Deuteronomy 26:1-11). However, this is probably a rather idealized picture: in general, it was the act of offering, not any accompanying words, that was the central concern.

Nevertheless, the Bible contains many words used in worship, both the prayers of individuals and the corporate expressions of praise, lamentation, and prayer that we find in the Psalms. The impression we get from the Old Testament is that people felt free to pray anywhere and at any time, and that, although there were many formulae on which they tended to draw, they often prayed **extempore**. There are lengthy prayers of repentance and entreaty in Nehemiah 9 and Daniel 9 that give us an idea of the style of prayer in vogue in the post-exilic period. In these we find lengthy repeated expressions of penitence, often going back over the history of the nation and presenting the current generation's sins as part of a continuum of disobedience. Solomon's great prayer at the dedication of the Temple (1 Kings 8) is probably an example of the same kind,

 Following the comments of Mowinckel in his influential six-volume work on the Psalms, *Psalms in Israel's Worship* (1962), Craig Broyles states, 'Our principal source of information about ancient Israelite worship is the Psalms themselves' (Craig Broyles, 'The Conflict of Faith and Experience in the Psalms: A Form-critical and Theological Study', *Journal for the Study of the Old Testament,* Supplement Series 52, 1989).

Extempore prayer is prayer which has no set formula and is created by an individual on the spur of the moment.

and similarly comes from the exilic or post-exilic community rather than really going back to Solomon himself.

However, it is in the Psalms, and other psalm-like texts embedded in some of the other Old Testament books, that we find the most profound expressions of all the emotions that Israelites brought out into the open when they prayed and sang.

Prayer in times of trouble

Although the Old Testament is mostly about extraordinary people like leaders, prophets, the rich and famous, occasionally there are tales that seem to reflect the everyday life and prayer of ordinary people in ancient Israel. This may well be true of the story of Hannah in 1 Samuel 1–2. Hannah was, it is true, the mother of the great Samuel, but her story is told as though it reflects normal practices of prayer in Israel in early times.

Hannah suffered ridicule because she was unable to have children — a situation which in ancient society was assumed to be the result of a defect on the woman's part, almost her own fault and a punishment from God. On a visit to the temple at Shiloh she prayed that God would grant her a child, and promised that if he did she would dedicate him to God by sending him back to the temple to be a priest there. Thus, the story makes it clear that it was normal for people to pray in temples and shrines, and that when they did so they did it aloud. We can see this because Hannah exceptionally prays in silence, and this leads to a misunderstanding between her and the priest, Eli. Seeing her lips move, but no sound come from her mouth, he assumes she is babbling drunkenly, and rebukes her (1 Samuel 1:14). However, when she explains to him that 'I have been pouring out my soul before the LORD . . . speaking out of my great anxiety and vexation' (1:15–16), Eli adds his own blessing, and a prayer that God may hear her (1:17). In time, of course, Samuel is born.

Another example of prayers from a particular named individual in the Old Testament is the passages in the book of Jeremiah which are rather like the Psalms in style, but which appear to reflect specific episodes in the prophet's own life. Traditionally known as the 'Confessions' of Jeremiah, these passages (Jeremiah 11:18–12:6, 15:10–21, 17:14–18, 18:18–23, and 20:7–18) may give us further insight into how individuals prayed when they were in trouble:

> It was the LORD who made it known to me, and I knew;
>   then you showed me their evil deeds.
> But I was like a gentle lamb
>   led to the slaughter;
> And I did not know it was against me
>   that they devised schemes, saying,
> 'Let us destroy the tree with its fruit,
>   let us cut him off from the land of the living,
>   so that his name will no longer be remembered!'

The book of Psalms (in Hebrew *tehillim* [pronounced tauh-hill-eem, with the stress on the last syllable] or 'praises') is a collection of 150 religious prayers or poems which appear to have been designed to be sung or accompanied by music. Many were originally attributed to King David, but scholars now view them as a complex compilation of five smaller collections put together sometime after the Exile for use in the Temple. Thus the book of Psalms has been referred to as 'the hymnbook of the Second Temple', although most scholars now believe that many of the psalms date from much earlier periods in Israel's history. Whatever the origins of individual psalms, as a whole they provide an interesting insight into Israel's worship. They offer examples of both individual and community prayer, and they cover a wide variety of subjects, including the praise of God, laments, the king, liturgical celebrations, thanksgiving, and wisdom. Therefore, the Psalms have also formed an important part of Jewish and Christian worship through the ages.

> *But you, O LORD of hosts, who judge righteously,*
> *who try the heart and the mind,*
> *let me see your retribution upon them,*
> *for to you I have committed my cause.* (Jeremiah 11:18–20)

In this outpouring, the prophet accuses some unnamed group of people of conspiring against his life, and we know that people did because they thought he was a collaborator with the Babylonians. Jeremiah also identifies himself with the plight of the people as a whole, and offers a prayer of lament for them:

> *Is there no balm in Gilead?*
> *Is there no physician there?*
> *Why then has the health of my poor people*
> *not been restored?*
> *O that my head were a spring of water,*
> *and my eyes a fountain of tears,*
> *so that I might weep day and night*
> *for the slain of my poor people!* (Jeremiah 8:22–9:1)

Jeremiah even challenges the justice of God, in words that could come from the book of Job — and which may indicate that the author of Job was drawing on traditional laments about God's injustice:

> *You will be in the right, O LORD,*
> *when I lay charges against you;*
> *but let me put my case to you.*
> *Why does the way of the guilty prosper?*
> *Why do all who are treacherous thrive?* (Jeremiah 12:1)

Of course, it is possible that Jeremiah's Confessions do not really go back to the prophet. Some scholars believe they have been put in his book by later editors, and others think that the 'I' in them really stands for the nation as a whole, just as the 'I' in Lamentations 3 is a representative of Jerusalem as a whole, not simply an afflicted individual:

> *I am one who has seen affliction*
> *under the rod of God's wrath;*
> *he has driven me and brought me*
> *into darkness without any light;*
> *against me alone he turns his hand,*
> *again and again, all day long.* (Lamentations 3:1–3)

Yet, even if this is the case, it is surely plausible to think that an individual such as Jeremiah could have uttered these prayers, or else an editor would not have placed them in his book; and so individuals in Israel must have prayed in something like this way. Indeed, in most cultures that believe in God or gods individuals do pour out their distress in ways like this.

Thus, many of the psalms are prayers for help in time of trouble, and although there is the occasional psalm about the destruction of the Temple, such as Psalm 74, which can come from only one situation, few of them seem to reflect specific needs. For the most part the sufferings of the worshipper are described in general terms, and sometimes details are even mutually incompatible or at least form an unlikely combination: the worshipper in Psalm 22, for example, is surrounded both by enemies and by wild animals, his bones are out of joint and his mouth is dried up! Most likely, this represents symbolically any unpleasant set of circumstances from which one might ask God for deliverance, and it has been used in that way by generations of Jewish and Christian worshippers. Therefore, we can probably assume that the psalms are not one-off prayers but were meant for use and re-use on many occasions of distress. For example, there are prayers for help against enemies:

> *Hear my voice, O God, in my complaint;*
> *preserve my life from the dread enemy.*
> *Hide me from the secret plots of the wicked,*
> *from the scheming of evildoers,*
> *who whet their tongues like swords,*
> *who aim bitter words like arrows,*
> *shooting from ambush at the blameless;*
> *they shoot suddenly and without fear.* (Psalm 64:1–4)

Other psalms envisage severe illness:

> *O LORD, God of my salvation,*
> *when, at night, I cry out in your presence,*
> *let my prayer come before you;*
> *incline your ear to my cry.*
> *For my soul is full of troubles,*
> *and my life draws near to Sheol.*
> *I am counted among those who go down to the Pit;*
> *I am like those who have no help,*
> *like those forsaken among the dead,*
> *like the slain that lie in the grave,*
> *like those whom you remember no more,*
> *for they are cut off from your hand.* (Psalm 88:1–5)

Others speak of false friends:

> *It is not enemies who taunt me —*
> *I could bear that;*
> *it is not adversaries who deal insolently with me —*
> *I could hide from them.*
> *But it is you, my equal,*
> *my companion, my familiar friend,*
> *with whom I kept pleasant company;*
> *we walked in the house of God with the throng.*
> (Psalm 55:12–14)

Prayers of penitence

Other psalms show us that individuals who felt they had committed sins offered prayers of penitence to God, perhaps at the same time as offering sacrifice. Often people felt that illness was a sign to them that they must have sinned and so at such times they would pray both for forgiveness and for deliverance from trouble:

> *As for me, I said, 'O LORD, be gracious to me;*
> > *heal me, for I have sinned against you.'* (Psalm 41:4)

However, a sense of penitence might also overtake someone even when not in trouble:

> *Have mercy on me, O God,*
> > *according to your steadfast love;*
> *according to your abundant mercy*
> > *blot out my transgressions.*
> *Wash me thoroughly from my iniquity,*
> > *and cleanse me from my sin.*
> *For I know my transgressions,*
> > *and my sin is ever before me.* (Psalm 51:1–3)

From the book of Joel referred to above, we also know that, at least in post-exilic times, there were public gatherings for corporate lamentation and repentance, during which people thought of their personal sins as well as those of the nation as a whole.

Prayers of praise and thanksgiving

The book of Psalms contains many prayers of thanksgiving and praise. Some of these are mainly corporate in character, speaking of what God has done for 'us' (see, for example, Psalm 118), and often referring to the great events in the history of the nation (Psalm 136). However, others recall God's goodness to the individual, and are a way by which individuals can stay in touch with the God who has, they believe, treated them well:

> *I love the LORD, because he has heard*
> > *my voice and my supplications.*
> *Because he inclined his ear to me,*
> > *therefore I will call on him as long as I live.*
> *The snares of death encompassed me;*
> > *the pangs of Sheol laid hold on me;*
> > *I suffered distress and anguish.*
> *Then I called on the name of the LORD:*
> > *'O LORD, I pray, save my life!'*

> *Gracious is the LORD, and righteous;*
> > *our God is merciful.*
> *The LORD protects the simple;*
> > *when I was brought low, he saved me.* (Psalm 116:1–6)

Such psalms bear witness to the conviction that 'Weeping may linger for the night, but joy comes with the morning' (Psalm 30:5). In the end, it appears that the Israelites believed that God would always save those who pray to him, and such knowledge was a cause for great thanksgiving.

Of course, we can scarcely ever tell when particular psalms were written. Up until the nineteenth century, most of the psalms were believed to have been the work of David, and scholars attempted to link each psalm with a specific event in David's life. Once such a link with David was dismissed, scholars then assigned them a much later date and, indeed, described the **Psalter** as 'the hymn-book of the Second Temple' (thus Julius Wellhausen, 1844–1918). However, through the work of the Scandinavian scholar Sigmund Mowinckel (1884–1965) and his development of the application of form criticism to the Psalms, which began with his teacher Hermann Gunkel (1862–1932), many psalms have come to be seen as possibly pre-exilic in origin. This is because form criticism has encouraged people to recognize many different genres among the Psalms, and on that basis to theorize about the possible settings in worship that could have given rise to them.

The **Psalter** is the name given to the book of Psalms.

One great division among the Psalms is between those that express the sentiments of an individual and those that have a more corporate character. Most obviously, some present the worshipper as 'I' (e.g. Psalm 30) and others as 'we' (e.g. Psalm 79). However, this may not tell us as much as it appears to. Sometimes the 'I' in a psalm may represent a personification of the nation as if it were an individual, or may stand for the king, who is a representative figure (see, for example, Psalms 25 and 61, which both oscillate between individual and nation or king). On the other hand, even where a psalm uses 'we' the writer may have intended it to be sung by a soloist, rather than a choir or congregation. Indeed, in general, it is thought unlikely that Israelites engaged in corporate hymn-singing, either at local sanctuaries or in the Temple. More probably, people employed professional psalm-singers to utter particular types of prayers on their behalf: singing was thus a task for professionals, such as the families of singers, like the 'sons of Asaph', to whom some of the psalms are ascribed.

However, whatever the true origins of individual psalms or groups of psalms might have been, for an understanding of ancient Israel's worship it is also important to view the Psalter as a whole. Such an approach to the Psalms has been the focus of much recent scholarship and is important because it recognizes that the Psalter reflects the collective experience and understanding of those who used Hebrew poetry in their attempts to explore their individual and national relationship with God. Thus, the Psalms are not just the 'sacred words' of ancient Israel, but 'sacred words' which have the potential to be universally relevant.

'In brief, the Psalter has not arisen out of any self-conscious creation of systematic doctrine; it has emerged from the experiences of life and liturgy, and has been shaped dynamically by the various literary and theological concerns of the collectors and editors: hence its theological tensions, and its para-doxical views of life and God. This means that any contemporary reader, similarly shaped by diverse experi-ences of life and of liturgy, may also discover in the poetry concerns, both literary and theological, which have as much meaning now as then.' (S.E. Gillingham, *The Poems and Psalms of the Hebrew Bible,* Oxford University Press, 1984)

The Psalms 'are rich in recurring human experience. In them people in many different situations in life have seen reflected their own hopes and fears, have found words to express their own inner thankfulness or their need for forgiveness, and have caught a vision of the unchanging realities which underpin life.' (Robert Davidson, *A Beginner's Guide to the Old Testament,* Saint Andrew Press, 1992)

Unleavened bread is bread made without yeast. It is, therefore, flat bread as the yeast is the element that makes bread rise. The fact that the bread eaten at the festival of Passover is unleavened was interpreted as being the result of the flight of the Hebrews from Egypt, which left no time for the bread to rise! (See Exodus 12:39.) Nowadays the unleavened bread, tra-ditionally eaten by Jews at Passover, is called a matzo, and can be bought in supermarkets.

The word **exodus** literally means 'way out' and refers to the depar-ture of the Israelites from Egypt under the leadership of Moses. Exodus is also the name of the second book in the Old Testa-ment in which these events are retold.

SACRED TIMES

In modern Judaism, as in Christianity, the year is punctuated by a whole series of special days — feasts and fasts. Some of these go back to biblical times, and it is possible to trace their development by a careful study of the Old Testament evidence.

It is generally agreed that Israel in the pre-exilic period celebrated three main festivals. All these festivals are harvest festivals in origin and are prescribed in Exodus 23:14–17, part of the old law code usually referred to now as the Book of the Covenant:

- The Festival of Unleavened Bread is at the conclusion of the barley harvest in early spring. In Hebrew this is called *matzoth.*
- The Festival of Weeks or Pentecost is at the conclusion of the wheat harvest in late spring. In Hebrew this is called *shabuoth,* which means 'weeks', and it was eventually fixed as falling fifty days after the Festival of Unleavened Bread, hence 'Pentecost', which in Greek means 'fifty'.
- The Festival of Tabernacles or Booths is in the autumn at the end of the grape harvest. In Hebrew this is called *sukkoth.*

These festivals clearly make most sense after the settle-ment of the Israelites in Palestine when they became a more settled agricultural community, and they may even have been Israelite adaptations of native Canaanite agricultural festi-vals. However, there was another festival always attached to the festival of Unleavened Bread in pre-exilic times, and this was the feast of the Passover (Hebrew *pesach*). This feast celebrated the firstborn lambs and, since it seems to fit better with the more pastoral and nomadic side of Israel's life, some people think it is the most ancient of the Israelite festivals and has its origins in the wilderness period. By New Testament times, these two feasts had become one and the feast of the Passover included unleavened bread as one of its components, as it still does today.

However, in the book of Deuteronomy the festivals are no longer interpreted primarily as harvest thanksgivings, but as commemorations of the **Exodus** (see Deuteronomy 16, which is a much expanded version of the laws in Exodus 23). Because of this it is possible to give them exact dates — whereas originally they were presumably celebrated when the harvest was actually in, which would naturally vary from year to year. This development continues in the P source in the Pentateuch, and here each festival comes to commemorate a different event in the 'salvation history' of Israel. Passover + Unleavened Bread continues to be a celebration of the Exodus, but Weeks remembers the giv-ing of the Law on Sinai — as it still does in modern Judaism — and Tabernacles or Booths turns into a remembrance of the creation. Detailed regulations for these festivals can be found in Leviticus 23.

After the Exile, importance came to be attached also to what may be an older observance, but one which had not been prominent in pre-exilic times, the Day of Atonement (in Hebrew, Yom Kippur), when a goat was laden with the sins of the people and driven out into the desert (Leviticus 16). Some think this was a very old rite, reflecting life in the wilderness; others think it was actually invented after the Exile. The desert, of course, is very near to Jerusalem, so it could have its origins in the Temple-cult.

There is definite evidence for each of these festivals in the Old Testament texts, but in the twentieth century it was common to argue that there was also a New Year Festival in the autumn — perhaps linked to Tabernacles. This theory grew from the fact that other cultures we know about in the ancient Near East did celebrate the new year, and indeed modern Judaism has a New Year Festival called Rosh Hashanah. The existence of a New Year Festival in ancient Israel is a reasonable, if unprovable, hypothesis, but some scholars went further and proposed that the New Year Festival was also a celebration of YHWH's enthronement. They argued that such a festival was taken over from the Canaanites and was reflected in the psalms that speak of YHWH as king: Psalms 93, 97, and 99 in particular. Certainly, the Babylonians celebrated the god Marduk's enthronement, and it is possible that Canaanites did the same for Baal, and that Israel adopted this custom and 'Yahwized' it. However, here we are in the realm of fairly tenuous speculation. There is no denying that YHWH's kingship is a major theme in the Psalms, but most of our evidence suggests that he was seen as permanently enthroned over the Ark of the Covenant, rather than that he was ceremonially re-enthroned each year as Babylonian gods were.

Other Jewish festivals such as Purim and Hanukkah came into being late in the post-exilic period. Purim commemorates the events described in the book of Esther, and Hanukkah the rededication of the Temple by the Maccabees.

SACRED PLACES

Throughout the pre-exilic period, each town or village had its own shrine, known as a *bamah* or 'high place', often on a hilltop inside or just outside the inhabited area. There can be little doubt that these shrines had often been Canaanite sanctuaries, and the prophets regard them all as suspect for that reason: what went on there, they suggest, was basically a paganized form of religion in which the people worshipped the god Baal and indulged in 'fertility rites' involving sexual activity. This is the clear implication, for example, of the message of the prophet Hosea, and we find such things presented as still going on in the early post-exilic period in the collection known as Trito-Isaiah:

Are you not children of transgression,
   the offspring of deceit —
you that burn with lust among the oaks,
   under every green tree? (Isaiah 57:4–5)

However, we should not generalize these prophetic denunciations as though the whole religion of the pre-exilic sanctuaries had been non-Yahwistic. Probably many people did revere Baal alongside YHWH, and they may, as Hosea suggests, have addressed YHWH himself as 'My Baal', that is 'My Master' (see Hosea 2:16). 'Baal' was the title of the Canaanite god Hadad, and people in Israel may well have applied it to YHWH, quite innocently and with no thought of disloyalty. What is clear is that early Israelite religion was often **syncretistic**.

In addition to this multitude of local sanctuaries, in pre-exilic times a special status seems to have been attached to the place where the Ark of the Covenant was located. In the time of Samuel, this was at Shiloh, and the stories in 1 Samuel 1–4 suggest a temple had been built there. When David established his capital in Jerusalem, a city that had not previously belonged to Israel, he secured people's allegiance to it by moving the Ark of the Covenant there, but apparently housed it in a tent. According to 2 Samuel 7, the prophet Nathan was told by God to forbid David to build a temple. Whatever may be the truth of this, the biblical record is unanimous in telling us that it was David's son Solomon who first built a temple in Jerusalem. To judge from the account in 1 Kings 6, this temple was not an enormous structure but it was lavishly decorated using the finest materials. In many ways, it was perhaps less a cathedral than a royal chapel, and there was no intention of abolishing worship at the local *bamoth* (high places). Therefore, the first temple in Jerusalem was simply a site for the Ark of the Covenant and, probably, for special royal rituals, though we are never told what these were. Since it was a regular target for plunder, it must also have served as a treasury for much of the nation's wealth. However, this temple was more than just a national building for the focus

---

Something that is **syncretistic** is an amalgam of different ideas and practices from a variety of sources.

The name Isaiah means 'Yahweh is Salvation', but we do not really know who Isaiah is as the Old Testament book of Isaiah is actually a compilation of different types of prophecy that span quite a period of time. Most scholars agree that chapters 1–39 relate to a prophet, called Isaiah, who lived in Jerusalem and engaged in prophetic activity from 742 to 701 BCE. The next section of the book, chapters 40–55, however, has a distinct literary and theological style and clearly relates to a later period towards the end of the Exile, from 550 to 540 BCE. As these chapters come second, the prophet is referred to as Second or Deutero-Isaiah. In addition, some scholars argue that there is a distinct third section to the book in chapters 56–66 written around 530 to 500 BCE. This section follows many of the ideas apparent in the first and second sections of the book of Isaiah but demonstrates a particular concern for the need for sincere worship. As this section comes third, the author of these chapters is referred to as Third or Trito-Isaiah.

This layout of Solomon's Temple was very similar to the layout of the movable tent, or Tabernacle, which Moses was instructed to build during the wilderness period to house the Ark of the Covenant (see Exodus 25–27). However, many scholars believe that it was the layout of Solomon's Temple which inspired the description in Exodus of the Tabernacle built by Moses, rather than the other way around!

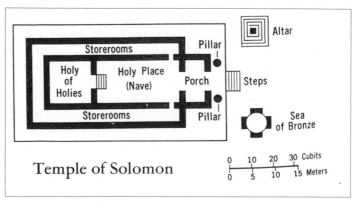

A plan of Solomon's Temple. © Copyright Hammond Inc, Maplewood, NJ

The stones which Herod the Great had cut to create a new retaining wall to support the esplanade to the Temple are the only visible remains of the Jewish Temple in Jerusalem today. This section of wall thus gained the name 'the Wailing Wall' as Jews adopted it as a suitable place to pray and to lament the destruction of the Temple.

(Photo: J. Bowden)

of worship, it was also a symbol of the power of the royal family of David and a visible manifestation of the covenant established between God and his people. Its destruction by the Babylonians in 587 BCE was, therefore, interpreted as symbolic of the destruction of the whole nation.

The shape of the Jerusalem Temple as the Old Testament describes it conforms to what is known about temples in the area from archaeological digs. It contained three areas: a large room for ordinary worshippers, a smaller one for the priests, and an even smaller one, the 'Holy of Holies', in which the Ark of the Covenant was housed, all arranged end to end in a pattern not unlike that of a normal western church with its nave, chancel, and sanctuary. Probably the book of Kings is relying on an old tradition about the Temple here, since temples in later times did not generally follow this pattern, so no one writing at a later period would have been likely to invent it.

The post-exilic Second Temple, sometimes referred to as Zerubbabel's Temple, since he oversaw its completion in 516 BCE, probably followed the lines of the first, but we have little detail about it, and it appears to have been less impressive than the original. Indeed, it was not until the days of Herod the Great, who reigned from 37 until 4 BCE, that the Temple was extended and enlarged to the scale it was in New Testament times — a much larger structure than Solomon's had ever been. In fact, the building work Herod began in 20 BCE was not finally completed until 65 CE, only five years before the Romans destroyed the Temple in 70 CE.

The experience of the Exile had, of necessity, changed the focus of Jewish worship and, even whilst the Second Temple

'Wherever the synagogues came from, the simple worship carried on there was an authentic reflection of an important strand in the spirituality of ancient Israel. For though the people rejoiced in the splendid magnificence of the Temple at Jerusalem, it had always been recognized that God's presence could not be restricted to one place. The consciousness that God was with them was more fundamental than the need for a holy place like the Temple.' (John Drane, *Introducing the Old Testament*, Lion, 2000)

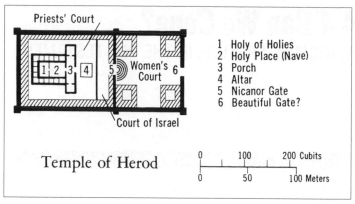

A plan of Herod's Temple. © Copyright Hammond Inc, Maplewood, NJ

A **synagogue** is a place where Jews meet to read and study the Scriptures and to pray together.

was in use, the practice that probably grew up in the Exile of coming together for non-sacrificial worship had become general among Jews, even in Palestine. This institution was what we know as the **synagogue**, though actual synagogue buildings are not found as early as this. However, on a day-to-day, week-to-week basis non-cultic worship in the synagogue was at the heart of Jewish regular religious practice; and, by New Testament times, for most Jews a trip to Jerusalem to offer sacrifice was only an occasional event.

4.4 Can We Cope?
WISDOM LITERATURE IN THE OLD TESTAMENT

THE BASICS

- Although later biblical wisdom writers questioned the validity of such a straightforward approach, living one's life in accordance with the insight the wisdom literature in the Old Testament provided was believed to make a person 'wise' about the way the world worked and to enable one to live a well-ordered and successful life.
- The wisdom tradition in Israel owed much to other wisdom traditions in the ancient Near East but it gradually became more integrated with the national religious traditions; wisdom was personified and linked specifically with the history of Israel and the Torah.

FROM ANCIENT TIMES, THREE books in the Old Testament have been referred to as books of 'wisdom'. They are Proverbs, Job, and Ecclesiastes. Alongside these, there are two books now in the **Apocrypha** that have 'wisdom' in their title: the Wisdom of Jesus son of Sira (Sirach or Ecclesiasticus, as it is also known) and the Wisdom of Solomon. The question is, 'What did people mean by calling these books "wisdom"?' Primarily it pointed to the idea that by reading them one would become wise, because they contain observations about the nature of human life lived with reference to God. Meditating on these observations would make people mature and endow them with

Apocrypha is the name given to the collection of books which are included in the Greek version of the Old Testament (the Septuagint) but not in the Hebrew Scriptures. These books are often also called 'deuterocanonical' books.

The Hebrew word for 'wisdom' is *hokmah,* and it is used with a diversity of meanings in a variety of contexts. Certain books in the Old Testament, such as Proverbs, Job, and Ecclesiastes, are categorized as being of the 'wisdom' genre; the book of Proverbs is arguably the clearest example of this as, in only thirty-one chapters, it uses the word 'wisdom' thirty-nine times and the word 'wise' forty-seven times. However, in addition, elements of 'wisdom' can also be found elsewhere in the Old Testament. For example, the German scholar Gerhard von Rad (1901–71) highlighted the wisdom elements of the story of Joseph (Genesis 37–50), in which Joseph is presented as a skilled administrator who acts wisely and perceives the plan and wisdom of God in the events around him and not, as with other patriarchs, as a result of direct revelation from God. Others have pointed to 'wisdom' influence in certain psalms, such as Psalms 111 and 119, and in parts of the prophetic books of Isaiah and Amos, to demonstrate the widespread influence of 'wisdom' in the life of ancient Israel.

'Wisdom as a description of a genre of material is a well-known usage of the term in scholarly circles to explain a phenomenon that extends throughout the world, in that the collection of wisdom sayings is a human activity common to all cultures.' (Katharine Dell, *'Get Wisdom, Get Insight': An Introduction to Israel's Wisdom Literature,* Darton, Longman and Todd, 2000)

insight and understanding. Of course, that was true in some measure of all the biblical books, but the wisdom books were seen as especially suitable for this purpose because of their form. Instead of containing narrative or prophecy or poetry, they consist mainly of individual sayings that point to important aspects of human life in society, and present in a condensed and forceful way conclusions that come from a lifetime's experience. Most of these are what we might call proverbs (sometimes the word 'aphorism' is used, borrowed from the Greek term *aphorismos*). The form is familiar to us from our own culture with sayings such as, 'Many hands make light work', 'Too many cooks spoil the broth', 'Look before you leap', and 'There's more than one way to skin a cat'.

Indeed, books of sayings and proverbs were commonplace in the ancient world, and modern discoveries have shown that Israelite wisdom books were often remarkably similar to their counterparts in other areas of the ancient Near East. The story of how such books came into being offers fascinating insights into ancient culture and ways of thought.

CHARACTERISTICS OF WISDOM BOOKS IN THE ANCIENT NEAR EAST

Advice for a variety of types of people

Around the end of the nineteenth century, archaeologists began to discover books similar to the Old Testament book of Proverbs in the archives of Egypt and Mesopotamia. Since there was a tradition of calling such books 'wisdom' in the Bible, they used the same term to describe these works, though in Egypt the usual term for them was 'instruction'. Egyptian wisdom books go back into the third millennium BCE, and include,

- The Instruction of **Ptah-hotep** (the oldest wisdom book known to us)
- The Instruction for King Meri-kare
- The Instruction of Ani
- The Instruction of **Amen-em-opet**.

Ptah-hotep lived and taught in Egypt between 2575 and 2134 BCE. His teachings have survived on papyrus sheets and on clay tablets, and are at the Bibliothèque Nationale in France.

Amen-em-opet lived and taught in Egypt between 1250 and 1000 BCE, and two versions of his 'wise words' were discovered in the 1900s. One version, now in the British Museum in London, is written on papyrus sheets and the other, now in a museum in Turin in Italy, is on clay tablets.

The last of these caused great excitement in the academic world because it was found that much of it was very close to a section of the biblical book of Proverbs, Proverbs 22:17–24:34. According to Proverbs 22:20, this section consists of 'thirty sayings', and Amen-em-opet contains thirty short 'chapters'. About half of them are astonishingly close to the contents of this part of Proverbs. For example:

> *Do not remove an ancient landmark*
> *   or encroach on the fields of the fatherless;*
> *for their redeemer is strong;*
> *   he will plead their cause against you.* (Proverbs 23:10–11)

> *Do not carry off the landmark*

at the boundaries of the arable land,
  nor disturb the position of the measuring-cord;
    be not greedy after a cubit of land,
  nor encroach upon the boundaries of a widow.

(Amen-em-opet 6)

Although the manuscript of Amen-em-opet that we have comes only from the seventh or sixth century, Egyptologists agree that the text is actually much older, and so, since Egyptians did not really borrow from Hebrew culture, the general consensus is that Proverbs is probably copying it, rather than vice versa. This has potentially very far-reaching implications, because we now know a great deal about how and why the Egyptian Instruction literature came to be written. Its home was the schools attached to the royal court of the Pharaoh, where scribes were trained to staff the extensive Egyptian civil service. The Egyptian material is intended not for all and sundry, but specifically for the educated elite of the country — those from whom administrators and officials were drawn. This is reflected in some of the sayings in Ptah-hotep, including the following rather cynical and crafty one:

If thou art one to whom petition is made, be calm as thou listenest to the petitioner's speech. Do not rebuff him before he has swept out his body, or before he has said that for which he came. A petitioner likes attention to his words better than the fulfilling of that for which he came.

Yet alongside these pieces of advice for the ruling class, the Egyptian Instructions also contain general everyday advice that would have been applicable to everyone:

Cast not thy heart in pursuit of riches,
(for) there is no ignoring Fate and Fortune.
Place not thy heart upon externals,
(for) every man belongs to his (appointed)
  hour. (Amen-em-opet 7)

Now much the same is true of Israel's wisdom literature. It advises on such matters as how to behave at a banquet, which would apply only to the upper classes:

When you sit down to eat with a ruler,
  observe carefully what is before you,
and put a knife to your throat
  if you have a big appetite. (Proverbs 23:1–2)

Are you seated at the table of the great?
  Do not be greedy at it,
  and do not say, 'How much food there is here!'...
Do not reach out your hand for everything you see,
  and do not crowd your neighbour at the dish....

 The wisdom literature in the Old Testament reflects a tradition which developed over a long time and which was influenced by a number of neighbouring civilizations. In their final form, most of the wisdom books of the Old Testament and Apocrypha appear to come from after the Exile. Job is one of the few works in the Old Testament that probably come from the time of Persian domination (say between 500 and 300 BCE), while Ecclesiastes is almost certainly from the Hellenistic age (probably the third century BCE). Sirach is from the second century BCE and the Wisdom of Solomon is later still, a work of the Jews in Egypt in the first century BCE. However, although there is no sure way of dating the book of Proverbs, most scholars think that even though it was certainly edited and supplemented in later times, it has a core which comes from a time before the Exile. Some scholars have identified a difference in style between wisdom that may date from before and wisdom that may date from after the Exile. In the first, they see a confident, trusting attitude towards humankind's ability to understand the ways of God, and in the second they see a more sceptical view which questions traditional assumptions and is prepared to comment on difficult questions about the nature and purpose of human life. Whatever the merits of such a distinction, what is clear is that the origins of the Israelite wisdom tradition reach back a long way into the nation's history and undoubtedly reflect her many experiences and her developing understanding of the world.

> *Eat what is set before you like a well-bred person,*
> *and do not chew greedily, or you will give offence.*
> (Sirach 31:12, 14, 16)

On the other hand, there are also sayings that presuppose the life of a peasant-farmer, and that must originally have been at home in the culture of a small town or village:

> *The lazy person does not plough in season;*
> *harvest comes, and there is nothing to be found.*
> (Proverbs 20:4)

> *The righteous know the needs of their animals,*
> *but the mercy of the wicked is cruel.* (Proverbs 12:10)

The most likely conclusion from this is that Israelite society had a tradition of popular or clan wisdom and that proverbs originated in the life of ordinary people — the same would be true, probably, of many English proverbs. However, they were collected together by a learned group, who added to them other sayings more specifically related to their own lifestyle as officials at the royal court. Indeed, Proverbs 25:1 refers to 'proverbs...that the officials of King Hezekiah of Judah copied'. This resulted, in both Egypt and Israel, in compendia of proverbs that do not reflect a consistent background and in which, therefore, homely sayings alternate with advice to officials. However, in general, it is probably with the official readership in mind that these compilations were created. It was felt that even people training for leadership could not afford to ignore the wise sayings handed down, probably by word of mouth, from the past, even though these reflected a different lifestyle from that of those who copied them out.

Attributed to a great king

Hebrew wisdom also shares the characteristic of Egyptian Instructions in attributing it to a great king or ruler from the past. In Egypt, Ptah-hotep, Ani, and Amen-em-opet are all meant to be rulers, and Meri-kare was a Pharaoh, and Israel attributed its 'wisdom' to Solomon, although his wisdom was seen as a divine gift,

> *God gave Solomon very great wisdom, discernment, and*
> *breadth of understanding as vast as the sand on the seashore,*
> *so that Solomon's wisdom surpassed the wisdom of all the*
> *people of the east, and all the wisdom of Egypt. . . . He com-*
> *posed three thousand proverbs. . . . He would speak of trees*
> *. . . of animals, and birds, and reptiles, and fish. People came*
> *from all the nations to hear the wisdom of Solomon.*
> (1 Kings 4:29–34; cf. Proverbs 1:1, 25:1, and Ecclesiastes 1:1)

The structure and style of the collections

Hebrew and Egyptian wisdom also display similarities in structure and style. They sometimes contain short paragraphs grouped by content alongside simple lists of proverbs. This is reflected in Proverbs 1–9, which is a set of little 'chapters' on a single theme rather than a random collection of sayings, such as we find in much of the rest of the book.

Furthermore, both types of collections address the reader as 'my son' (NRSV translates 'my child', but the original person addressed will almost certainly have been male). Sometimes this seems to be meant literally in Proverbs — for example, 'Hear, my child, your father's instruction, and do not reject your mother's teaching' (Proverbs 1:8), but at other times the father–son relationship is probably metaphorical, and refers to the student and his teacher. Such a relationship might support the idea that wisdom was something that was taught by scribes and officials in schools in Israel.

However, we do not know for certain that there were such schools in Israel before the **Exile**, although the officials, who certainly did exist, must have been trained somehow, and it is reasonable to think that the system was similar to that in Egypt. In Mesopotamia, too, there were schools from early times, and a similar group of learned 'scribes' who administered the state, and who were responsible for transmitting wisdom literature. In the book of Sirach, which we know is from the second century BCE, long after the Exile, we read for the first time explicitly of a school:

> In biblical studies, the **Exile** refers to the period in Israel's history in the sixth century BCE when many of its people were taken captive and deported from Israel to Babylon.

> *Draw near to me, you who are uneducated,*
> *and lodge in the house of instruction.* (Sirach 51:23)

The book also describes the characteristics of a learned scribe, and we see that such a person was (ideally) an administrator, diplomat, and counsellor, as well as a profound thinker:

> *He seeks out the wisdom of all the ancients,*
> *and is concerned with prophecies;*
> *he preserves the sayings of the famous*
> *and penetrates the subtleties of parables;*
> *he seeks out the hidden meaning of proverbs*
> *and is at home with the obscurities of parables.*
> *He serves among the great*
> *and appears before rulers;*
> *he travels in foreign lands*
> *and learns what is good and evil in the human lot.*
> (Sirach 39:1–4)

THE ETHOS OF WISDOM

What are the characteristics of a 'wise' life?

There has been a lot of discussion in biblical studies about the character of the life which books like Proverbs and Sirach commend. All agree that it is essentially a practical life. These books are not concerned with any kind of religious

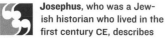

Josephus, who was a Jewish historian who lived in the first century CE, describes the wisdom books as 'precepts for the conduct of human life' (*Against Apion* I.8).

mysticism, but are meant for fairly hard-headed, sensible people living within the society of ancient Israel with its class structures and particular economic system. However, as we have seen, the proverbs preserved in wisdom books probably come from a range of different backgrounds such as the village, the city, and the royal court. They have been transmitted mainly for the benefit of an educated elite, but they do not all originally derive from this group and in many cases have their origin in simple family and village life.

This means that no completely consistent atmosphere or lifestyle emerges from the wisdom literature. Nevertheless, there are certain constant features. The books of Proverbs and Sirach — and many of the individual proverbs included in Ecclesiastes and Job — are all concerned with how to live a successful life. 'Success' is not a simple matter of becoming rich and powerful. It is a subtler concept: a life that is richly satisfying, not merely through outward trappings, but through inward contentment, though the realism of the wisdom writers means that they recognize this cannot be attained without enough to live on, and that achieving this requires hard work. Typical sayings which relate to this theme are:

> *A good name is to be chosen rather than great riches,*
> *and favour is better than silver or gold.* (Proverbs 22:1)

> *Do not love sleep, or else you will come to poverty;*
> *open your eyes, and you will have plenty of bread.*
> (Proverbs 20:13)

> *My child, eat honey, for it is good,*
> *and the drippings of the honeycomb are sweet to your taste.*
> *Know that wisdom is such to your soul;*
> *if you find it, you will find a future,*
> *and your hope will not be cut off.* (Proverbs 24:13–14)

> *A word fitly spoken*
> *is like apples of gold in a setting of silver.* (Proverbs 25:11)

> *Do you see persons wise in their own eyes?*
> *There is more hope for fools than for them.* (Proverbs 26:12)

Sometimes realism passes into something a little more cynical, with proverbs that register rather neutrally, without explicit approval or disapproval, the effects of human weakness:

> *'Bad, bad', says the buyer,*
> *then goes away and boasts.* (Proverbs 20:14)

> *A gift in secret averts anger;*
> *and a concealed bribe in the bosom, strong wrath.*
> (Proverbs 21:14)

However, in general, proverbs are strongly moral, encouraging honesty and virtue, and deploring unkind and immoral behaviour:

> *Whoever is kind to the poor lends to the LORD,*
> *and will be repaid in full.* (Proverbs 19:17)

> *Those who do violence to their father and*
> *chase away their mother*
> *are children who cause shame and bring reproach.*
> (Proverbs 19:26)

There is also a particular concern for self-control, which is seen in two frequently recurring themes: the evil of sexual immorality, and the harmful effects of drunkenness. Proverbs 1–9 contains a lot of material about the evil of adultery, and warns the reader (thought of as an impressionable young man) to avoid the wiles of the 'strange woman':

> *With much seductive speech she persuades him;*
> *with her smooth talk she compels him.*
> *Right away he follows her,*
> *and goes like an ox to the slaughter. . . .*
> *And now, my children, listen to me,*
> *and be attentive to the words of my mouth.*
> *Do not let your hearts turn aside to her ways;*
> *do not stray into her paths,*
> *for many are those she has laid low,*
> *and numerous are her victims.*
> *Her house is the way to **Sheol**,*
> *going down to the chambers of death.*
> (Proverbs 7:21–22, 24–27)

Sheol is the land of the dead; the general consensus of the Old Testament is that, though it is not 'hell', a place of torment, it is a sad and dark place where there is no life worth having.

Drunkenness, similarly, causes loss of self-control and brings shame on the drunkard:

> *Who has woe? Who has sorrow?*
> *Who has strife? Who has complaining?*
> *Who has wounds without cause?*
> *Who has redness of eyes?*
> *Those who linger late over wine,*
> *those who keep trying mixed wines.*
> *Do not look at wine when it is red,*
> *when it sparkles in the cup and goes down smoothly.*
> *At the last it bites like a serpent,*
> *and stings like an adder.*
> *Your eyes will see strange things,*
> *and your mind utter perverse things.* (Proverbs 23:29–33)

Nevertheless, the lifestyle commended is not **ascetic**. Marriage is praised, and moderate drinking is regarded as making for a happy life:

An **ascetic** is someone who, particularly for religious reasons, practises extreme self-discipline and abstains from all forms of pleasure.

> *... rejoice in the wife of your youth,*
> *a lovely deer, a graceful doe.*
> *May her breasts satisfy you at all times;*
> *may you be intoxicated always by her love.*
>
> (Proverbs 5:18–19)

> *Wine is very life to human beings*
> *if taken in moderation.*
> *What is life to one who is without wine?*
> *It has been created to make people happy.*
> *Wine drunk at the proper time and in moderation*
> *is rejoicing of heart and gladness of soul.* (Sirach 31:27–28)

Above all, being sensible is the great virtue for the wisdom books. Their strongest term of criticism is the word 'fool' (Hebrew *nabal*, pronounced naa-vaal, with the stress on the second syllable). Generalizing, we might say that where the prophets contrast the good and the evil, wisdom writers contrast the sensible person and the fool. Wisdom has to do with *coping*: leading a well-ordered and balanced life. Its ideal is the moderately successful, self-confident man who, without pride, can be conscious of his own uprightness, and who makes the world a better place for others.

Is the wisdom literature essentially non-religious?

The above description of what wisdom is, with its omission of any reference to God, prompts us to ask whether the wisdom literature is essentially non-religious. If by 'religious' we mean 'concerned with the practice of religious worship', then this is a fair assessment. This is because good moral conduct in the wisdom literature is prized above offering sacrifices: 'Guard your steps when you go to the house of God; to draw near to listen is better than the sacrifice offered by fools; for they do not know how to keep from doing evil' (Ecclesiastes 5:1). Indeed, wisdom writers are on the whole simply not very interested in what goes on in the Temple or at local sanctuaries. Yet, they are not **secular** in the modern sense, since they are often concerned with God and his requirements. In fact, many proverbs stress that 'the fear of the LORD is the beginning of wisdom' (e.g. Proverbs 9:10), indicating that wisdom was not just regarded as a form of superior human intelligence, but as a divine gift. Moreover, God is mentioned in every chapter of Proverbs! It has sometimes been suggested that wisdom began as a non-religious movement and only later started to incorporate these religious teachings, perhaps under the influence of the prophets. However, there is no real evidence of this, and it would be impossible to reconstruct a non-religious version of Proverbs. For that matter, Egyptian wisdom books also show a mixture of prudent advice with exhortations to pay heed to the gods, and the earliest Egyptian Instruction we have, Ptah-hotep, is probably also the most religious.

Katharine Dell says of the wisdom books of the Old Testament, 'They represent the teaching of the wise men of ancient Israel: their maxims distilled from the experiences of many generations, their advice to the young to understand and grow in maturity, their example tales and warnings.' (Katharine Dell, *'Get Wisdom, Get Insight': An Introduction to Israel's Wisdom Literature*, Darton, Longman and Todd, 2000).

The word **secular** suggests a view of the world which rejects religion, or regards it as of little importance.

Sometimes it is said that the theology of wisdom is a **natural theology**, and what is undeniable is that the kind of religion represented in the wisdom books is in many ways different from that of the sanctuaries or even of the prophets. God is not seen as the one who directed the history of Israel, nor as an active being who will shortly intervene in the running of the world. God is a more diffused influence, lying behind what goes on in the world, seeing that the wise are rewarded and the foolish get their just deserts, but not stepping in in person. It is interesting in this connection that the Egyptian Instructions often refer to 'the god' or 'the gods', but seldom to any specific god by name. It is as though they are concerned with 'the divine' as a rather vague category, a sort of world-ordering power, but not with the specific gods known from myths or worshipped in temples. Though Proverbs freely uses the divine name **YHWH**, it does not seem to be emphasizing what makes that God distinctive, but is alluding much more generally to 'the divine'. Ecclesiastes does not even use the name YHWH, but speaks simply of 'God' (in Hebrew *elohim*, pronounced elo-heem, with stress on the last syllable).

Natural theology is the view that God can be known to all from observation of, and reflection on, the world without the need for specific revelation from God.

YHWH is the primary way God's name appears in the Old Testament. It is simply four Hebrew consonants which many scholars believe may have been pronounced Yahweh. For a more detailed examination of this issue see 2.1 'Watchmaker or Living God?'

THE PERSONIFICATION OF WISDOM AND THE DISTINCTIVENESS OF LATER ISRAELITE WISDOM

A strange development occurred in Israelite wisdom literature, probably beginning shortly after the Exile, which we call the 'personification' of wisdom. Earlier texts in Proverbs use 'wisdom' as the term for a human skill or characteristic, in parallel with other words such as 'insight', 'shrewdness', and 'learning'. Thus, the book of Proverbs has this as its aim:

> *For learning about wisdom and instruction,*
> *   for understanding words of insight,*
> *for gaining instruction in wise dealing,*
> *   righteousness, justice, and equity;*
> *to teach shrewdness to the simple,*
> *   knowledge and prudence to the young —*
> *let the wise also hear and gain in learning,*
> *   and the discerning acquire skill,*
> *to understand a proverb and a figure,*
> *   the words of the wise and their riddles.* (Proverbs 1:2–6)

In this sense, 'Wisdom' becomes almost the name of a school subject. However, before long it comes to be personified as a female figure who invites people to share her banquet:

> *Wisdom has built her house,*
> *   she has hewn her seven pillars.*
> *She has slaughtered her animals, she has mixed her wine,*
> *   she has also set her table.*
> *She has sent out her servant-girls, she calls*
> *   from the highest places in the town,*

'You that are simple, turn in here!' (Proverbs 9:1–4)

Although this probably started as a mere literary convention, as poets might personify truth or beauty as if they were actual beings, simply to emphasize their importance, it seems that people eventually began to take the personification rather literally. So they believed that there was an entity called 'Wisdom' that really existed in some realm of its own. This may have been related to tendencies elsewhere in the ancient Near East. The Egyptians, for example, recognized a divine being called *ma'at,* a kind of principle of world order, which existed in some sense in its own right and with which the wise person could get in touch. Thus, wisdom became a sort of mythological being — as nearly divine as anything other than God could be in a **monotheistic** environment.

The next stage was to identify this being with the wisdom that God was thought to possess ('he too is wise', Isaiah 31:2), and Proverbs 8 speaks as though wisdom was made by God, and then became his assistant when he created the world:

> *The LORD created me at the beginning of his work,*
> *the first of his acts of long ago.*
> *Ages ago I was set up,*
> *at the first, before the beginning of the earth. . . .*
> *When he established the heavens, I was there,*
> *when he drew a circle on the face of the deep. . . .*
> *then I was beside him, like a master worker,*
> *and I was daily his delight,*
> *rejoicing before him always,*
> *rejoicing in his inhabited world,*
> *and delighting in the human race.*
>
> (Proverbs 8:22–23, 27, 30–31)

This puzzling development may reflect the tendency in post-exilic thinking for God to become so utterly **transcendent** that mediators are needed between himself and the world. God did not, it was felt, make the world directly, but through the agency of the divine Wisdom. Wisdom is thus almost turned into a goddess, since the Hebrew word for wisdom, *hokmah,* is feminine — almost turned into a goddess, but not quite, because Israel remained monotheistic. Nevertheless, in a world where there were many gods and goddesses Jews may have found it an advantage to believe in this semi-divine entity.

Yet, that is not quite the end of the story. In Sirach, probably a lot later than Proverbs 8, personified Wisdom is glorified still further. In it Wisdom is identified with the 'mist' that covered the ground at the creation according to Genesis 2:6 (a 'stream' in NRSV) and also with the pillar of cloud that led the Israelites through the wilderness (Exodus 13:21–22):

> *'I came forth from the mouth of the Most High,*
> *and covered the earth like a mist.*

A monotheist is someone who believes in only one God.

When applied to God, the term **transcendent** means that God is greater than the world and in some sense is beyond it and outside human experience.

I dwelt in the highest heavens,
*   and my throne was in a pillar of cloud.'* (Sirach 24:3–4)

However, the association with the pillar of cloud changes Wisdom from being a universal phenomenon to something especially connected with Israel; and the passage takes this idea further:

'*Then the Creator of all things gave me a command,*
*   and my Creator chose the place for my tent.*
He said, "Make your dwelling in Jacob,
*   and in Israel receive your inheritance".* . . . .
In the holy tent I ministered before him,
*   and so I was established in* **Zion**.
Thus in the beloved city he gave me a resting-place,
*   and in Jerusalem was my domain.*
I took root in an honoured people,
*   in the portion of the LORD, his heritage.'* (Sirach 24:8, 10–12)

> **Zion** is the name of the principal hill of Jerusalem but it is used poetically in the Old Testament to refer to the whole city of Jerusalem. Later generations referred to the entire nation of Israel as Zion, and the Jewish nationalist movement, whose aim was to establish a Jewish state in the land of Israel, attached the name Zionism to its cause.

From such a passage, we begin to suspect that Wisdom must have been identified with some other entity, peculiar to Israel. The solution to this riddle comes in verse 23:

All this is the book of the covenant of the Most High God,
*   the law that Moses commanded us*
*   as an inheritance for the congregations of Jacob.*

So, Wisdom is really the Torah, the Law revealed to Israel! With this identification, Jesus son of Sira takes what had been an aspect of what we called 'natural theology' — a theological system potentially known to all — and turns it into a specifically Israelite phenomenon. Thus, the personification of Wisdom ends as a way of glorifying the Law of Moses — an idea that would have been far from the minds of the authors of Proverbs.

 Anderson says of Jesus son of Sira's link between Wisdom and Torah, 'Here a Jewish sage, by identifying wisdom and Torah, brought the wisdom literature into the central stream of the Mosaic tradition. Wisdom was "nationalized", that is, related positively to the redemptive activity of God in Israel's history' (Bernhard W. Anderson, *The Living World of the Old Testament*, Longman, 1988).

It is noticeable that in other ways, too, Sirach integrates the more universal wisdom tradition with ideas that are specifically Jewish. In chapters 44–49, there is an extensive celebration of the nation's heroes, and there are frequent references to God's Law, in ways that would be out of place in Proverbs. The Wisdom of Solomon has an even more markedly Jewish character, with chapters 10–19 devoted to a retelling of the history of Israel, in which 'wisdom' rather than God is seen as acting to save the people. Thus, the wisdom tradition gradually became integrated with the national religious tradition. However, as we have seen, in earlier times it represented a rather distinctive way of thinking about religious questions, and had little interest in the history of Israel, or even in Israelites or Jews as special cases: it put forward moral principles that were based on human nature as such.

OBSERVATION VERSUS DOGMA

Wisdom begins with observation of the world. Proverbial sayings encapsulate insights derived from seeing how things actually turn out in human life, so that when people hear them, they say, 'How true!' However, because such proverbs get repeated over and over again, whereas human life keeps throwing up new situations, they can become clichés and may not continue to do justice to actual experience. Thus, sayings that were originally fresh and vivid observations, drawn from real life, may harden into platitudes that obscure more than they illuminate. For example, the wisdom writers express the valid observation that hard work is often repaid with success, and that dishonesty often leads to ruin, but they tend not to allow for exceptions. Yet, as we all know, there are hardworking people whose enterprises fail through no fault of their own, and there are criminals who become and remain rich. Consequently, proverbial wisdom does not fit all possible situations.

This problem became particularly acute when people started to write stories that dealt explicitly with the problem of the 'righteous sufferer'. All over the ancient Near East we find evidence of the basic story that is the plot of the book of Job, where a good man is afflicted for no moral reason. What seems to have happened is that the wisdom tradition began in effect to reflect on itself, and to see that its own certainties could not always be defended. These certainties are, in fact, found less in Proverbs and the other wisdom books than in certain psalms, and we can probably conclude from this that they were by no means the sole preserve of 'the wise', but were widely diffused in Israelite culture, as they were elsewhere in the ancient Near East. Particularly important examples are Psalms 1, 37, 49, 73, and 112. Take, for example, Psalm 37:

> For the wicked shall be cut off,
>> but those who wait for the LORD shall inherit
>>> the land.
> Yet a little while, and the wicked will be no more. . . .
> The LORD knows the days of the blameless,
>> and their heritage will abide for ever;
> they are not put to shame in evil times,
>> in the days of famine they have abundance. . . .
> I have been young, and now am old,
>> yet I have not seen the righteous forsaken
>>> or their children begging bread.' (Psalm 37:9–10, 18–19, 25)

One is tempted to reply, 'You should get out more', because surely no one in the ancient or the modern world could really claim this last sentence as a piece of observation. It is pure dogma, a claim made in the face of the evidence.

Indeed, this is the kind of attitude challenged in the book of Job. It sets up a situation which is completely incompatible with the dogma, since we know from the beginning

The 'Declarations of Innocence', from the Egyptian Book of the Dead, which consist of lists of things a person needs to say about how one has lived life well in order to guarantee a blessed afterlife, display parallels with Job's protest of his innocence in Job 31. In addition, an Assyrian poem about a man trying to work out why God is making him suffer, entitled 'I Will Praise the Lord of Wisdom', is so similar to the book of Job that it is sometimes referred to as a 'Babylonian Job'.

that Job is 'blameless and upright, one who feared God and turned away from evil' (Job 1:1), and yet he suffers the loss of all his property, most of his family, and his own health. His challenges to the dogma of the prosperity of the good thus ring true, and the book is one of the sharpest attacks on the conventional wisdom to be found in the Bible or, indeed, almost anywhere in the ancient world.

> *It is all one; therefore I say,*
> *   he [i.e. God] destroys both the blameless and the wicked.*
> *When disaster brings sudden death,*
> *   he mocks at the calamity of the innocent.*
> *The earth is given into the hand of the wicked;*
> *   he covers the eyes of its judges —*
> *   if it is not he, who then is it?* (Job 9:22–24)

Ecclesiastes also attacks the idea of an appropriate correspondence between conduct and reward. Everyone dies in the end, the preacher says: so what difference does it really make whether one is good or evil?

> *There is a vanity that takes place on earth, that there are righteous people who are treated according to the conduct of the wicked, and there are wicked people who are treated according to the conduct of the righteous. I said that this also is vanity [i.e. futility].* (Ecclesiastes 8:14)

> *The living know that they will die, but the dead know nothing; they have no more reward, and even the memory of them is lost. Their love and their hate and their envy have all perished; never again will they have any share in all that happens under the sun.* (Ecclesiastes 9:5–6)

Thus wisdom writers themselves began to mount a critique of wisdom. In this they were rather like the Greek philosopher **Socrates**, for whom good philosophy meant questioning received opinions — challenging people to think through accepted dogmas and to revise them where they were inadequate. Wisdom is, in effect, the nearest thing in the Old Testament to philosophy. It does include practical, everyday advice, but it also includes more reflective writing which is prepared to examine the meaning of life and the nature of suffering, and in this it can be interrogative and questioning in style, not always dogmatic or sure of itself.

'Wisdom is the art of living a good life, seeking what leads to life and not to death. It is a reflection on the great human questions: life, death, love, suffering, evil, men's relationship with God and with one another. Wisdom is universal and timeless. Suffering and death, life and love know no frontiers.' (Etienne Charpentier, *How to Read the Old Testament*, SCM, 1981)

Socrates (469–399 BCE) was an Athenian philosopher who felt he had a duty to teach through questioning people's beliefs. He never wrote anything himself, but his pupils, Plato and Xenophon, mention him and his teachings in their work. A public jury sentenced Socrates to death, by drinking hemlock, for corrupting the young with his teaching.

4.5 The Plot Thickens
ISRAEL'S HISTORIANS AND STORY-TELLERS

T H E   B A S I C S

- Almost half of the Old Testament is narrative and is most likely based on ancient oral traditions which in their present form reflect an extensive process of editing and reshaping.
- The narrative sections of the Old Testament contain a variety of types of literature but also share certain features that enable us to speak of an Old Testament narrative style.

STORY-TELLING IS PART OF every human culture. In societies that have not yet developed writing such story-telling is oral: stories are passed down the generations, and people gather to hear them. In our own culture, this oral level persists only in anecdotes and jokes, but where there is no writing people develop a good memory for much longer narratives. So, most scholars think that in ancient Israel stories must originally have been passed on by word of mouth and that large amounts of the narratives now found in the Bible were originally oral stories. There are a few accounts in the Old Testament of people actually telling stories — usually parables that have a 'moral' (Judges 9:7–15; 2 Samuel 12:1–4; 2 Kings 14:9) — but, of course, we do not possess any of this oral story-telling: there are no recordings of ancient Israelites telling stories! What we have are narratives that are the result of a lengthy process of the rewriting, editing, and reshaping of the stories people wrote down in ancient times.

However, there can be no denying the centrality of stories to Israelite culture, since about half of the Old Testament consists of narrative. All the books from Genesis to Esther (in the English Bible) are narrative, and so are some sections of Isaiah and Jeremiah, large parts of Daniel, the book of Jonah, and (in the Apocrypha) the books of Tobit, Judith, and Maccabees.

In our culture, we distinguish between many different

kinds of narrative writing. We would not lump together in a single book parts of a novel, myths, legends, anecdotes, jokes, extracts from the writings of academic historians, and lists taken from census returns. Yet, in ancient times people were much more inclined, when describing the past, simply to collect all the available material and blend it loosely together, without paying attention to differences of literary 'genre' or 'types' of writing. For this reason some Old Testament narrative books are puzzling to the modern reader because they seem to lurch from one kind of writing to another, without the writers apparently being aware of this or worrying about it.

This is most striking in the books of Kings, where we find material that looks as if it comes from a variety of different types of writing. For example, there are parts of the text which seem to be official royal documents, giving formal details of this or that king:

> *Amon was twenty-two years old when he began to reign; he reigned for two years in Jerusalem. His mother's name was Meshullemeth daughter of Haruz of Jotbah.* (2 Kings 21:19)

There are also stories such as those about Elijah and Elisha, which involve miracles and sound like folk tales, for example,

> *As they continued walking and talking, a chariot of fire and horses of fire separated the two of them, and Elijah ascended in a whirlwind into heaven.* (2 Kings 2:11)

In addition, the text contains passages that are more reflective in tone and give the historian's interpretation of events — usually in theological terms:

> *Still the LORD did not turn from the fierceness of his great wrath, by which his anger was kindled against Judah, because of all the provocations with which Manasseh had provoked him. The LORD said, 'I will remove Judah also out of my sight, as I have removed Israel. . . .'* (2 Kings 23:26–27)

Pentateuch is a common collective term for the first five books of the Old Testament — Genesis, Exodus, Leviticus, Numbers, and Deuteronomy. It is derived from the Greek word *pente* meaning 'five'. In the Jewish tradition, these are sometimes referred to as the five books of Moses.

Therefore, studying the narrative books of the Old Testament involves being alert to differences of genre, as well as asking about when the books were put together into the form we now find in our Bibles. The **Pentateuch**, the Deuteronomistic History, and the Chronicler's History are the titles given to the major narrative works in the Old Testament, but it must be remembered that these are all made up of earlier materials — which often belong to quite different genres, and so probably once existed as separate works in their own right.

THE PENTATEUCH

The 'five books of Moses' — Genesis, Exodus, Leviticus, Numbers, and Deuteronomy — tell a continuous story that runs from the creation of the world down to the moment when the Israelites are poised on the brink of crossing the Jordan and entering the Promised Land. They end with the death of Moses (Deuteronomy 34). Of all the narrative works in the Old Testament, the Pentateuch probably has the most complicated origins. A lot of the material must surely be very old, and reflect tales about their ancestors that circulated among the Israelites long before anyone wrote it all down, but we have no access to these early traditions, only to the finished product in the form of the five books.

According to perhaps the most influential theory in Old Testament study, the Documentary Hypothesis of Karl Heinz Graf (1815–69) and Julius Wellhausen (1844–1918), the Pentateuch results from the weaving together of several originally independent documents or sources. According to this theory, the oldest of these 'sources' of the Pentateuch begins in Genesis 2:4b with the account of the creation of the first human beings. It also contains most of the memorable stories in the Pentateuch, for example, the stories about Abraham, Isaac, and Jacob, the early life of Moses, the wanderings of the tribes in the desert after the Exodus from Egypt. One of its defining features is that it calls the God of Israel by his proper name, **YHWH**, throughout, whereas later sources think that the name was revealed for the first time to Moses. As a result, it is known as the J or the Yahwist source — since those who first developed this theory were German scholars and in German the name of God is spelled Jahwe.

The second source, also rich in stories, abstains from using the divine name until it has been revealed to Moses (Exodus 6) and calls God simply 'God'. In Hebrew 'God' is *elohim,* so the source is known as the E or Elohist source. It is likely that J and E were combined at some point to form an early version of Genesis–Numbers; it used to be said confidently that this took place well before the Exile. Scholars regarded J as a work from the period of the early monarchy, probably written in the southern kingdom of Judah; E they dated a bit later, perhaps in the eighth century (the age of the great prophets) and attributed it to writers in the northern kingdom of Israel.

However, nowadays scholars tend to be wary of these precise theories. Some E material may be simply a variant version of J, where two slightly different accounts of the same event have been preserved side by side. In addition, the date of writing is also widely disputed, with some now saying that J cannot be earlier than the **Exile** because it seems to depend on the stories of the prophets in, for example, its way of talking about Moses. The best we can probably say is that there is a thread of early narratives in the Pentateuch, running through the four books from Genesis to Numbers, which contains material that is not completely self-consistent, especially on the question of when God's proper name first began to be used. Most of the famous stories in the Pentateuch come from this document, such as the stories of Abraham and Isaac, and the story of the **Exodus** with its plagues.

YHWH is the primary way God's name appears in the Old Testament. It is simply four Hebrew consonants which many scholars believe may have been pronounced Yahweh. For a more detailed examination of this issue see 2.1 'Watchmaker or Living God?'

In biblical studies, the **Exile** refers to the period in Israel's history in the sixth century BCE when many of its people were taken captive and deported from Israel to Babylon.

The word **exodus** literally means 'way out' and refers to the departure of the Israelites from Egypt under the leadership of Moses.

The Pentateuch also contains some strikingly different writing, comprising few detailed stories but including a great deal of legal material to do with the ordering of the Jewish community. It is mainly found in the central section of the Pentateuch, beginning in Exodus 25, continuing throughout Leviticus, and running through Numbers up to about chapter 19. Since its main interest is in ritual and sacrifice, this material is known as the Priestly source (P) and, following the work of Julius Wellhausen, has been seen as a largely post-exilic document (though it may rest on older traditions). In many ways it is the foundation text for later Judaism with its detailed ritual legislation, and it gives the whole Pentateuch its overall tone as not simply a narrative text but also a law book.

The odd thing is that there is also P-type material outside this central section of the Pentateuch. The **genealogies** in Genesis 5 and 10, for example, share the style of the P source; and so do some very important parts of Genesis, notably the story of the creation of the world in Genesis 1. Oddest of all, the story of the great Flood in Genesis 6–9 seems to have been produced by weaving together an original J source account with material much closer to the interests of the P source. The P source, like the E source, thinks of the name YHWH as unknown before the time of Moses, and in the Flood story there are verses that use the name and others that speak simply of 'God' (*elohim*). It is possible to extract two parallel (but incompatible) stories from Genesis 6–9, and this is the reason why the account as it stands is difficult to read as a coherent whole. By piecing together detailed evidence such as this scholars came to the conclusion that the P source was, in origin, just as much a complete history of the world as the combined JE source, though it covered events much more sketchily and often by means of lists and genealogies rather than through narrative. As the Pentateuch stands, however, it begins (Genesis 1) and ends (Deuteronomy 34) with P source material, and this suggests that the older J and E sources have somehow been worked into the framework of the basic P account.

The fourth element in the Pentateuch is the book of Deuteronomy, which also had a separate history of its own before it was incorporated into the Pentateuch. Some think it was the law book found in the Temple by King Josiah (2 Kings 22). Whether or not that is so, Deuteronomy seems to be largely a reworking of legal ideas already set out in Exodus 21–24 and so must be later than that section, which is traditionally ascribed to the E source. It seems to have been added on to an essentially complete document, Genesis–Numbers, as part of a drive to collect all the material to do with Moses — probably, therefore, sometime after the Exile. At the same time, there are odd verses in the Pentateuch where ideas reminiscent of Deuteronomy have been inserted, and these are known as D source material for obvious reasons. On the whole, however, Deuteronomy represents a separate element

Genealogies are lists of people's descendants, like a family tree.

in the Pentateuch, and reads like an afterthought. The people are already about to enter the Land at the end of Numbers, but Moses then detains them with an enormous speech (almost the whole of Deuteronomy is a speech by Moses) before his death, and the appointment of Joshua to take them across the Jordan.

Though Moses is said to have written certain passages (see Deuteronomy 31:9, 22, 24), the biblical text nowhere says that he was the author of the Pentateuch as a whole. It was only later Jewish and Christian tradition that called these 'the books of Moses', and proposed theories as to how he could have written them — including the account of his own death! Yet, the association of the books with Moses, the great lawgiver, certainly contributed to the very high status these books came to have in Judaism, where they have an authority far greater than that of the rest of the Hebrew Bible.

Christians treated the Old Testament more on a level, and early Christian writers can even speak of a 'Hexateuch' (in Greek *hex* means 'six') consisting of the Pentateuch plus the book of Joshua. It is possible that the Pentateuchal sources continue into Joshua: this was a popular theory in the late nineteenth and early twentieth centuries. Indeed, though this view is not widely shared, a recent scholar, R. E. Friedman (b. 1946), has revived an old theory that the J source originally included material now in not only the Pentateuch but all the historical books, including Joshua, Judges, Samuel, and Kings. If so, there was once what a few early Christian writers called an 'Enneateuch' (in Greek *ennea* means 'nine').

 'The Pentateuch reminds one of a medieval cathedral which by good fortune has escaped the vandalism of rigorous restoration and therefore now stands with all its different styles mixed up, so that a very trained eye is needed to discover the original plan.' (A. Bentzen, *Introduction to the Old Testament*, 1948)

However, most scholars think that the 'books of Moses' do form a body of texts distinct from the books that follow in our Bibles. In addition, most would agree that, as the Pentateuch stands in its present form, it is a product of a 'redactor' who lived sometime after the Exile and who attempted to weave these separate sources into a theological and historical whole.

THE 'DEUTERONOMISTIC HISTORY'

If the Pentateuch tells the story from the creation to the death of Moses, the four books that follow take the reader from the entry into the Promised Land, at the beginning of Joshua, to the Exile from it, at the end of 2 Kings. This way of putting it already suggests a certain unity of purpose among these books. For all the variety in the types of literature collected together there, the four 'historical' books do have a thematic unity, and also in many places a unity of style. They incorporate, as was said above, official records, legends, folk tale, and theological reflection. Yet taken together they present a single history, the history of Israel in the Promised Land. Moreover, this is a completed story, for by its end the people have forfeited the Land through their sin.

 The four books referred to here are Joshua, Judges, I and 2 Samuel, and I and 2 Kings. Note that the book of Ruth, which is placed between Judges and I Samuel in Christian Bibles, appears in a different place in the Hebrew Bible. For more about Ruth, see 3.5 'Loyal Subjects?' and for more about the differences between the Christian and Hebrew Bibles, see I.I 'Old Testament or Hebrew Bible?'

It is thus attractive to think that the books might have been compiled deliberately as a unity. This was often suggested in the nineteenth century, but it was first developed in

Martin Noth (pronounced 'note') was an important German Old Testament scholar. In addition to his work on the Deuteronomistic History, he was interested in the social and political structure of early Israel and suggested that the Israelite tribes were constituted as an amphictyony (for more on this see 4.1 'The Social Scene'). One of his most influential works was his *History of Israel* (1950). He is buried in Bethlehem.

Prologue is a term used for an introduction or introductory comment.

detail by **Martin Noth** (1902–68) in the 1930s. He called these books the 'Deuteronomistic History' because the criteria they applied when judging Israel, and especially its kings, were taken from the book of Deuteronomy — particularly from Deuteronomy 12, which lays down the rule that the people are to have only one sanctuary, not many. He suggested, in fact, that the historian had originally begun his work with the book of Deuteronomy itself as a kind of extended **prologue** and that it was a later generation that detached Deuteronomy from the History and tacked it on to the end of Numbers to form the Pentateuch. Until recently most scholars accepted this hypothesis, to such an extent that people sometimes speak of 'the Deuteronomistic History' as though there were part of the Bible actually called that in the text itself — which of course is not the case! It remains only a hypothesis, though an appealing one.

However, if the existence of the 'Deuteronomistic History' is accepted, it raises the question as to when it might have been put together. On the one hand, since it is conceived as a history of Israel in the Land, it cannot be earlier than the Exile in 587 BCE. On the other hand, since it shows no awareness that the Exile has ended or is going to end, probably it cannot be later than the 'return' around 537 BCE. This information indicates, therefore, a relatively brief window of fifty years in which it might have been compiled. Few works in the Old Testament can be so exactly dated! However, things are (as always) more complicated than this. There is every likelihood that the 'finished' work was added to after the Exile, with odd verses and explanations added, and perhaps even with whole chapters inserted. For example, Deuteronomy 4 appears to reflect the post-exilic situation. Furthermore, it is also possible that the work passed through several editions — maybe there was even an earlier, pre-exilic version that brought the story down to about the time of King Josiah in the seventh century, and that was then rounded off by a second editor when the disaster of the Exile occurred.

As is usual in Old Testament studies, there are many theories about all this, but what we can say for certain is that the editor or editors drew on some material that already existed and had been known well before the Exile. This includes:

- Stories about the prophets Elijah and Elisha, now found in 1 Kings 17–2 Kings 9.
- The 'Court History' of King David, sometimes also known as the 'Succession Narrative' because it concentrates on the question of who is to be David's successor on the throne of Judah. This can be found in 2 Samuel 9–20 and 1 Kings 1 and 2. (For more about this, see below.)
- Stories about the lives of Samuel and Saul, found in much of 1 Samuel.
- Royal annals — that is, official records about what happened in particular years of a given king's reign. Extracts from these are found throughout 1 and 2 Kings.

- Stories about the exploits of the 'judges', which were probably each transmitted independently and which the editor has blended into a harmonious account of the whole judges period.

In fact, there are probably few passages where the historian was writing freely. Mostly he seems to have taken existing documents and joined them together, often introducing his own concerns about the purity and obedience of Israel, and thus trying to explain why the history in the end went so disastrously wrong. In a number of key places there are long speeches by important people in the story, and these often show us the historian's own concerns. Examples are Joshua 24 (the last words of Joshua), 1 Samuel 12 (where Samuel hands over the reins of power to Saul), and 1 Kings 8 (Solomon's great prayer at the dedication of the Temple). By reading these passages we can get an idea of the historian's central interests.

THE BOOKS OF CHRONICLES

Ever since the people who translated the books of 1 and 2 Chronicles into Greek called them *ta paralipomena* ('the things omitted') they have been treated as though they were simply a supplement to the books of Samuel and Kings. However, although Chronicles essentially tells the same story as Samuel and Kings, it does so in a highly distinctive way — not just adding 'omitted' bits of the tale, but reshaping it to make very different points. Chronicles is almost certainly a work of the late Persian period, perhaps around the fourth century BCE, and it reflects a time when the history of Israel was no longer felt to have ended with the Exile, but had re-emerged from the darkness and begun again, even if in a more muted form. So Chronicles does not tell a story of decline and fall, but recounts the history of the Judean monarchy from the rise of David to the restoration of Judah after the Exile — ending with the triumphant announcement that Cyrus the Persian king has encouraged Judeans to go back and resettle their land (2 Chronicles 36:22–23). Although a lot of material is simply repeated from the books of 1 and 2 Kings, there is also much modification of the story.

The books which have the title 'Annals' in the Hebrew Bible were given the title 'Chronicles' by Saint Jerome (c. 342–420 CE), who translated the Bible into Latin. The full title he gave these books was 'Chronicle of the whole divine history'.

To begin with, central to the author's vision of Judah is the importance of the Temple and the sacrificial system. Instead of being a warrior-king, David is presented as primarily a priest-king, who organizes all the festivals and rituals of worship, and prepares all the materials so that his son Solomon can build the Temple. In this Chronicles shares a similar ideology to the P source of the Documentary Hypothesis (outlined above), probably written around the same time.

Secondly, in contrast with the Deuteronomistic History, the author of 1 and 2 Chronicles records immediate punishments for those who disobey God. The Deuteronomistic view of history affirmed that God rewards goodness and punishes sin, but often as a delayed action, so that the sins of kings might

'For the Chronicler, David was a holy and dedicated leader who followed Yahweh faithfully. . . . In short, David is shown to be totally consumed with zeal for the right worship of Yahweh. He becomes a second lawgiver almost as great as Moses. This picture of David as the founder of a community centred on the Temple becomes the standard by which the Chronicler then judges the rest of Israel's history.' (Lawrence Boadt, *Reading the Old Testament: An Introduction*, Paulist Press, 1984)

The Samaritans, who take their name from the royal city of Samaria in the northern kingdom of Israel, were Jews who had survived the Assyrian defeat of the northern kingdom in 721 BCE. At that time, many Jews were deported, but many also remained in the area, which was restored and established by the Assyrians as one of their provinces. According to 2 Kings 17 the Assyrians also imported a number of other peoples into this area from places like Babylon. These people appear to have added the worship of Yahweh to the worship of their own gods, and the Jews who had remained in Samaria intermarried with these foreign peoples and adopted their worship. Thus, the Jews from the southern kingdom of Judah who returned from exile to Jerusalem around 538 BCE did not regard those in Samaria as true Jews because they were descendants of a mixed population. For this reason they rejected the offers of the Samaritans to help rebuild the Temple in Jerusalem. This prompted the Samaritans to protest to the Persian court and to threaten armed retaliation. In the end, the Samaritans built their own Temple to Yahweh on Mt Gerizim, and the hostility between the Jews and the Samaritans became legendary. A small community of Samaritans still exists today, centred around the town of Nablus (ancient Shechem).

be avenged on their descendants, very much as it says in the Ten Commandments. In the Deuteronomistic History, God 'punishes children for the iniquity of parents, to the third and fourth generation', and the fall of Judah is presented, at least partly, as a punishment for the sins of King Manasseh in the previous century. In Chronicles, on the other hand, there is what has been called a 'doctrine of immediate retribution'. Consequently, 'bad' kings, such as Manasseh himself, are said to have repented, in order to explain the fact that they had long reigns (2 Chronicles 33), while 'good' kings who died prematurely are said to have been worse than they looked (see 2 Chronicles 35:20–27, on King Josiah). In the case of King David, the more disagreeable aspects of his reign are omitted — the adultery, the murder, and the family troubles are all missing, principally because it is in the fulfilment of the Davidic covenant that the author of Chronicles sees the future hope of Israel. Such examples reveal that there is a tendency here, which became marked in later Jewish history writing, to tell the story as it should have happened rather than as it did!

A further feature of Chronicles, which in fact it shares with the Deuteronomistic History, is the belief that the northern kingdom of Israel perished because it was so wicked — indeed, it does not even record the history of the north in detail. However, unlike some in the post-exilic community the author of Chronicles believed that at least individual northerners could deserve salvation, and could rejoin the Judean community and worship in the Temple. Thus, when King Hezekiah of the southern kingdom of Judah (716–687 BCE) holds a great Passover celebration he sends messengers to the north to try to get northerners to attend. According to the author of Chronicles at least some do so (2 Chronicles 30) and they are allowed to celebrate the festival even though they are less 'pure' than they strictly need to be. Perhaps, therefore, the author must have belonged to the party in post-exilic Judah that was open to the possibility of 'Samaritans' being regarded as true Jews, as against the exclusivism of characters such as Ezra and Nehemiah.

OTHER NARRATIVE TEXTS IN THE OLD TESTAMENT AND APOCRYPHA

There are other important narrative books that do not fall under the three great collections of Pentateuch, Deuteronomistic History, and Chronicles. Particularly significant for their historical information are the books of Ezra and Nehemiah, which in the Hebrew Bible form a single book. These may come from the same period as Chronicles — indeed, it used to be thought that they were by the same author — a long time after Ezra and Nehemiah themselves actually lived. This probably explains why the historical sequence of events is so confused, especially in the first few chapters of the book of Ezra. At least in the case of Nehemiah there may be a genuine personal 'diary' underlying the present text, though it has clearly been reworked.

Most of the other shorter narrative books of the Old Testament and **Apocrypha** are probably fictitious, and may have been read as such by their earliest readers; they are sometimes described nowadays as 'Jewish novels'. Clear examples are Esther, Jonah, and Ruth, which take place in a fictionalized past with almost fairy-tale features such as the great fish that swallows Jonah whole. However, the first six chapters of Daniel also come from the fictional imagination, involving kings such as 'Darius the Mede' who never existed historically but who are personifications of good and evil rule. The same is true of the two tales in the Apocrypha, **Tobit** and **Judith**, which purport to be about life in the Assyrian period but really tell us more about the life of Jews in the Jewish dispersion some long time after the Exile. Only 1 Maccabees is a genuinely 'historical' work, providing important information about the Jews under Hellenistic rule.

THE STYLE OF OLD TESTAMENT NARRATIVE TEXTS

The narrative texts of the Old Testament are varied in character, as we have seen. Yet, there are certain features that mark them out as belonging to a distinctive and highly interesting literary culture. You do not need to read far in the Old Testament to develop a 'feel' for the narrative style, and you are soon in a position to recognize an Old Testament narrative and distinguish it from, for example, a Greek myth. Some salient features are these:

- The narrative is very terse. There is hardly any description of what people look like, unless it is strictly relevant to the plot, and there are no descriptions of places.
- There are no more than three characters 'on stage' in any given scene, so that dialogues lack complexity.
- Hardly anything is said about what is going on in the characters' minds; this has to be inferred from what they say or do.
- Mention of God's involvement in the plot is irregular. Sometimes whole pages will pass with no mention of God, and at other times he is an active character in the story. One of the characteristic features of Hebrew narrative is this oscillation between a 'divine' and a 'human' perspective on events. Sometimes we even find two versions of a story, one with divine involvement and the other not — look at the accounts of the deliverance of Jerusalem from the Assyrians in 2 Kings 18–19.
- It is usually easy to tell where one story ends and a new one begins. To put it technically, stories exhibit 'closure'. No one ever had any difficulty — in selecting 'Bible stories' for a children's Bible, for example — in deciding what constitutes 'one story'. Occasionally stories are interwoven, but this is the exception.

A good way of observing these points in action is to read some of the stories of the Judges (Judges 6–9 or 13–16), or

Apocrypha is the name given to the collection of books which are included in the Greek version of the Old Testament (the Septuagint) but not in the Hebrew Scriptures. These books are often also called 'deuterocanonical' books.

Tobit is the righteous hero of a story about pious Jews. In spite of the opposition of kings and demons, and with the help of the angel Raphael, Tobit experienced a miracle cure for his blindness, and suitable Jewish marriages are arrranged for his relatives deported to Assyria in the reign of Shalmaneser. It is a romantic adventure story and is allegedly set in Nineveh in the eighth century BCE. However, most scholars agree that it in fact reflects the piety and morality of late Old Testament Judaism and was probably composed around 200 BCE.

Judith is the heroine of a dramatic story of how a beautiful widow saves her town, Bethulia, from the assault of the wicked Assyrian general, Holofernes, by flirting with and then beheading him. The story is set against an inaccurate historical background, with features such as Nebuchadnezzar (king of Babylon 605–562 BCE) called the king of Assyria. This, together with the book's emphasis on the Law and its hope of deliverance from foreign enemies, has caused some scholars to suggest that it was written in the Maccabean period to encourage the Jews in their time of persecution by the Seleucids (see 3.5 'Loyal Subjects?').

better still the Court History of David (2 Samuel 9–20 and 1 Kings 1 and 2). Here we have long continuous accounts, yet they are broken up into separate scenes, and in each the features mentioned can be observed. The Court History is at least as interesting a read as most modern novels, and a good deal shorter!

4.6 Taking Orders
LAW AND INSTRUCTION IN THE OLD TESTAMENT

T H E   B A S I C S

- 'Law' in the Old Testament refers to a complex body of texts that has much in common with law codes of the ancient Near East. However, it also displays evidence of its own unique forms, content, and authorization.
- The law in the Old Testament is not really a coherent law code as we might understand it today but rather a sort of commentary on how God wishes to help his people live according to his will.

I N THE BIBLE 'LAW' can mean roughly what it means in English: legal regulations by which society is ordered. However, it can also mean the whole system of religious obligations peculiar to Judaism, which go far beyond what can be legally enforced and which mark out the way life is to be led in all its aspects. We have subtitled this chapter 'law and instruction' because it is not only about law in the usual English sense, but also about this wider concept of guidance for living an observant life as a Jew. As we shall see, these two ideas turn out to be related, but the story of how this came about is a complicated one.

Legal material in the Bible can be found almost entirely in the **Pentateuch**. Later ages attributed all lawgiving to Moses, just as they attributed psalm-writing to David and wisdom to Solomon. So legal texts are to be found in the great central section of the Pentateuch that runs from the middle of Exodus to the middle of Numbers, and includes the whole of the book of Leviticus, because these are the teachings Moses is said to have received on Sinai and passed on immediately to the people. A second collection of laws forms the heart of Deuteronomy: Moses is supposed to have been given these laws on Sinai but told not to convey them to the Israelites until they were about to cross over into the Promised Land. Since Israel's laws are all in the Pentateuch, the Pentateuch as a whole was often called 'the Law' (Hebrew *torah*) in later times. When the New Testament refers to 'the law and the

Pentateuch is a common collective term for the first five books of the Old Testament — Genesis, Exodus, Leviticus, Numbers, and Deuteronomy. It is derived from the Greek word *pente* meaning 'five'. In the Jewish tradition, these are sometimes referred to as the five books of Moses.

prophets' it generally means 'the Pentateuch and all the other biblical books'. As we shall see, even the non-legal parts of the Pentateuch (the stories) came to function as *torah* in later times, as part of the shift by which people began to talk of the whole Jewish system as 'the law'.

LAW IN ISRAEL AND IN THE ANCIENT WORLD — SIMILARITIES AND DIFFERENCES

When documents from Mesopotamia began to be discovered from the end of the nineteenth century onwards, it turned out that a number were law codes, and that they bore a striking resemblance to some of the laws in the Old Testament. By considering the resemblances — but also the differences — we can come to appreciate some of the characteristic and distinctive features of biblical law.

The following legal texts from Mesopotamia are important for this comparison:

> The Code of Hammurabi (eighteenth century BCE)
> The Laws of Lipit-Ishtar (first half of second
>   millennium BCE)
> The Laws of Ur-Nammu (nineteenth century BCE)
> The Middle Assyrian Laws (fifteenth century BCE).

There are three main texts within the Pentateuch that can be compared with these:

'The distinctiveness of biblical law can be seen in its form, its ethics and its theology.' (G.I. Davies, 'Introduction to the Pentateuch', in *The Oxford Bible Commentary*, ed. John Barton and John Muddiman, Oxford University Press, 2001)

The Code of Hammurabi is one of the most famous ancient law codes. It comprises 282 laws engraved in cuneiform script on a black stone stele (pillar) 2.25 metres high. It is now on display in the Louvre Museum in Paris and was discovered in 1901 by a French archaeologist in the city of Susa, on the borders of present-day Iran and Iraq. Hammurabi was king of Babylon (1792–50 BCE) and his memorial stele had probably been taken as a trophy of war to Susa from Babylon at some point. The Code of Hammurabi is interesting to biblical scholars because it contains many striking similarities to some of the laws of the Old Testament. A picture of this stele is in chapter 1.4 'The Way They Tell It'.

The Laws of Lipit-Ishtar (first half of second millennium BCE). Lipit-Ishtar was a shepherd and farmer from Nippur, Iraq who became the ruler of Isin from about 1868 BCE to 1857 BCE. In the introduction to the laws, Lipit-Ishtar sets out how the gods Anu and Enil have called him 'to the princeship of the land in order to establish justice in the land, to banish complaints, to turn back enmity and rebellion by force of arms, and to bring well-being to the Sumerians and Akkadians'. Only a portion of these laws were found on stone tablets in the 1930s, but they are believed to be some of the earliest known codified laws.

The Laws of Ur-Nammu (nineteenth century BCE). Ur-Nammu was a Sumerian ruler (2112–2095 BCE) whose name is attached to the oldest system of laws recovered from the ancient Near East by archaeologists. Tablets with these laws have been discovered in Ur and in Nippur and are part of the collection of the British Museum in London. The laws in this code cover a wide range of issues, many to do with social institutions, and many of the punishments stipulated in this law code are fines rather than physical injury.

The Middle Assyrian Laws (fifteenth century BCE). The Middle Assyrian Laws are linked in their written form to Tiglath-Pileser I, king of Assyria (1115–1077 BCE), but may have their origins several centuries earlier. The laws were found written on fifteen baked clay tablets at Ashur and are owned by the Staatliches Museum in Berlin. Many of the laws are notable for the physical punishments they prescribe such as the amputation of limbs, flogging, the gouging out of eyes, and castration!

The 'Book of the Covenant' is so called on the basis of the ceremony described in Exodus 24:3–8 where Moses reads 'the book of the covenant' and the people promise to observe it, saying, 'All that the LORD has spoken we will do, and we will be obedient' (Exodus 24:7). However, the laws of 'the book of the covenant' do not seem to fit well with pastoral, nomadic life in the desert under Moses and seem, rather, to presuppose a more settled, agricultural, slave-owning society in which courts of law existed. Such conditions are typical of the later monarchy but it is difficult to be sure about the exact origins of these laws.

The 'Book of the Covenant' (Exodus 21–23)
The 'Holiness Code' (Leviticus 19–26)
The laws in Deuteronomy (Deuteronomy 12–26).

There are many more laws than this in the Pentateuch, but these are the ones that show most points of comparison with ancient Middle Eastern laws.

If you open the Code of Hammurabi almost at random, you immediately feel that you are in the same world as that of the Old Testament 'Book of the Covenant'. The best-known example of a parallel law is about a goring ox:

> *When an ox gores a man or a woman to death, the ox shall be stoned, and its flesh shall not be eaten; but the owner of the ox shall not be liable. If the ox has been accustomed to gore in the past, and its owner has been warned but has not restrained it, and it kills a man or a woman, the ox shall be stoned, and its owner also shall be put to death. If a ransom is imposed on the owner, then the owner shall pay whatever is imposed for the redemption of the victim's life. If it gores a boy or a girl, the owner shall be dealt with according to the same rule. If the ox gores a male or female slave, the owner shall pay to the slave-owner thirty shekels of silver, and the ox shall be stoned.*
>
> (Exodus 21:28–32)

> *If an ox, when it was walking along the street, gored a noble-man to death, that case is not subject to claim. If a nobleman's ox was a gorer and his city council had made it known to him that it was a gorer, but he did not pad its horns or tie up his ox, and that ox gored to death a member of the aristocracy, he shall give one half mina of silver.*
>
> (The Code of Hammurabi 250–51)

Despite the differences in detail, this is surely in some sense 'the same law': it is difficult to imagine that the two laws developed completely independently of each other. By the time dozens of such examples have been added up, the conclusion that seems obvious is that there must have been a common legal culture in the ancient world. It is even possible that Israel's lawgivers were familiar with the Code of Hammurabi, despite the fact that it is in Akkadian, not Hebrew: royal courts in Israel and Judah had people who were expert in foreign languages, and copies of the Code of Hammurabi have turned up at many places outside Babylonia, though not as yet in Palestine. However, it is also possible that laws such as these were widely diffused in the ancient world, so that the Hebrew writers need not have borrowed directly from the Code of Hammurabi; there may have been, for example, native Canaanite laws which were the local version of laws also familiar to the Babylonians.

We cannot say when Israel became familiar with laws of this kind, though since they imply a settled residential society they cannot really go back into Israel's desert period, but must, at the earliest, reflect life after the settlement. The existence of such laws in the Book of the Covenant is one of the features that shows how Israel shared in many of the assumptions and structures of neighbouring societies.

However, having observed the similarities between Israelite law and the laws of Mesopotamia, we must not ignore significant differences. These lie in three areas: form, content, and authorization.

The forms of Old Testament law

A **casuistic** law is one which is stated with the formula 'If a person does X, then the punishment is Y'.

Most laws both in the Old Testament and in other ancient cultures have a form known technically as **casuistic**. All the laws quoted above are of this type, and it might be called the natural way of formulating law. What is odd is that Old Testament laws contain another type altogether, known as **apodictic** or **apodeictic** law. The classic example of this is the Ten Commandments: 'you shall not murder'; 'you shall not commit adultery'; 'honour your father and your mother'. However, although such apodictic laws hardly occur in the law codes of Mesopotamia, they do occur within the law codes of Israel. For example,

An **apodictic** or **apodeictic** law is one which is stated in the imperative, with the formula 'Do not do X'. The imperative is usually, though not always, in the negative.

> *You shall not wrong or oppress a resident alien, for you were aliens in the land of Egypt. You shall not abuse any widow or orphan.* (Exodus 22:21–22)

Linked with this distinctiveness of form is another feature that can be observed in the case just quoted: the provision of what are called motive clauses — explanations of why the law should be kept. The law about not ill-treating resident aliens points to Israel's own experience as slaves in Egypt to give an incentive for keeping the law. Other laws work with other motivations:

> *If you take your neighbour's cloak in pawn, you shall restore it before the sun goes down; for it may be your neighbour's only clothing to use as cover; in what else shall that person sleep? And if your neighbour cries out to me, I will listen, for I am compassionate.* (Exodus 22:26–27)

Here the motive clauses appeal to common sense or common compassion — if the poor are reduced to pawning the last scrap of outer clothing they have, so that they have nothing else even to sleep in, how can it be right to keep it overnight? However, the motive clauses also contain a threat: if the oppressed poor cry out to God, he will hear them because he, unlike the rapacious lender, is compassionate.

The fact that motive clauses are a distinctive feature of Israelite law might make us pause for thought and ask whether a text that contains clauses such as these is really law at all in the everyday sense of the word. In fact, it looks more as though a law is being referred to but then commented on, and a text that does that is not itself a piece of law, but a kind of ethical guidance. We might think of something like the Highway Code, which quotes from traffic laws, but in itself it is more a practical guide than an actual legal text. It explains to the reader why the laws are as they are, and encourages us to keep them by appealing to common sense, enlightened self-interest, and care for the well-being of others.

Thus already within what we have called Israelite 'law codes' there are indications that something is going on that was unusual in the ancient world — a kind of sermon or commentary on law from a moral perspective. That would fit with what we can deduce about the Ten Commandments, too, with their surprising inclusion of the prohibition of coveting, something which is essentially a non-enforceable 'law'! It all suggests that we do not have in the Old Testament 'raw' law of the sort to be found in the Code of Hammurabi, but more a series of reflections on various laws — laws that nevertheless were presumably actually in force. We can, of course, extract actual laws from the Old Testament, but as it stands it represents something more than just pure law.

Contents

Rather similar conclusions can be drawn if we look at the typical contents of Old Testament laws. Undoubtedly they reflect many of the same situations as the Code of Hammurabi or other ancient Mesopotamian codes — human life in a settled society that needs to be regulated for the common good. Within this, there are some ways in which Old Testament law is more 'advanced' than the codes of Mesopotamia, all of which are, incidentally, a lot older. One example is that there is a distinction between the punishments suitable for crimes against the person and the punishments suitable for crimes involving property or possessions. For example, according to the Code of Hammurabi, a thief who cannot make repayment should be put to death whereas the Old Testament says he is to be sold as a slave (Exodus 22:1–4). Thus, human life is viewed as more precious than possessions. Old Testament law always requires the death penalty for murder, and never lets the murderer off with a fine as was common in other cultures. This may seem harsher, but it undoubtedly represents a higher estimation of the value of human life. As Genesis 9:6 puts it, 'Whoever sheds the blood of a human, by a human shall that person's blood be shed; for in his own image God made humankind.' Another example is the comparative absence of physical mutilation as a punishment — whereas it is sickeningly common in, for example, the Middle Assyrian Laws, such as the law that states, 'If one citizen forces the wife of another to let him kiss her, then his lower lip is drawn along the edge of an axe blade and cut off' (Middle Assyrian Code, article 9). However, just as noteworthy is the fact that, unlike the Code of Hammurabi which reveals different laws for different classes of society, Israelite law is intended for everyone, regardless of class, and covers whole areas of activity that do not appear at all in most ancient law codes. The most obvious example is the regulation of sacrifice, and of worship generally. Laws about such matters appear at huge length in the book of Leviticus, but they are already present in the oldest set of laws in the Old Testament, the Book of the Covenant:

> *Three times in the year you shall hold a festival for me. You shall observe the festival of unleavened bread. . . . You shall observe the festival of harvest. . . . You shall observe the festival of ingathering. . . . Three times in the year all your males shall appear before the Lord GOD.* (Exodus 23:14–17)

In other cultures there were, of course, festivals of many kinds, and they were regulated by custom; but legislation about them does not appear in the law codes that have been discovered. Israelite law is unusual in including such laws alongside 'social' legislation, as though the world of sacrifice and festival and the world of social relations formed a continuum.

This could be interpreted in one of two ways. On the one hand, we might say that it reflects a unique insight, the insight that the areas of contact with God and with fellow human beings are not distinct areas, but belong together. There is no 'secular/sacred' divide in the Old Testament. On the other hand, we might approach the question from a more sociological point of view, and ask: If Israelite law codes uniquely contain laws about the sacred, what does this tell us about their origin and purpose? As to origin, it might suggest (for example) that the laws were preserved by priests in Israel, rather than by civil servants and judges as in Mesopotamia. As to purpose, it might be yet another reason for thinking that what we have here is not exactly 'law' in the same sense as the Code of Hammurabi is law, but more a religious exposition of law which therefore includes 'sacred' obligations alongside 'social' ones. Thus, the Old Testament evidence seems to edge us closer to seeing 'legal' texts as something other than ordinary law. The laws of the Old Testament are instruction in what God desires, rather than a set of laws enforceable in the courts — and, so, not much like what we usually mean by 'law' in our own society.

Authorization

In the area of authorization, there is another clear contrast between Old Testament law and the laws of other ancient cultures. Though Hammurabi says that the sun god Shamash inspired him, it is clear all the way through the Code of Hammurabi that this is the king's law. It is issued in his name and bears his authority. As a matter of fact, it is unlikely that Hammurabi or his lawyers devised the laws in the Code of Hammurabi themselves. It is more likely that they were simply traditional laws which were being codified. However, their re-issue in this codified form is clearly seen as an act of royal supremacy.

In contrast, no law in the Old Testament is ever attributed to anyone but YHWH, speaking through Moses. More specifically, there is no royal law in Israel. No doubt kings issued edicts about particular matters, but there is no record that they codified law in the way Hammurabi is supposed to have done. The oldest code, the Book of the Covenant, does not even mention the king — which leads some to think it must be older than the monarchy, and perhaps go back to the days of the judges. Interestingly, even when the king is mentioned in the laws of Deuteronomy, in Deuteronomy 17:14–20, it is entirely to limit his rights and powers! He is even told to make himself a copy of 'this law' (i.e. Deuteronomy itself) and to reflect on it all the days of his life (17:18–19). This could hardly be further from the idea of the king as a law-maker.

Now there is certainly an important theological point here. In formulating the laws by which the nation was to live, Israelite lawgivers saw them as divinely revealed, and as authorized by God himself, not by any human authority. However, there may again be a social dimension, too. We learn from Hosea that it was the priests, not royal officials, whose task was to maintain and teach the law:

> *My people are destroyed for lack of knowledge;*
> *because you have rejected knowledge,*
> *I reject you from being a priest to me.*
> *And since you have forgotten the law of your God,*
> *I also will forget your children.* (Hosea 4:6)

Thus, the law in Israel clearly had a divine sanction, not merely a royal one. This idea is also reflected in the way it is all attributed to Moses, who was the original priestly leader of the people, not any kind of king. The Book of the Covenant already envisages that in hard cases the priests of the sanctuary will be involved in giving judgement:

> *In any case of disputed ownership involving ox, donkey, sheep, clothing, or any other loss, of which one party says, 'This is mine', the case of both parties shall come before God; the one whom God condemns shall pay double to the other.* (Exodus 22:9)

So, despite the existence of royal courts, and of the old tradition of justice 'in the gate', there was a religious element to law in Israel which made it unusual in its context.

THE DEVELOPMENT OF ISRAEL'S LAW

The place of the Ten Commandments

Perhaps the most famous and in many ways influential part of the law in the Old Testament is the Ten Commandments. These commandments stand at the heart of Israelite law

A **covenant** is a solemn, binding, mutual agreement between two parties; the covenants between God and his people are an important feature of the Old Testament. For more information, see 2.2 'The Chosen People?'

'One who breaks these commands sets himself outside the established life of God's people. To transgress is not to commit a misdemeanour but to break the very fibre of which the divine–human relation consists. Nevertheless, the presence of the two positive commands would reveal another function of the commandments. The Decalogue serves not only to chart the outer boundary, but also to provide positive content for life within the circle of the covenant. The Decalogue looks both outward and inward; it guards against the way of death and points to the way of life.' (Brevard S. Childs, *Exodus: A Commentary*, SCM Press, 1974)

The technical term often used for religious law is 'fas' and the technical term for civil law is 'ius'. These are Latin words.

'Barely 300 words long in English, the Ten Commandments form the foundation of our legal system, are enshrined in the heart of our parliamentary structures and lie at the very core of Western civilization. In words so brief that they would make only a palm-size piece of text in a newspaper, this great arch of divine law encompasses family rights, property rights, the rights of the individual and even the rights of God.' (J. John, *Ten: Living the Ten Commandments in the 21st Century*, Kingsway, 2000)

and are found in Exodus 20:1–17, in Deuteronomy 5:1–21 and again, in a slightly different form, in Exodus 34:10–28. The Old Testament presents the Ten Commandments as part of the Law given by God directly to Moses on Mt Sinai for the benefit of the people of Israel who were on their way out of slavery in Egypt — and thus Moses is presented in Israelite tradition as the great lawgiver. They form the basis of the **covenant** agreement and are clearly meant to set out the way God expects his people to live. As they stand, there is a consistent use of the second person singular for the addressee, perhaps indicating that every individual is directly responsible to God, and there is a predominant use of the apodictic form — both unusual features in a legal series. In addition, the commandments are an example of a unique feature of Israelite legislation since they are divided almost equally between religious laws and civil laws. Yet, as they stand, they are not really laws at all in a strict sense because they provide no indication of the punishment for disobeying them; hence they are often referred to as the Decalogue, literally the 'ten words'.

Moreover, these ten statements of what God requires of his people are in their current form perhaps not as universally applicable as we might imagine. Since they mention houses, slaves, wives, and livestock, their content would appear to be aimed mainly at a settled population of middle-class, property-owning men! However, it is possible that in an original form all these commandments were formulated negatively and briefly, each one in a single clause free from expansions, examples, and explanations. In such a format, the commandments could conceivably have originated from the time of Moses and provided a nucleus of law around which considerable expansion took place over time. In this sense, Moses might correctly be seen as the author of the Law in the Old

---

THE TEN COMMANDMENTS

1. You shall have no other gods before me.
2. You shall not make or worship idols.
3. You shall not make wrongful use of the name of God.
4. Remember the Sabbath day and keep it holy.
5. Honour your father and your mother.
6. You shall not commit murder.
7. You shall not commit adultery.
8. You shall not steal.
9. You shall not bear false witness against your neighbour.
10. You shall not covet anything that belongs to your neighbour.

Note that the Jewish tradition interprets 'I am the LORD your God' (Exodus 20:2) as a commandment to believe in the existence of God and so lists it as the first commandment, combining numbers 1 and 2 above to create the second commandment. Other Christian traditions sometimes combine numbers 1 and 2 above to create the first commandment and divide number 10 above into 'You shall not covet your neighbour's house' and 'You shall not covet your neighbour's wife, slave, ox, or donkey or anything that belongs to your neighbour'.

Testament. However, it is extremely difficult to be precise as to these commandments' real date and place of origin, and most scholars believe they are considerably later than the time of Moses.

The relationship between the Book of the Covenant, the Deuteronomic laws, and the Holiness Code

One of the solid conclusions established by Old Testament scholars is that Deuteronomy represents an updated form of the Book of the Covenant. They have come to this conclusion because Deuteronomy contains themes that the older Book of the Covenant does not deal with at all, but wherever they handle similar issues Deuteronomy always shows itself to be at a later stage in the development of legal traditions. The classic case is the law about slaves:

> *When you buy a male Hebrew slave, he shall serve for six years, but in the seventh he shall go out a free person, without debt. If he comes in single, he shall go out single; if he comes in married, then his wife shall go out with him. If his master gives him a wife and she bears him sons or daughters, the wife and her children shall be her master's and he shall go out alone. . . .*
> *When a man sells his daughter as a slave, she shall not go out as the male slaves do.* (Exodus 21:2–4, 7)

> *If a member of your community, whether a Hebrew man or a Hebrew woman, is sold to you and works for you for six years, in the seventh year you shall set that person free. And when you send a male slave out from you a free person, you shall not send him out empty-handed. Provide liberally out of your flock, your threshing-floor, and your wine press, thus giving to him some of the bounty with which the LORD your God has blessed you. . . .*
> *You shall do the same with regard to your female slave.*
> (Deuteronomy 15:12–14, 17b)

In Deuteronomy the law about release applies equally to men and women, rather than only to men; and not only must slaves be released in the seventh year, they must also be provided for. In comparing these two laws scholars have concluded that Deuteronomic law must surely represent an updating of the older law in Exodus.

This view is compatible with the widespread belief that the Book of the Covenant comes from the time of the judges, and Deuteronomy from the seventh century BCE. However, it does not depend on these theories, since we can trace a development from one to the other across a wide range of issues simply by comparing the two texts.

There also seems to be a certain development from Deuteronomy to the Holiness Code (Leviticus 19–26). This code lays down many humanitarian practices similar to those commended in Deuteronomy:

> *When you reap the harvest of your land, you shall not reap*

to the very edges of your field, or gather the gleanings of your vineyard. You shall not strip your vineyard bare, or gather the fallen grapes of your vineyard; you shall leave them for the poor and the alien. (Leviticus 19:9–10)

However, it also greatly heightens the motivations based on the character of God. Such motivations, as we have seen, are to be found in the Book of the Covenant, but they start to proliferate in the Holiness Code. The whole basis of the Holiness Code (and the reason why modern scholars call it that) is the opening command, 'You shall be holy, for I the LORD your God am holy' (Leviticus 19:2), and each major section ends, 'I am the LORD your God' or 'I am the LORD'. It is as though all the laws derive so directly from God that he must be mentioned every time. Sometimes the formula seems to be a warning, in the sense that God is saying, 'I am to be reckoned with'. At other times, it is a word of comfort — but always it marks the laws out as divine in origin.

Here again we encounter the likelihood that what we are reading is not 'law' in the literal sense, but a kind of sermon on the law. With both Deuteronomy and the Holiness Code we could reconstruct an underlying, straightforward legal text without motive clauses or references to God. However, it is doubtful whether we should be attempting to reconstruct something that never really existed in ancient Israel. Deuteronomy in particular seems to be a rather utopian document, legislating for an ideal Israel rather than for the actual historical realities of life in the Land. The impracticality of its idea of the king, mentioned above, is a good example of this. This is because there was surely no period in the history of Israel when it would have been feasible to have a king who was uninterested in horses, silver and gold, and wives, and who spent his time meditating on the book of Deuteronomy to avoid 'exalting himself above other members of the community' (see Deuteronomy 17:14–20). This 'king' of the laws of Deuteronomy is thus an imaginary figure, and the book that describes him is a blueprint for an imaginary Israel. This is not to say that it was not seriously meant, but it is not a law code in the ordinary sense. It is a religious document setting out an ideal.

Thus, when we trace the development of law in Israel we find again that we are often dealing with texts that depend on actual law and presuppose it, but which in themselves are not 'legal' in the ordinary sense of the word.

THE DEVELOPMENT OF THE 'TORAH'

The idea of law as a religious document setting out an ideal, rather than a law code in the strict sense of the word, came to dominate Jewish thought in the form of the concept of the *torah*. Although even the Book of the Covenant contains a few motive clauses and religious references, it is with the book of Deuteronomy that we see a major shift in the direction of what may be called 'preached' law. Thus in

Deuteronomy, the law is seen as providing not simply rules for cases of crime or dispute, but a way of life: law as a positive, rather than as a negative, restraining force in society. Deuteronomy thinks in terms of God's decrees not as merely a way of controlling wrongdoing, but as a positive inspiration for living a good life:

> See, just as the LORD my God has charged me, I now teach you statutes and ordinances for you to observe in the land that you are about to enter and occupy. You must observe them diligently, for this will show your wisdom and discernment to the peoples, who, when they hear all these statutes, will say, 'Surely this great nation is a wise and discerning people!' For what other great nation has a god so near to it as the LORD our God is whenever we call to him? And what other great nation has statutes and ordinances as just as this entire law that I am setting before you today?
>
> (Deuteronomy 4:5–8)

With these words, Moses presents the laws in Deuteronomy as essentially a gift of God, by which he means to help Israel to live in fellowship with him. They are less demands than blessings, and Israel is lucky to have them — the envy of other nations. Unless we understand that, we shall not get far in grasping the development of the idea of the *torah* in Judaism, for which 'law' is ultimately the wrong word. The *torah* is the means by which Israel draws near to God, we are told in this passage from Deuteronomy, and that is a long way from 'law' in the everyday sense.

In **post-exilic** Judaism there developed a belief that the whole of life was to be regulated by a constant attention to God. This was particularly characteristic, in New Testament times, of the Pharisees. They were not at all the hypocritical, nit-picking people they have become in the Christian imagination, but were Jews — mostly laymen — who strove to live lives as pure as would be required if they were priests and if as such they lived always in the Temple (which no one did). To do this they had to make the laws in the Pentateuch extend to cover every aspect of daily life, so that at every moment of the day their every activity would honour God. It is a vision that is still alive in Orthodox Judaism, as it has been in some Christian religious communities. Its full flowering came later than the biblical period we are studying in this book, but its beginnings can be clearly seen in Deuteronomy and in the Holiness Code. In this way of thinking, 'law' becomes a way of life. In post-exilic Judaism the laws in the Pentateuch remained in force as law, but they also began to have this character as outlining the way people ought to live. One way of putting this would be to say that law passed over into ethics, but this must not be taken to mean that the detailed laws became only symbolic: Jews still felt (and feel) obliged to keep them to the letter.

Thus, the body of texts we refer to as 'law' in the Old

 The English novelist C.S. Lewis (1898–1963), who wrote a number of popular books about Christianity, describes in very positive terms the wholehearted attitude to the observance of the Law. With reference to the glorification of the Law in Psalm 119 he writes: 'The Order of the Divine mind, embodied in the Divine Law, is beautiful. What should a man do but try to reproduce it, so far as possible, in his daily life? His "delight" is in those statutes (16); to study them is like finding treasure (14); they affect him like music, are his "songs" (54); they taste like honey (103); they are better than silver and gold (72). As one's eyes are more and more opened, one sees more and more in them, and it excites wonder (18).' (C.S. Lewis, *Reflections on the Psalms*, Fontana Books, 1961, p. 53)

The term **post-exilic** is used to denote the period in Israel's history after the Exile in the sixth century BCE when many of Israel's people were taken captive and deported to Babylon.

The group of Jews known as Pharisees was a relatively small group within ancient Judaism who believed it was of the utmost importance to observe strictly every detail of the Law. Their name comes from the Aramaic word meaning 'separated ones' possibly because, in order to keep themselves as religiously pure as possible, they tried to keep themselves separate from those who did not observe the Law as strictly as they did. However, the origin of this group is not altogether clear but they seem to have emerged in the Hasmonean period (c. 166–137 BCE). We know of their existence from the writings of Josephus, a Jewish historian who lived in the first century CE, from some allusions in the Talmud, the Jewish commentary on the rabbinic law, and from the, generally negative, references to them in the New Testament.

Testament is complex. It is not merely complex in that it grew up by stages and at different times, but also in that it contains material of different types. At its root there undoubtedly lies a body of actual enforceable legal codes, and it is probably in the Book of the Covenant (Exodus 21–24) that we come closest to seeing how this may have looked in early times. However, from at least as early as the time of Deuteronomy, Israelite writers began to use actual laws as a basis for teaching how people should live a good life that goes well beyond simply avoiding certain 'illegal' actions. Over the course of time the laws developed into 'the Law', the *torah,* God's plan for living well as a Jew. In the form in which we have it, the Old Testament reflects that vision. This means that it cannot be compared directly with the law codes of ancient Mesopotamia, which are just that: codes. At most we can say that Israelite law rests on legal traditions that ultimately go back to the same sorts of situation as Mesopotamian codes, but have been transformed into religious teaching as they have been edited — not least as they have been incorporated into the Pentateuch, the story of Israel's beginnings, and attributed to Moses. *Torah* is much more than law.

4.7 The Number of the Beast
APOCALYPTIC LITERATURE IN THE OLD TESTAMENT

T H E   B A S I C S

- Apocalyptic literature is literature that the author believes contains secret revelations about impending events — often the end of an era — to provide comfort and encouragement to people oppressed by their current situation.
- Apocalyptic literature in the Bible is generally post-exilic and is often presented as the writings of an important figure from the past — angels, visions, and symbolic interpretations are commonplace in the writings and add to the sense of mystery.

THE WORDS **APOCALYPSE** AND **apocalyptic** are used in everyday speech to refer to ideas about the end of the world — a 'doomsday scenario' — but this is only part of what they imply in biblical studies. Apocalyptic literature in the Bible and the early Jewish and Christian worlds is literature that is concerned primarily with God's revelation of secrets to specially chosen people. It is referred to in that way because the most famous book of that kind, the New Testament book of Revelation, is called in Greek *apokalupsis Ioannou*, the 'revelation of John'. *Apokaluptein* in Greek simply means 'to reveal' but most of what is revealed in apocalyptic literature is concerned with 'the end' at least of the present world order, even if seldom of the universe as a whole. So the common use of 'apocalyptic' is partly justified although, as we shall see, there can be revelation of secrets of other kinds, too. However, it is this emphasis on revelation that unites all the works, both inside and outside the Bible, usually called apocalyptic.

The only book in the Old Testament generally described as apocalyptic is the book of Daniel although there are a few other texts sometimes thought of as at least on the way to apocalyptic ('proto-apocalyptic'). These are Zechariah, especially chapters 9–14, Joel, and the so-called 'Isaiah Apocalypse' in Isaiah 24–27. Most apocalyptic literature is outside the Bible, among the literature usually called the **Pseudepigrapha**, such as the various books of Enoch, the

The word **apocalypse** comes from the Greek word meaning to 'uncover' or 'reveal', and biblical literature termed **apocalyptic** is literature designed to reveal secret knowledge. Since much of this secret knowledge had to do with future disasters the term 'apocalypse' is now widely used in connection with disaster scenarios concerning the end of the world.

Pseudepigrapha is the term applied to writings attributed falsely to people other than their actual authors. In Jewish writings the people chosen were often characters previously mentioned in biblical history, and it was often done to lend the writing authority and authenticity.

'Apocalyptic can be briefly characterized as an exilic and post-exilic development of prophetic style, in which heavenly secrets about a cosmic struggle and eschatological victory are revealed in symbolic form and explained by angels to a seer who writes down his message under the pseudonym of some ancient personage.'(Carroll Stuhlmueller CP, 'Post-Exilic Period: Spirit, Apocalyptic' in *The Jerome Biblical Commentary*, Chapman, 1970)

The term **post-exilic** is used to denote the period in Israel's history after the Exile in the sixth century BCE when many of its people were taken captive and deported to Babylon; the term 'pre-exilic' denotes the period before this event.

If something is **Hellenistic** it relates to Greek history, language or culture. This term is particularly used to refer to the period following the death of Alexander the Great (late fourth century BCE) until the time of Augustus (first century BCE).

 The book of Daniel is an example of pseudepigraphy, as Daniel is in fact named in Ezekiel 14:14 alongside Noah and Job as a proverbially righteous man, and it can be divided into three distinct parts. The first six chapters tell the story of a prophet called Daniel who lived during the time of the Exile in Babylon in the sixth century BCE. These stories, including such well-known episodes as Shadrach, Meshach, and Abednego in the fiery furnace (Daniel 3:1–30), Daniel in the lions' den (Daniel 6:2–28), and Belshazzar's feast and the writing on the wall (Daniel 5:1–6:1), are about pious Jews who keep their faith at all costs. As such, they were intended to encourage those who, at the time the stories were being written, were suffering religious persecution in the Maccabean period (see 3.5 'Loyal Subjects?'). Chapters 13–14 make up the third section of the book — only found in the Greek text and so usually placed in the Apocrypha — in which other deeds of Daniel are recounted in a similar style. (These chapters appear in the Apocrypha as Susanna, Bel and the Dragon, and the Song of the Three Jews.) However, in the middle section of the book, chapters 7–12, the author deliberately employs an apocalyptic style and sets out a series of four visions in which Daniel is shown all the events in Israel's history for the centuries to come. Since the author is writing around 164 BCE in the Maccabean period, but pretends to be writing four centuries earlier at the time of the Exile, Daniel, of course, has no problems in interpreting these visions and accurately 'foretelling' the future! As a result, there is a message of hope for the readers because God is shown as being in complete control of history and as overcoming the evil enemies of his people in the end and establishing his kingdom on earth.

book of Jubilees, and a number of books ascribed to Ezra. (One of these, 4 Ezra, is in the Apocrypha, sometimes called '2 Esdras'.) All of the apocalyptic writings are from **post-exilic** times, and many are from the **Hellenistic** period.

TOWARDS AN UNDERSTANDING OF APOCALYPTIC WRITING

A number of features of post-exilic thought, such as revelation, authority, and the role of intermediaries, have to be understood if we are to grasp how apocalyptic books worked in the minds of their authors and readers.

The need for revelation

In pre-exilic wisdom there is a cheerful assumption that the right way for human beings to follow can be known by anyone who is willing to make an effort. Achieving wisdom requires effort, but such effort is always rewarded:

It is important not to confuse the words apocalyptic and apocryphal. The term 'apocrypha' is applied to the collection of books that are included in the Greek version of the Old Testament but not in the Hebrew Scriptures, but nowadays it can also be applied to any book or story which appears to be of dubious authenticity. (For more on the Apocrypha and the canon of the Old Testament, see 1.1 'Old Testament or Hebrew Bible?'.)

> *If you . . . cry out for insight,*
> *and raise your voice for understanding;*
> *if you seek it like silver,*
> *and search for it as for hidden treasures —*
> *then you will understand the fear of the LORD*
> *and find the knowledge of God.* (Proverbs 2:3–5)

However, in post-exilic writings this idea comes under attack. The author of Job 28, for example, deliberately contrasts the quest for wisdom with that for silver, and argues that though the latter can succeed, the former is beyond mortal capacity:

'Surely there is a mine for silver,
  and a place for gold to be refined. . . .

'But where shall wisdom be found?
  And where is the place of understanding?
Mortals do not know the way to it,
  and it is not found in the land of the living.' (Job 28:1, 12–13)

Thus, there developed a kind of pessimism about human abilities: unaided, mortals cannot discover the things that matter in life. On the other hand, there was room for optimism because God himself might choose to reveal these hidden matters. As Deuteronomy puts it, in the Law God has disclosed the way of life, and by keeping the Law Israel will show that it has acquired the wisdom that really matters (see Deuteronomy 4:5–8). However, the point is that the Law could not have been attained by human striving; it depended on God speaking to Moses.

This idea that really important knowledge can be attained only if God gives it is central to the apocalyptic vision of the world, but it is not found only in apocalyptic texts as it was a common element of all post-exilic thought. Its clearest statement, though, is probably in the book of Daniel:

'He reveals deep and hidden things,
  he knows what is in the darkness,
and light dwells with him.' (Daniel 2:22)

Daniel says this after God has revealed to him not only the interpretation of a mysterious dream experienced by the Babylonian king, but actually the content of the dream, which the king has forgotten: a feat which, as the wise men of Babylon acknowledge, is beyond the skill 'of any magician or enchanter' (2:10). The writer thus rejoices in the fact that 'there is a God in heaven who reveals mysteries' (2:28), and who can tell people what no one could ever discover unaided. The heroes of apocalypses such as Daniel are 'in the know'; ordinary people are not.

The authority of the past

One of the most obvious features of prophecy in pre-exilic and early post-exilic Israel is its constant insistence that God is about to do something new. For Amos or Isaiah, God had chosen Israel in the past, but now there was a real danger that he would cast them off; and this was a startling message. People heard the prophets, some with fear and some with loathing, but all with an awareness that these people were saying things no one had said before, and saying it with the direct authority of God. When King Zedekiah of the southern kingdom of Judah was in despair at the siege of Jerusalem by the Babylonians in 587 BCE, he turned to the prophet Jeremiah. This was because he believed Jeremiah was in touch with God and could tell him what to do — the fact that he ignored Jeremiah's advice does not mean he did not believe it; he was probably simply limited in his freedom of action by powerful advisers. Thus, prophecy was conceived of as an active force in the present.

At some point after the Exile — certainly later than Haggai, Zechariah, and Malachi — an idea grew up that true prophecy belonged to the past. Amos, Isaiah, Jeremiah may all have had new things to say in their own day, but in the present age such people no longer existed. The author of a later section of the book of Zechariah even seems to think that a claim to be a prophet would be rightly punished:

> And if any prophets appear again, their fathers and mothers who bore them will say to them, 'You shall not live, for you speak lies in the name of the LORD'; and their fathers and their mothers who bore them shall pierce them through when they prophesy. (Zechariah 13:3)

This does not mean that no one claimed to be a prophet in this period — indeed, unless they did it is not clear why there should be such a passage as this — but it means that there was some kind of 'official' belief that any such claim would necessarily be false. Prophecy belonged to the past.

Of course, for many in post-exilic times all important things belonged to the past. The Law belonged to the past: it had been given by Moses, and no one now would dare to change it or add to it. Psalmody belonged to the past, too, having been written by David, and so did wisdom, whose author was Solomon. People felt that they were living in a secondary or derivative age, treasuring the great works of the past but not producing any themselves. The golden age of originality was over.

The author of the book of Ecclesiastes is often referred to as **Qoheleth** since the first verse of the book declares the content to be the words of 'Qoheleth'— the Hebrew word for a preacher.

Now this does not mean that no one in fact had any new ideas or wrote any new works. In post-exilic Israel, as in any nation at any time, there were creative and original thinkers who continued to produce new literature. Yet it became necessary to deny one's own originality, even as one was practising it! If you had a prophetic vision or revelation, you had to ascribe it to a past prophet. This might be done by adding it to that prophet's book — thus the prohibition of prophecy itself is (obviously) not presented as a fresh prophetic revelation; it is ascribed to Zechariah. If you wanted to suggest a new interpretation of the Law, you must either slip it into the Pentateuch, or else say that it was a tradition that Moses received but which happened not to have been known until now. If, like **Qoheleth**, you wrote a new wisdom book, you ascribed it to Solomon, the fount of all wisdom (Ecclesiastes 1:1, 'The words of the Teacher, the son of David, king in Jerusalem'; cf. the Wisdom of Solomon in the Apocrypha).

So, when the author of Daniel, who lived in the critical period of the Maccabean revolt in the second century BCE, wanted to explain and interpret what was happening and to encourage people by promising God's deliverance, he did not do what Amos or Isaiah had done and deliver some prophetic oracles in his own name. Instead, he took on the persona of Daniel, a famous ancient prophet mentioned in Ezekiel 14:14, and said that this Daniel had lived during the exilic age, was in fact a contemporary of Jeremiah and Ezekiel, and that he had correctly foreseen the events of the Maccabean period. The author then described all that 'was to' happen from the time of 'Daniel' until the second century, and he got it right because, of course, in reality it had all already happened. However, in the process he was able to depict 'Daniel' as supernaturally knowledgeable about events which, for him, still lay in the future. When he then came up to the events of his own (the real author's) time, what he predicted seemed credible because it came from a source, 'Daniel', who had already proved so reliable. Thus, ascribing prophecies that were in reality quite new to a famous figure from the past gave them huge prestige, and meant that people would be predisposed to believe in them.

In fact, we can tell exactly where the real author slips from pretending to prophesy events that are really in the past to actually predicting what for him is still genuinely in the future precisely because he then starts to get the story wrong! The transition occurs in Daniel 11:40. Up until this point Daniel 11 has very accurately summarized what happened to Israel under the successors of Alexander the Great, until the account reaches the Maccabean period. However, when he begins to explain what will happen next, his predictions no longer conform to what actually happened. This is precisely how we know when he really lived: it must have been just around the time when Antiochus Epiphanes set up an image in the Temple, that is, about 167 BCE, since up until that point he is well informed. After that, the story becomes fantasy, because it is real (and inaccurate) prediction.

One important feature of late post-exilic times is thus **pseudonymity**, and the pseudo-authors are always people from the remote past, never contemporaries. We see this most clearly in apocalyptic writing, with texts ascribed not only to Daniel but to Ezra and even Enoch, who lived not long after the creation according to Genesis 5:18–24. Nevertheless, we also see it in other types of literature such as narrative. Post-exilic stories (including those in Daniel 1–6) are never actually about post-exilic times. Rather they are projected back into pre-exilic times. We find this in the book of Jonah, the story of a prophet who lived in the eighth century BCE according to 2 Kings 14:25, and in the book of Ruth, a story about women in the judges period. It is also evident in the book of Tobit, about the exiles from the northern kingdom in the eighth century, and in the book of Judith, which is a tale set in an imaginary past when Nebuchadnezzar allegedly reigned over the Assyrians.

The post-exilic age was thus what we might call an

Pseudonymity is when a work is attributed to a person other than its real author.

antiquarian age — interested in the past, as more important than the present.

Intermediaries

Another important development after the Exile that influenced the apocalyptic style was the belief in figures who were intermediaries between God and the human world, which we normally refer to as angels. In a way, this shows how difficult it is to be a monotheist. No sooner had Judaism settled into a pure **monotheism**, denying the very existence of gods other than **YHWH**, than all the gods came back in through the window in the form of angels — beings less than God himself, yet super-human. Some scholars think the remoteness of the single all-powerful God led people to feel that semi-divine beings were needed to bridge the gap between God and the world; others think this really is just a kind of purified **polytheism**, the old belief in many gods adjusted so as not to conflict with monotheism.

Whatever the reasons, there is no doubt that angelic beings are important in post-exilic literature, and not only in apocalyptic texts. The book of Job begins with a scene in the divine court, when the 'sons of God' come to present themselves for a meeting with YHWH. The 'Adversary' (Satan) is apparently one of them, as he is also in the book of Zechariah (3:1) — not yet the devil of later Judaism and Christianity, but a member of the heavenly court, though ill-disposed towards human beings, part of a kind of divine Public Prosecution Service. However, there are other angels in the book of Zechariah, who help in acting out a kind of pageant of the events that God is about to bring about (see Zechariah 1–2). Moreover, an angel is definitely not a sweet and gentle being, but a terrifying figure:

> *I looked up and saw a man clothed in linen, with a belt of gold from Uphaz round his waist. His body was like beryl, his face*

The term **monotheism** refers to the belief in only one God.

YHWH is the primary way God's name appears in the Old Testament. It is simply four Hebrew consonants which many scholars believe may have been pronounced Yahweh. For a more detailed examination of this issue, see 2.1 'Watchmaker or Living God?'

The term **polytheism** refers to the belief in many gods.

Zoroastrianism is the religion based on the life and work of a Persian prophet named Zoroaster (also known as Zarathushtra). His exact dates are unknown, although many place his birth in Persia in the seventh century BCE. The religion views fire, which represents truth and righteousness, as sacred and centres on the eternal struggle between good and evil in the world. Zoroaster believed in one god — Ahura Mazda — who was lord of all, but many lesser deities, spirits, and angels were incorporated into this religion with the roles of god's assistants. He also preached the idea of a judgement at death resulting in eternal reward in heaven or eternal punishment in hell and judgement of the whole of creation at the end of time when good will finally triumph over evil and the dead will be resurrected. Such ideas may well have influenced the biblical authors when they came into contact with them during the Persian era.

There are around 140,000 followers of Zoroastrianism today living mainly in Iran (ancient Persia) and in India, where they are known as 'Parsis' (Persians) because of their Persian origins. One of the most visibly distinctive practices of Zoroastrianism is that dead bodies, regarded as polluting to the earth, are not cremated or buried but are placed on top of towers for birds of prey to eat.

like lightning, his eyes like flaming torches, his arms and legs like the gleam of burnished bronze, and the sound of his words like the roar of a multitude. (Daniel 10:5–6)

It is perhaps no wonder that at this sight Daniel 'retained no strength' (10:8). There is much more about angels in some other apocalypses, such as 1 Enoch, where (as also in Daniel 8:16 and 12:1) they have individual names and specific duties, but a belief in such beings was normal in post-exilic Judaism. Some think it is part of the legacy of Persian dominion, since the Persian religion, Zoroastrianism, makes much of angels, and Jews could have 'borrowed' their angels from there. On the other hand, we do have the mysterious figure of the 'angel of YHWH' already in the Pentateuch and histories, so maybe the appearance of angels in post-exilic Judaism was a native development.

There are other mediating powers, too, in this later period, such as Wisdom, which do not appear in a human form but seem to have a similar role in acting as go-betweens in human relations with God. Thus, apocalyptic writers were not alone in seeing the divine realm as peopled with beings that were less than God, yet more than human.

THE APOCALYPTIC IMAGINATION

In addition to these concepts that were common to most literature written in the post-exilic period, there are several other features we need to explore relating to what the Old Testament scholar John Collins has called 'the apocalyptic imagination' (1998).

A divine plan for history

For apocalyptic writers, God plans the history of Israel, or even of the world, in advance. Even as late as the Deuteronomistic History we have a sense that events unfold largely according to human actions, though God from time to time steps in and works a miracle. Whole narratives in the Deuteronomistic History, and especially 2 Samuel 9–20, the so-called 'Court History of David' or 'Succession Narrative', operate basically with human motivation, and we feel that events could have turned out differently if one character or another had made a different decision. In apocalyptic works, on the other hand, there is a strong sense of **determinism**.

Determinism is the belief that history is mapped out in advance.

We see this in Daniel 2, where there is a vision of a statue made of gold, silver, bronze, iron, and clay. The statue is said to represent the history of the world, passing from a golden empire (that of the Babylonians), through empires of silver and bronze (Persian dominion and the rule of Alexander the Great), to a much more disappointing end in the rule of Alexander's successors. The final 'clay' element of the statue stands for the reign of Antiochus Epiphanes, which God will shatter. In this, there is a sense that nations rise and fall at the divine command, and there is not much anyone can do to alter the predetermined cycle of world empires.

However, this does not mean that the actions of individuals are decided by God in advance. On the contrary, people have to choose whether or not to accommodate themselves to what God is planning, either obeying his commands or rebelling against him. Thus, individuals will be rewarded or punished for their choices, just as in earlier strands of the Old Testament. Yet on the international scale there is no room for human decision-making: God has already made his decrees.

The most extreme example of this tendency is to be found outside the Bible, in the Book of Jubilees. Here the early history of Israel is told to Moses by an angel, and all the events are fitted rigidly into a pattern dictated by 'jubilees' — that is, periods of forty-nine years (since forty-nine is representative of the completely perfect length of time, given that the number seven represented perfection). God so arranges matters that all significant events happen at crucial points in relation to jubilees. Not much room is left here for human choice!

The fact that the imagined author of apocalypses, Daniel or whoever it may be, is thought of as living a long time ago increases this deterministic effect. On the one hand, many pre-exilic prophets 'predicted' particular events in the near future, such as the defeat of Israel by the Assyrians. However, such a prediction may imply nothing more than heightened insight into political affairs on the world stage and does not necessarily mean that God is thought to have planned the event long in advance; it may simply be his immediate reaction to what Israel is currently doing. On the other hand, to predict whole chains of events stretching over several centuries is bound to give the reader the impression that God had it all mapped out. In fact, this may not be the real author's main intention, and he may be using the detailed prediction of events that, for him, have already happened as a way of making his hero seem more reliable. Inevitably, however, the reader comes away with a feeling that history unfolds as a planned series of events, and that there is nothing anyone can do to alter it. This attitude is well summed up in Daniel 2:

> *'Blessed be the name of God from age to age,*
>   *for wisdom and power are his.*
> He changes *times and seasons,*
>   *deposes kings and sets up kings. . . .'*
> (Daniel 2:20–21, our emphasis)

Visions and their interpretation

Since apocalyptic writing is primarily about revelation — God's revelation of secrets — its main form is the account of visions. In this it differs from the 'revelations' given to the prophets, which seem to have been received in the form of oracles which they were to utter in God's name. Apocalyptic writers are said to have got their knowledge through visions, usually interpreted for them by an angel, and chapters 7–12 of Daniel consist almost entirely of such interpreted visions. This form goes back to at least the time of Zechariah so, whilst it is not necessarily a sign of very late composition, it is typical of apocalyptic writing. Zechariah provides the classic model for a vision and its interpretation:

> *In the night I saw a man riding on a red horse! He was standing among the myrtle trees in the glen; and behind him were red, sorrel, and white horses. Then I said, 'What are these, my lord?' The angel who talked with me said to me, 'I will show you what they are.' So the man who was standing among the myrtle trees answered, 'They are those whom the* LORD *has sent to patrol the earth.'* (Zechariah 1:8–10)

A particular feature of these visions is that they are normally symbolic. What the visionary sees is not what will actually happen, but a kind of symbol of it. Thus, in Zechariah 1, the horses do not stand for real horses, but are a symbolic way of portraying the fact that God can see all over the world, just as he would be able to if he sent out spies on horseback. In Daniel's visions, the history of Israel is presented in terms of battles between various kinds of animals. In Daniel 8 a goat and a ram symbolize, respectively, the kings of Syria and Egypt. In chapter 7 the nations are represented by composite animals, such as a sphinx, and the fourth animal (which stands for Antiochus Epiphanes) is so horrible it can barely be described, but it has iron teeth and many horns. Then Israel is symbolized by a human figure (Daniel 7:13), 'one like a son of man' as the original Aramaic puts it.

Although such figures clearly are symbolic, we probably should not say that they are 'merely' symbolic. What the visionary sees is a kind of pageant being played out, which symbolizes the events that are to happen on earth. Yet it may

 There are a number of people called Zechariah in the Old Testament, and it is important not to confuse the Zechariah who was briefly king of the northern kingdom of Israel (753/752–752/751 BCE), with the post-exilic prophet Zechariah, whose book appears in the Old Testament. The book of Zechariah can be divided into two parts. Chapters 9–14 are of unknown authorship and disputed date, but chapters 1–8, which are a series of night visions, are generally attributed to the prophet Zechariah, who appears to be writing around 520–518 BCE.

COMMON SYMBOLS IN APOCALYPTIC WRITING

The parts of the body
Eyes symbolized knowledge.
White hair symbolized eternity or majesty.
Hands symbolized power.
Legs symbolized stability.

Animals
A lion symbolized royalty.
An ox symbolized strength.
The horns of an animal symbolized power.
A sea-monster symbolized evil.
A lamb symbolized sacrifice.
The wings of a bird symbolized agility.

Colours
The colour white symbolized victory, purity, and joy.
The colour red symbolized bloodshed and martyrdom.
The colour black symbolized death.

Clothing
A crown or ring symbolized kingly status.
A long robe symbolized priestly status.

Numbers
4 symbolized the four corners of the earth.
7 symbolized perfection.
12 symbolized the people of Israel.
1000 symbolized a multitude.

be that this pageant is thought of as having a real existence of its own in a kind of heavenly world. Israel is 'symbolized' by the human figure in Daniel 7:13, yet it may be that that human figure has a real existence. Perhaps he is the angel that represents Israel in the council of God: Michael, maybe, 'the great prince, the protector of your people' (Daniel 12:1). Apocalyptic writers seem to have thought there were two parallel worlds, the heavenly and the earthly: what happened in one mirrored — perhaps even caused — what happened in the other. This also contributes to the sense that events are predetermined. What will take place on earth has already happened, in the symbolic realm, in heaven. These are strange ideas, but they may go back to much earlier conceptions such as the divine council, as described in 1 Kings 22:19–23.

Eschatology

From the Greek word *eschatos* meaning 'last', the term **eschatology** in biblical studies refers to everything to do with belief in an end. In Christian theology, it has come to be connected specifically with the 'four last things': death, judgement, heaven, and hell.

In biblical studies the word **eschatology** refers to everything that is connected with belief in an 'end', whether the end of an epoch, the end of human history, or even the end of the entire universe. In fact, there is little in biblical or post-biblical apocalypses about the end of the universe, although the New Testament book of Revelation, envisaging 'a new heaven and a new earth' (21:1), goes further than almost any other apocalyptic writing in this respect. However, many apocalypses do deal with some really crucial break or discontinuity in world history.

An example would be the way Daniel speaks of the end of the four great world empires that have dominated all of human history so far, and their replacement by the rule of the 'people of the holy ones of the Most High' (Daniel 7:27), in other words, by Israel. This is saying more than that Israel, too, will have its day on the world stage, it is saying that Israel's rule will last forever. That is the kind of thing we mean in Old Testament studies by eschatology. Such an idea goes well beyond the pre-exilic prophetic idea that a crucial change was coming for Israel. Daniel's eschatology even extends to the resurrection of the dead:

> *Many of those who sleep in the dust of the earth shall awake, some to everlasting life, and some to shame and everlasting contempt. Those who are wise shall shine like the brightness of the sky, and those who lead many to righteousness, like the stars for ever and ever.* (Daniel 12:2–3)

However, most apocalypses speak of earthly events, and mainly envisage the restoration of glory to Israel in a new world order.

It is also important to realize that apocalyptic works need not be eschatological in their concerns, even though many are. The book of Jubilees, for example, is clearly an apocalypse, since it is the revelation of God through an angel to Moses. However, the secret information passed on in this work is not concerned with the future at all, but with the past history of the world and the **patriarchs**. The book of 1 Enoch does contain some eschatological sections, but it also has a lot of astronomical information which we should nowadays call scientific, for example about the way the sun moves round the sky through the year (1 Enoch 72–82, the so-called 'Book of the Heavenly Luminaries'). Predominantly, it was the coming 'end' that concerned apocalyptic writers; but they did have other interests, too.

It is also important to see that those apocalypses that are eschatological in character nearly always operate with a belief that the end is near — near, that is, for the actual author and readers. Of course, because the apocalypse is attributed to someone in remote antiquity, that person will present the coming events as far distant for him — as when Daniel is told to 'keep the words secret and the book sealed until the time of the end' (12:4). However, that is part of the fiction whereby the vision is said to have been received long ago. The actual writer almost always believed that the events predicted were about to take place in his own lifetime. In this the apocalyptic writers were exactly like the prophets: they spoke of what they thought would happen very soon.

WHO WERE THE APOCALYPTISTS?

The fact that the apocalyptic writers thought the events they were writing about would happen very soon may help us to identify the people who wrote these strange books. They were people who thought that the immediate future would bring about a decisive change in the state of things. In that sense, they were indeed like the prophets, people with an urgent message for their contemporaries. The question is why they dressed their messages up in this guise of visions experienced by someone long ago.

The attribution of such visions and prophecies to a long-dead figure, as we have already stated, was the result of the prevalent post-exilic theory that real prophecy had ceased. Thus, it was no longer possible for someone who had what would once have been regarded as a prophetic 'call' to issue **oracles** in his or her own name, because prophecy was not supposed to exist any longer. However, this does not explain why the revelation was expressed as a vision. The normal form of expression for the prophets of old, after all, was in terms of a word which YHWH had put in their mouth, rather than a vision they had seen. Of course, some of the pre-exilic prophets did have occasional visions, but certainly not in the highly symbolic form characteristic of apocalyptic writers.

The simplest explanation is that the apocalyptists described visions because they themselves had experienced these visions. In other words, the vision attributed to Daniel or Enoch or some other ancient figure was a vision the actual writer had experienced himself, or was based upon one. Such an explanation might also be supported by the fact that later prophets, such as Ezekiel and Zechariah, had received their

Patriarchs is a term used in biblical studies to describe the key ancestors or father figures of the Israelites, specifically Abraham, Isaac, Jacob, and Jacob's twelve sons after whom the later tribes of Israel were named.

An **oracle**, in this sense, is a short saying given in the name of God.

⚑ Each of the letters in the Hebrew and in the Greek alphabets have numeric equivalents. The word 'gematria' is used to describe the study of the numeric equivalents and relationships found in words.

⚑ The idea of secret revelations being available to people through the Bible itself is something that appears to have endless fascination for people. The scientist Sir Isaac Newton (1643–1727) was convinced there was a hidden code in the Bible that would reveal the future, and he even learned Hebrew in order to try to uncover it. More recently an Israeli mathematician, Dr Eliyahu Rips, working on earlier theories, discovered a hidden code that appears to reveal the details of events that took place, and are still to take place, thousands of years after the books of the Bible were written. This hidden code, it is claimed, is revealed when you set out the Hebrew text of the Old Testament, without spaces, as a continuous string of letters in rows of equal length. Words and phrases that cross vertically, horizontally, and diagonally are then revealed by examining Equidistant Letter Sequences — that is, by selecting equally spaced letters in the text. According to this code, events such as the moon landing, the Second World War, and the assassination of the Israeli Prime Minister Yitzhak Rabin are foretold and, since Hebrew letters all have numerical values, even the dates and times of these events are revealed. Thus, the Old Testament has been described as 'a giant crossword puzzle . . . hidden under the original Hebrew of the Old Testament is a complex network of words and phrases, a new revelation' (Michael Drosnin, *The Bible Code*, Orion, 1997). Inevitably, other scholars have been quick to reject such theories on the basis that Equidistant Letter Sequences are a random phenomenon that can be made to work in any language in any text of reasonable length. Moreover, with Equidistant Letter Sequences you generally have to know the information you are looking for before you find it!

revelations in the form of visions and thus the tradition of messages from God received through visions simply continued to develop as time went by. Indeed, when later writers describe earlier prophecy, they tend to think of the prophets as having had visions, to a much greater extent than the prophetic books really suggest. Therefore, by the time the author of Daniel was writing in the second century BCE it may have been natural for him to ascribe his own visions to a past prophetical figure like Daniel. It was a matter of reading present experience back into the past.

Yet, this does not fully explain the cryptic character of some of the visions, the fact that they can be understood only with the help of the interpreting angel. Some scholars think that the visions were cryptic because they were politically subversive. The apocalyptists, they think, came from among people on the margins of society, who would have been in danger from the authorities if they had been open about their message. The author of Daniel, for example, lived under the tyranny of Antiochus Epiphanes, and for him to have said in so many words that God was about to overthrow Antiochus would have been dangerous. Hence he dressed his message up in terms of beasts and rams and goats, and hoped that the authorities would not be able to decipher it. This explanation is the one often suggested in relation to the book of Revelation where the 'beast' (13:11–18) is given a mysterious number: 666. As Hebrew letters also serve as numerals, most interpreters think that this is code for the Emperor Nero (Roman Emperor 54–68 CE), whose name, written in Hebrew, 'adds up' to this total. The author was speaking, on this view, to an in-group, people who shared his own status as a persecuted Christian, and he could not safely attack Nero openly, but he could provide a hint for anyone 'with understanding' (Revelation 13:18).

Certainly in later times, in both Judaism and Christianity, it has often been small and marginalized groups that have written apocalyptic works; that was true as late as the Middle Ages and, indeed, in more recent times. However, the presence of symbolism needing an interpreter seems to be part of the very nature of apocalyptic writing, as it had already been of some earlier prophecy. Look, for example, at Amos 8:1 or Jeremiah 1:11, or at the whole of Ezekiel 9: in all these places the prophet sees something whose inner meaning can be explained only by God. Moreover, as often in apocalyptic writing, an explicit explanation in fact follows, and surely cryptic visions that are then explained in the text itself can hardly have been meant to conceal information from the authorities! Even though the apocalyptists belonged to marginalized groups, as had some earlier prophets, it is probably not their cryptic style that points to this, but rather their sense of an impending overthrow of the status quo. There can be little doubt that the author of Daniel was among the small groups of people who remained faithful to Judaism during the persecutions of the second century BCE, and wrote for their comfort. In using cryptic symbolism he was probably simply conforming to the style that by his day had become normal and perhaps, after all, he had actually seen mysterious visions which really did need an interpretation.

Apocalyptic is a type of writing that often seems very strange to many modern readers. It cultivates an atmosphere of mystery, and sometimes approaches a kind of science or fantasy fiction in style. Such a style of writing has remained popular to this day with people who try to use it to calculate when 'the end' will come, but at the time it was written, it was intended to provide real comfort for oppressed people, and it conveyed a vivid sense that God had communicated with his people. Once we understand the conventions with which it operates, it introduces us to a mysterious world in which people had visions of heaven and hell, but derived from these courage to stand fast in times of persecution.

Section 5

Methods, Text, and Interpretation

5.1 Cut and Paste
SOURCE CRITICISM AND THE OLD TESTAMENT

THE BASICS

- Source criticism analyses the structure, vocabulary, and style of a text to identify separate sources and attempt to date them.
- Detailed examination of the first five books of the Old Testament using source criticism seems to indicate the presence of at least four separate sources: J, E, D, and P. The identification of the characteristics of these sources, and of their dates, has revolutionized biblical scholarship.

ANYONE WHO USES A computer is familiar with combining two documents, or placing bits of one document inside another, using a 'cut and paste' procedure. It may seem surprising that this technique was practised before computers existed, because a moment's thought will convince you that the process is quite laborious if texts are being copied by hand, or even on an old-fashioned typewriter. However, the need has always existed. Two people draft different versions of documents needed for a committee, or write alternative accounts of some event; and then one of them, or perhaps a third person, has to blend them together to produce a smooth single document. Sometimes, with old technologies, this was done by literally 'cutting and pasting', sometimes by copying out the whole finished document. Even when the product is physically a single text, however, the joins sometimes show through — abrupt changes of style, or tell-tale signs such as differences in the spelling of the same word or different ideas about what should go in capital letters. Committee-produced documents rarely read completely smoothly.

One of the earliest discoveries of modern biblical scholarship ('modern' in a relative sense — it goes back to at least the seventeenth century) was that many biblical books contained evidence of this kind of cutting and pasting. This way of looking at biblical texts is known as the 'source-critical' approach, and it is at its most developed in studies of the

Pentateuch is a common collective term for the first five books of the Old Testament — Genesis, Exodus, Leviticus, Numbers, and Deuteronomy. It is derived from the Greek word *pente* meaning 'five'. In the Jewish tradition, these are sometimes referred to as the five books of Moses.

Pentateuch where it was first noticed. Basically, there are two sorts of evidence that suggest the Pentateuch is a 'composite' piece of writing and the result of splicing together a number of source-documents.

Firstly, the same story sometimes occurs more than once, with variations. For example, there is a story about how one of Israel's ancestors was placed in danger at the court of a foreign king because the king wanted to take his wife and might have killed him to get her, but he escaped by passing her off as his sister. This can be found in Genesis 12:10–20, 20:1–18, and 26:6–11. It is not very plausible either that exactly the same incident took place three times, or that a single author would have deliberately told the same story three times. It looks, therefore, as if variant versions of essentially the same story have all been incorporated in the final text of Genesis. A second example of this can be found in the stories about creation where in Genesis 1 human beings are created after the animals (1:24–26) but in Genesis 2 they are created first (2:4–21). Since it is hard to see how anyone could have deliberately produced this contradiction, there is thus a suspicion that we are dealing here with two originally separate documents.

Secondly, there are texts that seem incoherent as they stand, but where it is possible to separate out two parallel strands, each of which on its own is coherent. The classic case is the story of the Flood in Genesis 6–9. If you read this story quickly, you get a general impression that makes overall sense. But if you read it with rather close attention to the details, it starts to come apart. For example, how many animals went into the ark? Pairs of every kind of animal, according to 6:19–20, but seven pairs of 'clean' animals and one pair of 'unclean' ones, according to 7:2–3. How long did the Flood last? Forty days according to 7:17, but 150 according to 7:24. If you were to retell the story, you would have to make choices between these variants, as happens, for example, in children's Bibles.

Of course, not everyone believes that the Pentateuch is a mosaic of different sources, but it is the most widespread explanation for phenomena such as these. Indeed, source criticism has become a sophisticated tool over a couple of centuries, and much modern Old Testament scholarship rests on a source-critical foundation.

SOURCE CRITICISM IN PRACTICE

Source criticism works primarily by noting, often at quite a minute level, the sort of discrepancies mentioned above in connection with the stories of creation and the flood. Its first aim is to separate out the different strands in a text. If we had a manuscript that had been physically cut and pasted this would be easy, but all we have is a text that has been handed down over the centuries as a finished whole, and a lot of detailed observation is needed to spot the tell-tale signs that more than one source-text has been used. Take the following passage about Moses from Exodus 24:

> 1. *Then he said to Moses, 'Come up to the* LORD, *you and Aaron, Nadab, and Abihu, and seventy of the elders of Israel, and worship at a distance. 2. Moses alone shall come near the* LORD; *but the others shall not come near, and the people shall not come up with him.' 3. Moses came and told the people all the words of the* LORD *and all the ordinances; and all the people answered with one voice, and said, 'All the words that the* LORD *has spoken we will do.' 4. And Moses wrote down all the words of the* LORD. *He rose early in the morning and built an altar at the foot of the mountain, and set up twelve pillars, corresponding to the twelve tribes of Israel. 5. He sent young men of the people of Israel, who offered burnt-offerings and sacrificed oxen as offerings of well-being to the* LORD. *6. Moses took half of the blood and put it in basins, and half of the blood he dashed against the altar. 7. Then he took the book of the covenant, and read it in the hearing of the people; and they said, 'All that the* LORD *has spoken we will do, and we will be obedient.' 8. Moses took the blood and dashed it on the people, and said, 'See the blood of the covenant that the* LORD *has made with you in accordance with all these words.' 9. Then Moses and Aaron, Nadab, and Abihu, and seventy of the elders of Israel went up, 10. and they saw the God of Israel. Under his feet there was something like a pavement of sapphire stone, like the very heaven for clearness. 11. He did not lay his hand on the chief men of the people of Israel; also they beheld God, and they ate and drank. 12. The* LORD *said to Moses, 'Come up to me on the mountain, and wait there; and I will give you the tablets of stone, with the law and the commandment, which I have written for their instruction.' 13. So Moses set out with his assistant Joshua, and Moses went up into the mountain of God. 14. To the elders he said, 'Wait here for us, until we come to you again; for Aaron and Hur are with you; whoever has a dispute may go to them.' 15. Then Moses went up on the mountain, and the cloud covered the mountain. 16. The glory of the* LORD *settled on Mount Sinai, and the cloud covered it for six days; and on the seventh day he called to Moses out of the cloud. 17. Now the appearance of the glory of the* LORD *was like a devouring fire on the top of the mountain in the sight of the people of Israel. 18. Moses entered the cloud, and went up on the mountain. Moses was on the mountain for forty days and forty nights.* (NRSV, slightly altered)

On a fairly casual reading we get a general impression of Moses and various other people having a vision of God, and of Moses receiving the Law. However, if we pay closer attention to the text there are some puzzles and inconsistencies. For example, if Moses went up the mountain in verse 9, how can God have told him to come up the mountain in verse 12? He was already there. Then again, if he went up in verse 15, how can he have gone up again in verse 18?

There is also the question of who went up the mountain

with Moses. According to verses 1 and 9 it was Aaron, Nadab, Abihu, and seventy elders; but according to verse 13 it was Joshua, not previously mentioned; and Hur — also not previously mentioned — and Aaron stayed with the elders, who did not go up with Moses. Then in verse 18 Moses seems to go up alone.

The passage also seems to contain inconsistencies relating to when Moses actually received the laws for the people to obey. In verses 3–8 he already has a book which **YHWH** has given him, and the people promise to obey its laws. Yet in verse 12 he is told to go up the mountain to receive the laws.

Furthermore, verses 9–11 refer to the deity as 'God'; the rest of the passage calls him by his proper name, YHWH ('the Lord'). It is also striking that in verses 9–11 God seems to be fully visible to the group on the mountain, whereas in verses 15–18 all that can be seen is 'the glory of the Lord', and he is hidden in a cloud. In fact, it begins to look as though verses 9–11 do not fit very well with the rest of the passage, especially as verse 12 speaks as though going up the mountain were a new thought.

Thus, close analysis reveals that this passage is not fully coherent as it stands, and we suspect the presence of **doublets** — if we wanted to film this scene, we would have to make some choices. Verses 12–15 seem to tell one straightforward story, in which Moses has his assistant Joshua with him, and the two of them are summoned up the mountain, leaving behind Aaron and Hur to govern the people in their absence. Verses 16–18 speak of a solitary ascent by Moses, and here the mountain is shrouded in cloud, and God's appearance is like fire. Verses 1–11 are another version again, in which Moses has already received the Law, but then goes up with a whole entourage of leading Israelites to enjoy a meal in God's presence; and in this account all of the leaders, not Moses alone, see God.

Whether or not the details of this reconstruction are correct, it should be possible to see that there is at least a problem to be solved. Source critics solve it as we have done here, by thinking in terms of several stories, not fully compatible with each other, that have been copied out and in some cases interwoven, to produce a final, complicated account that makes sense in general terms but is inconsistent in its detail.

Source critics in the last two centuries studied every passage in the Pentateuch with this perspective, and they soon noticed that in many composite passages there were little units that correlated in important ways with little units in others. For example, there were passages that called God 'YHWH' and others that called him simply 'God', in Hebrew *Elohim* (pronounced el-oa-heem, with the stress on the last syllable); but the former also tended to share a common theological approach, as did the latter, and to have a recognizable literary style, using distinctive terms. Thus, there are two ways in Hebrew to say 'make a covenant': one is liter-

YHWH is the primary way God's name appears in the Old Testament. It is simply four Hebrew consonants which many scholars believe may have been pronounced Yahweh. In English translations of the Old Testament the words 'the LORD' often appear where the written Hebrew is YHWH.

In this context, **doublets** refer to alternative versions of the same story.

ally 'to cut a covenant', and the other literally 'to establish a covenant'. Passages that call God YHWH tend to favour 'cut' and passages that call him 'God' tend to favour 'establish'. This kind of observation can be repeated over many examples, suggesting that the same author was at work in all the 'YHWH' passages, and a second author at work in all the 'God' ones. Thus, the idea grew that the Pentateuch was not simply an assemblage of many fragments, but the weaving together of just a few longer and originally continuous documents — a theory often referred to as the Documentary Hypothesis.

THE DOCUMENTARY HYPOTHESIS — FOUR SOURCES J, E, D, P?

By putting together detailed evidence of this kind from the whole Pentateuch, scholars by the end of the nineteenth century had arrived at the conclusion that there were four essentially continuous sources running through the whole Pentateuch — some thought they continued into Joshua and even beyond.

- One source thought the name YHWH had been used from very early times (Genesis 4:26), and had no difficulties about using it in stories well before the time of Moses. This source also often displays quite a primitive view of God, describing him in **anthropomorphic** terms. It also contains most of the vivid stories in the Pentateuch and shows little interest in matters of law and ritual. In addition, these stories appear to be concentrated on the southern kingdom of Judah and call God's holy mountain 'Sinai' and the natives of the land 'Canaanites'.

- A second, mainly narrative, source was like the first in many ways but had a preference for avoiding the name of YHWH and called God simply *elohim*, 'God', rather than using a proper name for him, until the point in Exodus where his proper name, YHWH, was revealed to Moses (Exodus 3:15). The source is also characterized by presenting God as one who does not walk and talk with humans on the earth, but who reveals himself in dreams and voices from heaven. In addition, these stories appear to be concentrated on the northern kingdom of Israel and call God's holy mountain 'Horeb' and the natives of the land 'Amorites'.

- The book of Deuteronomy was, on the whole, a separate block, but it had parallels in odd verses and phrases found in Genesis–Numbers that seemed not to belong to any of the other three sources. This source tends to emphasize God's love for his people and to stress that God has acted in and through history because they are his 'chosen people'. In addition, the source is keen on obedience to the Law.

- Another source also called God simply *elohim*, 'God', rather than using a proper name for him, until the point

When God is described in **anthropomorphic** terms, God is ascribed human characteristics. For example, God is described as 'walking in the garden' in Genesis 3:8.

Genealogies are lists of people's descendants, like a family tree.

in Exodus where his proper name, YHWH, was revealed to Moses (Exodus 3:15). This source was characterized by a detailed concern for ritual and ceremonial instructions, and had a generally ponderous style, ill-suited for telling vivid stories. In addition, this source is keen on **genealogies** and lists. As well as material in Genesis and the early parts of Exodus, this source also contained the great central block of laws in the Pentateuch, running from Exodus 25, all the way through Leviticus, and up to Numbers 10.

These four basic sources came in the course of time to be called respectively J (from the German spelling of YHWH, Jahwe), E (from *elohim*), D ('Deuteronomy-like'), and P (the 'priestly' source) — though other names for them were in use in the nineteenth century. Exactly what belonged in each one was (and remains) a matter of discussion, but by the early twentieth century the basic outlines were widely agreed. Some people thought (and think) that each of the sources is itself composite. The 'author' of J, it can be thought, was also a compiler of still earlier sources, which could be called J1, J2, J3. . . . Alternatively, after the sources were more or less complete, some of them may have been compiled into documents that were still less than the entire Pentateuch. Thus, many scholars thought that J and E had been blended together before the combined document was woven into P. The basic structure of four sources remains central to much study of the Pentateuch but, in principle, source criticism can proceed *ad infinitum!*

DATING THE SOURCES

It is important to see that establishing the sources of the Pentateuch does not, of itself, tell us anything about when it was written — even those who wish to maintain that Moses wrote the Pentateuch could say that he used a variety of earlier sources to do it. Nevertheless, trying to date the sources has been a crucial part of Old Testament study.

It is sometimes said that 'source critics have proved that Moses did not write the Pentateuch', but the work of one of the first Pentateuchal critics, Jean Astruc (1684–1766), shows that this is not true. In 1753, when he identified two different sources using different words for 'God', Jean Astruc thought that he had discovered the sources Moses had used in compiling the Pentateuch. Of course, there are indeed good reasons for thinking that the Pentateuch is not by Moses (mainly that it refers to so many things later than his time), but the existence of sources is not one of them.

In the nineteenth century, it was believed that the order of the sources should be PJED. This stemmed from the common belief that the P-source was the oldest of the sources. After all, it contained the essential rules by which Judaism ordered its life; it lay behind the first chapter of the Pentateuch, Genesis 1; and it definitely seemed to be the document into which the other sources were slotted. It was perhaps genuinely from Moses or, if not, then certainly from a very early time. It was sometimes referred to, in fact, as the 'basic document' in the Pentateuch. It was then felt that the J-source and the E-source came from a time somewhat later than the P-source, as they reflected the period of the Hebrew monarchy, with the E-source probably somewhat later than the J-source. Finally, Deuteronomy, and hence the D-source, was thought to be the latest source, going back no further than the seventh century BCE, because Deuteronomy was the law book King Josiah's officials had 'discovered' — or rather 'planted' — in the Temple according to 2 Kings 22:8.

It was the work of Julius Wellhausen (1844–1918) that decisively changed this relative dating and, in the process, brought about a revolution in the study of the Old Testament. Since the P-source was supposed to be earlier than the great **pre-exilic** prophets, such as Amos, Isaiah, and Jeremiah, Wellhausen presumed they would have quoted it; and he read these books in order to note the places where they showed knowledge of the P-source. To his surprise, he found that they did not. Then he turned his attention to the stories in Judges, Samuel, and Kings — stories of pre-exilic Israel — and again he could find no evidence that the people whose activities were described in these books had any knowledge of the 'basic document' of the Pentateuch. It thus seemed to him that people in pre-exilic Israel had acted as though the P-source did not exist since they showed no concern for any of its ritual laws or its theological assumptions. When he heard that another German scholar, Karl-Heinz Graf (1815–69), had suggested that 'the law is later than the prophets', Wellhausen felt that the scales had fallen from his eyes and he realized that the P-source was not the earliest source: it was the latest. It was not the foundation document of pre-exilic Israel, but the foundation document of post-exilic Judaism — the Judaism of Ezra and Nehemiah and the **post-exilic** prophets and Chronicles, and in due course of the Pharisees. The correct order for the sources was JEDP.

So, although Wellhausen did not actually discover the sources of the Pentateuch — though he did refine earlier analyses of them — he did re-date them. He re-dated them relative to each other, placing P last, but he also re-dated them absolutely, arguing that the J and E sources came from the later years of the Hebrew monarchy in the ninth century BCE, the D-source (as was customary since de Wette) from the seventh century BCE, and the P-source only from the fifth century BCE — well after the return from Exile.

Though this may sound like a mere detail of biblical scholarship, it was actually revolutionary. It produced an understanding of the development of religious belief in practice in ancient Israel that is significantly different from the impression the Bible itself gives us, when read at face value. For example, since all the institutions and ideas that made Judaism distinctive in the ancient world — the ritual laws, the **covenant** idea, and above all **monotheism** — were to be found much more clearly in the late P-source than they were in the early J-source, it became evident that these things were not there at Israel's beginnings, but emerged over time. This meant that they were not implicit in the religion of the **patriarchs** or Moses or even David, but came in at a much later date. Thus, it also became clear that the prophets were not transmitting an old tradition about God, but discovering much that was new in religion, and it is on them that later traditions of law rested, rather than vice versa. All this

 The identification of the book of Deuteronomy as the law book King Josiah's officials had 'discovered' in the Temple according to 2 Kings 22:8 was first argued in detail by W.M.L. de Wette (1780–1849). However, the idea had been around a very long time and had even been suggested by some in the early Christian Church such as St Jerome (c. 347–420).

The terms **pre-exilic** and **post-exilic** are used to denote the periods in Israel's history before ('pre') and after ('post') the Exile in the sixth century BCE when many of its people were taken captive and deported to Babylon.

 Datings are said to be relative when one event is placed in relation to another without regard to particular years or periods in history. Datings are said to be absolute when an event can be fixed in a particular year or period in history, usually with reference to events outside the Pentateuch. Thus, placing the P-source after the J and E-sources is a relative dating, but saying that the P-source comes from the fifth century BCE is an absolute dating.

A **covenant** is a solemn, binding, mutual agreement between two parties; the covenants between God and his people are an important feature of the Old Testament. The Hebrew word for covenant is *berith* (pronounced buh-reeth, with the stress on the second syllable).

The term **monotheism** refers to the belief in only one God.

Patriarchs is a term used in biblical studies to describe the key ancestors or father figures of the Israelites, specifically Abraham, Isaac, Jacob, and Jacob's twelve sons after whom the later tribes of Israel were named.

Speaking of the Documentary Hypothesis, the scholar S. H. Hooke (1874–1968) said, 'The scheme gave to the "shapelessness" of the Pentateuchal material an apparent order and rationality which carried conviction.'

Among the scholarly positions worth mentioning here are those of John Van Seters and H. H. Schmid. Van Seters' theory for a late date for the J-source rests on his comparisons with comparable writing from other cultures, and Schmid, whose theory highlights the prophetic features of the J-source and the fact that there are key traditions in the J-source that are absent from other pre-exilic Israelite literature, suggests a seventh-century or sixth-century BCE date for its composition. Of course, it should also be noted that the American literary critic H. Bloom has suggested that the J-source was the work of a woman, and R. Rendtorff, on the other hand, suggests that the J-source does not exist as a separate entity at all!

was startlingly new in biblical scholarship, and it produces a picture of Israel that is sharply different from that which a straightforward reading of the Old Testament would suggest. Thus source criticism, which can seem small-scale and nit-picking in its attention to minute detail, turned out in reality to give us a wholly new picture of everything in the Old Testament.

Since Wellhausen there have been many fresh developments in source criticism. Some scholars, particularly Jewish scholars, have undertaken a wholesale reassessment of the date of the P-source and have argued that, even if late in its *final* form, it rests on much older traditions and should not be taken as simply post-exilic. Others have suggested that the supposedly 'early' J-source is in fact far later, maybe even as late as the P-source; while others again have disputed whether there really was ever an E document, which, as Wellhausen acknowledged, is pretty fragmentary. In general, however, modern biblical scholarship takes Wellhausen's basic scheme as its starting-point; no one has ever brought about so huge a shift in perspective as he did, and all subsequent biblical studies are 'after Wellhausen' — there can be no putting back the clock to a time before his breakthrough.

SOURCE CRITICISM OUTSIDE THE PENTATEUCH

Source criticism has been practised in most detail on the Pentateuch, but the basic method is obviously applicable to other ancient (and modern) texts, biblical and non-biblical. J. H. Tigay (*b.* 1941) has shown that many ancient literary works were put together in the same way as the Pentateuch: the Mesopotamian Epic of Gilgamesh, for example, similarly combines several sources.

Within the Old Testament, the other narrative books lend themselves to the same kind of analysis. The first book of Samuel, for example, contains two different accounts ('doublets') of the way David was first introduced to Saul. In 1 Samuel 17 David first emerges from obscurity when he kills Goliath, but in 1 Samuel 16:18 Saul has already got to know David as one whose lyre-playing acts as a kind of music therapy for him. Clearly both stories cannot be true as accounts of how Saul *first* encountered David, and it is a reasonable hypothesis that they come from two different sources.

This is an example of our first type of inconsistency — two versions of the same event. The other type, a muddled narrative woven from two strands, can be found in Joshua 3–4, which describes how the Israelites crossed the River Jordan to enter the Promised Land. The story is too long to summarize here, but it is worth reading it carefully, and trying to visualize the scene being described. Rather as in the case of Moses' repeated ascent of Mount Sinai, here the people seem to cross and re-cross the Jordan; and it is not clear whether they take stones out of the Jordan, or put stones in it. Imagine you were trying to make an accurate film version of the events being described, and you will soon see why source critics argue that it is a blend of more than one account. Once again, the basic plot is clear, but the details are hazy and obscure. Obscurity is the source critic's friend!

QUESTIONS ABOUT SOURCE CRITICISM

The work of source critics has illuminated the biblical text in many ways, and in the work of Wellhausen its implications revolutionized our whole way of thinking about ancient Israel. However, it leaves some questions unanswered, and two of these are especially important.

Firstly, even if we agree that the biblical texts were produced in the way source critics suppose, we should ask why. Why should someone, faced with two coherent though incompatible accounts of an event, weave them together to make a single incoherent one? In the light of this question, it is perhaps not surprising that some people have found this so implausible that they have questioned whether the source critics can really be right in their analysis. Such people might think that maybe an account such as the Flood story is more coherent than it looks or that traditional readers, who instinctively think of Genesis 2 as a kind of explanation of details within Genesis 1 rather than as an alternative version, are right after all. Indeed, some might reach the conclusion that perhaps source critics are being too clever by half with stories that were not told with so much attention to detail as modern readers bring to bear upon them. At any rate, we cannot ignore the question why anyone should do what the source critics claim to have shown was in fact done. Of course, the answer might be that the process was the result of a kind of respect for older documents and a feeling that they could not be simply bypassed. Nevertheless, it is perhaps a strange kind of respect which so reworks old documents that they are no longer themselves.

Secondly, although source criticism may get us back to an earlier stage in the composition of the Pentateuch than any other approach, the question is whether it can get us back to the earliest stage of all, the original stories. After all, these stories may have been passed around by word of mouth for a long time before they were written down. In the end, all history, even in modern times, goes back to events that are recalled and retold before they are put in writing. Indeed, Wellhausen himself said that even the stories in the J–source were themselves older than the source in which they were eventually written down, and must rest ultimately on legend and folktale. However, he thought there was no chance that we would ever be able to reconstruct these early oral versions of the stories, a position adherents of the form-critical method soon began to think was unduly pessimistic.

 The Epic of Gilgamesh is a Babylonian story featuring the adventures of Gilgamesh, a tyrant king of Uruk, and his friend Enkidu. Enkidu is originally created by the gods to be a companion who will encourage Gilgamesh to put his energies into adventures rather than being a tyrant. This plan works well until Gilgamesh rejects the advances of the goddess Ishtar, and the gods decide that Enkidu should die as a punishment for Gilgamesh's arrogance. Seeing his friend die, Gilgamesh then sets out on a fruitless quest to find a cure for his own mortality. The full story covers ten or more clay tablets, and the many copies of it which have been found all over the ancient Near East suggest it was a very popular tale from around 2000–1000 BCE. The Epic of Gilgamesh is particularly well known to scholars of the Old Testament because of the similarities between its story of a world-wide flood and the biblical flood story.

For more about this, see 3.1 'Tall Stories?'

5.2 Word of Mouth
FORM CRITICISM AND THE OLD TESTAMENT

T H E   B A S I C S

■ Form criticism analyses the structural forms of a text and attempts to relate them to their oral origins and transmission within a community.

■ Detailed examination of the Old Testament using form criticism has illuminated understanding of the ancient oral forms that may lie behind the Old Testament texts. For example, stories of characters such as Abraham and Jacob seem to indicate the presence of individual anecdotes about regional heroes, which were only later collected into cycles of stories about the ancestors of all Israel; detailed examination of the Psalms seems to reveal forms of early Israelite liturgy.

ORAL FORMS

In traditional societies, most communication takes place in an oral form. People tell stories, make speeches, and pass on information by word of mouth; and even though we think of modern western culture as highly literate, such oral communication is still very important to us. Jokes and anecdotes circulate mainly in an oral form, and much of our political and social life still depends on the impression other people make on us when they speak. However, in ancient societies such as that of Israel, where literacy was much less widespread and written documents were far rarer, such orality was central to people's life. The identification of this originally oral literature, which may lie behind our existing written texts, is the quest of the branch of biblical studies called form criticism, and from it scholars hope to learn more about the social and religious life of ancient Israel.

Just as there are many types or genres of writing, there are also many different types of oral expressions. We mentioned two above: jokes and anecdotes. A joke can be identified by a number of formal features. It begins by setting up a situation, often an unusual one ('A penguin went into a pub . . .') and then usually contains some brief quoted speech or dialogue ('. . . and asked the barman, "Have you seen my brother?"'). It is rounded off with a punchline, which exploits something incongruous in the story ('He said, "I don't know. What does he look like?"'). The exact details of the wording rarely matter, provided the story is told so as to lead up to the punchline.

An anecdote is rather like a joke in being a self-contained story, but it does not have to have a punchline. It depends on the persons involved being well known, so that there is an underlying assumption that we want to know about them. Characteristically, neither jokes nor anecdotes have to be rooted in exact historical contexts. No one faced with the joke about the penguin asks, 'Where was the pub?' or 'Did that happen last week or the week before?': such questions show a misunderstanding of the type of speech a joke is. An anecdote needs to fit broadly into its subject's life history, but we are not particular about exact times and places — and everyone knows that similar anecdotes are told about different people. They are 'floating' stories.

Other oral genres include short nursery rhymes, usually passed down by word of mouth rather than from books, and quite lengthy stories, such as fairy-tales, which may be transmitted in a lot of detail. Such stories often also include vital catch phrases — think of Red Riding Hood or the Three Little Pigs, where everyone remembers, and passes on to children, phrases such as 'All the better to eat you with' and 'I'll huff and I'll puff and I'll blow your house down'.

In the late nineteenth century oral genres in traditional societies began to be studied academically and, in particular, collections of folk tales were made such as the famous collections of the **Brothers Grimm**, who travelled around gathering stories from traditional story-tellers. It was not long before it began to occur to biblical scholars that some of the material in the Old Testament might originally have existed in an oral form. The work of Hermann Gunkel (1862–1932) was especially central in developing this idea; he tried to reconstruct earlier forms of stories that have come down to us through the work of later compilers and writers, such as the compilers of the sources in the **Pentateuch**.

> The German brothers Jacob Grimm (1785–1863) and Wilhelm Grimm (1786–1859) began collecting folk tales and legends in 1806. A number of volumes were published and included such well-known tales as Cinderella, Sleeping Beauty, and Tom Thumb.

FORM CRITICISM AND THE PENTATEUCH

The German biblical scholar Julius Wellhausen (1844–1918) had believed that the Pentateuchal sources must rest on originally oral traditions, but that we could not get back behind the present literary versions of the stories about the Israelite ancestors. Gunkel, however, thought that it was possible to take the stories out of their present connected literary context and to study each story in its own right as an independent 'legend' which might have had an existence quite apart from the context in which it had been placed by the compilers of the Pentateuch. In this way, he imagined that the stories of Abraham, Isaac, and Jacob were originally told orally, just as happens in many traditional societies to this day, around the camp fire in the evening or during religious festivals. Each story in Genesis would have formed a freestanding unit, just like a joke or an anecdote; only later did the compilers of the Pentateuchal sources

> **Pentateuch** is a common collective term for the first five books of the Old Testament — Genesis, Exodus, Leviticus, Numbers, and Deuteronomy. It is derived from the Greek word *pente* meaning 'five'. In the Jewish tradition, these are sometimes referred to as the five books of Moses.

weave them all together to form a continuous and coherent account.

The stories of the ancestors, as originally told, may have fallen into different types. One is the ***aetiological legend*** which explains some custom or natural phenomenon. Thus, the story that Lot's wife was turned into a pillar of salt when she looked back at the ruins of Sodom (Genesis 19:26), would have developed as an explanation of a strange pillar-like structure in the desert. In the same way, the tale of Jacob wrestling with the 'angel' (Genesis 32:22–32) could be viewed as an explanation of why Israelites did not eat a particular portion of the legs of animals (see Genesis 32:32). Sometimes such stories also seem to have passed through several stages of development, so that Jacob's wrestling-match may at some even earlier stage have been told to explain some strange 'spooky' phenomenon encountered at the ford of the Jabbok, which was then later converted into an aetiology of the particular food custom involved. Gunkel thought, though, that it was not originally part of a connected tale about Jacob's journey home from Mesopotamia, but a 'floating' tradition about Jacob, in the manner of an anecdote. Thus, he believed that the Jacob stories gradually came to be a corpus of orally transmitted material through which people would know a lot of 'Jacob tales', though they would not have a connected 'biography' of him. Only when the J source was put together was each story assigned a place at some particular point in Jacob's journeyings.

The form-critical interest in stories as originally independent units thus leads on to a study of how the units came to be grouped together, even at the pre-literary stage. Many 'anecdotes' or 'legends' about Abraham, Isaac, or Jacob came to form complexes of oral tradition, so that we can speak of a 'Jacob cycle' of stories. According to form-critical analysis such a group of stories about Jacob will originally have been independent of the Abraham and Isaac cycles; only much later, though still before the written sources came into existence, did the idea develop that the three ancestors formed the three generations of a single family. Gunkel also tended to think that cycles of stories about a particular hero were localized: thus Abraham was acknowledged as their ancestor by tribes in the region of Hebron, which is where many of the stories about him are located (see Genesis 13:18, 14:13, 18:1). As Israel developed into a nation, the stories came to be seen as concerning the ancestors of the *whole* people, but originally they were the tales belonging to a small local group — people of Hebron revered the memory of Abraham, people of Beer-sheba that of Isaac (see Genesis 28:10). It was only much later that they came to be seen as the ancestors of all Israel, and given a dating many years before other heroes, such as Joseph or Moses.

Form criticism is strictly the study of each small unit in its own right, and putting together theories about the amalgamation of the stories into larger complexes (which eventually

A story which is **aetiological**, based on the Greek word *aitia* meaning 'cause', is a story which is an explanation of the origins of something.

became the basis for the source-editors to work on) is known as tradition history or traditio-historical criticism. It can be practised on later tales too. For example, the stories about Elijah and Elisha are also somewhat free-floating. They were tied down to the reigns of particular kings by the authors of the books of Kings when they provided a framework for these tales, but in themselves they seem to fit rather loosely into this framework: often they refer to 'the king' rather than to any particular monarch by name. Furthermore, the tales of the two prophets are sometimes similar. Compare, for example, 2 Kings 4 with 1 Kings 17: in both chapters the prophet raises a dead child to life. This may have been a piece of floating prophetic tradition, much like an anecdote told of several different famous people.

'Sitz im Leben' and the Pentateuchal material

As we have seen, different types of oral material belong in different social settings. Legends may have their origin in gatherings around the camp fire. Aetiologies probably grow up when people teach their children and try to answer their questions ('Why is that pillar there in the desert?'; 'Why do we not eat that piece of meat?'). The social setting of an oral form is known in German as its *Sitz im Leben*. The term refers to the type of social context within which a tale was told rather than the actual setting of the people it is about or the historical period or circumstances in which the story came into existence. Thus, the *Sitz im Leben* of the stories about Isaac may (if form critics are right) be the Israelite community in Beer-sheba passing on its ancestral stories from one generation to the next at a public gathering. This says nothing about the real life of Isaac, his actual relationship to Abraham or Jacob, or when he really lived. It is a theory about the stories and the social context in which the tales about him were told and retold.

Many scholars think the *Sitz im Leben* of Israelite legends was often liturgical or cultic — in other words, that it was during public worship that the stories were recounted. This is partly because it seems to have been mainly for communal worship that people in Israel gathered together in large numbers, and partly because some of the stories seem to teach something about Israelite religious customs — as with the food regulation with which the story of Jacob's wrestling-match ends (Genesis 32:32). Nevertheless, we should not overlook the possibility of 'secular' public occasions, such as gatherings of the people 'in the gate' to transact the business of towns or cities, or purely informal occasions such as Gunkel's 'camp fires'. In many traditional societies the inhabitants of villages gather together after the day's work is done and exchange stories, or listen to professional or semi-professional tale-tellers recounting old legends and tales, and this is highly plausible as the original context for Israelite story-telling, too.

The German phrase *Sitz im Leben* is usually translated into English as 'setting in life'; it refers to the social context in the life of a community in which a particular biblical story or saying was developed and transmitted.

The implications of form criticism for the historicity of Pentateuchal stories

A 'legend', in the technical sense the term has in biblical studies, is a story about times past which was recounted orally over the generations before it was written down. The stories in Genesis may thus be called legends to distinguish them from chronicles (such as the official notices about the kings in the books of Kings) or from fiction (as in Ruth or Jonah, which are freely written works that probably never had an oral existence). The term 'legend' does not contain within itself the idea that the story in question is untrue, although the word does tend to imply that in everyday English — as it would if we told someone that the story of David, say, was 'only a legend'.

Nevertheless, form criticism does tend to make the historicity of the stories it studies seem rather less likely. For Wellhausen, the stories of the **patriarchs** were really more or less fiction, reflecting the ideas and customs of the age in which the sources were compiled. Gunkel argued that, on the contrary, we could get back to some generations earlier than the written sources, and reconstruct the stories as they had been recounted by several — perhaps many — generations of story-tellers, thus taking the accounts back to a time well before the written sources. However, although this sounds like good news for anyone who wants to defend the stories' contact with historical reality, the impression is misleading, because Gunkel did not think we could make contact with the real Abraham, Isaac, and Jacob: only with the earliest stories about them. Moreover, he felt that these stories might well have no historical substance at all and might be legends in the everyday sense of the term. For Gunkel, it was simply impossible to tell.

Some of his categories also seem to have a lack of historicity more or less built into them. Thus, an aetiological legend provides a reason for a custom, and the implication is normally that this reason is one people have worked out, rather than being the real historical reason. If we say that the story of Lot's wife is a way of explaining the presence of an odd, salt-covered pillar in the desert, we are presumably implying that people *made the story up* to explain the phenomenon, and hence that Lot's wife was not really turned into a pillar of salt. However, there can be perfectly true aetiologies. For example, the story of the Last Supper in the Gospels is an aetiological legend explaining why Christians celebrate the Eucharist (Mass or Holy Communion), but very few people would deduce from this that the Last Supper never happened. People in Britain light bonfires on 5 November to commemorate the defeat of the plot led by Guy Fawkes, but (even though autumn bonfires of course already existed before him) we could not deduce from this that Guy Fawkes is a fictional or 'legendary' figure. The custom really is related to the event it is claimed to be related to.

Nevertheless, the general tendency of form criticism in

Patriarchs is a term used in biblical studies to describe the key ancestors or father figures of the Israelites, specifically Abraham, Isaac, Jacob, and Jacob's twelve sons after whom the later tribes of Israel were named.

Old Testament studies is to make the historicity of the events described in legends dubious. Gunkel's work did not undermine Wellhausen's claim that 'we attain to no historical knowledge of the patriarchs'; all it did was to push back much further the date at which the stories of the patriarchs (in some form) were known and told. Its great contribution was to help us to imagine the kinds of social context in ancient Israel in which the telling may have taken place. It also served to replace the source-critical idea of the stories as written by a kind of novelist or chronicler with a picture of a whole society engaged in transmitting the tales of its ancestors through traditional story-telling.

FORM CRITICISM AND THE PSALMS

Another area in which Gunkel pioneered form criticism was the study of the Psalms. The traditional view by the late nineteenth century had come to be that the psalms were lyric poems written by individual poets to express various human emotions. Nearly all of these poets, it was held, lived in **post-exilic** times, that is, later than the sixth century BCE. Gunkel had the idea, which seems rather obvious once suggested but which was by no means obvious at the time, that the biblical psalms were really based on texts that had been used liturgically in public worship, and had only later been turned into expressions of individual religious emotion. He pointed out that many of them are cast in a 'we' form, for example:

> *As we have heard, so have we seen*
> > *in the city of the LORD of hosts,*
> *in the city of our God,*
> > *which God establishes for ever.*
> *We ponder your steadfast love, O God,*
> > *in the midst of your temple.* (Psalm 48:8–9)

Others are prayers for the king, or for the success of the whole people in battle:

> *the king trusts in the LORD,*
> > *and through the steadfast love of the Most High he shall not*
> > > *be moved.*
> *Your hand will find out all your enemies;*
> > *your right hand will find out those who hate you.* . . .
>
> *Be exalted, O LORD, in your strength!*
> > *We will sing and praise your power.* (Psalm 21:7-8, 13)

Such psalms could conceivably be lyric poems meant for reading by individuals, but they sound very like texts for public use. Their probable *Sitz im Leben* is not private reading in someone's study or living-room, but liturgical use at a time of war; and Psalm 48:9 certainly suggests that the place where such use would have occurred is the Temple.

This suggestion adds to our knowledge in two ways.

The term **post-exilic** is used to denote the period in Israel's history after the Exile in the sixth century BCE when many of its people were taken captive and deported to Babylon.

Firstly, it tells us more about the psalms themselves: that they (or some of them) are public texts that were probably used repeatedly in situations calling for prayer to God. Secondly, it also tells us more about public worship in Israel: that this worship included the singing of psalms. This second point seems to be confirmed by a few passages in the Old Testament that speak explicitly of psalm-singing in the liturgy. For example, in 2 Chronicles 6:41, the people sing an excerpt from Psalm 132, and in 1 Chronicles 16 it is said that various psalms were sung after the Ark of the Covenant had been brought to Jerusalem in the time of David. Older commentators thought this was a reading back of later custom into earlier times, but Gunkel's proposal was that it was a fairly accurate reflection of what actually did happen even in the **pre-exilic** Temple.

A student of Gunkel's, the Norwegian scholar Sigmund Mowinckel (1884–1965), took the proposal a stage further. He argued that the biblical psalms were not merely modelled on poems that were used in the early liturgy, but that many of them were, indeed, the very texts that Israelites had used. Thus, the old idea that the Psalms are post-exilic was replaced with the theory that many of them were quite early, perhaps even going back to the time of David himself. Therefore, as with the legends of Genesis, a form-critical approach again tended to favour an earlier dating of texts than had previously been accepted.

Mowinckel went much further than Gunkel in reconstructing the settings in which the Psalms were used. In the case of Psalm 118, for example, he envisaged a solemn procession towards the Temple, singing verses 1–18 in celebration of victory in battle:

Out of my distress I called on the LORD;
the LORD answered me and set me in a broad place. . . .

All nations surrounded me;
in the name of the LORD I cut them off! (Psalm 118:5, 10)

At verse 19 the procession stops at the Temple gate and the people ask to be admitted:

Open to me the gates of righteousness,
that I may enter through them,
and give thanks to the LORD.

In verse 20 the priests inside the Temple reply that only the righteous may enter:

This is the gate of the LORD;
the righteous shall enter through it.

But the people evidently pass the test, because in the next verse (21) they rejoice that they have been allowed to enter:

The Ark of the Covenant (not to be confused with Noah's Ark which uses a different Hebrew word!) is an important part of Old Testament history. It was a large wooden box covered with gold which was constructed according to God's specific instructions (Exodus 25:10–22) and was said to contain the two tablets on which God had written the Law. For more about this see 3.6 'Digging Up the Old Testament'.

The term **pre-exilic** is used to denote the period in Israel's history before the Exile in the sixth century BCE when many of its people were taken captive and deported to Babylon.

I thank you that you have answered me
    and have become my salvation.

Verse 26 contains a blessing by the priests in response to a prayer for blessing in the preceding verse:

Save us, we beseech you, O LORD!
    O LORD, we beseech you, give us success!

Blessed is the one who comes in the name of the LORD.
    We bless you from the house of the LORD.

The psalm even contains a 'rubric' (a stage-direction):

Bind the festal procession with branches,
    up to the horns of the altar. (Psalm 118:27b)

This reconstruction goes far beyond anything we can possibly know for certain, but it makes it plausible that the Psalms were indeed used liturgically, and that we can form at least some idea of the types of 'service' in which they occurred. They may have been limited in their use to the Temple in Jerusalem, and not have been used at local sanctuaries, though some seem to come from the northern kingdom and may have been in use at temples there. Psalm 80, for example, speaks of 'Ephraim and Benjamin and Manasseh' (v. 2), which suggests a northern origin.

Gunkel distinguished between individual and communal laments, and individual and communal thanksgivings, within the psalms, and certainly some are in the first person singular ('I') and some in the first person plural ('we'). The problem here, as Mowinckel saw, is that sometimes the community can be personified as an individual (as above in Psalm 118: '*I* thank you that you have answered me'), while an individual speaker, conversely, may sometimes speak for the whole community and so say 'we'. Nevertheless, there is a distinction between psalms such as 118 that are clearly concerned with the plight of the people as a group and those that seem to be about the woes of individual Israelites, such as Psalm 22:

For dogs are all around me;
    a company of evildoers encircles me.
My hands and feet have shrivelled,
I can count all my bones.
They stare and gloat over me;
they divide my clothes among themselves,
    and for my clothing they cast lots. (Psalm 22:16–18)

Many of the psalms that contain this kind of lament seem to be multi-purpose, since the sufferer is enduring many, sometimes incompatible, sufferings — note Psalm 69, where he has been engulfed by water and his throat is dry! Probably the *Sitz im Leben* of such psalms is not public liturgy, but a visit to the Temple to offer prayer undertaken not by the sufferer him- or herself but by a professional psalm-singer, who would recite the prayer on the sufferer's behalf.

OTHER OLD TESTAMENT FORMS IDENTIFIED BY FORM CRITICISM

Legends and psalms have been among the most important forms studied by form critics, but there are others besides. Proverbial sayings have perhaps yielded most information to a form-critical style of enquiry, though this is partly because there are so many parallels in other ancient cultures. It is not difficult to see that such sayings have their natural *Sitz im Leben* in some kind of educational environment, and the fact that we know so much about scribal schools in Egypt and Mesopotamia has made form-critical study of proverbs less speculative. One can easily imagine, though, a family setting for transmitting many proverbs, since this remains even today the main context in which children learn traditional proverbial sayings such as 'Many hands make light work' or 'Where there's a will, there's a way'.

Legal forms are also common in the Old Testament. We can identify formulas of acquittal in court ('X is righteous', see Genesis 38:26; Psalm 51:4; Lamentations 1:18) and, of course, actual legal formulations such as the 'If X, then Y' or 'casuistic' way of framing laws.

Prophetic speech also provides material for form criticism. It was form critics who realized that the formula 'Thus says the LORD', which opens so many prophetic oracles, must rest on the form of speech used by ambassadors in the ancient world to announce their master's message, as in 2 Kings 18:19: 'The Rabshakeh said to them, "Say to Hezekiah: Thus says the great king, the king of Assyria. . ."'. This has important implications for our understanding of the prophets. They did not see themselves as speaking off their own bat, but rather as official spokesmen for **YHWH** — no more independent than an ambassador is of the king who sends him. In Amos we even find a kind of playing with forms properly at home elsewhere, as he poses as a dirge-singer (Amos 5:2), a priest summoning people to worship (Amos 4:4–5), or a teacher of proverbs (Amos 3:3–6). In each of these cases he adapts a common form by filling it with a message of doom.

YHWH is the primary way God's name appears in the Old Testament. It is simply four Hebrew consonants which many scholars believe may have been pronounced Yahweh. In English translations of the Old Testament the words 'the LORD' often appear where the written Hebrew is YHWH. For a more detailed examination of this issue see 2.1 'Watchmaker or Living God?'

INSIGHTS OF FORM CRITICISM

In general, form criticism reminds us that, underlying the written form of our present Old Testament, there must have been live speech: story-telling, public pronouncements in various contexts, worship, legal decision-making, all couched in oral forms of expression. Sometimes a form-critical approach enables us to dig below the surface of the Old Testament text, and reconstruct what went on in Israelite society. In the case of the stories that make up so much of the Old Testament text, we can speculate fruitfully about how they were origi-

'Form Criticism performs a valuable service in its concern with classifying types of literature within the biblical texts. By enquiring after the typical it highlights what is individual in any piece of literature, and by identifying the type or genre of the passage in question it offers a major interpretative key to the passage.' (David J. A. Clines, 'Methods in Old Testament Study' in *Beginning Old Testament Study,* ed. John Rogerson, 2nd edn., SPCK, 1998)

nally used, and even how they were reshaped over the generations, until they reached the form that was eventually set down in writing. Thus, form-critical study of the *Sitz im Leben* of many oral forms, and especially of the sacred poetry found in the book of Psalms, has made it possible to reconstruct what went on in the social and religious life of ancient Israel, well beyond what we learn from straightforward descriptions of social institutions in the historical books.

5.3 Edit and Format
REDACTION CRITICISM AND THE OLD TESTAMENT

THE BASICS

- Redaction criticism analyses identifiable sources within a text and attempts to discover what creative or theological motives prompted the final author to combine the material in a particular way.
- Examination of biblical texts with redaction criticism has illuminated understanding of the biblical texts as they appear in their final form. It reveals that the editor or final author, by ordering material in a particular way and by adding material, had great power to influence the way a text is understood and interpreted.

I F WE ARE FACED with a document put together from two originally separate sources, it seems natural to think that we are dealing with two writers who can be studied as separate entities. Yet, really we are dealing with three writers: the authors of the two sources, and the person who put the sources together. Similarly, if we are studying a text made up of many originally oral fragments, it makes sense to ask not only about the origin of those fragments, but also about the compiler who grouped them into a single document. In both cases, we should probably call the person responsible for the finished document an editor. However, in German, people speak of the *Redaktor,* and so attempts to study the editor are known traditionally as 'redaction criticism'.

Redaction criticism is a difficult art. Sometimes we have a good idea of what the redactor's sources originally were because they are preserved in another place. For example, the books of Chronicles are largely a reworking of the material in the books of Samuel and Kings, and we can compare the original with what the editors of Chronicles have done with it. However, in the **Pentateuch** the task is much harder, because we do not have the original unedited sources but have to reconstruct them out of the finished product. Separating sources out, and then trying to work out what was going on in the mind of the person who put them together, is no easy assignment.

Pentateuch is a common collective term for the first five books of the Old Testament — Genesis, Exodus, Leviticus, Numbers, and Deuteronomy. It is derived from the Greek word *pente* meaning 'five'. In the Jewish tradition, these are sometimes referred to as the five books of Moses.

ARRANGEMENT OF THE TEXT

When several different documents are being woven together, the order in which a redactor arranges them can be significant.

The creation stories

Genesis 1–2 is a good example of this. Working with the idea that there are four literary sources which lie behind the Pentateuch, we can say that Genesis 1:1–2:4a is probably from the so-called Priestly source (P), and is later in origin than Genesis 2:2b–25, which comes from the 'Yahwist' (J). These two accounts of creation are very different. In the P account, human beings are created last in the order of things, after all the animals, and man and woman are created together. In J, man is created before the animals, and then woman is created last of all. The two stories are clearly not compatible: the animals must have been created either before or after human beings — both versions cannot be true. Yet, generations of readers have not been very much disturbed by the discrepancy, and people who claim that Genesis is literal truth hardly ever seem aware that they are affirming two incompatible things. The reason is that the two stories have been joined together so that the reader is predisposed to think they must be coherent. What happens when we read Genesis 1–2 is that we tend to think of the second (J) story as a kind of elaboration of one stage in the P version. Genesis 1:27 tells of the creation of humankind, and when we then hear of the creation of man again in Genesis 2:7 we instinctively feel, not that the story is starting up again from scratch, but that we are being given more detailed information on something that has already been mentioned. In our minds we read the story as if Genesis 2:7 said, 'When God created human beings (see above), he did it by taking dust from the ground…'. This understanding then blocks us from noticing the discrepancy about the creation of the animals, which turns into an unimportant detail.

A similar example is to be found in Exodus 24:1–18, where the casual reader gets the impression that Moses went up Mount Sinai to speak with God and then came down again, even though the details are a bit blurry. On the other hand, the reader who is really attending to the detail can see easily enough that Moses keeps on going up and down and is sometimes in the wrong place! For a more detailed analysis of this example, see 5.1 'Cut and Paste'.

Thus, for a very long time most readers were not alert to the difference between the two stories. Once you read them as separate, the differences are very striking. However, so long as you read them as a continuous account, what you get is a slightly out-of-focus story that nevertheless conveys what probably seems the most important point, namely that God created everything there is. Now the person who made the Genesis story read in this way was the redactor, the one who placed Genesis 1 and Genesis 2 next to each other. The P author was trying to tell us that the animals were created first, and that human beings came later, and represented the pinnacle of creation. The J author was giving us an account of how the first man was formed, then the animals to be his companions — an experiment that failed — and finally a woman as a more fitting companion for him. These are two entirely different stories, but the redactor who put them together was trying to convey a general sense that God is responsible for all there is, animals and humans alike, and that the exact detail of the process of creation does not matter so very much. In this, he was spectacularly successful, because almost everyone reads Genesis in this way. Only critical scholarship noticed the original discrepancy and found a satisfying explanation for it — the theory of two sources.

The early history of Israel

Another good example of the work of a redactor in arranging the text was highlighted by the work of **Martin Noth**, who wrote about the 'Deuteronomistic History'. He pointed out a strange arrangement of the events around the time of the conquest of Palestine under Moses and Joshua. The Pentateuchal narrative links together Israelite victories over two kings who lived east of the River Jordan, Sihon, king of Heshbon, and Og, king of Bashan. The detailed stories of these victories are in Numbers 21, but Deuteronomy 2:16–3:7 relates how the Israelites defeated these kings, apparently one immediately after the other. Indeed, these campaigns came to be so much linked that they could be recalled together by the psalmists: Psalms 135 and 136 both join them together:

> *He struck down many nations*
>   *and killed mighty kings —*
> *Sihon, king of the Amorites,*
>   *and Og, king of Bashan,*
>   *and all the kingdoms of Canaan. . . .*
> (Psalm 135:10–11; cf. 136:18–20)

What is odd about this is that the territory of the two kings is widely separated, Moab being a long way south of Bashan, so that the impression of a single campaign against the two kings is rather implausible. Noth suggested that the reason why they are recorded together is that the author of the Deuteronomistic History had a theory that all the conquests east of the Jordan happened under Moses, all those west of the Jordan under Joshua. Therefore, he moved the material around to ensure that the narrative followed this scheme. The stories themselves may well be older, and it is easy to imagine that form critics could study how and why they were originally told, but each story would have been a separate entity: they would have had no connection with each other. It is the historian who has edited the account so as to bring them together and thus present a unitary 'history of the conquest of Transjordan' out of originally diverse stories. This suggestion of Noth's is a piece of redaction criticism, a theory about the work of the editor.

REDACTIONAL ADDITIONS

Sometimes redactors *add* to the material they are working on rather than merely arranging it. Naturally we can tell they have done so only if their work is noticeably different from what surrounds it — if you add a sentence to a document

Martin Noth (pronounced 'note') was an important German Old Testament scholar. In addition to his work on the Deuteronomistic History, he was interested in the social and political structure of early Israel and suggested that the Israelite tribes were constituted as an amphictyony (for more on this see 4.1 'The Social Scene'). One of his most influential works was his *History of Israel* (1950). He is buried in Bethlehem.

that is in exactly the same style as the original, your work will go undetected.

However, one place where the redactor's hand can be clearly seen is at the beginning of 1 Kings, where David, on his deathbed, is giving instructions to Solomon, his son and successor:

> 'I am about to go the way of all the earth. Be strong, be courageous, and keep the charge of the LORD your God, walking in his ways and keeping his statutes, his commandments, his ordinances, and his testimonies, as it is written in the law of Moses, so that you may prosper in all that you do and wherever you turn. Then the LORD will establish his word that he spoke concerning me, "If your heirs take heed to their way, to walk before me in faithfulness with all their heart and with all their soul, there shall not fail you a successor on the throne of Israel."

> 'Moreover, you know also what Joab son of Zeruiah did to me, how he dealt with the two commanders of the armies of Israel, Abner son of Ner, and Amasa son of Jether, whom he murdered, retaliating in time of peace for blood that had been shed in war, and putting the blood of war on the belt around his waist, and on the sandals on his feet. Act therefore according to your wisdom, but do not let his grey hair go down to Sheol in peace. . . . There is also with you Shimei son of Gera, the Benjaminite from Bahurim, who cursed me with a terrible curse on the day when I went down to Mahanaim; but when he came down to meet me at the Jordan, I swore to him by the LORD, "I will not put you to death with the sword." Therefore do not hold him guiltless, for you are a wise man; you will know what you ought to do to him, and you must bring his grey head down with blood to Sheol.'

(1 Kings 2:2–6, 8–9)

Most readers will quickly see that there is a contrast, to put it no more strongly, between the pious sentiments of the first paragraph of this speech and the vindictive character of the second. One might suspect that there are two different sources here which have recorded David's last words, but there is a more probable explanation for what has happened. The original speech, which is part of the so-called Succession Narrative or Court History of David, probably consisted of the words, 'I am about to go the way of all the earth. Be strong, be courageous'. It then continued with what is now the second paragraph, spelling out what form Solomon's 'courage' was to take: settling David's old scores. Particularly noticeable is the advice about Shimei. Shimei had cursed David when he was fleeing from Jerusalem at the time of his son Absalom's rebellion, but David had promised not to take vengeance for this, saying that perhaps God had told him to curse (2 Samuel 16:10). What he now says, in effect, is that he promised not to kill Shimei himself, but made no promises about what Solomon might do! Solomon should act according to his 'wisdom', here meaning his political shrewdness, getting rid of those who had been a trouble to his father and so making his own rule more secure.

This is completely in keeping with what we know of the character of David from the rest of the Court History. On the other hand, the remainder of the opening paragraph, with its advice to 'keep the charge of the LORD your God', is much more typical of the language of the Deuteronomistic History, the larger narrative of Israel's history into which the Court History has been incorporated. The talk of **YHWH**'s 'statutes, commandments, ordinances, and testimonies', and the reference to the Law of Moses, are characteristic of the major speeches that punctuate this work. So is the fact that the promise to David's dynasty is made conditional on his good behaviour, a conditionalizing of the **covenant** which does not appear in the older traditions we find in 2 Samuel 7 and in the Psalms about the king such as Psalms 2 or 110.

The simplest explanation is, therefore, that most of this first paragraph belongs to the editor of the Deuteronomistic History who was faced with a deathbed speech quite out of keeping with his own ideas about the need for the king to be pious and law-abiding. Though he did not change the words of the source he was working with, he inserted some more material which had the effect of blunting its edge, connecting the new material to the old with the word 'moreover', which is often found in the Old Testament as a link between source-material and redactional additions. Thus, the end result is a speech in which the more bloodthirsty elements are toned down by the addition of a pious framework. Solomon is told to carry out a couple of specific acts of revenge, but overall he is meant to regulate his conduct according to the Law of Moses. The effect is to make what are clearly going to be assassinations sound a bit like judicial executions — that, at least, is the way a reader who is trying to find a unity in the passage is bound to read it.

Redactors are thus very powerful people. They present us with traditional material, but they find subtle ways of forcing us to read it against its natural sense, by adding bits of their own. They throw us off the scent of the original meaning, and make the text mean what *they* want it to mean.

REDACTORS OR AUTHORS?

Sometimes a redactor may be so creative that in effect we might describe him as an author. It is true that authors, in the modern sense, do not usually recycle older documents because they would be accused of **plagiarism**. However, if one's use of old material is sufficiently creative, the result is going to be a new work in its own right. This will be particularly clear if the material being recycled was not already in the form of a few self-contained documents — as most scholars think the Pentateuchal sources were — but consisted merely of fragments that needed to be pulled together to make a whole.

YHWH is the primary way God's name appears in the Old Testament. It is simply four Hebrew consonants that many scholars believe may have been pronounced Yahweh. For a more detailed examination of this issue see 2.1 'Watchmaker or Living God?'

A **covenant** is a solemn, binding, mutual agreement between two parties; the covenants between God and his people are an important feature of the Old Testament. For more information on the concept of covenant in the Old Testament, see 2.2 'The Chosen People?'

 '. . . [W]hen scholars speak of a redactor today they are thinking more often of a figure who may only have had in front of him a single document or account, and amplified it by the addition of words or sentences which would alter its overall meaning to present more clearly the teachings which he himself believed to be most important for his day.' (John Barton and John Muddiman, *The Oxford Bible Commentary*, Oxford University Press, 2001)

To accuse an author of **plagiarism** is to accuse him or her of trying to present someone else's writing or ideas as his or her own.

An example of a redactor who was an author in this sense might be the compiler of Proverbs. This redactor took many individual proverbs and a few collections that already existed, and produced out of them a single book. In origin, the individual sayings probably came from a wide diversity of backgrounds. Some were at home in the court, some in village life, some in schools. The collections, too, were diverse in character. For example, the section from Proverbs 22:17 to 24:34 was a short treatise probably intended for fledgling officials, modelled on similar Egyptian instructions, and the material in chapters 1–9 seems to reflect the education of young men in a wider setting. Indeed, this section even shows signs of redaction within itself, since it also contains later, more theological layers such as 8:22–31 about the divine Wisdom. Therefore, as a whole, the book is intended for readers of all kinds, and offers practical guidance for living along with religious reflections. It may be called a work of spirituality, since it teaches how by living a moderate and well-ordered life one can be pleasing to God. However, the redactor of Proverbs did not succeed in introducing as much thematic order into most of Proverbs 10:1–22:16, which generally consists of individual sayings in no particular order. Nevertheless, even in this section a unifying theme occasionally emerges for a few verses — for example:

> *The plans of the mind belong to mortals,*
>   *but the answer of the tongue is from the LORD.*
> *All one's ways may be pure in one's own eyes,*
>   *but the LORD weighs the spirit.*
> *Commit your work to the LORD,*
>   *and your plans will be established.*
> *The LORD has made everything for its purpose,*
>   *even the wicked for the day of trouble.* (Proverbs 16:1–4)

In this, the work of the redactor is evident because these four proverbs convey more when grouped together than they do if taken individually. They express a belief in divine providence, in a God who exercises control over the world and overrules both human intentions and human judgements; and they act as an encouragement to put oneself into the hands of a God who can be trusted. Thus, the redactor has done far more than merely collect proverbs together: he has used proverbs to make a larger and more complex point than any individual saying can make.

An even more striking case of a redactor who had original ideas of his own is the person who put the book of Ecclesiastes into its present form. The words of **Qoheleth** seem to have been largely sceptical in character, expressing doubt about all accepted ideas of God and providence. In particular, they called into question the common notion that the world is run on principles of justice. Like the author of Job, Qoheleth had observed that 'there are righteous people who are treated according to the conduct of the wicked,

Qoheleth is the alternative name for the book of Ecclesiastes. Ecclesiastes is the Greek translation of the Hebrew word *qoheleth*, which means 'preacher'. The book gets its name from its first verse which declares the content to be the words of 'Qoheleth'— a preacher. Thus, the author of the book is often just referred to as 'Qoheleth'.

and there are wicked people who are treated according to the conduct of the righteous' (Ecclesiastes 8:14). The overall conclusion was that 'all is vanity', i.e. futility (1:2). Yet astonishingly, Ecclesiastes has often been used by Christians and Jews to encourage people to lead a good and holy life in the hope of receiving a rich reward. This is largely because a redactor added some words to the end of the book:

> *Fear God, and keep his commandments; for that is the whole duty of everyone. For God will bring every deed into judgement, including every secret thing, whether good or evil.*
> (Ecclesiastes 12:13–14)

That 'God will bring every deed into judgement' was just what Qoheleth had denied. However, by placing this statement at the end of the book, the redactor gave it a decisive twist in a more 'orthodox' direction. He also added some touches of the same kind to the passages that come immediately before: 'Remember your creator in the days of your youth' (12:1); 'know that for all these things God will bring you into judgement' (11:9). Thus, by the time the reader comes to the end of the book, Qoheleth's more sceptical utterances get forgotten, and the whole book turns into a guide to righteous living, much like Proverbs.

Beginnings and ends of books are crucially important, because the beginning sets up expectations that carry you through the whole work, and the end tells you where you have got to, what the experience of reading this particular book amounts to. The importance of the two ends of the book is strikingly illustrated by Job. Job, like Ecclesiastes, is a highly sceptical work, and in the dialogue that forms its core every accepted doctrine about divine justice comes under fire from Job himself. Yet the first chapter tells us that he was 'blameless and upright' (Job 1:1) and that he rebuked his wife when she encouraged him to curse God because of his sufferings (Job 2:10); and the last chapter tells us that God rewarded him for his righteousness. This sets up the expectations with which generations of readers came to the book, and they blocked out the amazingly unorthodox things Job said by believing that they must somehow be incorporated into the picture of him as 'blameless and upright'. Consequently, the 'patience' or 'endurance' of Job has been proverbial at least since the New Testament letter of James, where the phrase occurs (James 5:11), and is found in practically all commentaries on the book from ancient until quite modern times. No one could believe that a work that began and ended in such an orthodox way could have a central content that was so very different. The redactor who put the book into its present form thus influenced the interpretation to a huge extent.

In a way, redaction criticism is simply the next logical step after source and form criticism. First you take the biblical books apart to see how they were compiled; then you study

Bernhard W. Anderson describes the redactors of the Bible as 'the anonymous interpreters of the tradition who have too often been ignored or underrated in modern biblical study', and he says, 'These editors were not just tampering with the tradition or touching it up for publication. They were interpreters who believed that the sacred heritage was relevant to their time' (Bernhard W. Anderson, *The Living World of the Old Testament,* 4th edn., Longman, 1988).

the process of compilation itself. Yet, in another way redaction criticism can lead us away from an interest in questions about the origins of the biblical text altogether, and towards an appreciation of it as it now stands. The more a redactor is like an author, the less interest we may feel in what his raw materials were — for he has done such original things with them that the finished product may well be more interesting than what lies behind it.

In Pentateuchal study the redactor is sometimes symbolized by the letter R. Thus R(JE) means the person who wove the J and E sources together, and R(JEDP) would be the writer responsible for the final form of the Pentateuch. The great Jewish scholar Franz Rosenzweig once said that R should be interpreted to mean *rabbenu,* the Hebrew for 'our teacher', because it is to the biblical redactors that we owe the text that is actually there when we open our Bibles. J and E and the original Qoheleth and so on are, in a sense, hypothetical people: we reconstruct what they wrote as best we can, but can never be certain we have got it right. However, R is always real, the author of the text as we actually possess it. *Someone* must have put biblical books into the form which exists today — indeed, someone (or more likely several people) put the whole Bible into its present form. These people are the 'Rs' of the Bible, the redactors who are the real authors of the books as they have actually come down to us.

5.4 A Good Read?
LITERARY CRITICISM AND THE OLD TESTAMENT

THE BASICS

- Literary criticism focuses on reading a text in its final form and exploring what it means to a particular reader or community of readers. It has attempted to reverse the trend of taking the biblical texts apart and has illuminated understanding of how people in different ages can read and interpret the biblical texts as a unity.
- Examination of the final form of biblical texts reveals literary devices and characteristics common to much great literature and encourages people to respond to the text in the context of their own experiences and interests.

Source criticism is concerned with analysing the structure, vocabulary, and style of a text in order to identify separate sources within the text and attempt to date them. For more detail, see 5.1 'Cut and Paste'.

Form criticism is concerned with analysing the structural forms of a text and attempts to relate them to their oral origins and transmission within a community. For more detail, see 5.2 'Word of Mouth'.

Redaction criticism is concerned with analysing identifiable sources within a text and attempts to discover what creative or theological motives prompted the final author to present the material in a particular way. For more detail, see 5.3 'Edit and Format'.

The term **secular literary critics** is often applied to people who study literature in general and have no special religious commitment to the Bible.

A **close reading** is a reading that pays attention to the way the text is constructed as a whole and the way it develops its themes.

T HE MOOD IN BIBLICAL criticism has developed over the last few decades from a concern for the earliest stages of the biblical text towards a greater interest in the finished product. **Source criticism, form criticism**, and **redaction criticism** continue to be practised, but many people who study the Bible have moved in the direction of what may be called a 'literary' concern and, at least in the English-speaking world, such a concern now tends to dominate biblical study. This literary approach became popular from about the 1970s onwards when **secular literary critics** began to take an interest in biblical books. They were generally not bothered with all the earlier stages in a text's growth that source and form critics can painstakingly reconstruct. They wanted instead to read the books as they were, in their 'final form', and to read them as finished wholes, not as collections of bits and pieces. This kind of literary criticism is a little like redaction criticism in its concern for the final edition of the text, but unlike it in not taking any interest in what the redactor's raw materials were. Literary critics simply read the text as it lies before us in the Bible. Sometimes they argue that the biblical books are so well constructed, from a literary perspective, that source-critical and form-critical explanations are implausible anyway. However, for the most part they simply bypass such methods and go straight for what in literary studies is called a **close reading** of the text.

EXAMPLES OF CLOSE READINGS OF THE OLD TESTAMENT

Erich Auerbach (1892–1957)

One of the first people in modern times to take an interest in literary aspects of the Old Testament was the German literary critic Erich Auerbach. His book *Mimesis: The Representation of Reality in Western Literature* was written while he was teaching in Turkey during the Second World War. He had very few books around him, so he was obliged to study the detail of the texts he was writing about — a wide range from the whole of western literature, ancient and modern — without being able to consult older commentaries on them. The result was a fresh and original book. He included in it an important chapter comparing Genesis 22, the story of Abraham's near-sacrifice of his son Isaac, with a scene from Homer's *Iliad*. He tried to show that whereas the *The Iliad* presents all the incidents in the story it tells with attention only to 'surface' impressions, the Old Testament narrative is 'fraught with background'. By this he meant that it hints at many things that are not made explicit, and invites the reader to get below the surface of the story. We are not concerned here with whether Auerbach was right about **Homer**, but we may well think that he had a good feel for the biblical narrative:

> *After these things God tested Abraham. He said to him, 'Abraham!' And he said, 'Here I am.' He said, 'Take your son, your only son Isaac, whom you love, and go to the land of Moriah, and offer him there as a burnt-offering on one of the mountains that I shall show you.' So Abraham rose early in the morning, saddled his donkey, and took two of his young men with him, and his son Isaac; he cut the wood for the burnt-offering, and set out and went to the place in the distance that God had shown him. On the third day Abraham looked up and saw the place far away. Then Abraham said to his young men, 'Stay here with the donkey; the boy and I will go over there; we will worship, and then we will come back to you.' Abraham took the wood of the burnt-offering and laid it on his son Isaac, and he himself carried the fire and the knife. So the two of them walked on together. Isaac said to his father Abraham, 'Father!' And he said, 'Here I am, my son.' He said, 'The fire and the wood are here, but where is the lamb for a burnt-offering?' Abraham said, 'God himself will provide the lamb for a burnt-offering, my son.' So the two of them walked on together.' (Genesis 22:1–8)*

Auerbach suggests that what makes this story so poignant are the things that are not stated in it. Nothing at all is said of the emotions of either Abraham or Isaac. We are not told how God revealed the place for the sacrifice. When Isaac asks Abraham about the lamb, Abraham answers without really answering, but we have the impression that Isaac may well have realized the truth. Twice we read, 'So the two of

Homer is known as the great Greek poet who is responsible for *The Iliad* and *The Odyssey*, epic poems about the Trojan War (*The Iliad*) and the twenty-year journey of Odysseus, king of Ithaca, home from this war (*The Odyssey*). However, scholars are not very sure at all who Homer was, when he lived or where he lived. Some theories suggest he lived and wrote in the twelfth century BCE, in the era of the Trojan War; others suggest that he lived and wrote in the ninth or eighth century BCE and that he collected and edited a large number of oral sources in order to produce his epics. One writer, in a claim regarded as ridiculous by serious scholars, has even pointed out that if Homer's name were spelled backwards and in Hebrew it would be a form of Solomon's name; and he has, therefore, suggested that King Solomon was in fact the real Homer!

them walked on together', but the writer does not point out — because he does not need to — how much has changed between the first and the second time, since by now the truth has dawned on Isaac. The repetition of this sentence also increases the sense of something fated, a series of events over which the actors have no control: they walk their appointed path. The horror of the incident is much stronger when narrated in this spare, bleak way than it would be if there were much more dialogue and much more description of emotions. All of that is only hinted at, and the reader fills it in from his or her knowledge of human nature. All this is what Auerbach means by saying that the text is 'fraught with background'.

Note how this reading is different from anything we have described so far. Auerbach is not interested in when the text was written, or which source of the **Pentateuch** it comes from. He does not look for breaks or awkwardness in the text that might show it is made up from several underlying fragments. He is not concerned, either, with its possible historical truth, or — as has often been suggested — its function in the history of child-sacrifice in Israel. What interests him is its literary character, as a skilfully written narrative. His com-mentary on it is the kind of thing we would expect in a work of literary criticism on any other text, ancient or modern.

Pentateuch is a common collective term for the first five books of the Old Testament — Genesis, Exodus, Leviticus, Numbers, and Deuteronomy. It is derived from the Greek word *pente* meaning 'five'. In the Jewish tradition, these are sometimes referred to as the five books of Moses.

Robert Alter

More recently, literary study of the Old Testament has come from Robert Alter (b. 1935), who is Professor of Hebrew and Comparative Literature at the University of California, Berkeley. His earlier writing was on the work of Fielding, Stendahl, and Kafka, as well as some modern Israeli literature, and he became interested in the Bible for literary, not religious or theological reasons. Alter thinks that much of the work of traditional biblical critics has been misguided: they have been so busy taking the text apart ('excavative' is his name for what they have done, a kind of textual 'archaeology') that they have failed to read it and to appreciate the literary skill with which it was written. His most recent work is a study of the story of David (*The David Story: A Translation with Commentary of 1 & 2 Samuel*, 1999). He pays close attention to the Hebrew text — just as close as any source critic — but sees it as a well-constructed narrative, not as an assemblage of bits and pieces.

One of Alter's discoveries is what he calls the *type scene*. This is a stock incident that occurs in the stories of several different people in the Old Testament. One example is the scene at a well, when the hero of the story meets the heroine at the village well, where the flocks are being watered. There are examples in Genesis 24:10–27, Genesis 29:1–12, and Exodus 2:15–22. Whereas traditional critics might try to establish that one of these depended on another, as with the three 'wife-sister' stories in Genesis 12:10–20,

20:1–18, and 26:6–11, Alter is interested in their function in the finished text, as a way of giving a pattern to the stories of the Hebrew ancestors. He thinks they are part of the repertoire of Israelite story-tellers. Obviously if this is so we cannot establish anything about the historical reliability of the tories: they are simply recurring motifs with a literary function. Like a repeated theme in a piece of music, each time we meet one of them we recognize an old friend, and this gives a particular kind of literary pleasure or satisfaction.

Other literary scholars have noticed additional commonly occurring motifs, which are sometimes referred to as *topoi*. The Greek word *topos* (singular)/*topoi* (plural) simply means 'place' or 'places', but it is used in a technical sense for incidents that are related about many people, rather like the recurring features one finds in anecdotes told of different people. For example, the theme of the weaker defeating the stronger is such a *topos*. We find it in the stories of Jacob and Esau in Genesis (Genesis 27–33), and in the story of David and Goliath (1 Samuel 17). A related theme, the choice of the apparently unlikeliest candidate, occurs in the accounts of God's choice of Saul (1 Samuel 10:17–24) and then of David (1 Samuel 16). This is also a theme familiar to us from the story of Cinderella, reminding us that such *topoi* are commonplace in the literature of many nations.

Another particularly striking *topos* is the story of someone who carries a letter containing instructions for his own execution, which again is found in many cultures. The biblical example is Uriah the Hittite, taking to the general Joab a letter that instructs Joab to place him in the most dangerous part of a battle (2 Samuel 11:14–15). However, the motif is familiar to readers of English literature because it occurs in William Shakespeare's *Hamlet,* with the messengers Rosencrantz and Guildenstern. Shakespeare probably did not borrow it directly from 2 Samuel: it is a motif that circulates in the literature of many countries.

Thus, where form critics would be interested in tracing the origins and development of such motifs, the concern of critics such as Alter is for the way they are used in biblical narrative. He is interested in how the biblical writers deploy such *topoi* to give meaning and structure to the stories they want to tell and finds considerable literary skill in the way such traditional features are blended into the specifics of stories about the heroes of Israel. He is not interested in when, where, and how this happened, but in the literary result of the process: vivid and exciting stories.

THE ROLE OF THE READER

In recent years biblical studies have come to be influenced by various movements in general literary criticism. One of these is 'reader response criticism'. This comes in two forms, which we may call regular and strong.

Reader response criticism (regular)

The regular form of reader response criticism stresses that it takes two to make a literary interpretation, the author and the reader. Texts do not simply lie around with meanings inherent in them: the reader has to extract the meaning. The theory is that this is in itself a creative process, since the reader does not merely register, passively, what is there, but contributes to the meaning through his or her own critical intelligence. The easiest place to see this is in the New Testament **parables**. It is not enough in reading a parable to decode what the writer or speaker meant: a proper reading involves the reader in an appropriate response to the speaker's message. Thus, the reader has to feel addressed by the parable, warned or threatened or encouraged.

In fact, the same is true of all literary texts that really engage our interest. In the example above, from Genesis 22, it is the reader who fills in the gaps in the text, speculating about how much Isaac knew of what was really going on, noting the meaningful silence in which Abraham and Isaac go on their way, feeling the unexpressed pain of the father called upon to sacrifice his only son. None of this lies there on the surface: the reader has to dig it out. One of the main proponents of reader response criticism, the German literary critic Wolfgang Iser, talks explicitly of gaps (*Leerstellen* in German) in texts, which it is the job of the reader to fill in. Much of the pleasure in reading a piece of literature consists in filling them in correctly, so as to re-create the original vision of the author. That is why we enjoy texts that contain lots of gaps, and tend to get bored with stories in which everything is spelled out explicitly.

In Old Testament studies reader response criticism of this kind can contribute fruitfully to a literary reading of the texts. For example, Danna Nolan Fewell and David Gunn have presented a reading of the book of Ruth in which they notice what previous readers seem to have overlooked, the gaps or silences in the text. The story is often held up as a small masterpiece of writing, in which all the characters behave in an exemplary way. However, Fewell and Gunn point out some strange silences. For example, when Naomi returns to her homeland she tells everyone that she is totally unsupported because her husband and sons are dead, yet makes no mention of the fact that Ruth is with her and is in fact supporting her. This and other ways in which she seems to ignore Ruth's contribution to her well-being make these scholars sceptical of how 'ideal' a person Naomi really is, and they challenge us to question our own attitudes towards the relationships between the generations and between people in difficult circumstances. They are not suggesting that the story-teller necessarily *intended* us to raise such awkward questions, but they think that as readers we have the right to raise them — indeed, perhaps a duty to do so. Thus, we as readers contribute to the meaning the story has: it is not fixed in stone by the original author.

A **parable** is a story told to illustrate a particular moral or spiritual teaching. Much of Jesus' teaching in the New Testament is in the form of parables.

'The text is a static, fixed reality, just words, until the imagination of the reader renders it alive and makes it a dynamic force in shaping the future by allowing a reading of its narrative to influence contemporary understanding of life experience.' (Mary E. Mills, *Historical Israel: Biblical Israel — Studying Joshua to 2 Kings*, Cassell, 1999)

The book of **Ruth** tells the story of a woman from Moab, across the Jordan, who comes to settle in the land of Israel because she will not abandon her mother-in-law, Naomi, when both of them have been widowed. Ruth there finds a husband, Boaz, and bears him a son (who becomes in due course the ancestor of King David), thus ensuring that the 'names' of both her husband and her father-in-law are not 'lost', as people in Israel thought they were in cases where there were no heirs. For more information about this book, see 3.5 'Loyal Subjects?'

Reader response criticism (strong)

There is also a strong version of reader response criticism, put forward by the American literary critic Stanley Fish in his essay 'Is There a Text in This Class?' According to Fish, the reader does all the work in establishing the meaning of a text. Reading is like a 'bring and share' meal: the author brings the words, but the reader brings the meanings. There is no 'original' meaning in any text, nor does the author exercise any control over what the text means. Texts are assemblages of words, and the meaning of these words comes into being in the act of reading them.

Not many biblical scholars are prepared to go this far in ascribing meaning to the reader. One aspect of Fish's theory, however, that may make it quite attractive to some in the world of biblical studies is his emphasis on what he calls 'interpretive communities'. In practice he is not saying that each individual reader can make just anything of any text, but rather that readers are shaped by their membership in groups for whom given texts have a particular resonance. A poetry reading group, for example, will tend to interpret any text as a piece of poetry, with the conventions that we usually apply to poetry — for example, that its statements are not statements of fact, but evoke emotions and reactions. If you gave such a group a piece of scientific writing to read, they might try to read it as if it were poetry, with interesting results. Similarly, we might say, a Bible reading group will bring certain assumptions to the reading of a biblical passage. Among these assumptions are that the text has a profound meaning, not a trivial one, and that it concerns human life lived under God, rather than being purely secular. Bible readers tend to belong to a religious 'interpretive community' and thus tend to look for religious meanings in the biblical text.

Traditional biblical criticism resists this way of looking at the Bible and says that the meaning of each text is the meaning intended by its original writer. However, this is one of the aspects of biblical criticism that religious believers have often had problems with, since they may want to argue that the biblical texts, being inspired by God, can have meanings that go beyond those intended by their original authors, and that the eye of faith can sometimes discern what those meanings are. If one thinks about the Bible in this way, then Fish's theories may not seem such a problem after all. The price to be paid, though, is that the biblical text ceases to be available for the kind of investigation biblical criticism has usually gone in for, and much of what we have written in this book becomes irrelevant!

RECEPTION HISTORY

Sensitivity to the literary aspects of the Bible need not, of course, lead in this rather radical direction. We do not have to think of the meaning of the text as totally fluid in order to be able to appreciate it as a literary work in its finished form. In doing redaction criticism of the composite books in the

Bible, scholars were taking an interest in the finished text as opposed to the sources from which it is made up; and there are books in the Bible that are not composite anyway — Ruth is probably an example — but were written straight through just like a modern story or poem. In such cases, a literary approach will seem to many readers the natural one.

Such a way of reading the text can still be 'historical'. It is concerned with understanding the finished texts in their ancient Israelite/Jewish context, not with lifting them out of that context and reading them as though they were modern works. By some time in the Second Temple period, most of the books of the Old Testament were roughly in the form we now have them, and people were even beginning to see them as a **canon**. By then, all evidence that some of the texts had come together by 'cut and paste' methods had long been forgotten, and the books were read as single, continuous works. Jews in the fourth century BCE did not know about J, E, D, and P, the four sources for the Pentateuch; they knew about Genesis, Exodus, Leviticus, and so on — just like a modern reader who has never studied biblical criticism. For this reason, it is interesting to see how they read all these books.

To see how readers from the Second Temple period read these books we have to have evidence about Bible reading from this later period. Fortunately, there is some evidence, in the form of the very latest books of the Old Testament and **Apocrypha** and in texts such as the **Dead Sea Scrolls**, and of course in the New Testament, which often quotes and comments on the Old. Here we can see that people did treat the texts as finished wholes. They read the histories, for example, as a continuous work, glossing over the awkwardnesses that have led modern scholars to think in terms of sources. Often they treated the texts as highly relevant to their own day, much as Bible readers today do, if they are religious. Sometimes this took the form of thinking that the ancient text was actually foretelling events of the reader's day — an example is when Daniel says that Jeremiah's prophecy of a seventy-year exile was really referring to the age of Antiochus Epiphanes and the Maccabees (Daniel 9:2). The New Testament is full of such discoveries of 'prophecies' (i.e. predictions) in the Old Testament books. For example, in 1 Corinthians 10 the apostle Paul refers to the story of how many of the Israelites were killed by snakes for disobedience during the wanderings in the wilderness (Numbers 21:5–6), and adds, 'These things happened to them to serve as an example, *and they were written down to instruct us*' (1 Corinthians 10:11, our emphasis). He then argues that 'we' shall also be punished if we forsake God.

The Dead Sea Scrolls contain a number of texts called *pesharim* (pronounced pe-shar-eem, with the stress on the final syllable), which means 'commentaries'. These, like Paul, try to show contemporary meanings in the ancient texts. For example, the Dead Sea Commentary on the book of **Habakkuk** (*pesher Habakkuk*) sees the obscure events referred to in that

The word **canon** comes from a Greek term referring to a measuring rod, and it is used to denote a fixed list of those books accepted as being genuine, authoritative, and inspired for a particular religion.

Apocrypha is the name given to the collection of books which are included in the Greek version of the Old Testament (the Septuagint) but not in the Hebrew Scriptures.

The **Dead Sea Scrolls** is the collective name given to a large number of manuscripts, including some of the earliest manuscripts of the Old Testament, discovered in caves at Qumran near the northwestern edge of the Dead Sea in 1947. For more information, see 3.6 'Digging Up the Old Testament'.

The book of Habakkuk contains the prophecies of the prophet Habakkuk, one of the twelve minor prophets of the Old Testament. Nothing much is known about his life, and the identity of the 'oppressor' referred to in his prophecies is obscure. The book, which most scholars agree is from the late seventh century BCE, deals with the issue of evil and why evil people appear to prosper. The prophet's conclusion is that God is the ultimate judge and deliverer and that, whatever the situation appears to be, those who are evil will not survive, but those who are righteous will live because they are faithful to God (Habakkuk 2:4–5).

The term **reception history** refers to the history of how the biblical books were received by those who had inherited them from the past.

book as predictions of the troubles and trials of the Dead Sea community itself.

Other texts were approached in different ways. The Psalms, for example, were not thought of as the hymn-book of Solomon's Temple, but primarily as texts through which people could express the whole range of their emotions before God in any age. They have functioned like that in both Judaism and Christianity down to the present day. They can be studied as poems in any culture can be studied, as texts expressing human feelings in a sophisticated way. Again, we know that the Dead Sea community valued them and used them since a number of scrolls containing various selections of Psalms turned up among the finds at Qumran. The community also wrote psalms of its own, the *hodayot* (pronounced hoe-die-ot, with the stress on the final syllable), and these were modelled quite closely on the biblical Psalms and used the same literary techniques.

This study of how biblical texts were read by later generations is known technically as **reception history,** and it is an area of growing interest in biblical studies today. In principle one could ask about the way the Bible or parts of it were read in any period — in early Judaism or the early Church, in the Middle Ages, or at the Reformation in the sixteenth century. In a way, modern literary readings, as well as readings by particular interest groups such as feminists, ecologists or Liberation theologians, are also part of the text's reception, since they show us how people read it today. This is a long way from traditional concern for what the books conveyed to their original readers, but it is an equally valid interest.

FEMINIST AND LIBERATION INTERPRETATIONS OF THE BIBLICAL TEXT

In dealing with the interpretation of the biblical text as a whole, it is worth mentioning a couple of specific readings of the Bible by particular interest groups such as feminist and Liberation theologians. Such groups do not place their main focus on the text itself, but upon the text in relation to a specific issue which is of importance to them.

Feminist theology and the Old Testament

Feminist theology originally grew out of the Women's Movements in the nineteenth and early twentieth centuries CE. These were concerned with achieving more equality for women in terms of voting, employment, and pay, and led to a 'second wave' of feminism in the 1960s which challenged the assumption that women were inferior to men and drew attention to the ways in which male-dominated societies had viewed women in the past. This inevitably led to an examination of the biblical texts from such a perspective.

As a result, some feminist theologians reject the biblical text and the faith which is founded on it as irredeemably **misogynistic.** They highlight the fact that the Bible and its dependent religions are 'male-authored' and 'male-centred',

To be **misogynistic** is to display a hatred of women.

especially in their characterization of God, and they claim that the text's deeply rooted sexism has too often been used to justify the subordination of women. Such a view highlights the basic portrayal of women in the Old Testament as either good wives and mothers or wicked seductresses. On the one hand, then, women in the Bible are portrayed as child-bearers and homemakers whose power and authority are limited to their immediate family context. On the other hand, women in the Bible are portrayed as a source of evil, tempting men to turn their backs on God and his commandments. Neither image, such feminist theologians claim, is credible or helpful. The work of Mary Daly (b. 1928) is associated with such an analysis. For her, the image of God and of women in the Scriptures and the way such images are used in the Christian Church are simply examples of a patriarchal society projecting its views on to God so that such images can be used to subordinate women. The conclusion is that the tradition is so inherently **patriarchal** that women should reject Judaism and Christianity and seek out alternative traditions for themselves.

A **patriarchal** structure is one dominated by men.

Others, such as Phyllis Trible (b. 1932) and Rosemary Radford Ruether (b. 1936), try to work within the religious traditions linked with the Bible and advocate ways of reading it that highlight feminine concerns. Their approach draws attention to the feminine imagery associated with God, such as the image of God as a woman suckling her child (Isaiah 49:15) and the female figure of divine Wisdom involved in the work of God's creation. This approach also points to certain biblical texts which appear to be pro-women or concerned with the stories of women and, therefore, inspirational for women today. Furthermore, this view seeks to offer revisions of the male-centred language and approach and tries to recover the deeper meaning from the text which can then be applied in a way which is not gender-specific. Adherents of this view also sometimes point out that when viewed against its cultural, patriarchal, background the Bible could be said to be less sexist than one might expect.

 Even in the nineteenth century CE female writers were criticizing the Bible as an instrument of male domination. One wrote, 'I think that men have read their own selfish theories into the book, that theologians have not in the past sufficiently recognised the progressive quality of its revelation, nor adequately discriminated between its records of history and its principles of ethics and religion.' (Elizabeth Cady Stanton, *The Woman's Bible*, 1895)

Liberation Theology and the Old Testament

Liberation Theology emerged in the 1960s from Latin America where theologians drew a parallel between Israel's experience of slavery in Egypt and their experience of life for the poor and the needy under repressive political and military regimes. It claims that, in the same way that God heard his people cry out in their slavery and put in place a plan to lead them out of Egypt to a new land 'flowing with milk and honey', the poor of Latin America look to God for liberation. This liberation is envisaged in terms of the re-creation of their country as a place where regimes are just and dignified human life is possible for all. Thus, advocates of Liberation Theology highlight the themes of justice and righteousness in the Bible and point out that the Bible portrays God as one who has made a clear choice to be on the side of the poor,

 'A starting point of liberation theology is that the authentic voice of the Bible can be heard only in solidarity with the poor and the oppressed.' (John Rogerson, *An Introduction to the Bible*, Penguin, 1999)

the suffering, and the oppressed as opposed to the side of
wealthy, powerful oppressors. The ethical teaching of the
Old Testament prophets is particularly useful in this context,
with its emphasis on acting justly and upholding the rights of
the poor and the oppressed.

Interestingly, such an interpretation of the Bible goes further than many interpretations because it also obliges the
reader to engage in positive action to oppose poverty and injustice. It was this sort of obligation that inspired the Roman
Catholic Church's adoption of the 'Option for the Poor' put
forward by the bishops of Latin America in the 1960s and
1970s and which compelled people like **Oscar Romero** to
speak out against social injustice.

READING THE BIBLE AS SCRIPTURE

A final approach that ought to be mentioned is the move to
read the Bible 'as Scripture'. All the approaches we have discussed in this book so far are in principle open to believers
and non-believers alike. You do not, for example, have to be
a Christian to practise form criticism, or a Jew to be interested in a literary reading of the text. As a result, there is an
influential movement in biblical studies today, especially in
North America, that suspects the Bible has been surrendered
too much into the hands of readers with no religious commitment, and would like to 'reclaim the Bible for the Church',
as they sometimes put it. The movement, with major representatives such as Brevard S. Childs (*b.* 1923) and Walter
Brueggemann (*b.* 1932) in the USA, sometimes talks about
a 'canonical' approach to the Bible, sometimes about reading it 'as Scripture' — in other words, not from the carefully
neutral standpoint that seems to have characterized biblical
criticism over the last couple of centuries. In a way this is
asking biblical scholars to go back to reading the Bible in the
way ordinary believers read it, as a text that has something
powerful to say to us about God now, rather than as a means
by which we can reconstruct what people thought about God
at various points in the past.

We mention the 'canonical approach' here, because it
usually goes hand in hand with the belief that what the biblical interpreter should study is the finished form of biblical
books, not hypothetical earlier stages in their growth. In this,
it is quite similar to a 'literary' approach, even though its
underlying commitment is different. In both cases, attention
is fixed on what is there when we open a Bible, rather than
on what lies behind or underneath the present biblical text.
Only here, the justification for this is that it is the finished
books that Christianity and Judaism have bequeathed to us,
and therefore it is these books, not their hypothetical compo-
nent parts, which we are meant to read and upon which we
are meant to reflect. In support of such an approach, it can
be noted that the Church did not put the J-source or Second
Isaiah (Isaiah 40–55) into the canon. Instead, the Church put
the Pentateuch and *all* sixty-six chapters of the book of Isaiah

Oscar Romero (1917–80)
was the Roman Catholic
Archbishop of El Salvador
from 1977 to 1980. His experiences
of his country's corrupt government
inspired him to preach consistently
about the rights of the poor. He spoke
out against the brutality of the military and against the concentration of
the country's wealth in the hands of
the few. He became 'the voice of the
voiceless' and such a threat to the
government that he was assassinated
as he celebrated Mass on 24 March
1980. The words of the sermon he
had been preaching just before he
was shot included a call to action
typical of Liberation Theology: 'We
must do what we can. All of us can do
something.'

into the canon; and so it is these books in their entirety that we are meant to be reading.

Put like that, this might sound rather like a ban on intellectual curiosity: why should we not be interested in underlying documents if we can see that they must have existed? The idea, though, is to allow all the now traditional methods of biblical study, but to say that more is needed: a commitment to the scriptural status of the texts. The Bible is not just like any other book, but Holy Scripture, and we should not act as if this were not the case.

Any reader of this book who is not a Christian or a Jew will probably feel that this concern is simply irrelevant to their studies. However, even those who do have a religious commitment may find it rather restricting. In point of fact, in placing certain biblical books in the canon the Church said nothing about how they were to be read, and many of the discoveries on which biblical criticism rests were achieved by people who were themselves religious believers. Many religious insights have come through the painstaking work of analysis that biblical critics have undertaken, and it may be a bit too easy simply to say that we must move 'beyond' criticism to a 'canonical' perspective. Nevertheless, this movement of thought is influential at the time we are writing, and it will be interesting to see what new contributions it will make to the study of the Old Testament.

Index